T0271009

History of Insurance

Volume 8

History of Insurance

Volume 8

MARINE

Edited by
DAVID JENKINS
and TAKAU YONEYAMA

Routledge
Taylor & Francis Group
LONDON AND NEW YORK

First published 2000 by Pickering & Chatto (Publishers) Limited

Published 2016 by Routledge
2 Park Square, Milton Park, Abingdon, Oxon OX14 4RN
605 Third Avenue, New York, NY 10017

Routledge is an imprint of the Taylor & Francis Group, an informa business

BRITISH LIBRARY CATALOGUING IN PUBLICATION DATA
The history of insurance
1. Insurance — Great Britain — History
2. I. Jenkins, David T. II. Yoneyama, Takau
3. 368.9'41

ISBN 13: 978-1-13876-092-9 (hbk) (Vol-8)

LIBRARY OF CONGRESS CATALOGING-IN-PUBLICATION DATA
The history of insurance / edited by David Jenkins and Takau Yoneyama.
    p.cm.
Includes bibliographical references and index.
Contents: v. 1 16791816 — v. 2 17971877 — v. 3 16711762 — v.4 17741826 — v.5
18281848 — v.6 18481887 — v.7 16011910 —v.8 18101811.
    ISBN 1-85196-527-0 (set)
1. Insurance — Great Britain — History — Sources. 2. Insurance companies —
    Great Britain — History — Sources. I. Jenkins, David (David Trevor). II.
    Yoneyama, Takau, 1953

HG8597.H574 2000
368'.00941—de21

Typeset by Techset Ltd.,
Gateshead

CONTENTS

Volume 8

1810 Select Committee on Marine Insurance

BPP (226) 1810 IV 247, *Report from the Select Committee on Marine Insurance* (1810)
Observations on the manner of conducting marine insurances in Great Britain; and on the report of the Select Committee of the House of Commons, to whom that subject was referred, including a few remarks on joint-stock companies (London: Gale and Curtis, 1810)
Joseph Marryat, *Observations upon the Report of the Committee of Marine Insurance, with a few incidental remarks on a Pamphlet Lately Published, entitled 'A Letter to Jasper Vaux, Esq.,'; to which is added copy of a report, proposed as an amendment to the report adopted by the committee on marine insurance* (London: W. Hughes, 1810)
Considerations on the Dangers of Altering the Marine Insurance Laws of Great Britain; in the manner proposed by a bill, brought into Parliament for that purpose; And On the impolicy of granting, without the most accurate Legislative Enquiry, several Applications to Parliament, for sanctioning certain self-erected Joint Stock Companies for Insurance of Lives, Insurance against Fire, and for the Purchase and Sale of Annuities (1811)

The conduct of marine insurance had gradually become more complex and intricate during the later decades of the eighteenth century and the first few years of the nineteenth. Fraudulent activity, a large number of legal cases, complaints against underwriters and uncertainties of the law, in a business which to great extent depended upon previous case law, all led to the need to put marine insurance on a surer footing.

The Minutes of Evidence and Report of the 1810 Select Committee on Marine Insurance is of great importance both as a source for understanding how marine insurance was being conducted and as a major step forward in the regulation of the conduct of the business. The task of the Committee was to review previous legislation, including that which gave exclusive privilege for marine insurance to the two chartered companies (6 Geo. I, c.18), and to recommend improvements in the means of effecting marine insurance. Thirty-six merchants and underwriters gave detailed evidence to the Committee. That evidence provides the best available insight into how marine insurance was operating in Britain up to that time. Many of the practices established in the early eighteenth century still persisted in spite of the massive increase in Britain's overseas trade, the growing complexity of goods transported and the problems of trade during war. It considers the role of the two chartered companies, the Royal Exchange and the London Assurance, and of the increasing role of the Lloyds Coffee House. It provides an insight into contemporary levels of risk and the profitability of underwriting. It reveals the extent of private underwriting, including outside London, and refers to private underwriting in the United States, as well as to the establishment of a marine insurance company in Massachusetts in 1795. By 1810 it intimates that there were nineteen marine insurance companies in that State and that they were offering lower rates on transatlantic trade than their British counterparts. It also gives some evidence of marine companies on the continent of Europe. Evidence is given of the difficulty, on occasions, of placing risk, and of the implications of the failure of underwriters, although these were not generally great.

The evidence and report of the Committee gave rise to considerable debate, as is clear from the various observations reprinted here, which reflect the different interests and concerns of the parties involved.

R E P O R T

FROM THE

SELECT COMMITTEE ON MARINE INSURANCE;

(SESS. 1810.)

Ordered, by The House of Commons, *to be Re-printed*, 11 May 1824.

The SELECT COMMITTEE appointed to consider of an Act, made in the 6th year of King George the First, intituled, " An Act for better se-" curing certain powers aud privileges intended to be granted by his " Majesty by two Charters for Assurance of Ships and Merchandizes " at Sea, and for lending money upon Bottomry, and for restraining " several extravagant and unwarrantable practices therein mentioned;" —and of the state and means of effecting MARINE INSURANCE in Great Britain;—and to report the same, with their Observations and Opinion thereupon, from time to time, to The House:—And to whom the several Petitions, which have been presented to This House in this Session of Parliament, upon the subject of MARINE INSURANCE, were Referred;—And who were empowered to report the Minutes of the Evidence taken before Them ;——HAVE, pursuant to the Order of The House, considered these several matters ; and have agreed upon the following REPORT :

IN a country where Commerce in all its various branches has been carried to such unexampled extent, where we have so much of the produce of our soil and of our industry to exchange for that of the rest of the world, and from our insular situation so much to exchange among ourselves by the navigation of the seas, and where the most perfect and improved mode of this circulation is so much connected, not only with the comforts of individuals, but through the revenue with the safety of the State, no subject can be of more real and extensive importance than that which has been referred to Your Committee. Duly impressed with this opinion, they have collected such evidence as they thought best calculated to inform them of the present state of Marine Insurance in the country, and to guide their judgments as to any measures which it might be expedient to recommend to the House. The Minutes of this evidence accompany this Report ; and Your Committee, in submitting to the House the opinions which after the most diligent investigation they have formed, and the RESOLUTIONS to which these opinions have led them, proceed to consider the subject in the following natural order :

I. The nature of the exclusive privilege conferred upon *The Royal Exchange Assurance* and *The London Assurance* Companies, and the manner and extent of its exercise by those Companies.

II. Its effects upon Marine Insurance, and the state of and means of effecting Marine Insurance in this country.

III. The importance of a better system to the Commerce and Revenues of the Empire, and to all parties concerned.

I. The nature of the exclusive privilege, and the manner and extent of its exercise.

The Act of the 6th Geo. I. c. 18, provides for the incorporation of the Royal Exchange and London Assurance Companies, for the purpose of effecting Marine Insurances, to the total exclusion of all other corporations or bodies politic, and all societies and partnerships whatsoever, who are " restrained from granting, signing, or underwriting any policy or policies " of Insurance, or making any contract for Insurance of or upon any ship " or ships, goods or merchandizes, at sea or going to sea."—Sect. 12.

The Legislature, however, even of those times, when political economy was imperfectly understood, apparently distrusting the policy of the extraordinary privileges thus granted, provides for their determination at any period within the thirty-one years next ensuing, on giving three years previous notice and repayment of the monies which each of the Companies advanced to Government; and after the expiration of the said thirty-one years, a power is reserved to repeal those rights without any previous notice or any repayment, if they should be judged hurtful or inconvenient to the public; but with this declaration, " that the same corporations, or " any corporation or corporations with the like powers, privileges, benefits " and advantages, shall not be grantable again to any persons or corpora- " tions whatsoever, but shall remain suppressed for ever, as having been " found inconvenient and prejudicial to the public."

The sum which each Company engaged to pay Government, was 300,000 *l.* but they were severally excused the payment of one-half thereof by another Act of Parliament (7 Geo. I. c. 27, s. 26) from which it appears that each of them had obtained a separate charter for the assurance of houses and goods from fire, but without an exclusive privilege.

Thus neither Company paid more than 150,000 *l.* to the public, of which sum 38,750 *l.* was the consideration of their Fire-assurance charter; so that, in truth, neither paid for their exclusive privilege more than 111,250 *l.*

The exclusive privilege of the two Companies rests therefore altogether upon the 6th Geo. I. c. 18, which provides for its determination in the manner which has been stated.

It appears indisputable, that, the Companies having possessed their exclusive privileges more than twice the period of time for which they paid any valuable consideration, no claim can be set up for their continuation, should the House be of opinion that the existence of such privileges are according to the words of the Act, " hurtful or inconvenient to the public." From the sequel of this Report, it will appear that this is decidedly the opinion of Your Committee; and should the House adopt their recommendation, to repeal the exclusive privilege of the two Companies, but to preserve to them unimpaired all their other chartered rights, there is every reason to believe that this necessary sacrifice for the general good can be attended with little if any injury to the Companies themselves, as it is not probable that their Marine Insurance business will be diminished below that very limited extent to which they confine themselves.

It is not necessary for the present purpose of Your Committee to animadvert upon the several inconsistencies of the Act by which the two Companies were incorporated; nor to discuss the question, whether the House should hold itself bound by the very singular restriction of the rights of future Parliaments, to grant such powers and privileges to any Companies hereafter as might be abrogated from those now existing, because Your Committee could not recommend to the House to grant the same exclusive privileges to any Company.

The motives which induced the Legislature to grant these privileges in 1719 are set forth in the preamble of the Act, which among other things recites, " that it is found by experience, and that many particular persons " after they have received large premiums or consideration monies for or " towards the insuring ships, goods and merchandize at sea, having become " bankrupts, or otherwise failed in answering or complying with their " policies of assurance ; whereby they were particularly engaged to make " good or contribute towards the losses which merchants or traders have " sustained, to the ruin or impoverishment of many merchants and " traders, and to the discouragement of adventurers at sea, and to the " diminution of the trade, wealth, strength, and public revenues of this " kingdom :

" And whereas it is conceived, that if two several and distinct Corpora- " tions, with a competent joint stock to each of them belonging, and under " proper conditions, restrictions and regulations, were erected and esta- " blished for assurance of ships, goods or merchandizes, at sea or going to " sea, exclusive of all or any other corporations or bodies politic already " created or hereafter to be created, and likewise exclusive of such societies " or partnerships as now are or may hereafter be entered into for that pur- " pose, several merchants or traders who adventure their estates in such " ships, goods or merchandizes, at sea or going to sea (especially in remote " or hazardous voyages) would think it much safer for them to depend on " the policies or assurances of either of these two Corporations so to be " created and established, than on the policies or assurances of private or " particular persons."

On inquiring into the manner and extent of the exercise of these rights by the Companies, it appears evident that the intentions of the Legislature have been wholly disappointed. Whether these Companies have, as Companies are very apt to do, degenerated from their original principles, it is certain that at present, instead of relieving the Merchants, as the Act supposes they would, from the insolvency of individual Underwriters, the whole of their transactions are insignificant, when compared to the general Insurance business of the country ; and that instead of affording that relief, as the Act again supposes they would, " especially in remote and " hazardous voyages," it appears that both Companies seldom insure risks of this description. The chartered Companies do not insure quite four parts out of one hundred of the Insurances of Great Britain, so that for the remaining ninety-six parts the Merchants continue exposed to all the consequences from which the Act of Parliament meant to relieve them.

From the return made to Your Committee of the gross amount of value insured on sea risks by the two Companies, for the last five years, it appears that the average for those years amounts, for the Royal Exchange Assurance Company, to 3.720,000 *l.* and for the London, to 1,452,000 *l.*

Appendix 2.
Accounts.
N° 6, 7

The amount insured by the London Company would be hardly more than a single mercantile house might require ; and both added together would not exceed what two of the most considerable individual under- writers would write in one year.

That the extent of the Insurances done by the Companies does not amount to four parts in one hundred of the total insurances effected in

Great Britain, is apparent from an account which has been laid before Your Committee of the gross amount of the stamp duties paid upon policies of Marine Insurance for the last nine years. In the year 1800, the gross amount of those duties was 113,442*l.* 18*s.* of which 4,076*l.* 7*s.* 6*d.* was paid by the Royal Exchange Assurance Company, 1,279*l.* 7*s.* 6*d.* by the London Assurance Company, and 9,216*l.* 5*s.* 8*d.* by Scotland. In the last year the gross amount of these stamp duties for the Metropolis and for Scotland, was 348,592*l.* 1*s.* 10½*d.* of which 8,209*l.* 1*s.* 3*d.* was paid by the Royal Exchange Assurance Company, 4,729*l.* 15*s.* by the London Assurance Company, and 17,136*s.* 8*s.* 9*d.* by Scotland.

It is evident that the commerce of the country has very much outgrown the capital, and the whole system upon which these Companies were originally founded. But to clear up this part of the subject, it may be proper to submit some estimate of the insured and insurable property at the present time, compared with the period of the establishment of the chartered Companies.

Appendix of Accounts, N° 2.

From an Account laid before Your Committee, it appears that the total tonnage of British registered vessels in the year 1778 (being the earliest period at which the same can be made up) was 1,363,488; but the tonnage of such vessels in the last year amounted to 2,368,468.

Appendix of Accounts, N° 1.

The exports and imports in the year 1719 amounted only to 12,202,215*l.* but in the last year they amounted to 80,708,823*l.* of official value, exclusive of the imports from the East Indies and China.

Appendix of Accounts, N° 3.

The extent of the trade and commerce of the empire at the present period, will further appear from the number of ships and vessels cleared outwards and inwards for the last three years. The number in the last year was no fewer than 37,607.

The total amount of the sums insured by the Royal Exchange Assurance Company in the last year amounted to 3,905,755*l.* and the total Insurances effected by the London Assurance Company in the last year amounted to 2,250,000 *l.*

But the total sum insured in Great Britain in the last year amounted to 162,538,905 *l.* as will appear from the following Statement:

The amount of the 5*s.* stamp duty in the city of London in the year 1809, was 311,787*l.*; consequently there was insured to the amount of   £. - 124,714,800

The amount of the 2*s.* 6*d.* duty was 19,577*l.*; consequently there was insured to the amount of - - - - - - - - - 15,763,600

The 5*s.* and 2*s.* 6*d.* duties are not distinguished for Scotland, but the total amount being 17,136*l.* if the same proportion be taken that the 2*s.* 6*d.* duty bears to the 5*s.* duty in England, that is about 7*l.* per cent, this will give of 5*s.* duty for Scotland 15,844*l.*; consequently there was insured to the amount of - - - - - - - - 6,360,600

And this will leave of 2*s.* 6*d.* duty, the amount of 1,241*l.*; upon which there must have been insured - - - - - - - 992,900

No return has been made of the stamp duties on Marine Policies in the parts of England, exclusive of the metropolis, the distributors not having distinguished them in their returns to the Head Office; but supposing them to be double those of Scotland, this will give insured by the 5*s.* duty - - - - - - - - - 12,721,200

And by the 2*s.* 6*d.* - - - - - - - - - 1,985,800

Total sum insured - - - £. 162,538,900

Large as this sum is, it amounts to little more than one-half of the sum

sum that might have been insured in Great Britain in the last year, as will appear from the following Estimate :

		£.	
The amount of the imports for the last year was	-	30,406,560	
The exports	- - - - -	50,301,763	£.
Official value	- -	————	80,708,823

(Exclusive of the imports from the East Indies and China.)

Difference between real and official value, say 50 *l.* per cent	-	-	- 40,354,421

£. 121,063,244

Tonnage of British vessels for the year 1809, 2,368,468 tons, at 10 *l.* per ton - - - - - - - - - - - -	-	23,684,680
Freight, at 5 *l.* per ton - - - - - - - - -	-	11,342,340
Tonnage of foreign vessels, 1,459,046, at 20 *l.* per ton -	-	29,180,920
Freight, at 10 *l.* per ton - - - - - - -	-	14,590,460
Difference between the tonnage of British vessels cleared inwards and outwards (3,070,725) for the year 1809, and the tonnage (2,368,468) of registered British vessels for the year 1809, being 702,257 tons, at 10 *l.* per ton - - - - - - - - - -	-	7,022,570
Freight, at 5 *l.* per ton - - - - - - -	-	3,511,285
Value of goods carried coastwise, say one-half of the exports and imports		60,531,622
Value of foreign adventures upon British capital, Irish insurances, American and other foreign insurances effected in Great Britain -	-	50,000,000

Total that might have been insured, exclusive of imports } from the East Indies and China - - - - } - - £. 320,927,121

If the above statement be correct (and it is conceived not to be over stated) the total sum that might have been insured in Great Britain in the last year, was - - - - - - - £. 320,927,121

But the sum actually insured was only - - - 162,538,900

Leaving a sum uninsured to the amount of - £. 158,388,221

Whether the proportion is taken from the stamp duties or the amount of the sums insured, it will be found that the two chartered Companies insured less than four parts out of one hundred of the whole Insurances effected in Great Britain.

It thus appears, that the Marine Insurance business of these Companies is of an extent disproportioned to the demands of the country, and wholly inadequate to the unbounded expectations of the Legislature.

Several of the Merchants called before Your Committee, concur in stating, that though they would much prefer making their Insurances with the Companies, and would pay a higher premium to them than the risk is supposed to be worth by the Underwriters at Lloyd's Coffee-house, yet that owing to the cautious system of the Companies they are seldom able to deal with them.

It appears probable that the Companies, by relaxing in some degree the rigour of their terms, might command much additional business. Indeed when it is considered that the capital at first raised by these Companies did not exceed 600,000 *l.* and that they carry their Fire and Life Insurances to a much more considerable extent than their Marine Insurances, the limits they prescribe to themselves may be very wise and proper.

The capital of the Royal Exchange Company appears to have been much increased by their success, and is stated now to be worth about two millions. What changes have taken place in that of the London Assurance Company does not appear, Your Committee having made no inquiry into that fact. So much, however, is evident, that in the present times, when the value of insurable property of every description is so much increased, the capitals which in the year 1719 were by Parliament thought sufficient to afford the public a proper security for sea risks only, in the then contracted state of trade, must be very inadequate to answer the addition since made of fire and life risks, besides the immensely increased value of the property subject to these three distinct species of Insurance.

Though, therefore, the cautious conduct of these Companies may be proper, and consistent with their interest and with their duties, yet the intention of the Legislature in granting them an exclusive right of effecting, as Companies, Marine Insurances, are evidently defeated. They do not, and they cannot afford any adequate accommodation to the Merchants. And though these transactions, as far as they go, are of service (and it is not intended by Your Committee to recommend any thing to prevent their continuance) yet their right to exclude all other societies and corporations from doing what they can with their monopoly so inadequately perform themselves, appears to be decidedly, according to the words of the Act of Incorporation, " inconvenient and prejudicial to the public," and as such may and should be repealed. The framers of the Act in question seem to have thought that Insurances are best done by Companies; whatever may be the opinion of the House on this point at present, there can be little doubt of the absurdity of suffering a monopoly to exixt, more effectual in its hindrance than its performance, where such a monopoly can, as in the present instance, be repealed without any violation of public faith.

II. The effect of the exclusive privilege upon Marine Insurance, and the state of and means of effecting Marine Insurances in this Country.

The most obvious effect has been to drive the business of Marine Insurance into a situation directly the reverse of that intended by the Act of Parliament ; that is, it has been obliged to resort almost entirely to individual security, from the consequences of which it was the object of the Act to relieve merchants and traders.

Its effect in the city of London has been to compel individuals to assemble together, in order to underwrite separately while it has prevented them from associating to make Insurances jointly. Hence the establishment of Lloyd's Coffee-house, where every person meaning to underwrite must attend during the time necessary for that purpose. But the first Merchants in the city of London do not and cannot attend Lloyd's Coffee-house. This exclusive privilege, therefore, operates as a monopoly, not merely to the Companies, but to Lloyd's Coffee-house.

It will appear from the Evidence, that the Merchants pretty generally complain of the mode of transacting business at the Coffee-house, which, on the other hand, is as generally defended by the Underwriters and Brokers. Without pretending positively to decide between such contradictory opinions, Your Committee, in forming theirs, think it most prudent to confine themselves to obvious deductions from general principles, and from such facts as appear well established.

From individuals being prevented from associating as in other trades, much inconvenience must infallibly result both to the insurer and insured, and the security of the latter must be lessened. The necessity of applying to so many single persons, either for signing a policy or for settling a loss, and the having in case of death no surviving partner to settle with, are, with many other circumstances which it is unnecessary to detail, such obvious disadvantages, that there can be little doubt that partnerships and associations will be formed, if the law should permit it; and at all events, Merchants and Underwriters, being left to manage their concerns unfettered by any restrictions, will soon fall into that system best suited to their general convenience.

That there is great difficulty and trouble in effecting Insurances, may be safely inferred from the singularly high compensation retained by the Brokers. It appears that they retain for their agency about twenty-five per cent of the total balances of premiums paid by them to the Underwriters, so that one-fourth part of the total profits on underwriting is received by the Brokers.

A practice appears to prevail at the Coffee-house, which is the subject of very general complaint among the Merchants. During the months of August, September, October, November and December, a great number of the Underwriters withdraw from Lloyd's Coffee-house. The Merchants ascribe this to a dislike to winter risks. But whether it be from this cause, or, as the Underwriters allege, for the purpose of relaxation, the consequences are still the same. At this season of the year, when the peril is greatest, and when there are the largest sums to be insured, the means of effecting that Insurance at the Coffee-house are lessened. The Jamaica July fleet, the latest West India fleet, the Baltic, the Mediterranean and Newfoundland convoys, the homeward bound East-Indiamen, not to mention the numerous fleets and vessels taking their departure from Great Britain to Ireland, are mostly then at sea, and, with the exception of part of the West India July and August fleets, are to insure in these months. Some opinion of the consequences arising from Underwriters withdrawing from the Coffee-house in the autumn and winter months, may be formed from the following Account of the sums insured by an Underwriter who attended there every month last year:

	Sums Insured.	Premiums.
	£.	£.
1809. January	25,600	1,853
February	25,100	1,934
March	23,000	1,751
April	26,250	2,860
May	27,900	2,831
June	21,200	2,207
July	24,000	2,554
Amount for the first seven months - £.	173,050	15,990
August	52,000	5,685
September	74,600	8,823
October	45,500	7,401
November	30,000	4,113
December	28,200	4,389
Amount in the last five months - - £.	230,300	30,411

The amount of the sums insured by the Underwriter in the last five months in the year, therefore, exceeded the amount of the sums insured by him in the first seven months by the sum of 57,250 *l.*

Not only is the difficulty of insuring increased by this practice, but, owing to the diminished competition, such Insurances as are done are at a more extravagant premium. If the cause assigned by Underwriters for their absence at this period be the true one, it would be remedied by associations in partnerships, as the partners may attend alternately, without the firm being at any time absent from the Coffee-house.

The out-ports of the kingdom are exposed to very great hardships by the Insurance Law as it now stands. The Merchants of Liverpool, Bristol, Hull, &c. cannot legally associate together. They can have no joint security for their Insurances. They are denied the right, because it is exclusively granted to two Companies in the metropolis, from which they can derive little or no benefit. This is manifestly unjust, and has been found to be so inconvenient, that the rights of the Companies have been disregarded ; and it appears, that notwithstanding the prohibition and the penalties by which it is protected, that there are upwards of twenty known Associations in different parts of England for the purposes of Marine Insurances.

See Evi-
dence of
Mr. Cheape.
Two of these exist in London, the one called The Friendly Assurance, the other The London Union Society. The former is an Association of Proprietors of eighty-three regular Transports, and it has produced to them a great saving in the amount of their Insurance. Last year it appears, that of their averages and losses the amount which each member of the Association will have to pay is only 1 ¼ *l.* per cent ; whereas if they had gone into Lloyd's Coffee-house to get the same risks covered, they would have been obliged to pay a premium of from 9*l.* to 11 *l.* per cent.

See Evi-
dence of
Mr. Wilson.
The other of these societies established in London is an Association of Owners of Vessels trading to the port of London. The number of persons associated is about eighty, and the number of vessels which they insured last year was about ninety, at an expense of 5*l.* 10*s.* per cent ; whereas if the same Insurances had been made in Lloyd's Coffee-house, they would have cost, if transports 9*l.*, if colliers from 18*l* to 20*l.* per cent.

See Evi-
dence of
Mr Gillespy.
The capital of similar Associations established in other parts of England, is estimated at a million, by a person well acquainted with them.

A further effect of this exclusive privilege therefore has been to drive ship-owners into a course which is illegal, but which ought not to be suffered to remain so.

Your Committee refrain from entering upon various other details, by which the defects of the present mode of transacting Marine Insurances would be explained, conceiving that they are sufficiently manifest : And they therefore proceed to the last point reserved for consideration.

III. The importance of a better system to the Commerce and Revenue of the Empire, and to the parties concerned.

That mode of effecting Marine Insurances must be the best, which gives the best security at the cheapest rate.

And that which gives the best security at the cheapest rate, is the enabling Merchants to insure each other.

If such a system shall be established, it is probable that the price paid for Insurance will not much exceed the aggregate value of the losses sustained on each class of risks insured. The advantage to the Merchant from a cheap rate of good Insurance is so great, that no profit he could make from a participation of premium in any association he might enter into for this purpose could overbalance it, and his interest would therefore lead him to keep the premium of Insurance always as low as possible.

The premium he pays is in truth either a diminution of his profit, or a clog upon his trade.

Dr. Adam Smith, though unfriendly to joint stock companies in general, makes four exceptions; viz. " The only trades which it seems possible " for a joint stock company to carry on *without an exclusive privilege*, " are those of which all the operations are capable of being reduced to " what is called a routine, or to such a uniformity of method as admits " of little or no variation; of this kind is, first, the banking trade; " secondly, the trade of Insurance from fire and from *sea risk and capture* " *in time of war*; thirdly, the trade of making and maintaining a navi- " gable cut or canal; and, fourthly, the similar trade of bringing water " for the supply of a great city." He appears, however, to have been " under a mistake in one respect, for he adds " that neither the London " Assurance nor the Royal Exchange Assurance Companies have any " such (exclusive) privilege." *Wealth of Nations, vol. 3, p. 146.* *Ibid. p. 147.*

The superiority of Companies for the purposes of Marine Insurance, for facility, security and cheapness, appears from the concurring testimonies of all the Merchants who have been examined, and may be inferred from the fact, that wherever there is no restriction (that is, every where but in Great Britain,) Insurances are invariably done by Companies.

In Hamburgh there were thirty-six Marine Insurance Companies; two at Stockholm, one at Gottenburgh, and five at Copenhagen. In every part of America the Insurances are done by incorporate Companies. In the state of Massachusets alone there are nineteen Companies; at Boston there are seven; at New York, six; at Philadelphia, eight; at Baltimore, five; at Norfolk, one; at Charlestown, two; at New Orleans, one; and in our own settlements there are, at Newfoundland one Marine Insurance Company; at Halifax, one; in Jamaica, one; in Barbadoes, two; and in the East Indies, thirteen. *See Evidence of Mr. Rucker, Mr. Molling, Mr. Jones.*

In Ireland there are three Marine Insurance Companies; and one of these, viz. the Belfast Insurance Company, has an agent who underwrites for them in Lloyd's Coffee-house.

The advantages of joint over separate Insurances are further shown by the establishment of so many societies in different parts of England, in violation of the rights of the existing Companies.

But it is not the intention of Your Committee to recommend the enforcement of any particular system by law; but, on the contrary, to release this branch of business from the restraints now existing, and to leave it to shape itself as it then infallibly would do, in conformity with the true interest of the public.

Should the House still be of opinion that chartered Companies with exclusive privileges afford the best means of Insurance, it would undoubtedly become the duty of Your Committee to recommend that one or more such establishments be formed under the regulation of Parliament, for the purpose of securing to the Merchants those advantages which the existing institutions are incapable of affording. But they hope that the House will concur with them in thinking, that though Companies and Associations for Marine Insurances may be useful or desirable, yet that it would be inexpedient and unwise to protect any of them by privileges or exemptions from which others should be excluded.

It is certainly of the utmost importance that there should be the means of effecting Marine Insurances with economy and security. The Merchant, by being permitted by his correspondent abroad to insure at home, not only derives a profit therefrom, but adds much to the security of his trade. And if the complaints which it is said Foreign Merchants make to London Insurances be well-founded, there can be little doubt that where the restraints of law shall be removed, this country will, in this as in most other operations of trade, manifest its accustomed superiority.

By an uneconomical Insurance (and what stronger proof can exist that it is uneconomical, than where the brokerage even amounts to one-fourth of the Underwriter's profits,) the prices of all imported articles consumed are enhanced. The same is the case with the raw materials for our manufactures, and in the exportation of manufactured articles. We shall, on a return of peace, want every advantage that wisdom can devise, to meet the competition arising from low wages on the Continent.

The great consumption by Government of stores from the Baltic and other parts of the world; the number of hired transports in its service; the shipments it must make to various quarters; the contracts it is necessarily engaged in; all concur to give the public a direct interest in this question.

The revenue of the country receives also an important contribution, which has been increasing, and may be further increased, by an improved system of Marine Insurance. In the last year the Stamp Duty on policies amounted to 348,592 *l.* 1 *s.* 10 ½ *d.* exclusive of the duties paid at the outports in England, which are not distinguished in the returns from other stamp duties remitted from the country. From an Estimate in a preceding part of this Report, it appears that a sum of not less than 158 millions is either left annually uninsured, or insured by means which evade or escape the duty. Much of this, and certainly much additional foreign property, might be expected to be insured under a better system, by which this source of revenue might be further increased. While these important considerations induce Your Committee to call the attention of the House to the defects in the present system of Marine Insurance, they have great satisfaction in stating as their belief, that an adoption of the substance of the Resolutions which they submit to the House, will be productive of general benefit to all parties concerned.

The existing Companies can have no difficulty at any time of extending their Marine Insurances to any amount they may think consistent with the extent of their capitals, and their other engagements and avocations. It is not even pretended that they will lose any share of their business by any competition which the repeal of their exclusive privileges can create.

The individual Underwriters will have the relief and facility in their business which partnerships afford; one man may suffice for what four or five are now employed at, and they will no longer be obliged to let their business stand still when they may be occasionally absent. Both the Companies and the Underwriters will derive their proportion of that general increase of Insurances expected from an improvement of the system.

The Brokers will also partake of this increase; for there can be no reason to suppose that this, any more than any other business, can be transacted without such intermediate agency. Their trouble will be very much diminished, by dealing with partnerships which are always at hand, instead of a great number of individuals frequently scattered about the country.

The concern of the Merchants generally in this change, and consequently of the great commercial interests of the State in all its various ramifications, is still more manifest, and would be of a description to outweigh any partial injury to other classes, if such had been, as it is not, apprehended by Your Committee.

The voice of the great and respectable body of general Merchants appears so unanimous on this occasion, and the nature of their present complaints have been so extensively enlarged upon in the course of this Report, that Your Committee will conclude with submitting to the House the RESOLUTIONS they have come to after the most attentive inquiry into this important subject ; viz.

Resolved,

That it is the opinion of this Committee, That property requiring to be insured against sea and enemies risk, should have all the security which can be found for it, whether that security exists in chartered Companies, in other Companies, or through Individuals.

Resolved,

That it is the opinion of this Committee, That the exclusive privilege for Marine Insurance of the two chartered Companies should be repealed, saving their charters and their powers and privileges in all other respects ; and that leave should be given to bring in a Bill for this purpose.

Resolved,

That it is the opinion of this Committee, That with respect to the two Petitions which have been referred to them, it should be left to the discretion of the Petitioners to bring their respective cases under the consideration of the House, by Bills for carrying into effect the prayer of their Petitions, if they shall think proper so to do.

18 *April* 1810.

APPENDIX.

MINUTES OF EVIDENCE

TAKEN BEFORE THE

SELECT COMMITTEE appointed to consider of the State and Means of effecting MARINE INSURANCE in Great Britain.

Lunæ; 26° die Februarii, 1810.

WILLIAM MANNING, Esq. in the Chair.

John Dederick Rucker, Esq. called in; and Examined.

DID you sign the petition?—No, I did not.

You are a partner in the house of Messrs. Rucker and Brothers?—Yes, I am.

J. D. Rucker, Esq.

Have you insurances of every description to make, and to a large amount?—Yes, I have.

State the amount of the premiums upon insurances you effected last year?—The premium of insurances which we effected last year amounts to about 100,000*l*.

Were many of these insurances effected with the companies?—No, very few.

Would you in general insure with the companies, and to a larger extent than you now do, if they would enable you so to do?—Yes; I certainly would always prefer to insure with the companies, if they were inclined to underwrite upon equitable terms.

Does it consist with your knowledge, that the narrow scale upon which the companies transact business is matter of general complaint amongst the merchants of the city of London?—As far as I have had an opportunity of observing, I believe it has been a very general complaint against the companies.

Does it consist with your knowledge, that the state of insurance in Great Britain is matter of general complaint upon the Continent?—Yes, I am convinced it is a matter of general complaint.

Do you speak from your personal knowledge?—Yes, I do.

Can you state the number of marine insurance companies established abroad?—I can only state the number of insurance companies established at Hamburgh, where I formerly resided myself.

State the number of insurance companies at Hamburgh?—There were about thirty or thirty-five.

At what time are you speaking of?—The greater part of these companies were only established since 1803.

Supposing a company or companies for marine insurance established in Great Britain, with a sufficient capital, and transacting their business in a proper manner, does it appear to you that many insurances, which would otherwise be done upon the Continent, would be effected in this country?—Yes, I am clearly of opinion that they would.

State your reasons for that opinion?—I have many reasons for that opinion : the general complaint which exists upon the Continent against the underwriters in general here, and the difficulty which they have experienced in settling their losses, has hitherto prevented them, and made them averse from giving their orders for insurances to this country ; but I am of opinion that if a company or companies should be established, that would be willing to underwrite more extensively and upon more liberal terms than the companies that now exist, or the underwriters at Lloyd's, it would enable merchants here to effect their insurances more to the satisfaction of the merchants abroad, and I have no doubt would induce them to extend their orders to this country. I may also mention, that the establishment of a great number of insurance companies at Hamburgh, had the effect of drawing a great

J. D. Rucker,
Esq.

many more insurances from hence, as well as from other parts of the Continent to Hamburgh.

Is it a general condition made by your correspondents that you should guarantee the underwriters?—Yes, it is almost made a general condition.

State your reasons for submitting to this condition?—If we were always to refuse it, we should most likely lose some of our best connections.

You believe this condition to have arisen from the delays and losses which merchants abroad sustained in the recovery of sums insured here?—Yes; I am convinced that that has been the cause of it.

Do you think this condition a hardship, and submit to it only from the apprehension of losing the employment of your correspondents?—Yes, I consider it as a hardship, and would rather not submit to it, as I do not consider the small commission which is generally allowed to guarantee the safety of the underwriters as adequate to the risk.

Does it appear to you that you would be relieved from it by the establishment of a company or companies in Great Britain willing to take, and adequate to, the risks which you have to insure?—Yes, I have no doubt that the establishment of a company or companies, willing to transact their business upon liberal and more extensive terms, would relieve us from the necessity of guaranteeing the underwriters.

In the months of September, October and November, have you not frequently found great difficulty in effecting your insurances at Lloyd's Coffee-house?—Yes; we have, particularly during that period, met with very great difficulties to complete our insurances.

State what are the reasons?—I believe that the chief reason for it was owing to the general absence of the principal underwriters at Lloyd's, who generally leave Lloyd's Coffee-house about that time, in order to avoid writing during that particular season.

Is the Committee to understand, that during those months Lloyd's Coffee-house is almost totally deserted by the principal underwriters?—Yes; I speak from experience.

Have you found difficulty in settling losses upon insurances done here?—Yes, I certainly have met with very great difficulty.

Have you had frequent instances of those difficulties?—Yes, we have met with many difficulties.

Have you experienced those difficulties lately?—Yes, lately.

When you stated your premiums to be about 100,000*l.* did you mean the gross premiums before any returns were made upon them?—Yes

Can you state nearly what the amount of your net premiums may have been last year?—I suppose that the amount of the returns which we shall have to set off against our premiums the last year will amount to 20 or 30,000*l*, which will leave a net amount of 70 or 80,000*l*.

Is the Committee to understand that you paid to the amount of 70 or 80,000*l.* premium in the course of last year?—The premium which we have, and shall have to pay, will amount to about that sum I suppose.

Is the reason which prevents you from insuring with the two chartered companies their refusal to take the sum you may have to insure, or is it on account of the high premium demanded by them?—Sometimes these are our reasons, but more generally because they are not willing to underwrite at any premium.

What is the nature of the risks which the companies are not willing to underwrite at any premium?—Most of the risks from the Continent, and in particular those from the Baltic

Please to state any instance in which the companies have so refused?—We received an order from Hamburgh, in the month of August, to insure the sum of 22,000*l* or 24,000*l.* upon a good ship from Tonningen to London, and the companies refused to underwrite this risk at any premium, but in the month of October they wrote several risks to us of a similar nature at even a less premium than we were obliged to pay at Lloyd's The premium which we paid at Lloyd's, in the first instance, will show, that it must have been generally considered as a fair risk, as we only paid three guineas per cent, and did about 18,000*l*

State the name of the ship?—The Franciscow, Captain Grothman

You have stated that you were ordered to insure to the amount of 22,000*l* how happens it that you could only effect insurance to the amount of 18,000*l.* upon the above ship?—This is a point which I wish to mention particularly, as it exposed us to considerable risk, in not being able to complete the whole of the order on account of the unwillingness of the company to take any part of this risk Another house received a similar order, and nearly to the same amount, to insure on the same ship; and I understand they were not able to effect the whole.

J. D. Rucker, Esq.

Is the Committee to understand that you could not effect insurance upon this risk to the amount of 22,000 L. in Lloyd's Coffee-house, in the month of August last?—Not to our satisfaction.

When you say not to your satisfaction, do you mean that the premium at which you could effect it was not to your satisfaction, or that the character of the underwriters was not such as you liked?—Certainly, we were prevented by both causes; their not being willing to underwrite at any premium, and partly because we did not like the underwriters.

Were you limited in point of premium?—No, we were not.

What addition to the original premium did you offer after you had effected the 18,000 L.?—We doubled the premium.

Does it ever happen, where the risk is a fair one, that there is any difficulty in effecting the insurance at Lloyd's Coffee-house with underwriters of the first character, to the amount of 22,000 L.?—I believe not to the amount of 22,000 l.; but in the instance I mentioned the sum was nearly double.

Does any such difficulty occur when the sum is 40,000 L.?—Yes; I think the instance I have stated is a proof of it.

Do you effect your own insurance, or do you employ a policy broker?—We employ brokers.

What is the name of the broker?—We employ several brokers.

Did you put this particular insurance into the hands of one or more brokers?—I put it into the hands of four or five.

Is the Committee then to understand, that there is, generally speaking, a difficulty in effecting insurances with the underwriters at Lloyd's to the amount of 40,000 l. on one ship?—Yes, I think that difficulty exists.

Was this insurance upon the ship or goods?—Upon the goods.

Was there any guarantee that secured the underwriters, in this particular instance, against capture or seizure in foreign ports?—There was no particular guarantee; it was against all risk; but as well a British as a Danish licence was on board.

Are the insurances for which you receive orders from the Continent principally upon foreign ships?—Yes, they are.

Are they not altogether foreign ships?—They are all foreign ships; from those ports from which the British flag is excluded.

Is not your business, with reference to insurances, almost solely confined to those ports?—No, by no means.

Are not the insurances for which you receive orders from ports from which the British flag is not excluded, also generally upon foreign ships?—They are not; they are generally upon British ships.

Was the ship mentioned in a former answer (the ship Franciscow) recorded in the register book at Lloyd's?—I cannot positively say, but I believe she was.

Do you not, in point of fact, know that the Franciscow was a very bad ship?—No, I do not; I am convinced, on the contrary, that she was a very fine ship.

Was she out of time when the insurance was proposed?—No, she certainly was not out of time when we began to do the insurance.

To what then do you attribute the impossibility of effecting insurance upon so small a sum as 44,000 l.?—The insufficiency of the means of doing insurances here.

Have you ever heard of insurances having been effected at Lloyd's to the amount of 100,000 l. upon one ship?—Not upon merchantmen.

You have stated that foreigners object to insure in England, on account of the difficulty experienced in settling losses with underwriters; is the Committee then to understand that the body of underwriters in England is in low estimation abroad?—I am sorry to say that I am perfectly of that opinion.

What is the commission usually allowed for guaranteeing the underwriters?—We never do it at less than a half per cent upon the capital insured.

You have stated that the good underwriters are generally absent in the months of September, October and November, and that you are thereby exposed to difficulties in insuring at Lloyd's during those months; have you, upon those occasions, offered your risks to the two companies?—Yes, repeatedly.

And have your proposals been refused?—Yes, they have.

Has such refusal been owing to the nature of the risk, or to the smallness of the premium offered by you?—I suppose it must have been owing generally to the nature of the risk that has prevented them; but in most instances they were not willing to fix any premium; or at least it was so unproportionable that we were not able to give it.

J. D. Rucker,
Esq.

If a new insurance company were to be established, have you any reason to believe that such a company would take risks so refused by the two existing companies, and to avoid taking which risks, you have stated the principal underwriters absent themselves from Lloyd's?—I believe that would be the case; I am not sufficiently acquainted with the plan upon which this new marine insurance company is to be established.

Do you believe that any new insurance company could possess a better knowledge of the business of underwriting than is now possessed by the underwriters at Lloyd's, and the two chartered companies?—I believe that they are sufficiently acquainted with insurance business. However, I suppose they (the new insurance company) could underwrite upon more extensive and liberal terms, and that the greater competition would produce that effect.

How long has your commercial house been established in London?—The house in which I am a partner has not been established in London above five or six years.

What description of insurances does your house effect, exclusive of those to the ports of the Continent of Europe?—A great many to and from the West Indies.

Have you ever found any difficulty in effecting those West India insurances?—Not so many difficulties.

What difficulties have you found in effecting insurances to and from the West Indies?—The same difficulty which I have stated before: that of not being able to insure with facility the amount which we had to do.

What is the largest amount on which you have been ordered to effect insurance at any time from the West Indies?—To the best of my recollection, from 20,000 *l.* to 25,000 *l.* upon one ship.

Do you mean to state that you have not been able to effect insurance from 20,000 *l.* to 25,000 *l.* upon a West India ship, either at Lloyd's, or with the two chartered companies?—We met with difficulties in effecting these insurances, owing to large sums being done upon the same ship by other persons.

What do you conceive to be the largest amount, in point of value, that a West India ship is capable of carrying in West India commodities?—It depends entirely upon the size of the ship; but I should not suppose much above the amount of 50,000 *l.* or 60,000 *l.*

Have the complaints made to you from the Continent of the present state of insurance business in this country applied to the rate of premiums, or to the want of solidity in the underwriters?—Not so much to the state of the premiums as to the want of solidity in the underwriters.

At what period were those complaints first made?—I believe they are of very old standing.

At what period were they first made to you?—I speak from my own experience, having been established abroad for several years before I came to this country.

Where were you established abroad before you came to this country?—At Hamburgh.

Are not the insurances done at Hamburgh done upon enemy's property?—Yes.

Is not the insurance of enemy's property prohibited by law in Great Britain?—I believe it is.

Have not the insurances which you are principally in the habit of effecting included the risk of capture and seizure in the ports of the enemy?—Yes, a great number have.

Do the chartered companies insure against that risk?—No, I believe they do not.

Then have not all those insurances been effected by the underwriters at Lloyd's?—I suppose they have; but I know that some such insurances have been effected abroad.

Can you state the profit and loss upon your account on guaranteeing the underwriters?—No, I cannot: we have been very fortunate in general in having very few losses. My experience is not long enough to speak precisely.

How then can you state the guaranteeing the underwriters to be a hardship?—Because in the few losses which we have had to settle we have had several instances of bankruptcy.

Have the losses in those bankruptcies made the guaranteeing of the underwriters a losing concern or not?—Not to us, as our losses were so few.

Did the Franciscow arrive safe or not?—She arrived safe.

Are not the months of September, October and November the months when the great business from the Baltic is principally carrying on?—Yes.

Do not merchants as well as underwriters frequent watering places in the autumn?—I suppose they do.

How do you know the motives of the underwriters in going to watering places?—I cannot positively say that I know their motives, but I suppose, as it generally happens at that time of the year, that their motives are to avoid underwriting.

Have not those insurances, which you stated yourself to have effected, generally been against all risks?—Generally all risks, but not that of British capture.

Do not all risks include British capture?—No, they hardly ever include the risk of British capture.

What proportion of your correspondents for whom you transact business have their insurances effected here, compared with those who have them effected at Hamburgh or at the place of their residence?—The proportion of those who do their business abroad is very small at present, owing to many circumstances which compel them to effect their insurances in this country; a number of circumstances connected with the present state of the Continent, compel them to give their orders for insurances to this country.

Is not the principal circumstance that compels them to make their insurances in this country, a desire to avoid publicity in the business that is prohibited?—Certainly.

You have stated, that you do part of your business at Lloyd's and part with the companies; can you state to the Committee whether the premiums asked by the companies are considerably higher than those asked by the coffee-house?—In general we have found them to be higher than at Lloyd's.

Can you state to the·Committee what proportion the one bears to the other, taking them generally?—From two to five per cent more.

Do you mean upon the premium?—I mean upon the premium; upon small premiums they ask two per cent more, and upon large premiums from five to eight per cent more.

Do you mean, for instance, that on a risk for which the coffee-house would ask six, the companies would ask eight?—Yes, that is the proportion I mean.

Then that would be 33⅓ per cent upon the premium?—Yes, it would.

Although you have yourself not been above six or seven years established in London, your family has been very long established in this country?—Yes, for a great number of years.

And has been one of the most considerable houses connected with the trade with the continent?—Yes.

Do you, in point of fact, know any instance where the companies have asked eight per cent for what could be effected by respectable underwriters at six per cent?—I do not remember at this moment any particular instance, but we have had a great many.

Then you can speak positively to the fact, although you do not recollect a particular instance when such difference occurred?—Yes, I can speak positively to the fact.

J. D. Rucker, Esq.

Martis, 27° die Februarii, 1810.

WILLIAM MANNING, Esq. in the Chair.

Frederick Molling, Jun. Esq. called in; and Examined.

DESCRIBE in what trade you are?—Hamburgh merchants.

You are a partner in the house of Spitter, Molling and Company?—Yes.

Your house executes a great variety of insurances?—They do.

What might be the amount of the premiums you paid in the last year?—Nearly 40,000 *l.*

Do you speak of net or gross premiums?—Gross premiums.

Subject to returns?—Yes.

Your house receives *del credire* commissions?—Frequently we do.

Do you execute them?—We always decline them.

Why do you decline them?—In consequence of losses we have formerly sustained at Lloyd's, by failure of the underwriters.

Would such *del credire* commissions be necessary if there was a company or companies willing to take, and adequate to the risks you have to insure?—We should accept of those del credire commissions having respectable bodies to do the insurances with.

F. Molling, Esq.

F. Melling,
Esq.

Has your house exported goods to the continent to a great amount?—Very largely.

How much in any one year?—Since I have been a partner, I can speak to from five to six hundred thousand pounds.

Have those goods been insured here or abroad?—Chiefly insured abroad.

Where?—Chiefly in Hamburgh.

Why have you insured abroad?—Because we would not take upon ourselves the responsibility of the insurance.

Have you ever found difficulty in effecting insurances?—At certain times we have.

How has such difficulty arisen?—In consequence in the close of the year, August, September and October, of the coffee-house being deserted by the principal of the respectable part of the underwriters.

Has your own broker always been able to effect your insurances?—Not in every case.

If there were a company or companies established in Great Britain, equal and willing to take the risks required to be insured; does it appear to you that insurances would be effected here which would otherwise be effected abroad?—Certainly there would.

State the grounds upon which you form that opinion?—In the first place, as exporters of goods, we should do the insurances here ourselves, having better security, and our friends abroad would save another commission, which they are obliged to pay in Hamburgh, in consequence of the insurance not being done here.

Are the insurances on the continent done by companies or individuals?—I can only speak to Hamburgh; they are chiefly done by companies there.

Can you state the number of insurance companies abroad?—They are very much increased since I left Hamburgh.

You have stated, that you have frequently experienced difficulties in effecting insurances at Lloyd's, have those insurances which you have found a difficulty in effecting, been upon what may be considered good risks?—Very good risks.

Are they such risks as the two chartered companies would take?—They would, but with a warranty against capture and seizure in ports of the enemy.

Would not individual underwriters insure the same risks with the same guarantee? —That I cannot answer.

Do you believe that there would be any difficulty in effecting such insurances with respectable underwriters under such guarantee?—We found in the close of the last year a policy that could not be continued by respectable underwriters.

Of what nature was that policy?—A policy to the Baltic against all risks.

At what season of the year?—I think it was in the beginning of September we effected the insurance.

To what amount?—I believe about 8,000*l.*

Did you offer any additional premium, and what?—We continued at the same premium as we began it.

The Committee is to understand no additional premium beyond that at which the policy was opened was offered?—No.

If an additional premium had been offered, do you believe the insurance could have been effected?—I do not think it could.

Is the risk to which you now allude one which would have been taken by the two chartered companies?—They always refuse to write so late to the Baltic as that policy was effected.

Is it not the practice to give an additional premium to the Baltic as the season advances?—Certainly, but this was a high premium.

When was this policy opened?—I cannot exactly state the date.

What was the premium?—I think twenty-five guineas per cent; but it was from Gottenburgh to the Baltic, not from London.

With what returns?—With five, and five returns for convoy.

You have stated two instances where insurance could not be effected either with the chartered companies or at Lloyd's, state whether you have any reason to believe that any new companies which might be formed, carrying on their business upon principles of prudence and reason, would be likely to take such risks as have so been refused at Lloyd's and by the chartered companies?—I have reason to believe it.

Be pleased to state the ground of that belief?—That the premiums given are adequate to the risk.

Do you then believe that the underwriters who now frequent Lloyd's, and the two

existing chartered companies, are less capable of judging of the value of premiums
than any companies would be which might be hereafter established?—I should consider if there were new companies, they would be more open to general business.

Do you thereby mean to say, that their eagerness to obtain business would make
them less cautious than the present underwriters, and the present chartered companies?—There would be more competition.

Have you any notion of the number of individual underwriters who now frequent
Lloyd's coffee-house?—No, I have not.

Do you believe from your knowledge of Lloyd's, that there are at least 500 individuals who now underwrite?—I suppose there may be.

Do you believe that the establishment of one or more companies would produce
a greater competition than at present exists amongst so many individuals, acting
each for his own individual interest?—I consider that it would.

Upon what grounds do you so consider?—The premiums would be more settled,
and the office would take it probably at the same premium with individual underwriters at Lloyd's.

Is not the principal part of your insurances effected upon risks to and from the
Baltic?—No, they are not.

Is it not then to and from other ports in the possession of the enemy?—Our
principal insurances last year were to Sweden, which were not then enemy's ports.

Have you made out any account of the profit and loss of your house in consequence
of guaranteeing underwriters?—Since I have been a partner we have never guaranteed, and I have not looked into it.

Then you cannot speak from your own knowledge as to the state of your profit and
loss in consequence of guaranteeing underwriters?—We never guaranteed.

Do you not know that considerable demands have been made upon the underwriters on cargoes bound to the ports of the enemy for sums alleged to have been
paid by the assured to the French officers, in order to procure their admission?—
We never have paid those demands.

Do you not know that large demands of that sort have been made upon the
underwriters?—I cannot answer that question from my own knowledge.

Do either of the existing chartered companies insure against capture and seizure
in the ports of the enemy?—I believe not.

Are not risks of that description insured at Lloyd's by individual underwriters?—
Certainly they are.

Have you ever found any difficulty at Lloyd's in effecting what are called regular
risks, insurances on British ships sailing with convoy?—We have had so little to do
with British ships for the last five years that I have been in the house, that I cannot
say that we have.

Do you know that such risks are generally considered as good risks?—Certainly.

If a new chartered company were established, supported by very extensive commercial interests in this metropolis, would they not possess a very large show of this
description of regular risk?—Certainly, I suppose they would.

Do you not believe that the two chartered companies now existing, have found by
long experience that those regular risks are more advantageous than risks of that
hazardous description, which include capture and seizure in the ports of the enemy?
—Chartered companies do not accept of those risks.

Can they not judge from the experience of others as well as from their own experience?—I believe that money has been made by insurances for all risks.

Do you suppose that the chartered companies would decline risks which they
conceived to be advantageous?—I suppose not.

If they do not consider them as advantageous, and decline writing them under that
conviction, would not experience be very likely to produce the same conviction in the
minds of the directors of any new company?—That would depend upon whether
the directors of new companies might not think those risks good.

If a new company were to write against capture and seizure in the ports of the
enemy indiscriminately, might not the seizure of all the vessels in the ports of the enemy
trading with this country, involve them in losses beyond the amount of their capital?
—If they wrote indiscriminately they would perhaps be large sufferers by it.

Is it possible for a company doing a vast mass of business, to class their risks in
the same manner as an individual underwriter can do?—I should consider they
would look to the parties who insure.

Do you not consider the seizure of all vessels coming from this country in the
ports of the enemy as a very improbable circumstance?—I consider that vessels going

F. Milling,
Esq.

F. Molling, Esq.

to enemy's ports, are provided with such papers, that preparations are made there to receive them in a friendly manner.

Then am I to understand, that you do not consider their seizure in those ports as a circumstance likely to take place?—I do not consider it so.

Then why do you pay so large a premium to insure against that risk?—It is a premium that we seldom pay ourselves; we frequently take upon ourselves the risk of seizure in port.

Does it consist with your knowledge, that the method of transacting insurances here, is matter of general complaint among the merchants abroad?—It certainly is; I have had many complaints of it.

Does it consist with your knowledge, that foreign merchants find considerable difficulties in settling their losses with underwriters here; and is it your opinion that such difficulties induce them to insure abroad?—Yes.

Has the custom of guaranteeing the underwriters arisen solely in consequence of the losses sustained by foreign merchants on insurances done here, or has it arisen from other causes?—It is in consequence of the merchants abroad wishing to have security, the insurances abroad being chiefly done by companies.

You do not mean to say it is the want of credit of the gentlemen at Lloyd's that has induced this custom of guaranteeing insurance?—It is for want of the merchants abroad confiding in the underwriters, but looking up to the person that effected their insurances.

Have you experienced any difficulty in getting losses settled on insurances done here?—We have found frequent delays.

Have you experienced those difficulties lately?—Not so much lately as we used formerly, in consequence of our being very particular whose names we receive upon our policies.

What is the Committee to understand by formerly?—I speak of five or six years back.

You have stated, that the complaints against the London underwriters are very general abroad; do you know whether any such complaints exist abroad against the insurance companies abroad?—They are generally more easily settled abroad than here.

Do you know instances where complaints have been made?—I never heard of any.

Do you believe there would be any difficulty in effecting an insurance to the amount of 40,000 *l.* amongst the most respectable underwriters at Lloyd's, on what is generally considered as good risk?—That is a larger sum than we have had to do, and I cannot answer to it.

Have you never heard that an insurance to the amount of 100,000 *l.* has been so done at Lloyd's?—No, I never have.

You having stated, that at a certain time of the year when the winter risks are current, the principal underwriters at Lloyds are often absent; if they were not absent, and they were the underwriters who saw and wrote on your good policies, would you not have a fair call upon them to take a line upon more disadvantageous ones?—We should have a call upon them, but probably they would decline writing them.

Do not the premiums advance in the winter months in proportion to the increase of the risk?—They do.

As you transact your business at Lloyd's by a broker, how do you state from your own knowledge that underwriters absent themselves in the winter months?—Because we have asked our brokers why such names were not there, and they have said they were not in town.

That you have only from hearsay?—We have it from our brokers.

As the premiums advance in the winter months in proportion to the risk, how can it be for the advantage of the underwriters to absent themselves at that season of the year?—It cannot be to their advantage.

Do not merchants here frequently guarantee the buyers of goods consigned to them by their foreign correspondents, as well as guarantee the underwriters upon their policy?—Yes certainly.

Is not the property insured by merchants on the continent principally enemy's property?—No; scarcely any insurances are done at present on the continent.

What description of British property is generally insured on the continent?—At present not any.

Is there not one inducement to merchants here to insure if possible in England, that they may be thereby enabled to hold the policies as a security?—That is a very great inducement.

George Simson, Esq. a Member of the House, was Examined.

YOU are of the house of Bruce, De Ponthieu & Company?—I am.

Has your house ever found any difficulty in effecting its insurances?—Yes, it has.

State the particulars?—In the year 1799, upon the ship Scaleby Castle, consigned from Bombay to London, an insurance of 161,000*l.* was directed to be made upon the ship and cargo; the sum the house were enabled to effect at Lloyd's was 93,100*l.*; they made their other insurances 10,000*l.* at the Royal Exchange, 16,000*l.* at Manchester, 11,400*l.* at Bristol, 10,000*l.* at Liverpool, and 8,100*l.* at Glasgow, making altogether 148,600*l.*, which was all they could make in England, as they stated in their letter to India; the rest remained uncovered.

Was application made to the London Insurance Company?—I understood application was made to them, but they declined insuring on account of the ship being manned with Lascars.

Have you ever experienced any similar difficulty?—In the year 1801, upon the same ship, we were not able to complete our insurances; the Royal Exchange charged 2 per cent additional premium. On the second voyage we did at Lloyd's 102,800*l.* at 10 guineas, at the Royal Exchange 10,000*l.* at 12 guineas; we had a small additional insurance at Hull of 4,000*l.*, which was upon the same terms as at Lloyd's. On the former insurance this letter was written by the house of Law, Bruce & Company, in England, to the house of Bruce, Fawcett & Company, in Bombay, saying, " We have insured on the Scaleby Castle 109,000*l.*; viz. 93,000*l.* here, 10,000*l.* at Manchester, and 6,000*l.* at Hull, and in consequence of your directions shall proceed as far as possible. We have great doubts that it will be practicable to do above 25,000*l.* more. We have already all the responsible private underwriters on our London policy, and must now apply to the public offices. We expect one only of them will take any risk, and that will not be more than 10,000*l.*, with an advanced premium. We shall write to Bristol immediately, and perhaps to Glasgow, for insurance at these places." That was dated the 26th of April; on the 10th of May they wrote, " After all our endeavours it will not be possible to complete your order for insurance on the Scaleby Castle; we have done to the following extent, all but the Royal Exchange Insurance Office, at 10 guineas.

London.						
Private Underwriters	-					92,600
Royal Exchange Office						10,000
						102,600
Manchester	-	-	-	-	-	10,000
Hull	-	-	-	-	-	6,000
Glasgow	-	-	-	-	-	4,700
Greenock	-	-	-	-	-	3,400
Bristol	-	-	-	-	-	11,400
Liverpool	-	-	-	-	-	10,000
					£.	148,100

What was the amount of the sum required in the second instance you have mentioned?—I think this completed the order.

Have you any other difficulties to state for the information of the Committee?—None.

Do you find that the chartered companies charge a higher premium upon the same risk than you pay at Lloyd's Coffee-house?—We do.

State the difference?—Two per cent on India risks.

Can you state the amount of the insurances of your house for any certain number of years back?—I think for these thirteen years past they have amounted to about eight millions and an half property, the gross premiums upon those insurances were probably about 750,000*l.*

Would your house insure to a large extent with the companies, if they would take a larger portion of your risks?—If they would do it on terms equally advantageous.

Is the narrow scale on which the companies do business matter of general complaint in the city of London?—We understand that they never take above 10,000*l.* on one policy, we have never been able to prevail upon them to take more.

You are a partner in the house of Bruce, Fawcett & Company at Bombay —Yes, and have been for twenty years and upwards.

G. Simson, Esq

Can you state the number of marine insurance companies in India?—I think about six in Calcutta, four at Madras, there were five but one I think has expired, and one at Bombay, there were two at Bombay.

Does the company to which you belong insure with the offices in India?—Very largely.

Can you state to what extent?—The office at Bombay, where they make the greater part of their insurances, take from 25,000 *l.* to 30,000 *l.* on one ship, that is principally in the trade from India to China, and from different parts in India, and also to this country.

Do you know the rate of premium upon those risks?—Rather higher than in this country.

Are the insurances effected with the companies in India chiefly confined to coasting risks in India?—The principal part of our trade is in the coasting trade in India, and therefore our insurances are upon those voyages; and also in risks to this country, and we have many policies transmitted from India to us on insurances made there, covering risks from India to England.

You have stated, that you have twice found a difficulty in insuring the Scaleby Castle, are you aware of any particular reason why the underwriters object to that ship?—I imagine there is no reason, she is one of the finest ships in the world, she is the finest merchant ship that was ever built, I believe.

In the year 1799, was not the ship Scaleby Castle on her first voyage, a ship of upwards of 1,200 tons burthen, and fitted out in India and manned with Lascars, and not known or registered at Lloyd's?—She was a new ship, consequently could not be known; her measurement is upwards of 1,200 tons.

What premium was paid to the underwriters at Lloyd's upon that first voyage?—Ten guineas.

Was any additional premium offered to the underwriters in order to induce them to increase their subscriptions?—I am not aware that there was any additional premium offered.

If such additional premium had been offered, might not the order for the insurance have been completed?—Perhaps they might have been induced to take a greater risk, if they had been tempted with a very high premium.

You have stated the amount of your premiums for thirteen years past, can you state the amount of the returns, averages, and losses that went against those premiums?—I cannot exactly, but I believe, for the first five years, half the premiums were profit to the coffee-house.

Has that been the case for the last eight years?—I have not made up any account to ascertain it, but I apprehend not quite so profitable as for the first five years, though profitable.

Are you not aware that the losses on East India ships for the last eight years have very much exceeded the premiums?—Except in one instance the losses on our policies have been very trifling; with the exception of the Skelton Castle, I think not.

The question relates generally, not to the particular concerns of your house?—The losses by Indiamen have been very great the last year.

Are not many of the country voyages, as they are called in India, necessarily insured there for want of opportunity to cover those risks in due time by writing to Great Britain?—At present they are; formerly opportunities were more frequent; there was a monthly overland dispatch from India in former times, but the state of Europe prevents it now.

Is it not an inducement to many parties resident in India to insure there, that they can then recover their property upon the spot, without waiting the period of time that must elapse before they can realize their funds, if they are insured in Great Britain?—I think not; an insurance in Great Britain can be realized by drawing upon their agents when the loss happens.

Is it not necessary to wait until they know the loss is recovered, before they can draw upon their agents?—I should think not, they would consider it as assets in the hands of their agents.

Is it not in the ordinary course of things, that wherever extensive commercial establishments are formed, establishments for effecting insurances, by which commerce is to be secured, should be formed also?—That is very natural.

Are there any regular packets established between this country and India?—None.

If regular packets were established instead of overland dispatches, would not more Indian assurances be effected in this country?—I think there would.

What proportion do the cases your house has sustained, in consequence of the insolvency of underwriters at Lloyd's, bear to the eight millions and a half insured by you?—Our losses have been very trifling indeed.

Can you state to what amount?—I cannot exactly, but I think they are so small that we have never charged them to our constituents, but taken them to ourselves.

You have never thought it worth while?—No.

G. Simson,
Esq.

Mr. *James Lindsay* called in ; and Examined.

I BELIEVE you are an insurance broker?—I am.

You manage the business of Messrs. Thomas Gregg & Company?—I do.

How long have you known the chartered companies and Lloyd's Coffee-house?—I have been in business perhaps twelve years, I believe I may say eight or nine I have been acquainted with them.

Mr.
J. Lindsay.

Have you observed that after the first of August, and that during the months of August, September, October, November and December of every year, a great number of underwriters withdraw from Lloyd's Coffee-house?—Almost every year I have observed that.

Were the number of underwriters that withdrew from the coffee-house in those months very remarkable the last year?—I think they were more so than in any other year.

What has appeared to you to be the cause of the underwriters absenting themselves from Lloyd's Coffee-house during those months?—A general dislike to winter risks I consider as a most material reason.

Do you find greater difficulties during those months in effecting your insurances than in other months of the year?—We do.

Does it consist with your knowledge that the Jamaica fleet, which leaves that island on or before the 26th of July ; the Leeward Island fleet, which takes its departure on the 1st of August ; the West India fleet, which leaves the island in October; the Baltic homeward-bound convoys, the Newfoundland convoys, the Mediterranean convoys, the homeward-bound East India fleets, not to mention the various fleets and vessels which depart from Great Britain and Ireland in those months, are all at sea?—I cannot exactly speak to all of these, but to nearly the whole of them ; Newfoundland and the Mediterranean I am not so well acquainted with.

With the exception of the Jamaica July fleet and the Leeward Island fleet, part of which may have been insured in the months of June and July, are not all those fleets and vessels to be insured in those five months?—I should conceive that most of them were.

Does it appear to you that in those five months there are more fleets and vessels to insure than in the other seven months of the year?—I cannot precisely say.

Are you in the habit of making insurances with the two chartered companies With the Royal Exchange.

Would you insure more, and more frequently with the Royal Exchange Insurance, if you could do so?—Certainly.

State the causes which prevent you?—The risks are required to be more defined, and the premium is in general larger ; in addition to that, there are clauses in the Royal Exchange policies and other restrictions, which are not imposed by underwriters at Lloyd's.

Do not the insurance companies always fill up their own policies in the manner they think proper?—They fill them up under your eye ; you sit by them at the time of their doing it.

Does not the manner in which they fill them up frequently prevent you from insuring with them?—I have often found it so.

State some instances.—Very lately I had occasion to insure a vessel from Oporto, which I was refused at the Royal Exchange insuring, unless I would insert a warranty of free from capture in the port of Oporto, which I did not consider myself authorized by the assured to do.

Can you state any other instance?—I had another instance to insure from Sicily on a cargo of brimstone and barilla, on both of which articles they required the insertion of a particular clause ; brimstone to be free of average entirely, and a deduction of five per cent from any average on barilla.

Can you state any further instances for the information of the Committee?—Not any particular ones; in general, they require the exact voyage to be laid down more strictly than the underwriters at Lloyd's Coffee-house do.

With reference to Lloyd's Coffee-house, do not you always make up the policy yourself in the manner you think best adapted to the risk to be insured and the circumstances of the case?—Yes.

Is the rate of premium charged by the Royal Exchange Insurance, in general higher than you pay on the same risk at the coffee-house?—I think it is.

State the difference.—It will vary according to the risk, but I should imagine generally from a fifth to a sixth higher.

Have you taken an account from the convoy books at Lloyd's of the number of sail which came from the Baltic to Great Britain from July to December last?— I have.

Produce it.

[The witness produced it, and it was read, as follows :]

July and Aug. -	Wrangler, G. B. consisting of	-	161 Sail.
Aug. 4. -	Hebe, A. S. - - -	-	32
11. -	Ned Elvin, S. W. - -	-	33
-	Melpomene, M. W. -	-	210
Sep. 19. -	Charles, A. S. - -	-	20
October -	Owen Glendower, S. W.	-	255
October -	Plantagenet and Tarter, M. W.	-	355
November -	Bellerophon, M. W. -	-	151
-	Chanticleer, S. W. -	-	67
-	Charles, A. S. - -	-	29
-	Hebe, A. S. - -	-	15
-	Sheldrake, S. W. - -	-	9
-	Curlew, S. W. - -	-	15
-	Edgar, M. W. - -	-	95
-	St. George, M. W. -	-	139
-	Phœbe, M. W. - -	-	23
December -	Minotaur - - -	-	158

1,767 Sail.

The average value of each Ship, her Freight, and Cargo, at a moderate computation,
2,000 *l.* - 4,000 *l.* - 10,000 *l.* = 16,000 is 28,272,000 *l.*

You have calculated the total value to have been 28,272,000 *l.*?—Yes.

Upon what data have you proceeded in making this calculation?—From the opinions of those who were interested in the Baltic trade.

Have you ever found it impracticable, in consequence of the absence of some of the underwriters in the fall of the year, to effect such insurances as you may have had to make?—Not impossible certainly, but very difficult.

In point of fact, though difficult, such insurances have been effected notwithstanding the absence of some of the underwriters?—It may be attained by increasing the premium considerably above what you would have to pay if there were more underwriters and greater competition.

You have stated difficulties in making insurances with the Royal Exchange Company, in consequence of certain clauses and terms inserted in their policies; have you, in consequence of such difficulties which prevented you from insuring with the Royal Exchange, effected those insurances with facility at Lloyd's Coffee-house?— I have always effected the insurance; I have never left it undone.

From your experience at Lloyd's, can you state whether there would be any difficulty in effecting an insurance there to the amount of 40,000 *l.* upon a good risk in one ship?—None, I should imagine, on a good risk in one ship.

In your opinion could such an insurance be effected to the amount of 100,000 *l.*? —I should imagine it could.

Do you mean to state, that many of the underwriters make a practice of absenting themselves from Lloyd's for five months of the year?—Perhaps not wholly five, but nearly so.

Do not gentlemen in general go to watering places in the autumn as well as underwriters?—I believe they do.

Do not the premiums rise in proportion as the winter season advances?—They rise certainly, and probably in proportion; that is, according to the opinion of the person who is to take the risk, whether it is in proportion or not.

The fewer competitors there are, have not those that remain the better choice of risks, and the greater probability of insuring to advantage?—As far as respects the underwriter, yes; but not as far as respects the assured.

Is it likely, that if the prospect of advantage was greater to the underwriter he would absent himself at the period when that circumstance happens?—I cannot enter into what passes in the mind of the underwriter, nor his motives for going; I can only state the fact.

Is your house in the habit of guaranteeing the underwriters, when desired so to do by your principals?—I do not recollect any instance of our doing so, or being asked.

Can you state what proportion of insolvent underwriters you have had on the business your house has transacted?—We have had, comparatively speaking, few insolvent underwriters.

Can you give any idea of the proportion they bear to the amount of the goods you have insured?—I cannot; but very trifling.

You have stated the value of the ships and cargoes that came from the Baltic last year to exceed twenty-eight millions; if a new chartered company is to be established, and to take the risk of capture and seizure in the port of the enemy, might not such a company be ruined in case of such an event taking place?—It would depend upon the capital of that company.

Is it not within your knowledge that all prudent underwriters class their risks, and stop, that they may not take beyond a certain amount on any particular sort of risk?—I have no doubt they do.

Would it be possible for an office, comprising a great majority of the whole commercial interest of this metropolis, and doing business in proportion, to exercise the same daily caution?—That would depend upon the ability of their sitting director or directors.

Would it be possible to do it with so large a mass of business as must pass through their office?—I should imagine it would be possible; it would be more difficult, perhaps.

Have you ever experienced any difficulties in getting losses settled upon insurances done here?—I have experienced difficulties, but I have always got over them.

Without litigation?—I think I can remember only two law suits.

Within what period of time?—Eight or nine years.

John Milford, Esq. called in; and Examined.

STATE your profession?—A merchant.

Have you ever found any difficulty in getting an insurance to a considerable amount effected?—Yes, on one occasion great difficulty.

State the circumstances?—About eighteen months since I sent two ships to South America on a trading voyage under His Majesty's license, and on those ships I had to insure the sum of 128,000 *l.* I applied to my usual brokers, who could not effect more than 60,000 *l.* of that sum; in consequence, I was under the necessity of applying to five or six other brokers, and after a considerable delay I effected my insurance, having also been under the necessity of sending to Liverpool to get the policies effected, where I had 16,000 *l.* effected; and further, I applied to the chartered companies, and the London Assurance Company underwrote the sum of 3,000 *l.* on one ship, but refused to take more, declaring that they wished to see how risks of this description turned out before they would extend their risk.

Was the risk you have just mentioned in your opinion a good risk?—Yes.

Have you any further difficulties to state to the Committee?—No.

Had those ships a Spanish licence as well as a British licence?—No.

Is there any warranty of their being free from capture and seizure in the ports of the enemy?—None; they were not sent on a voyage to go into ports of the enemy, they were sent on a trading voyage to South America.

Were not those vessels to carry on a contraband trade on the coast of Spanish South America?—At the time they were sent I did not deem it a contraband trade, because we were at war with Spain.

Was not the trade contraband even after we were at peace with Spain?—I understood, after we were at peace with Spain it was contraband, and contrary to the colonial laws of the Spanish government.

If this trade is not permitted to an ally is it permitted to an enemy ?—I consider that it is by the laws of nations.

Do you mean to state that it is permitted by the Spaniards ?—No.

Was the whole insurance at length completed?—Yes.

Without the necessity of giving any additional premium ?—Yes.

Jovis, 1° *die Martii,* 1810.

WILLIAM MANNING, Esq. in the Chair.

Mr. *William Bridgman,* called in ; and Examined.

YOU hold a situation in the house of Messrs. Porcher & Co. ?—I do.

From your situation in that house are you enabled to give the Committee some account of the marine insurance companies established in the East Indies; the amount of insurances upon goods sent from thence to Great Britain, appearing from policies you have seen, or other circumstances within your knowledge, and the amount insured with those companies, upon consignments sent to the house of Messrs. Porcher & Co. for the last seven years?—I have made a statement of it, which I will deliver in : there are seven in Calcutta, five in Madras, and one in Bombay ; but I have reason to believe that three of the Madras insurance companies are dissolved, or at least act no longer.

State the amount insured by those companies on consignments to your house?— In the year 1803, 53,775 *l.* ; in the year 1804, 310,384*l.* 5 *s.* 9*d.* ; in the year 1805, 189,412*l.* 17*s.* ; in the year 1806, 171,588*l.* 6*s.* 8*d.* ; in the year 1807, 86,864*l.*; in the year 1808, 176,194*l.* 7*s.* 6*d.* ; in the year 1809, 49,542*l.* 19*s.* ; making a total of 1,037,761 *l.* 6*s.* 11*d.*

Do you not understand other houses in the East India trade are in the same situation with yourselves, of having their insurances effected partly in India?— Certainly ; every house of agency I believe has.

Do not the insurance companies in India generally make their policies payable in London ?—Generally, whenever required by the assured.

Are you aware of any instances where such losses so made payable in London have not been paid there ?—I know two instances.

State them ?—They happened in our own house ; we were agents for the Exchange Insurance Company, and for the Carnatic ; we had not funds, and of course did not pay the policies.

Do you not, as merchants, find considerable inconvenience from the practice of insuring in India?—I hardly know what to say upon that subject ; we prefer insurances in this country undoubtedly, because we have people that we know to apply to in case of loss, and the Indian policies are payable only six months after the loss is known; and if it is a very large sum of money, it may be inconvenient to remain so long out of the money.

Does it not expose you frequently to an inconvenient advance of capital?— I do not know that it has happened to us, but such a thing may be contemplated to happen.

Does the property so insured from India belong to your house, or to persons resident in India ?—To persons resident in India, who make consignments for sale to our house.

Do you know any thing of the rate of premium taken by the insurance companies in India, compared with the rate of premium current in England?—I think, generally speaking, it has been as nearly equal as may be ; rather higher than lower in India than at Lloyd's.

Supposing the rate of premium nearly equal, is it not more natural that the India merchant should make his insurances in India than in England?—The only reason I can give for his wishing so to do, is the difficulty of advices reaching this country, and he might be uninsured by that means.

Might not that be obviated, if regular packets were appointed between the two countries ?—Certainly.

In point of fact, would it not be more to the advantage of your house that the insurance should be effected in England than in India, although the effect to the proprietor of the goods in India in either case would be the same ?—Certainly, we derive a commission upon the insurance effected.

It is, then, to the advantage of the agent in England that the insurances should be effected here rather than in India?—Doubtless.

In the two instances referred to by you, where the money insured was not paid from want of effects by your house, is it within your knowledge that it was paid by any other house in England?—I know it was not.

Was it, then, paid by the insurance company in India?—In one case we drew bills as agents for a policy effected for about 6,000*l.*; and when those bills were presented in Madras, they were not accepted, the company there alleging that they had remitted funds to us for the purpose of liquidating the losses; the bills of course came back, and the remittances came forward, and we then paid the loss. In the other instance, it is not yet paid in England to my knowledge: it may have been paid in India, but I believe it is not.

Then the loss and inconvenience arising from the nonpayment, when demanded in England, falls upon the proprietor of the goods in India, and not upon the agent in England?—No; in most cases I think it would fall upon the agent in England, inasmuch as the greater probability is, that he would have made advances. The inconvenience, therefore, in that case, would fall on the London agent, but not the loss, provided the proprietor had the ability to repay the advance made by his agent.

Generally speaking, is it not more the interest of the agent in England, than of the proprietor of the property in India, that the insurances should be effected here?—That it is difficult to answer in a general way; because there may be cases in which it would operate more to the advantage of the proprietor in India, and others in which it would solely rest with the agent in this country. It is difficult to answer the question generally.

With reference to your own house, do you not conceive that it is always more to your interest to effect the insurances on property consigned to you in England, than for such insurances to have been effected by the proprietors in India?—Certainly it is.

Do you know whether the merchants resident in India are interested in the insurance companies established there?—Partially so; I believe not universally so.

In instances where such proprietors are also interested in the insurance companies, have they not an additional motive for preferring India to England for effecting their insurances?—Certainly: wishing to carry business to their own office.

Does not this of itself furnish a reason and cause for the establishment of insurance companies in India?—It is difficult to say; that might be one reason; whether it is the sole reason I am not competent to say.

If you were resident in India, consigning goods of great value to England, would it not be your interest to effect the insurance of such property with any insurance company in India in which you might have an interest?—I think it would.

Can you state what proportion of the sums insured by the companies in India are made payable in Great Britain in case of loss?—The whole, I believe, on policies for goods consigned to this country.

Are the risks on country voyages insured in India generally made payable in this country in case of loss?—I believe never: it has never occurred to me to know an instance of it.

Then the parties carrying on the country trade in India prefer, in case of loss, receiving the money in India?—So I conceive.

You have stated an instance in which your house refused to pay a loss of 6,000*l.* for one of those India companies; can you state whether any of those companies have ever failed?—I believe not.

Are there any regular means in India of ordering insurances in Great Britain, either by packets or overland dispatches?—There have not been any overland dispatches of late years; we used to receive overland dispatches; the packets are very uncertain; it lies with the governor in council to dispatch a packet whenever he thinks proper, but there is no regular packet.

Then are not insurance companies in India necessary establishments for the security of the commerce carried on there?—I think they are.

Would that necessity be obviated by the establishment of any new insurance companies in England?—That it is very difficult to answer; because unless there were regular communications, people would not chuse to trust to the uncertain conveyances that we now have from India; they come in fleets, and probably the very fleet by which you order the insurance the property is shipped. If there were regular packets I have no doubt a vast deal of insurance might be done in this country that is now done in India.

Mr.
W. Bridgman.

Would the establishment of any new insurance companies in Great Britain afford additional facilities to the effecting of Indian insurances here, unless additional means of communication were also furnished?—I think not.

How long has the practice prevailed of insuring in India?—I can only speak from the year 1803, from my own knowledge, but I believe, for some years prior to that.

Was it not before the period when the regular packets, or the overland dispatches, ceased to come?—Yes, certainly.

Therefore the Committee is not to understand that you give it as your opinion, that the practice of insuring in India is solely owing to the difficulty of communication by letter?—Not solely.

Have you any general knowledge of the extent of the country trade of India?—No, I have not.

Do you not believe it to be very considerable?—It certainly is considerable.

To the extent of many millions per annum?—I should think so, but I cannot speak accurately.

Do you believe the country trade of India sufficient of itself for the support of several insurance companies?—Of several, certainly; but whether to the extent they are now established I am unable to form any opinion.

Mr. *John Barr*, called in; and Examined.

Mr.
J. Barr.

DO you not hold a situation in the house of Messrs. Paxton, Cockerell, Trail and Company?—I do.

In what branch of trade are those gentlemen concerned?—East India agents.

Was it not in your department to attend to the insurances of the house?—It was for one year; from April 1804 to April 1805.

You have been in their house since, have you not?—Yes, I am there still.

And acquainted with the general nature of their affairs?—Yes; but not with the insurances only for that year.

Are any considerable portion of the insurances on consignments to the house of Messrs. Paxton, Cockerell, Trail and Company, effected in India?—Yes.

What proportion of the whole do you suppose?—I cannot speak to that point.

Have any instances occurred in which you found a difficulty in effecting the insurances of the house?—Yes.

Be so good as to state them.—On the 28th of April 1804 I effected an insurance on ship or ships from Calcutta to London for 119,050*l.*, to which there were 167 names, and on the 2d of May 1804 another for 174,400*l.*, to which there were 194 names. In doing the latter one I found considerable difficulty in procuring respectable underwriters; many of those to whom I applied to increase the sum which they had subscribed declining to do it until such time as the names of the ships on which they had already underwritten were declared. I had another policy to do, amounting to 250,000*l.* on ship or ships from India; but after the difficulty I had experienced before, I was advised not to attempt getting any more effected till I should be enabled to make a declaration of the interest on the preceding policies. About the end of September accounts were received of the capture of the Althea, though still no advices came respecting the interest of the two first mentioned policies. Towards the middle of October the list came to hand of the distribution of the whole of the interest of the first policy and part of the second, whence it was ascertained that 43,755 *l.* attached to these two policies were shipped on the Althea. In consequence of this capture the premium on ship or ships from India rose from 15 to 25 guineas; and as the time of covering the interest of the 250,000*l.* could no longer be delayed with safety, I was obliged to get it done at this heavy premium on the 12th of November 1804.

Where was that insurance ultimately done?—All at Lloyd's.

In the course of effecting your insurances, did you do any with the public companies?—None.

Why did you do none with the public companies?—We were informed that they took a larger premium, and therefore avoided applying to them.

Should you not have been willing to have paid the public companies something more than the underwriters at Lloyd's?—Very likely we might; but the sum they would take was only 10,000*l.* which is a very small part of any of those policies.

You would have thought yourself justified in paying them something more than the other underwriters?—Very likely we should, something more.

Why should you prefer companies to the other underwriters?—On account of the risk of failure among the underwriters.

Is it not also a convenience to have larger sums done?—A very great convenience.

Did you offer any part of those risks to either of the two chartered companies?—To neither.

Were there any failures among the underwriters, who were subject to the loss upon the Althea, amounting to 47,000 *l*?—Very trifling; there was only the sum of 490 *l.* 10 *s.* 10 *d.* not recovered, a small sum considering the amount of the policies, viz. 293,450 *l.* and the number of individuals to recover from.

With reference to this particular insurance, the whole was paid by the underwriters?—Nearly the whole loss by the Althea was paid by the underwriters.

Are not insurances upon ship or ships always more difficult to be effected than on ships distinctly named?—Always.

Have you any knowledge of insurance companies established in India?—I have merely heard of them during my residence in India.

How long did you reside in India?—Between nine and ten years.

Had you not an opportunity during that period of knowing that the country trade of India was very considerable?- Yes.

Would not that trade require the establishment of insurance companies in India, in order that the country risks might be covered?—Yes; it was for that purpose that the insurance offices were established there.

It was, then, for the purpose of insuring the country trade in India, that the insurance companies were established?—Yes; and also to insure the risks from India to England.

Do you believe it would be practicable to insure the country trade in India, without the existence of some insurance companies there?—I do not.

Had you been in the habit of doing insurances at Lloyd's previous to 1804, when you shewed those policies for Messrs. Paxton, Cockerell, Trail and Co.?—I had not.

Had you had any means of forming a general acquaintance with the great body of the underwriters there?—None, but referring to the former policies which had been done for the house through a broker.

Might not that circumstance account in some degree for the difficulty you found in effecting the two first policies?--No doubt it might.

Towards the latter end of the year you did effect the whole of the 250,000 *l.* which you were instructed to get insured?—I did.

You have stated the number of names that you had on the policies for the two first sums insured, can you state the number of names you had on the last policy insured for 250,000 *l.*?—I could by reference to my books, but not without.

In what lines was the last policy of 250,000*l.* begun?—In lines of 5,000*l.* each.

Then you found no difficulty in persuading the underwriters to take larger lines when you gave a larger premium?—None.

What was the amount of that premium?—Twenty-five guineas.

What returns were there upon it?—I cannot state the particulars, I can give it in on a future day; but the returns were so many for different descriptions of ships that I could not positively speak from memory.

What would have been the usual rate of such a risk?—Fifteen guineas was what I had had it done at; I believe it had been done as low as ten guineas.

Had you not had so large a sum to do, do you not think you would have done it at a more reasonable rate?—I do not; and the reason was, there were a great many smaller sums done at the same premium after the capture of the Althea, before I began to do that large policy.

Do you know the amount of the loss that was paid upon the Althea by the underwriter's at Lloyd's Coffee-house?—Only the loss upon our policies.

You have never heard the estimated value of that ship and cargo?—I cannot state it from recollection.

Can you state what was the net premium left upon that policy done at twenty-five guineas per cent on the regular ships of the season, exceeding 800 tons and upwards, after deducting all the returns?—I think it was twelve guineas.

In the same proportion what would have remained of the net premium at the gross premium of fifteen guineas?—I cannot exactly speak to that, but I think eight.

Mr. *William Lumley* called in; and Examined.

YOU are in the house of Messrs. Paxton, Cockerell and Co.?—I am.

Are you able, from you situation in that house, to inform the Committee, of the number of marine insurance companies established in the East Indies?—There are seven at Calcutta; I believe five at Madras; the other presidencies I am not so well acquainted with.

What amount of sum do they generally insure upon each ship?—About a lack of rupees, or 12,500 *l.*; they generally limit each ship to that sum.

Can you state to the Committee the amount of insurances upon goods sent to Europe, done by any of those companies for any certain period, and the amount of consignments to your house for the last seven years, which appear to have been insured in India?—I can only speak with regard to the Calcutta Insurance Company, for which our house are agents; the policies they have advised from the year 1803 to the end of the year 1808, amount in pounds sterling to 581,600 *l.* The consignments to our house insured in India, within the last seven years, amounted to about a million of money.

When you state the amount of insurances effected by this company in India, for which you are the agents, you confine yourself solely to those which are made payable in London?—Yes, solely.

You have no advice from them of such part of their insurances as are made payable in India?—No.

Do you make the insurances in London on any part of the consignments that come to you from India?—Yes, we do.

What proportion of the whole do you suppose?—I really cannot say.

Do you think it amounts to one half?—No, it does not.

A fourth part?—No, it has not done lately.

Does it not expose your house, and other India houses, occasionally to considerable inconvenience, having the insurance effected in India on consignments to you?—We have not hitherto experienced any inconvenience.

What do you understand to be the motives which induce them to prefer India to London for their insurances?—I cannot state, I have never heard them give any reasons.

Do you attend to the branch of insurances in the house of Paxton, Cockerell, and Company?—No further than by giving orders to the brokers to insure.

Have you ever found any difficulty in making your insurances to the amount you have wished?—I believe there have been some difficulties some years back.

Do you effect your insurances mostly in Lloyd's coffee-house or with the public companies?—Lloyd's Coffee-house.

Why do you prefer Lloyd's Coffee-house to the public companies?—We never have had occasion to trouble the public companies, we have always gone to Lloyd's.

Should you not at an equal premium prefer the companies to the coffee-house?—I really cannot say.

Have any of the correspondents of your house in India assigned the difficulties of effecting insurances in Great Britain, or the insolvency of the underwriters there, as reasons for their preferring to insure in India?—No.

Can you state what proportion the amount of losses by insolvent underwriters bears to the whole sum insured on the policies you have effected in Great Britain?—No, I cannot, but it is very trifling.

Have your house always been able to effect their insurances at Lloyd's, even without applying to the public companies?—Yes.

Mr. *John William Russell*, called in; and Examined.

YOU hold a situation in the house of Messrs. David Scott and Company?—I am a clerk in that house.

From the situation you hold in that house, are you enabled to give an account of the number of marine insurance companies established in the East Indies?—I have seen policies of many of those insurance companies, and I believe the number to be thirteen established in India.

Is not the house of David Scott and Company agent for some of these companies? —They are for two of them.

Mr.
J. W. Russell.

From the situation you hold in that house, are you enabled to give an account of the number of marine insurance companies established in the East Indies, the nature and extent of the insurances effected by them, and the amount insured with those companies on consignments sent to the house of Messrs. David Scott and Company, for the last seven years?—I have made a statement upon those subjects, which, with the permission of the Committee, I will read.

The following are the titles and the number of the Insurance Companies established in India mostly since the year 1797, viz.

AT CALCUTTA.

Asiatic Insurance Company
Calcutta Insurance Company
Calcutta Insurance Office
Ganges Insurance Society
Hindostan Insurance Society
India Insurance Company
Phœnix Insurance Society

} 7

AT MADRAS.

Old Madras Insurance Company
New Ditto
Carnatic Insurance Company
Exchange Insurance Company
Madras Equitable Insurance Company

} 5

AT BOMBAY.

A Branch of the Calcutta Insurance Office   1

Insurance Companies established in India   13

I have seen policies granted by all or most of the Calcutta Insurance Companies above named, and by some of the Madras offices; my knowledge of the remainder is derived from the East India Directory and from private information. I am not competent to prove the cause of the origin of the East India Insurance Companies. I can therefore only suggest, that the increase of the private trade consignments to Europe, and the difficulties and uncertainty of timely communication to the Consignees in Europe, rendered the establishment of insurance companies on the spot a very expedient measure. I have known frequent instances where, from the ignorance the merchants in India were under as to the quantity and quality of the tonnage which would be allotted to them by the Company's Board of Trade, they have been under the necessity of ordering their insurances to be done in Europe a season before, to cover the whole of their consignments of the following season, i. e. to open a policy at Lloyd's perhaps to the amount of 100,000 l. on ship or ships of the whole season, a policy which is not only a more expensive mode of insurance, but more difficult to get effected, since it gives to the underwriter no choice of election of ships, regular ships, extra or country built; the difficulty alluded to might also sometimes operate to the admission of certain names upon the policy, which were taken more upon the necessity of completing the insurance than from choice; thus, when a loss happened, occasional defalcations in the recoveries ensued; but whether such a consideration had any weight with the merchants of India, in their determination of establishing insurance companies, I cannot depose. The nature of the insurances undertaken by the India Insurance Companies is two-fold, viz. "the insuring of property shipped to Europe or America, and the insurance of the trade between India and China, &c. i. e. the country trade of India."

As to the extent of their insurances to Europe, the following is a statement of policies insured by the company, intituled, "The Calcutta Insurance Office," on goods shipped to Europe, from the establishment of that company, in 1798, to the spring of 1809, and made payable in case of loss by David Scott and Company as agents, viz.

Mr.
J. W. Russell.

From March 1798 to March 1799 Policies £. 248,005 Sterling.

1799 to	-	1800	-	149,692
1800 to	-	1801	-	182,889
1801 to	-	1802	-	310,144
1802 to	-	1803	-	227,478
1803 to	-	1804	-	323,686
1804 to	-	1805	-	272,804
1805 to	-	1806	-	140,502
1806 to	-	1807	-	229,885
1807 to	-	1808	-	155,820
1808 to	-	1809	-	170,282

Insured in 11 years by one Office in Calcutta, on risks payable in Europe   -   - } £. 2,411,157

So that the average of the insurances effected by "The Calcutta Insurance Office," payable in Europe for the preceding 11 years, is equal in amount to 220,000 *l.* per annum.

The following is a statement of the amount of policies made payable in Europe by "The Ganges Insurance Society," since the period when David Scott and Company became agents to that company, viz.

Policies insured in 1807   -   -   -   -   per £. 118,420

1808   -   -   -   -   -   173,832

The Register of policies for 1809, has not yet been completely furnished or received.

Insured in 2 years by one office in Calcutta, on risks payable in Europe   -   -   -   -   - } 292,252

By the foregoing statement it appears, that "The Calcutta Insurance Office" had, in the years 1807 and 1808, a greater sum at risk on policies to Europe than "The Ganges Insurance Society," (the latter is indeed an establishment of more recent date than the former); considering, however, that a portion of the risks insured to Europe are (at the option of the proprietor) made payable in India, it may fairly be presumed, that the aggregate sum of insurances effected by the offices in India upon risks to Europe, is not less than 1,500,000*l.* per annum.

Of the extent of insurance made with those offices upon the country trade and shipping of India I am not informed, but I believe it to be very considerable; in proof of which I would give the following extract, taken by me from the copy of a memorial addressed by the merchants, agents, ship owners, and underwriters of Calcutta, to the Lords Commissioners of the Admiralty respecting the losses sustained by capture of ships and vessels in the Indian Seas.

The copy is in the possession of David Scott and Company, and the memorial itself is understood to have been presented and delivered to the Lords of the Admiralty, by the hands of a member of the honourable House of Commons:

" Abstract of losses by capture of ships and vessels in the Indian Seas, accounted for and paid by the different insurance companies of Calcutta, from 1798 to the 1st of October 1807,

By the Calcutta Insurance Office -	-	3,746,939	Sicca Rupees.
India Insurance Company -	-	2,397,858	
Phœnix Insurance Company	-	2,050,456	
Calcutta Insurance Company	-	2,120,125	
Asiatic Insurance Company	-	1,715,041	
Hindostan Insurance Company -		950,183	
Ganges Insurance Company	-	736,520	

Sicca Rupees - 13,717,122

Amounting in sterling to   -   -   -   -   £. 1,714,640 5

To which add, losses by capture paid for by private underwriters and insurance companies at Bombay and Madras, estimated at sicca rupees 3,000,000. or   -   375,000

Total Sterling,   -   - £. 2,089,640 5

Mr.
J. W. Russell.

Signed,
Fairlie, Gilmore & Co. Secretary Calcutta Insurance Office.
Hogue, Davidson & Co. Agents India Insurance Company.
Scott, Wilson & Co. Agents Phœnix Insurance Company.
J. M'Traggart, Secretary Calcutta Insurance Company.
Alexander and Co. Agents Asiatic Insurance Company.
Joseph Barretto & Co. Agents Hindostan Insurance Company.
Campbell and Radcliffe, Agents Ganges Insurance Company.

By another statement in the same memorial, also signed by the agents I have mentioned, it appears that the losses sustained by the Calcutta Insurance Companies, &c. in two months alone of the year 1807, (viz. by the capture of 20 ships or vessels in the Bay of Bengal, during the months of September and October in that year) amounted to more than 300,000*l.* sterling. These statements are detailed by me, as being the only information that I am enabled to afford in regard to the extent of insurances effected by the offices in India upon the country trade and shipping of India. The following is as accurate a Report as can be given of the amount insured in India, upon consignments made to David Scott & Co. for the last seven years; distinguishing each year :

In 1803 about	£. 221,940
1804	275,500
1805	402,800
1806	142,250
1807	214,460
1808	258,500
1809	251,500
Insurances in India upon consignments to David Scott & Co. for seven years, about	1,766,950

In the course of the business of Messrs. David Scott & Company, do they not sometimes make their insurances in London?—Yes, they do.

What proportion of their whole business do you conceive to be insured in London, and what in India?—Since the establishment of the offices in India I conceive that the proportion insured in London has not been equal to one third of the amount of the insurances effected in India on consignments to Europe.

Veneris, 2° die Martii, 1810.

WILLIAM MANNING, Esq. in the Chair.

Samuel Williams, Esq. called in ; and Examined.

S. Williams,
Esq.

YOU are an American merchant established in London?—Yes.

How long have you been established here?—Seven or eight years.

Your business is American business generally, in its several branches, is it not? —Yes.

Do you not receive in the course of your business considerable remittances from the Continent for American consignments there?—Yes.

Where are those goods generally insured?—In America.

Are they not sometimes insured by you in this country?— Very seldom, nineteen-twentieths are insured in America.

Are those insurances effected in America done with companies, or with individuals?—Companies, I believe, generally, so I have been informed by my correspondents.

In stating that the insurances are principally effected in America, do you mean on the business of your correspondents generally, or only what goes to the continent?—On my consignments generally.

You receive also consignments from America to this country?—I do.

Have you any opportunity of knowing what number of Marine Insurance Companies are established in the United States of America?—I know chiefly those in Massachusets, those I know from the American register or calendar of the year 1808 ; it appears that there were in that year nineteen incorporated companies in that state.

Do you not know that there are also a number of companies in the other states of America?—Yes, I have done business for some in other states.

S. *Williams*,
Esq.

But your particular information applies only to Massachusets ?—Yes, in American price-currents I have seen lists of the insurance companies in different towns.

Are those companies generally incorporated companies?—I know they are in Massachusets, and presume they are in the other states.

Are not those companies incorporated for the purpose of insurances, but without an exclusive right so to do?—Yes, they have no exclusive right.

Has it not been found from experience in America that insurances are best done by companies?—I believe so.

Was it not formerly the case that there were a great number of private under-writers in the different towns?—Yes, all those companies have been established since I left America.

The business was formerly done by private underwriters?—Yes.

Do you not conclude from thence, as this business has been left perfectly free, that merchants naturally find it more for their interest to insure with companies than with private individuals?—Yes.

Do you consider the companies established in America as offering a fair security in insurances?—Very fair security.

Should you, in the course of your business, consider them as safe as insurances done at Lloyd's?—I have considered them as safer.

In what respect have you considered them safer?—I have considered them so much safer, that I have allowed my correspondents to draw upon me and to insure their property in America.

Is it not from an opinion that companies well regulated, always afford a better security than can be afforded by individuals?—Certainly.

Does not the present state of the law which prevents any two persons combining for the purpose of signing a policy, tend very much to diminish the security derived from private underwriters in this country?—I think so.

Do you know whether the incorporation of different companies in America has been a subject of complaint from the merchants there, or whether they have not generally considered them as conveniencies afforded to their trade?—I have never heard a single complaint against them.

Do you not from your experience believe, that since these companies have been established the American trade has been insured more at home than it used to be?—Certainly.

Was it not formerly insured to a more considerable extent than it now is in this country?—Much more.

Has not the mode of doing the insurance business at Lloyd's been the subject of much complaint with the merchants in America?—I never heard of any; as my correspondents have no insurance effected here, it has not come to my knowledge.

What is the mode of incorporating these companies in America?—By the Act of the State Legislatures.

The subscribers in these corporations are responsible only for the sums they have subscribed!—Yes.

Are there any private underwriters in America at this moment?—I believe there are some.

Was the number of underwriters greater in America, previous to the establish-ment of those companies than at present?—No, I suppose not; there is a larger sum insured now in America than there was formerly.

Do you effect much insurance at Lloyd's Coffee-house?—Yes.

Is it your opinion that insurances to a very considerable amount may be made with private underwriters at Lloyd's of undoubted solidity?—Yes, it is my opinion that there may be.

You left America before the establishment of these companies?—Yes, the first company incorporated in Massachusets was in the year 1795, and I left it in 1793.

How do you obtain your information as to the estimation in which those com-panies are held in that country?—From all the Americans whom I am in the habit of seeing.

Do you know nearly the annual amount of the exports from the United States of America?—I do not.

Is not the greater part of those exports produce of the colonies of those powers with whom Great Britain is at war?—I think not.

Is not a great proportion of their exports produce of that description?—A very large proportion, I believe.

S. *Williams,*
Esq.

Are not such commodities, particularly when brought to the ports of the enemy, liable to the suspicion of being enemy's property?—Every thing bound to an enemy's port is liable to suspicion.

Have not vessels with such cargoes and such destinations been frequently brought in for adjudication by British cruizers?—Yes.

Are not British underwriters exonerated by law from paying in case of British capture?—Yes.

Does not this circumstance induce American shippers to insure their produce in countries where the law is no bar to their immediate recovery?—No doubt it is.

Would this objection to their insuring in England be remedied by the establishment of any new insurance companies?—No.

Is it not also an inducement to merchants residing in America to insure on the spot, that they can immediately command their funds, and recover them themselves in case of loss, instead of insuring them in a distant country, where they must recover by agents, and pay them a commission for their trouble?—No doubt.

Are not the proprietors of the insurance companies in America for the most part merchants?—I do not know how that is; I believe they are.

Is not the dividing the profits on their own insurance business, another additional inducement to them to insure at home in their own offices?—Yes.

Is it to be expected that a rising and enterprizing country like America, should forego either the advantages to individuals, or the security to commerce in general, that is derived from the establishment of insurance companies?—No.

What proportion do the bad debts you have made among underwriters in Great Britain bear to the sums you have insured?—Small; I have been fortunate in my insurances.

State as nearly as possible?—I cannot, it is very small indeed.

Scarcely worth mentioning?—No.

Have you kept any account of the dividends paid by individual underwriters who have failed, and compared it with the dividends paid by the houses in which they were partners?—I have not.

On what have you founded your opinion of the security of the assured being lessened by the law which prohibits writing in firms or partnerships?—I have been fortunate in my business, but I have heard others speak of the losses they have sustained by the failure of underwriters.

The evidence given by you on that point is merely matter of opinion?—With respect to myself it is.

Did you ever suffer any loss from the failure of any company in America?—Never.

Did you ever know any of the insurance companies there fail?—No; no such circumstance has come to my knowledge.

Has not their business been very extensive?—Very extensive.

You have stated, that one inducement to insure in America arises from our insurances not covering British capture; is it not a common practice here to insure against British capture by what is called a separate clause?—There are some such policies.

Is it not a common practice with American houses?—I believe not; it has not been my practice.

Do you not know that such insurances can be done without difficulty at Lloyd's?—Yes.

You have stated, that you make some insurances with the underwriters at Lloyd's, do you ever insure also with the public companies here?—Never, I have only made one attempt to insure there.

What was the result of that?—Some difficulty arose in effecting it, and nothing was done.

Did you abstain from repeating your attempts from an opinion that those companies did not take risks at reasonable rates?—Yes, and because they did not take American risks, I believe.

Do you not know that many underwriters at Lloyd's refuse to write against British capture, under any circumstances whatever?—Yes.

Are the insurance companies with which you are acquainted in America, bound only to the extent of their individual subscriptions, or they are bound to the whole extent of their private fortunes?—To the extent only, I believe, of their subscriptions.

Then are they chartered companies?—They are all chartered companies that I know.

You have stated that you are in the habit of insuring annually to a considerable

S. Williams, Esq.

extent at Lloyd's, have you ever found any difficulty in effecting your insurances there?—Sometimes; not very frequently.

Have you found any difficulties which you can state to the Committee?—No, I do not recollect any.

Have the instances been frequent?—Not very frequent.

Have they generally been in the latter months of the year?—Yes.

What is your principal ground of preference to the insurances of America over those of Lloyd's coffee-house?—I thought myself always more secure by having them effected in America; I allow my correspondents to draw in anticipation.

Have the difficulties you have found in effecting insurances at Lloyd's been as to the extent of the sum you wished to cover, or the rate of the premium?—It has principally arisen from the rate of the premium in the last months of the year; it has arisen also from the absence of the underwriters who principally wrote for me.

Would you find any difficulty in finding other underwriters in the absence of those with whom you usually transacted business?—I found some difficulty in the last winter months, and was obliged to put the policies into the hands of brokers

Did those brokers, into whose hands you put your policies, effect your insurances? —Yes.

Is not your acquaintance among the underwriters at Lloyd's limited?—Rather so.

You do not believe that the companies in America have been established in consequence of any difficulties experienced in effecting insurances in this country? —No.

Jenkin Jones, Esq. called in; and Examined.

J. Jones, Esq.

YOU are secretary to the Phœnix Fire Office?—Yes, I am.

Have you not lately travelled in North America and the West Indies, on the business of that company?—I have travelled throughout the United States of America, and the British American Provinces, as well as the West India Islands.

During your residence in America, did you make any particular inquiry respecting the companies for marine insurances established in the United States?—I made very particular inquiries, it was a part of my object when I went on the mission.

Can you state to the Committee the number of those companies that you ascertained to be established in different places, the amount of their respective capitals, and whether they are chartered or not?—I believe the list I have of them is extremely imperfect, but I have the Acts of Incorporation of about thirty in my possession. I know that in the Northern States there are a vast number more than I am well acquainted with, and that the aggregate capital employed must be infinitely greater than that mentioned in this list; those of which I give in a list are those whose Acts of Incorporation or Acts of Settlement I have; some of them are by deeds of partnership among themselves, others by Acts of the Legislature of the States. I believe almost all the sea-ports in New Hampshire and Massachusets have them, perhaps on a smaller scale than those contained in my list.

[*The witness delivered in the list as follows:*]

Boston, seven companies—four incorporated, three private.

New York, six companies—three with 500,000 dollars; two with 250,000 dollars; Philadelphia, eight companies—six incorporated; two under articles of partnership; Capitals of seven of them, 3,300,000 dollars.

Baltimore, five incorporated—three have a capital of 928,000.

Norfolk, one 400,000.

Charleston, two companies—one, May 1804, 350,000.

New Orleans, one, 200,000, May 1805.

Barbadoes, two.

Newfoundland, one.

Nova Scotia, one.

Are there any of those companies that have privileges of exclusion of any other. There is no such thing known, I believe; there is not such a thing in any branch of trade in America.

Can you state whether you found any such companies established in Canada, Nova Scotia or Newfoundland?—In Canada, there is none established at present. I had some negociation on the subject, but it came to no particular issue. In Newfoundland there is one, and one in Nova Scotia.

Did you find it to be the opinion of the merchants in America, and in the Northern Colonies, that their trade was satisfactorily insured by means of their companies?—Certainly.

As you have made the state of insurance in America a particular subject of inquiry, did you hear any complaints among the merchants there as to the state of insurance in this country;—Yes; I think there were two considerable branches of complaint made to me whilst I was in America, as well as whilst I was in the North of Europe in some preceding years; the first branch I think applies particularly to the state of the insurance law, and the habits of our courts of justice, following invariably the courts of admiralty in the doctrine of blockade, and all the decisions of those courts obnoxious to neutrals; the other complaint applies generally to the difficulty of recovery.

You found generally that the merchants there thought our underwriters upon the whole were litigious?—I heard a general complaint of litigiousness, and a complaint of the loss of money occasionally.

Do you not believe, that if it were not for those objections Americans would insure a greater proportion of their property in Great Britain than they do?—I think that more of it might be procured by English insurers, by a different system. The responsibility of a public company would undoubtedly add very considerably to the body of their business.

In what manner do you suppose a public company to afford more satisfactory means of insurance than private individuals?—I think, in the first place, the confidence is greater in it for fair dealing, and, generally speaking, the security more certain.

Did you learn whether there were any individual underwriters in America?—Yes, there are some still remaining in the southern states; there are some, I know, in Baltimore.

Can you inform the Committee whether there are any marine insurance companies established in the West Indies?—There are two at Barbadoes, which are mentioned in the list I have given in.

Can you inform the Committee, of your own knowledge, what number of insurance companies there are established on the continent?—I cannot give the exact number, but there are a very considerable number in the North of Europe; two at Stockholm, one at Gottenburgh; there were five at Copenhagen, I think.

Have you not universally found, in the course of your inquiries, that when no restrictions existed by law as to any particular mode of insuring, companies were generally formed and had the preference?—Undoubtedly; the course of the American business has completely exemplified that preference, for private underwriters have nearly disappeared.

State the greatest and smallest capital of the two companies established, mentioned in this list?—About 115,000 *l.* sterling is the largest, and 44,500 *l.* the smallest.

Are you acquainted with Lloyd's Coffee-house?—No, not particularly; I have a general knowledge.

Do you not believe that there are many individuals at Lloyd's Coffee-house, whose fortunes greatly exceed the largest capital of any of the companies established in America?—I dare say there are; I have not the smallest doubt of it; but the capitals of those companies are the deposited capitals, and very often the individuals are liable beyond the amount of those capitals.

Of the companies in that list, be pleased to state such of them as are responsible beyond the amount of the subscriptions?—That would be out of my power, without referring to the different documents from which this list has been drawn out, the acts of incorporation, or the deeds of partnership.

In general, are the incorporated companies subject to a greater responsibility than to the amount of their respective subscriptions?—I should suppose the majority were not; what proportion are, I really do not know, without referring to the acts.

Do not you believe, that there are, at least, 100 individuals at Lloyd's, whose private fortunes exceed the greatest capital stated to belong to the insurance companies in the list delivered in?—No doubt. I have not the smallest doubt that there is an infinitely greater aggregate capital employed by individuals in the insurance trade here, than by the companies in America: but I suppose the obligations upon it are as infinitely greater too.

Then it cannot be on the ground of the want of solidity in the underwriters that objections are entertained against insuring in England?—Not generally, but I imagine, among the private underwriters, there are a great many who have not amenable

J. Jones,
Esq.

funds beyond their premiums; there are occasional losses from the insolvency of underwriters.

You have stated, that the two grounds of complaint against making insurances in England are, first, the system of our courts of law; and secondly, the difficulty of recovery; the establishment of a new marine insurance company or companies in this country would not then remove those complaints without a change of the present system of our courts of law?—I do not think that follows at all; it will depend upon the conduct of that company; a company would, perhaps, be actuated by more liberal principles than individuals, and might satisfactorily accomplish the objects of the assured by such a course of proceeding, without innovation upon the established law.

Upon what do you ground your opinion that new marine insurance companies would act in the way you have just described?—I speak from the general feeling I know to pervade a public board, as less selfish, less acute in the pursuit of its own interest, and less careful of it, generally speaking, than an individual, and more disposed, I think, to act on liberal principles.

Your belief, as to the advantage to be derived from a new marine insurance company would be founded upon their not being governed by the rules which prevail in our courts of justice, as our present underwriters are?—That is not the exact amount of the answer—I think they would be more liberal in their construction, and be more disposed to apply them fairly; a general rule would not be applied indiscriminately to every particular case within its letter.

You were the projector of this new marine insurance company, for which a petition has been delivered to this House?—Originally I was, but I have no connection with it now; it was set on foot by myself, with a view to additional benefit to the Phœnix Office.

Is the rate of premium in America, generally speaking, higher or lower than it is in England?—It is generally higher.

Can you say in what proportion?—Not without turning immediately to the returns I have in my possession. I should suppose, generally speaking, that it is as much as one-third higher; a two-guinea premium here would be a three-guinea premium very often in America.

Is this high rate of premium not to be ascribed to the want of individual underwriters in America?—I suppose an enlarged competition, whether by individual underwriters or by companies, would naturally tend to lower the premiums, but capital bears a much higher profit in America than it does in England, and it does in marine insurance as well as in other trades.

Is it not your opinion, that if all the insurances in this country were effected by companies instead of private underwriters, the rate of premium would naturally rise?—It would depend upon the extent of competition; but I think the general habit of a company is to trade to fewer advantages for itself than an individual. I apprehend that a public company would be, undoubtedly, a dearer resort for insurances, but I think there would be a compensation in the security of it.

You mean to say, that the premiums of insurance would be higher, if the business were carried on by companies instead of being carried on by individuals?—It would depend, I think, very much on the extent of the competition by companies; for instance, at the present moment the competition of companies for fire insurances has brought the price in most branches below what will absolutely pay for the risk.

Is not the competition arising from 1,500 individual underwriters greater than any competition that might be expected if the whole insurance business of the country were carried on by companies?—I am quite of a different opinion?—I think the country would be crowded by insurance companies in the first instance; that would reduce the price of insurance very materially.

Why do you believe that the price of insurance would be reduced more by companies, than that competition which now exists among individuals?—I think, with the superabundance of capital which exists, and the disposition to speculation, that there would fifty subscriptions filled up in a short space of time, and I suppose the private underwriters would then resolve themselves into companies.

Why should that have the effect of reducing the premium?—The eagerness for business always naturally does that, particularly for speculative business.

Do you believe the eagerness for business would be greater among the companies, than among the 1,500 individuals who now carry on that business?—I should think it would depend very much upon the nature and extended state of the general competition.

You do not believe that the American companies have been established in consequence of any difficulties experienced in effecting insurances in England, or of the want of solidity of the English underwriters?—I should think those causes had contributed with others; but the difficulty of effecting insurances in England, so as to suit the time and occasion of the American shipper, has been a primary cause of the American companies.

Have you any specific cases to state of the litigious spirit of the underwriters at Lloyd's, which you have heard mentioned as a subject of complaint abroad?—I have from time to time heard several cases cited, but I never preserved any memorandum of them, nor have I any distinct recollection of such cases.

Have you any circumstance to state of losses by the insolvency of underwriters at Lloyd's?—Not specifically; the complaints were directed more particularly against the solidity of the Liverpool underwriters, but specifically I cannot state circumstances.

Are you a subscriber to the petition presented to this house for this new marine insurance company?—I am not.

You have no interest in it?—No, I have not.

But you were the original projector of the scheme in its present state?—I was the original mover of bringing to issue the question, whether the grants to the present companies were in perpetuity, or were capable of admitting of a further establishment.

You have stated, that the premiums in America are generally higher than those here?—I think they are.

Do you think the premiums on American coasting voyages, and their trade to the West Indies is higher?—No, it is lower on those voyages; they know the voyages better a great deal.

The increase you allude to is principally on European voyages?—European and East India voyages.

What premium is charged in the offices in America from thence to the West Indies?—They have, in general, a very accurate account of the state of the West Indies, what are the cruizers in it, and so on; but the voyages are much better known in America.

In insurances against fire, do not the premiums increase with the increase of the sum insured?—They did; they do not now. The competition has entirely taken off that increase within the last few years.

J. Jones, Esq.

Lunæ, 5° die Martii, 1810.

WILLIAM MANNING, Esq. in the Chair.

James Forsyth, Esq. called in; and Examined.

I BELIEVE you are an underwriter at Lloyd's Coffee-house?—I am.

How long have you frequented that coffee-house?—About twenty-three years on my own account; some years previously as a clerk to my uncle.

In the course of that period have you generally found, that after the 1st of August, and during that month and the months of September, October, November, and December, a greater number of underwriters absent themselves from Lloyd's Coffee-house?—It has been very often the case, but particularly last year.

Do you state, that the number who so absented themselves in those months was particularly remarkable the last year?—Yes.

Have you made an abstract showing the amount of the premiums in each of those months in the last year upon policies underwritten by you, and in each of the five months preceding the month of August?—I have made an abstract for the whole year, showing each month: this is the account:

An Account, showing the sums insured by James Forsyth, and the Premiums thereon, each month of the year 1809.

January insured	-	£. 25,600	amount of Premiums	-	£. 1,853
February	- - -	25,100	- - - - - - -	-	1,934
March	- - -	23,000	- - - - - - -	-	1,751
April	- - - -	26,250	- - - - - - -	-	2,860
May	- - - -	27,900	- - - - - - -	-	2,831
June	- -	21,200	- - - - - - -	-	2,207

J. Forsyth, Esq.

J. Forsyth,
Esq.

July	£.24,000	£.2,554
August	52,000	5,685
September	74,600	8,823
October	45,500	7,401
November	30,000	4,113
December	28,200	4,389
	£. 403,350	£. 46,401

Can you account for the reason of the absence of the underwriters being particularly general the last year?—I should think the reason was, that they may have suffered the former year, as they do many years in the winter months, and of course they have gone away; but another reason was, that a great deal of business was doing in the coffee-house last year, which made the difficulty the greater of doing insurances.

Do you mean to say, it was partly in consequence of there being a great deal of business doing in the coffee-house last year, that the absence of the underwriters took place?—That was partly the reason, and of course the difficulty the merchants had in doing their business was the greater.

Are you one of the subscribers to the petition to this house for the establishment of a joint stock company, for the purpose of effecting marine insurances?—I am.

Are you acquainted with the plan and principles upon which such a company, if established, propose to conduct their business?—I am as much acquainted as others of the Committee; but I conceive I cannot say I am acquainted, because that would depend upon future considerations.

You are then a member of the committee?—I am a member of the committee.

If such a joint stock company should be established, are you to have any particular situation either as director or secretary for conducting the business?—Not that I know of.

There is no such plan in contemplation with reference to yourself?—Certainly not, with the explanation that companies of that kind are first formed by a committee, and I conceive that who may be directors afterwards will depend upon the majority of the subscribers, whether by ballot or any other mode.

Have you not had reason given to you from some member of the committee to expect to be elected to some situation of trust or management in the said company, if it shall take place?—Never.

Do you know the extent of sum which such a company would be likely to take upon any one good risk?—Surely I cannot, when the company is not yet formed.

Have you reason to believe that such a company would take a larger sum than is now generally taken by the two existing chartered companies?—I can form no idea upon that.

Then it never has been stated by the committee, in the way of observation or conversation, that such a company would take a larger sum than the two existing companies?—Not to me; I never heard of any such idea.

Do you think it likely that such an event would take place?—I must explain a little previously, that I rather think the proposed company, if they become a company, would take a larger sum than the present companies do, but I really do not know what those companies ever may have taken; I have done business with them both, but it is impossible for me to say what may be their rules.

Have you seen the subscribers to the petition?—I have seen some, and others not.

Do not the subscribers constitute a great majority of merchants and traders in the city of London, who are in the habit of effecting insurances?—I believe they do; I conceive so.

State as nearly as you can what proportion you believe that majority to be?—I cannot form an idea.

You believe it to be a very great proportion?—Yes, I do.

Is it not then naturally to be expected, that such merchants and traders as are subscribers to the proposed new joint stock company would prefer that company to individual underwriters?—At the same premium I conceive they would.

Would the effect of this be to withdraw such business from Lloyd's, and to give it to the proposed new company?—That is very much matter of opinion; I think in the first place it will draw a great deal of business to London.

Will it not transfer the business now effected by such traders and merchants at Lloyd's, from the coffee-house to the proposed new company?—No, if my first opinion be right, that it will bring business to London?—I think it may be the means of transferring business to Lloyd's Coffee-house; because, if business comes from any part of the country, or from any other part of Europe, or from America, to this place, it must be done either by this company or Lloyd's Coffee-house, so that in my view of the case I should say it would bring business to Lloyd's Coffee-house.

Do you mean to state, that in consequence of the establishment of this new company there would be such an increase to the general insurance business of the country as not only to give as much as the new company would take, but also to increase the business now done by private underwriters?—I rather incline to that opinion.

State your grounds for that opinion?—I have already stated them; I think the formation of a new company might bring insurance from different parts of the kingdom, and of Europe, from America, from the East and West Indies, to London; and when insurances once come to London they cannot return again, but must be done in London, and then the principals sending them would make their calculations for the future.

In the event of the establishment of a Joint Stock Company, would not, in your opinion, all insurances coming within the sum such a company would take, and which the subscribers may have to effect, be of course offered to such company in preference to individual underwriters at equal premiums?—I can hardly answer that question; it must depend upon the merchant; at equal premiums I think they would.

Would you yourself, having insurances to effect, and being a subscriber to this new company, offer such insurances to the company in preference to individuals at Lloyd's at equal premiums?—That must depend upon the premiums, and upon the advantages that the new company or the underwriter holds out.

What are those advantages you allude to?—They consist in short or long credit, and in discount, advantages besides the premiums.

Supposing the advantage of premium, credit and discount, the same in both instances, would you not then prefer the company to individuals?—I think I should, on account of security, the same as I should like to buy cheap any other article. I conceive a premium of insurance an article of trade, and of course, as a merchant, I make my calculation, and take which I like best.

You would give such preference to the company in consequence of your being a subscriber to that company?—By no means; it would be my duty as a good merchant to go to the companies, or such individual as I could deal best with.

The terms being the same, would it not be your interest to prefer giving business to a company in which you were interested, rather than give it to individuals at Lloyd's?—It might be my interest, but as a merchant I should not do my duty to my employer; it would be my duty as a merchant to study his interest, and not because I was a subscriber to any company to give my business to that company.

How would you be wanting in duty to your correspondent by preferring the company, the terms being the same with the company as with individual underwriters? —If the terms were the same, I say I should prefer the company on account of their security, but on no other account.

Would not the system of Joint Stock Companies have a tendency to narrow, in the first instance, and in time, to destroy altogether, the business of the present underwriters?—I think not.

Supposing this however to be the effect of the establishment of such companies, would it not necessarily follow that competition would be lessened, and the rate of insurance increased?—No, I think the competition would be increased.

Do you mean to say that the competition would be increased by the destruction of the system of individual underwriting?—I do not admit the probability of the destruction of the system of private underwriting.

Have you been in the habit of absenting yourself from Lloyd's as an underwriter, during the autumnal months?—I was absent five months of the year 1807, and about six weeks in 1808; independent of that, I do not think I have been absent from London above three or four weeks at one time for these many years.

Then during the twenty-three years you have been an underwriter, you have not absented yourself from Lloyd's during the fall of the year?—No, save as above stated.

Is not the constantly sitting in a crowded room at Lloyd's found by many of the underwriters prejudicial to their health?—I really cannot tell, I never found it hurt me.

Have you not heard it complained of by others?—Certainly.

Is not that inconvenience more particularly felt during the hot summer months?— During the hot summer months, and during the winter, from the obvious reason of being much confined in a warm room, or going out of a warm room into the cold air.

J. Forsyth,
Esq.

But the relaxation that is the result of constantly sitting in a close and crowded room, must be most felt during the summer months?—I do not know; it has been my good fortune to enjoy good health; I think it is a great inconvenience both in summer and in winter.

Is underwriting a line of business that can be safely confided to an inexperienced substitute?—I should say not, I would not trust an inexperienced substitute myself.

Do you conceive that underwriting in the fall of the year has been generally a losing concern?—That is quite matter of opinion, it depends upon the premium you take.

As you have been an underwriter twenty-three years, you can speak upon this point from experience as well as from opinion?—I can, and I have found that it has not been in my own experience such a bad business at that time of the year, because I exact a high premium.

I observe that your premiums during the four last months of the year 1809, amount to more than the premiums of the first eight months, was not the greater extent of your writing during the months of September, October, November and December, from an expectation that you were then writing to more advantage than at the other periods of the year?—No doubt of it.

Does not the premium from England to the continent to various ports, and for instance to Heligoland, advance in the proportion of from one guinea in the summer to twelve guineas in the winter?—From a guinea and a half in the summer to twelve guineas in the winter; I did not myself write many at a guinea and a half, I thought the premium too low.

Is not the season in which the gradations of this advance of premiums takes place, that is, between the months of September and December, a constant period of contest between the underwriters and the assured?—It certainly is more than in the summer months; there must be all through the year a contest between the underwriters and the brokers, but it is greater in the winter months when the premiums are rising.

Are not the difficulties in effecting insurances at that time rather owing to the unwillingness of the underwriters to write without an advance of premium, rather than for any other cause?—No, not altogether; I ascribe that difficulty to gentlemen leaving the Coffee-house, some to go into the country for pleasure, and others who really are in London will not come into the coffee-house; the two causes both operate against the merchant.

By those who go into the country for pleasure, do you mean those who go to the watering-places?—To watering-places, or to any where out of London.

Do you not believe that many of those who go to the watering-places, go there for health as well as for pleasure?—I cannot tell; but if the coffee-house be thinned of underwriters the merchant is placed under a difficulty.

Do not the underwriters who remain at Lloyd's at that season of the year, like yourself, write more largely than they otherwise would do, owing to the absence of other underwriters?—It follows of necessity.

The orders for insurance then are still effected, notwithstanding the absence of particular underwriters?—That I cannot answer; from my own knowledge they may be effected in London, or they may be sent to the out ports, or they may be returned.

Have you had any instances in your own house of being unable to effect any orders for insurance at that season of the year —Yes, though I do not remember it to have occurred the last year.

State any instance which has occurred?—In former years it is perfectly in my memory to have sent orders to the out-ports.

Were those orders sent to the out-ports rather to avoid giving an advanced premium at Lloyd's, than from any other difficulty in getting the sum completed there?—There is no doubt that a high premium will command the insurance being done.

Is your house in the habit of guaranteeing their underwriters for foreign correspondents when desired so to do?—It is very little required.

When required, is the request complied with?—I do not remember that we ever refused it, but it is hardly in my memory its having been asked.

Can you state what proportion the losses by insolvent underwriters on insurances effected by your house bear to the amount of the property insured?—Really I cannot.

State to the best of your opinion and belief?—I do not know what opinion to give upon it; I might say that underwriters at times have failed certainly, and we have suffered losses by them.

Have those losses, comparatively speaking, been heavy or trifling?—I should say in my own experience they have not been heavy; if you allow me to go back to what I remember in the year 1782 or 1783, they were heavy.

J. Forsyth, Esq.

Since you have effected the insurances of your house, the losses by the insolvency of individual underwriters have been very trifling?—I should rather say they have not been heavy.

Do you recollect the loss of nearly the whole of an outward-bound West India Fleet captured by the Spanish Admiral Cordova?—I remember in a general way the capture of that fleet, and of the Quebec fleet the same year.

Were there not about that time many failures of underwriters?—Yes, there were.

Has such an accident as that since happened to your knowledge?—Not to the same extent, I think.

Has not the business of underwriting been generally more profitable during this and the last war than during the American war?—I cannot form any idea; there has been a great deal more business done.

Have there been during this or the last war any great misfortunes at sea, such as in former times we have experienced, to put to the test the solidity of the underwriters much?—No, I think there has not.

Does not that circumstance in some measure account for what appears to you to be the more solid state of the underwriters now than in the year 1782 or 1783, of which you have spoken?—Surely; and there is of course less fluctuation in the premiums.

When you say that underwriters absent themselves during the autumn months, do you not really believe that a great many of them absent themselves from the coffee-house for the purpose of avoiding the risks of that period?—I certainly think so; I feel no doubt of it.

You have stated that you understand a great number of the most respectable merchants of the city to be subscribers to the new projected company; are there not also among those subscribers some of the most respectable underwriters at Lloyd's?—Yes.

Do you think those underwriters would so have subscribed if they thought it would essentially injure their business at Lloyd's?—I should think not.

Do you think, that if in the new company individuals were limited to hold no more than five shares of 1,000*l.* each, any profit they could derive from an interest in the new company could compensate to them the loss of their business as underwriters?—I think it would be no compensation.

Among the subscribers to Lloyd's, are there not a great many who do not underwrite at all?—Certainly.

By getting a list of the subscribers to Lloyd's the Committee would not be able to judge from the number upon that list the number of underwriters there?—I think it would be no guide.

Are you aware that as the law now stands no two persons can associate for the purpose of underwriting?—I believe they cannot.

Do you not think that if the underwriters at Lloyd's were enabled, by a repeal of that Act, to associate among themselves, they would find a greater facility in executing their business by small associations or partnerships, as other trades are carried on, than by the present mode of each man being obliged to do his own business?—I can hardly give an opinion upon that.

Have you not heard that there exist friendly associations through the country for mutual marine insurance?—Yes, I have heard that such associations exist particularly in the north, at Newcastle and Shields perhaps; but I know nothing of their plans; I believe they are societies to insure one another's property.

Have you not also heard of some existing in London?—I do not know of any in London, and the knowledge I derive of others is from people coming with policies, who have said, this ship is insured at such a club at Newcastle or Shields.

Can you state to the Committee whether such associations pay the stamp duty upon their insurances?—I do not know; I never saw any of their policies.

Has there not been in Lloyd's coffee-house some attempt on the part of the more respectable underwriters to distinguish themselves from those they have considered as not so deserving of credit, by some subscriptions of stock, or by some other means?—I have heard of such a thing, but I cannot speak to it of my own knowledge.

You are not able to state the particulars to the Committee?—No.

Do you not believe from your own experience that a great many persons who frequent Lloyd's coffee-house, for the purpose of underwriting, are not deserving to

J. Forsyth, Esq.

be trusted to the extent of the sums they underwrite?—I should rather say, from my own knowledge, because my experience would lead me to avoid those people; there are many persons whom I should not trust.

Are not the merchants frequently obliged to trust persons of inferior credit, for want of being able to effect the whole amount of their insurances with good names?—Certainly.

To what amount do you suppose it is possible to effect an insurance with good names upon your policy?—It is impossible for me to answer that question; I should say 100,000 *l.* if I am allowed to give a good premium.

Do you ever show the polices of your house to men whom you consider as unworthy of credit, to the amount of the sums they underwrite?—Surely not.

Do you suppose that any house of respectability would show such men their policies?—They certainly would not knowingly.

Then they would only show them their policies by being deceived in their characters?—Yes.

What is your reason for thinking that other underwriters quit Lloyd's in the autumn months, because they find it disadvantageous at that period of the year, when you say you have found it advantageous yourself?—Because I exacted what I thought a sufficient premium for the change of season.

Cannot other underwriters do the same?—No doubt of it, but they may be of a different opinion, or they may be more timid, and not choose to remain in the coffee-house.

Was not a great proportion of the Dutch ships detained and afterwards condemned in the British ports in the year 1794, insured, and afterwards paid for at Lloyd's?—I cannot say.

Were not a great number of the American ships seized, and afterwards condemned by France and Spain in the year 1797, for navigating without the *Roll d'Equipage* required by treaty, paid for by Lloyd's?—I have no recollection of any particular year, but I should think some of those ships must have been paid for by the underwriters.

Were not a great number of ships condemned by the Emperor Paul in the ports of Russia, in the year 1799, paid for by the underwriters at Lloyd's?—I think they were.

Were not those events very heavy calamities upon the underwriters?—They did not strike me as very heavy; the American losses were gradual, and many of the Russian losses were recovered back.

Did the property on board the ships detained in the ports of Russia, being ultimately restored, prevent the inconvenience to the underwriters of paying the loss in the first instance?—I think not; I do not remember any particular failure of underwriters in consequence of that.

Was not the circumstance of there being but few failures in consequence of that event, a proof of the general solidity of the underwriters?—I think it was, but I speak not from experience but from observation, because my friends had at that time little or no connection with Russia.

If the number of underwriters was diminished, by their being permitted to write in partnerships, would not the lessening the number lessen the competition also?—No doubt, lessening the number of underwriters would lessen the competition; at the same time, if three or four men join their stocks, they would write larger sums.

Are not the accounts kept in the name of an individual underwriter very frequently in point of fact, for account of the house in which that underwriter is a partner?—They may be, because a mercantile house may keep their own books in any shape they please, and divide the profits as they please.

May not underwriters who think their present avocation would be injured by the establishment of this intended new Marine Insurance Company, take shares in that company as some compensation for the injury they expect to receive?—No, I think not.

Is not some compensation better than none at all?—I should suppose that an underwriter, or any other man, if he takes a share of a new company, expects some profit; but the shares being limited, I do not think it would enter into his head that it would compensate any loss he might sustain; we can try to calculate what the profit will be upon five shares, which is only an advance of 1,000 *l.*

Then you believe that underwriters accept those shares with a view to the profit, though not with a view to compensation?—Not as any compensation, certainly; I speak that from my own feeling more than any thing else.

J. Forsyth, Esq.

Do you know whether underwriters in bad credit at Lloyd's take a less premium than the underwriters who are in good credit?—I should think they did.

Then are not such underwriters of use to the general interests of commerce, by tending to keep down the rate of premiums?—No, I think they are of great disuse.

Do not respectable underwriters frequently find themselves obliged to accept premiums because other underwriters, not equally respectable, have written at those premiums?—I fancy they do.

To what cause do you attribute the existence of those societies in the north of England with whose existence you have stated yourself to be acquainted?—I conceive to save themselves premiums.

Do you conceive that if there was a greater facility of doing business at Lloyd's with the two chartered companies there would have been any call in the opinion of the persons of whom those societies consist for their formation?—I have no knowledge of the persons who have formed those societies, and therefore cannot answer that question; I derive my knowledge of them merely from brokers having come to me and said, this ship has been insured, or partly insured, at a club at Newcastle or Shields.

Mr. *John William Russell* again called in; and Examined.

Mr. J. W. Russell.

YOU have stated yourself as employed in the house of Messrs. David Scott and Company?—I am.

You have stated that Messrs. David Scott and Company have effected part of their insurances in this country?—Yes, they have.

Has the house ever found any difficulty in effecting such insurances?—I can state a recent instance, in which the house felt an inconvenience in effecting an insurance; it was an insurance effected on the ship and cargo of the Shah Ardasier, of 124,440 *l.* from Bombay to London; the order arrived on the 9th of December to the house, and the first of the policies at Lloyd's bears date on the same day, but the insurance was not completed at Lloyd's until the 27th of December, and was effected through the medium of five different brokers, besides the agent usually employed by the house; there was also a part of this insurance effected with the London and the Royal Exchange Assurance Offices, namely, 10,000 *l.* at the London Assurance Office, and 7,000 *l.* at the Royal Exchange Assurance Office, which I understood was respectively the extent to which those offices would insure upon the risk; that I state as an instance of inconvenience to the house, because they were obliged to employ five different brokers not usually employed by them.

You say that the policy was opened on the 9th of December, and was not completed till the 27th; were the brokers during that time exerting themselves for its completion?—I believe so.

Was the whole at last done at London, or was any sent to the out-ports?—The whole was done in London, with the exception of the 17,000 *l.* insured by the two chartered companies; the rest was by the underwriters.

What was the premium paid at Lloyd's?—Ten guineas, with the exception of 6,000 *l.* freight, which was done at 10*l.*, that done by the companies was at twelve guineas both on freight.

Was that ship lost?—She was burnt in Bombay harbour, with about one-third of her cargo on board.

If advice of that accident had come by a fast-sailing vessel, would it not have been possible, in consequence of the difficulty you found in effecting your insurance, that it might have reached you before that insurance was completely effected?—The ship was burnt in Bombay on the 13th of September, and had a fast-sailing vessel been leaving Bombay immediately afterwards, she might have arrived by the middle of December, in which case one half of the insurance would not have been effected.

Was she an India-built ship?—Yes.

Manned with Lascars?—Chiefly with Lascars, I believe.

Was she known in the register-book at Lloyd's?—She had been insured there before.

She had made a voyage?—Yes, and intermediate voyages to China, which were also insured at Lloyd's.

Does not it always happen that ships chiefly manned by Lascars are more difficult

Mr.
J. W. Russell.

to be insured, than ships manned by a proper proportion of European sailors?—We had two previous instances almost immediately previous to this; the David Scott and a ship called the William, both country-built ships, and manned in the same manner, in which we did not experience that difficulty.

Were the sums upon the two ships to which you have now referred, so great as that upon the ship Shah Ardasier?—They certainly were not so great, the sum insured upon the David Scott and her cargo, amounted to 74,000 *l.*, and upon the ship William and her cargo to 50,000 *l.*; the insurance on the David Scott was effected the latter end of September, and that on the William the beginning of December.

You have stated that of the 124,000 *l.* insured upon this ship, 17,000 *l.* was done by the two chartered companies, and that the ship was burnt; did you receive from the underwriters the whole of the remaining sum of 107,000 *l.*?—The loss has been adjusted at Lloyd's coffee-house, so far that the underwriters have signed the adjustment of it, but none of that loss has yet been received; the adjustment took place on the 29th of January, and according to the usage of Lloyd's the payment falls due in one month, but by the modern usage that is still further extended to a grace of a fortnight beyond the month, making six weeks.

In point of fact, are you aware that any of those underwriters have failed?—I believe, none.

Then you do not expect there will be any loss in this 107,000 *l.* insured by those underwriters?—That I cannot answer till the day of payment comes.

But you have no reason to believe there will be any such loss?—I have no particular reason to expect it.

What proportion do the losses your house has sustained by insolvent underwriters at Lloyd's bear to the amount of the property they have insured there?—I believe the proportion to be very trivial, but I cannot state it.

Was not the premium of ten guineas per cent. upon this country ship objected to by many of the underwriters at Lloyd's as being too low?—I believe there were such objections started.

Was any higher premium offered to the underwriters at Lloyd's?—There was not, to the best of my knowledge.

If a premium had been offered which the underwriters had thought adequate, would the same delay have taken place in effecting the insurance?—I think it very probable that in that case the insurance would have been sooner completed.

Is not the want of opportunity of writing from India for insurance a great obstacle to many insurances being effected in Europe?—I certainly conceive it to be so.

If the sum you had to insure had not been so large, do you not think you would have been able to have had it covered at a more reasonable premium?—Not at a more reasonable premium than this was effected, but at that premium without so much difficulty.

Was not the premium of ten guineas per cent. fully as high as you had given on similar risks?—Yes, in the same season rather higher; the cargo of this ship had the liberty of coming by ship or ships, therefore the ten shillings additional was given, though on other ships of the same season we had given only 10 *l.*

Does not the danger of the voyage increase in proportion to the lateness of the season at which the vessel arrives on the coast of England?—That is a question I am not competent strictly to answer, but I believe it to be so; but in the present instance of this ship the Ardasier, she, from the time when she was to have left Bombay, which was the beginning of October, should have been here in the month of January, and the ship William insured at ten per cent. arrived in the month of January; the ships were following each other from Bombay immediately.

Are the insurances upon goods coming consigned to your house made either in India or in England at the option of the house in India, from which the goods come consigned?—The house of David Scott and Company only make insurances when ordered.

Jovis, 8° die Martii, 1810.

The LORD BINNING in the Chair.

John Inglis, Esq. called in; and Examined.

YOU are a general merchant ?—Yes.

Do you in general insure with the chartered companies, or at Lloyd's?—My house has not for some years back had such extensive business to do in that line as formerly; they have chiefly done their insurances of late at Lloyd's Coffee-house; when they had extensive business they used to apply to the public offices, to Lloyd's, and to the out-ports frequently.

State the reasons of your not insuring with the chartered companies?—Our reason for not insuring with the chartered companies is in some measure accounted for by my last answer, that we have not had occasion to apply to them, but when we have applied to the public companies, we have found, they having particular clauses of average, and other conditions in their policies, we could effect our insurances at Lloyd's on better terms in these respects.

As a general merchant, are you satisfied with the present state of marine insurance in this country?—I have for some time past considered that greater facilities were necessary in making marine insurances, from the great extension of the trade.

Does it consist with your knowledge, that merchants in the city of London are dissatisfied with the present state of marine insurance?—The merchants generally, I believe, have had the same feeling upon the subject that I have had, that some further facilities were necessary to extend their means of making marine insurances.

Did your house lose considerably upon your insurances at the end of the American war?—There were at the close of the American war very considerable failures at Lloyd's Coffee-house, and my house suffered pretty considerably upon that occasion.

Does it appear to you that similar losses are to be apprehended at the close of the present war from similar causes ?—I think it very probable that there might ; if the business of insurance at Lloyd's Coffee-house was lessened by the close of the war, failures might happen, or persons would leave the coffee-house from the insufficiency of the business there to maintain their present degree of credit in it.

Do you recollect the capture of the Saint Eustatia fleet, the Quebec fleet, and the East and West India fleets, in the American war?—I was not much acquainted with the capture of the Eustatia fleet, but I perfectly recollect the capture of the Quebec fleet, in which trade I was very much engaged, as well as the West India trade.

Do you recollect the effect which those captures produced upon Lloyd's Coffee-house?—Perfectly well ; there were some considerable failures at that time, and others who were in better circumstances, and conceived themselves competent to their engagements, quitted the coffee-house from the great losses they had sustained, to give them time to look into their affairs and wind up their accounts.

Supposing a Baltic convoy to be lost, or any great capture to happen similar to the capture in the American war, which you have mentioned, does it appear to you that similar effects would be produced ?—I think it very probable, on any very great change of public circumstances, if the enemy, which is not impossible in their now situation, should bend their whole force to fitting out privateers, or a sudden rupture with America, either would be attended with very injurious effects to the underwriters at Lloyd's Coffee-house.

You have stated in a former part of your evidence, that your house had been in the habit of applying to the out-ports for insurance occasionally, did you apply to individual underwriters, or to clubs at those ports?—The merchants here do not belong to the clubs ; the clubs insure their own members, and merchants, when they apply to out-ports to get insurance done, write to the brokers there to get the business done for them.

Without regard to whether it is done by individual underwriters, or by the clubs?—Yes.

Does it consist with your knowledge, that there are now different associations of that description in the north of England ?—It does not consist immediately with my own personal knowledge ; I have seen the terms of insurance in part, and the number of ships they insure.

Does it consist with your knowledge that there are clubs of that description in London ?—I only know of one ; I have seen a printed paper they circulate among their members, and I believe in this day's newspaper there is an advertisement to form one.

J. Inglis,
Esq.

Do you conceive the main object those clubs have in associating together is the saving themselves premiums, or to what cause do you attribute their existence?—A member of one of the clubs, who gave me the printed paper I allude to, told me their reason for forming the club was the difficulty they met with at Lloyd's Coffee-house, in settling the averages upon their ships.

Were not the failures at the end of the American war general among merchants, as well as among underwriters?—No, they were not; two or three years after the American war there were very great failures, but that happened from a circumstance totally unconnected with Lloyd's Coffee-house, from excess of the shipments made to America, for which remittances were not received in due time.

To what cause do you attribute the failure of so many underwriters at the close of the American war?—I attribute that to the premiums being reduced to a peace-rate, that the brokers who kept account with insurers who had not large capitals, were not able to fill up their accounts by new premiums, so as to enable them to meet their losses.

Is not the close of a war an advantageous circumstance to underwriters, inasmuch as the policies they have written at premiums then run off at peace risk?—In so far as that goes it is certainly so, and a man of capital will derive that advantage from it, because he is enabled to proceed with his business, which those that have not a capital to meet previous losses cannot do.

What proportion do you suppose war-premiums generally bear to peace-premiums?—It is impossible to answer that question precisely, because the premiums to different parts of the world are various; probably double.

Then in case of peace taking place, does not the underwriter derive an advantage to the extent of one half the premiums he has written upon policies, in consideration of the war risk no longer attaching?—Upon the generality of risks, he certainly does for a short period.

Were there great failures among the underwriters at Lloyd's at the close of the late war?—They were not so extensive as at the end of the American war.

Were they at all extensive or numerous at the close of the late war?—I do not recollect that they were, I was not so much in the habit of knowing it, not having so much business to do at that time.

If they had been very extensive, must not you have known it from the number of insolvent underwriters whose names would have been entered on the policies effected by your house?—I think not, because the policies effected at that time by my house did not require us to take in any very great number of the insurers at Lloyd's Coffee-house.

Would you give the preference to Lloyd's if you were not satisfied of the solidity of the individual underwriters?—It would depend upon the rate of premium whether I would give the preference to Lloyd's, or the public offices; I am satisfied with the solidity of a great many of the insurers at Lloyd's Coffee-house, certainly.

Can you state what proportion the losses your house has sustained by the insolvency of the underwriters at Lloyd's Coffee-house bears to the sums you have insured there?—That question cannot be very well answered by me on behalf of my house, from the extent of the business they at present do; and for another reason, that we generally have accounts with the persons who underwrite to us, which help to set off the losses that we sustain.

Is your house in the habit of guaranteeing their underwriters to their foreign correspondents, when required so to do?—We have done it in some instances, but very rarely.

Do you guarantee, when it is the wish of your foreign correspondents that you should?—I should have no objection to do it for an adequate premium.

What premium does your house charge for guaranteeing underwriters?—In some instances one per cent, in others half.

Is your house in the habit of guaranteeing the buyers of produce consigned to you by foreign correspondents, when requested so to do?—In some instances

The habit of guaranteeing is not peculiar to underwriters, but proceeds from the general wish of foreign merchants to be covered against all possible risks in disposing of their property?—It is the custom in some particular branches of trade to guarantee all the sales made, and a premium is charged for it, generally of two per cent if it is for six or nine months credit.

Were there great failures among the underwriters at Lloyd's when the late Emperor Paul seized all the British ships in the ports of his dominions in the year 1799?—I do not remember that, but I rather suppose that the chief of the ships that were stopped there were not insured at Lloyd's Coffee-house.

Where do you suppose those ships were insured?—With the clubs in the north.
Do you mean that the cargoes of those ships were insured by the clubs in the north?—No, certainly not, but the ships.

Where do you suppose that the cargoes of those ships were insured?— At the ports they were destined for, I suppose, but it happened late in the season, when there were not a great many cargoes laden.

Do you know the number of cargoes that were seized on that occasion?— No, I do not.

Has your house lately been unable to complete any insurances you have received orders to effect?—We have not very lately had any such large orders as to induce us to have recourse in a general way to the country, but we have, within a few years, made considerable insurances at Glasgow, having larger sums to do than we found we could do at the coffee-house with our class of underwriters.

On such occasions has your house employed brokers, whose connections lay among different classes of underwriters at Lloyd's, before you sent the orders to Glasgow?—Yes, we have occasionally put the policies into other hands than our own immediate brokers.

Have those brokers been unable to complete the insurances in question?—Yes, they have with such underwriters as we chose to accept.

For what sums, and on what voyages, has your house been unable to affect their insurances at Lloyd's?—We have been unable to complete our insurances at Lloyd's, or the offices, upon particular ships from Quebec, and also upon cross-risks in the West Indies.

What were the sums which your house was unable to effect on any particular ship from Quebec to London?—We have insured at Glasgow from twelve to fifteen thousand pounds, which we could not effect here.

What was the whole sum ordered on any particular ship, which you found yourself unable to effect at Lloyd's coffee-house?—I cannot state that precisely, but probably one hundred thousand pounds on a direct risk from America, and on cross-risks in the West Indies from thirty to forty thousand pounds.

Do you mean to state that one hundred thousand pounds on a good ship from Quebec to London cannot be effected at Lloyd's coffee-house by good underwriters?—I mean to say by a particular house, because other houses may have large sums to do upon the same ship.

What do you imagine to be the utmost value of the cargo of any one of those ships?—A particular ship from Quebec might be worth 200,000*l.*

Is it your opinion that 200,000*l.* cannot be effected satisfactorily on one of the fur-ships from Quebec to London?—I think it cannot at Lloyd's coffee-house, because we found that it could not.

In such cases did your house offer any advance of premium?—No, I do not recollect that we did; but I have known instances when my house have taken their policies round to persons who did not attend at Lloyd's, and who were not considered as regular underwriters.

Will not underwriters take a larger line on obtaining a larger premium?—Probably there are a few underwriters who would take a larger sum on obtaining a larger premium; but it is not the interest of the merchant to do that when he can get it done at the out-ports.

Then the object of your house in sending those orders to the out-ports was to keep down the rate of premium?—To get it done at the current premium; but I doubt whether an advance of premium would have the effect, it might with respect to a few persons.

You never tried the experiment?—No.

Are you a subscriber to the petition for the establishment of a new Marine Insurance Company?—I am.

Are you a proprietor of shares in that intended new Company?—I have subscribed for shares.

Has not a deposit been paid upon those shares?—There has a subscription been paid; not a deposit, but a subscription to defray the expenses of the petition to Parliament.

Has not that deposit been paid according to the number of shares subscribed for?—Certainly.

Are you a member of the Committee of the intended new Marine Insurance Company?—I am.

You have stated, that there is a dissatisfaction among the merchants in the city

J. Inglis,
Esq.

as to the present means of effecting insurances?—I do not conceive I expressed myself so strongly, but I think there is a very general satisfaction in the city, and concurrence in the present measure by all the merchants.

Are the means at present afforded of effecting insurances, namely, by the two chartered companies and by Lloyd's, considered insufficient or inadequate?—I consider them so myself; the two companies may be presumed to be pretty nearly obsolete, when compared with the present extent of the business of the country; and the extension of the trade has brought to Lloyd's coffee-house a very great number of insurers in proportion to the number which used to be there at former times; but how far these numbers have added to the security of the merchant, or the reputation of the coffee-house, I am not prepared to give a positive opinion.

Do you believe, by a judicious selection of underwriters at Lloyd's coffee-house, insurances to any amount likely to be wanted in the present increased state of the trade of the country, can be effected?—I have not experienced it beyond the answer J gave to a similar question before; but I understand there have been a great many insurances transmitted to the country because they could not be effected in a satisfactory manner at Lloyd's coffee-house.

You have stated that you understood that the cause of the establishment of the clubs was asserted to be the difficulty in recovering their losses; is there not something in the nature of the risks effected by those clubs which naturally renders it difficult to effect insurances upon them at Lloyd's coffee-house?—The club I spoke of was one to insure transports. I never heard that there was any difficulty in insuring transports at Lloyd's coffee-house.

Is not the insurance of transports for nine or twelve months difficult to be effected, unless at a very high premium?—There is a regular and invariable premium for insuring transports, I believe, because it may be considered as a peace-premium for the time for which it is done; the transport being insured by the government against capture by the enemy; it is a premium against sea-risk only.

Do you conceive the underwriters as a body at present carrying on their business at Lloyd's, more or less solid than they were at the end of the American war, when the considerable failures alluded to in a former part of your evidence are stated to have taken place?—I am not so particularly acquainted with Lloyd's coffee-house at present as to answer that question precisely, but I conceive that the true principle of insurance is that of merchants meeting by some means or other to participate in their risks by insuring each other, and that a professional underwriter coming to Lloyd's without a known capital, is not of that class of insurers that merchants would wish to take upon their policies.

Does not the circumstance of the sum to be insured being large frequently induce the underwriter to ask a higher premium?—I have always understood that if they had information that a large sum was to be done, they would ask a higher premium.

Does not the power which the underwriter possesses of imposing upon the merchant a higher premium, necessarily arise from a want of competition?—It certainly does, from a want of competition among those leading persons in the coffee-house who fix the premiums; and I have known instances where orders have been sent to the country, and the insurances effected there at less premium than had been demanded at Lloyd's coffee-house.

Has not the trade of the country during the present and the last war had a protection from our naval force unexampled in any former wars?—There is no doubt of it.

Does not the circumstance of that protection prevent the solidity of the underwriters at the coffee-house being put to any severe test?—Unquestionably it has had that effect.

If, therefore, no great failures have of late taken place in the coffee-house, may it not to a great degree be owing to their business as underwriters having been from those circumstances more profitable than in former times?—It has certainly had that effect, and in a great degree, from this cause, that the enemy has never had it in his power to send out a fleet powerful enough to cope with our convoys, so as to take a whole fleet, and by that to cause a very great distress.

You have stated to the Committee that you are yourself a subscriber to this new company, are not almost all the merchants of respectability in the city equally subscribers to it?—I believe a very great proportion of them.

Could you name half a dozen houses of any note in the city, which are not subscribers to the institution?—I think not, without a considerable degree of reference to some list of merchants; not from my head, certainly.

J. Inglis, Esq.

Do you suppose it possible, that so general a concurrence of the mercantile interest of the city can arise from any cause but their expectations of general benefit to the trade of the country from such an institution?—I have certainly considered that such an institution, the direction of which was confided to persons now engaged in extensive trade, would render facilities to the business of insurance generally, and all the merchants I have conversed with on the subject have been of the same opinion.

Are not the premiums of insurance reduced in proportion to the reduction of the risk, occasioned by the superiority of our naval force?—It has certainly had the effect of reducing it more in this war than any former war with which I am acquainted.

Can you state what premium is now paid on a running ship from London to the West Indies?—It depends upon the strength of the ship, but I am not immediately acquainted with it.

Do you think the present premiums more than adequate to the risks?—I think not; not upon some voyages, certainly.

Are not the premiums at Lloyd's lower than those required by the public companies?—To answer generally I should say they are, but there have been instances where the companies have taken a less premium than the coffee-house.

Is not a lower rate of premiums taken at Lloyd's owing to the competition in consequence of the great number of individuals?—It is so, but that leads to dividing the coffee-house into classes, which I do not wish to enter into.

May not the difficulty in insuring transports be owing in a great degree to the owners insuring the best of them themselves in their clubs, and only sending the worst classes of them to be insured at Lloyd's?—It is very possible that may be the case, but it is not consistent with my knowledge.

Alexander Glennie, Esq. called in, and Examined.

YOU are a general merchant, are you not?—Yes.

What is the firm of your house?—James M'Kenzie and Alexander Glennie.

A. Glennie, Esq.

Does your house, in the course of their business, effect insurances to any considerable extent?—Yes, we have; formerly we used to effect insurances to a very considerable amount every year; we do yet, to a certain amount, but not near in the proportion we used to do before the companies in America were established.

Can you state to the Committee the causes which produced the establishment of the companies in America?—The causes, I believe, proceeded, first of all, from the general complaint in America of the high premiums that were required by our underwriters here, and by the difficulty there was of effecting some of their insurances, which are termed cross insurances, not direct from America to this country, but from America to different parts of the world, and back again; in consequence of the complaints that we continually had about the high premiums we were compelled to give on those risks, the merchants in America formed themselves at first into clubs, and those clubs afterwards applied to the government of America for charters, and I believe they have all been erected into chartered companies; and though they have generally effected the insurances at two thirds, and in many instances one half of the premiums we must have given here, they have divided very handsome profits.

Do you think that the premiums paid to those companies in America are generally lower than what is paid here, or is it merely on what may be more immediately considered American and West India voyages?—I believe as far as has come to my knowledge, the premiums on risks from the ports of America to the East or West Indies, or to the Mediterranean and back to America, have been generally about one half what would have been demanded by our underwriters here.

But not so the direct risk from America to this country?—No, the direct risk from America to this country, I believe, cannot be stated at more than perhaps one third less premium, and in many instances not quite that; in many instances nearly the same.

What has been the consequence to your house of the establishment of those companies?—The consequence has been we have lost the orders we used to receive for effecting insurances to a very considerable amount; I suppose we do not now effect insurances for 1,000*l.* where we used to do twenty, thirty or forty thousand pounds before.

Did you generally effect your insurances in this country with private underwriters, or

A. Glennie,
Esq.

with the chartered companies?—Where the chartered companies would take our risk, we have generally preferred doing our insurances with them, and in fact have always offered them as much as they would take; they were very limited in the amount they would take; when we had large sums to do we have been in the habits of resorting to Lloyd's coffee-house for what the public companies would not take.

What difference have you generally found between the premiums asked by the companies and the private underwriters?—I have given them sometimes one per cent more, but I have done my insurances at the public companies at less premium than I could effect them at Lloyd's; I have one instance of it in my books which will prove what I say; a risk that I had to effect from the Bahama Islands to London, upon a prize-ship carried in there, coming forward under an order of the court of Admiralty, I was appointed a commissioner by the court of Admiralty there, along with a Mr. Black, of Glasgow, to receive this cargo, and sell it for the account of whoever it might belong to; upon receiving the order I went to Lloyd's coffee-house; I disclosed the whole of the orders of the Vice-Admiralty court there; the underwriters at Lloyd's coffee-house asked me 30 guineas per cent; if the vessel had been one of the constant traders I should have got it done at eight guineas per cent, with a return of two guineas per cent for partial convoy; I thought their demand too much; I then went to the public offices, and they took the whole of the cargo at 18 guineas per cent; it was a sum much larger than they would take, and I was obliged to have recourse to Lloyd's coffee-house to effect the ship, which I believe is in all instances considered a better risk than the cargo; but notwithstanding that, I was compelled to give 25 guineas per cent at Lloyd's coffee-house upon the ship.

In general did you do much of your business with the companies, or was it principally done by private underwriters?—By far the major part of our business with Lloyd's coffee-house; we had many risks to do which the public companies would not take; they refuse all risks to or from an enemy's port on perfect neutral property, though warranted to be such.

Are they not in general more difficult about all cross-risks than the private underwriters?—I do not recollect that they ever took any cross-risk from me.

As a general merchant, state to the Committee whether you are satisfied with the present state of the marine insurance in this country?—Certainly not with the present mode of carrying on the business in Lloyd's coffee-house; if I could do all my business at the public offices I should undoubtedly prefer doing it with them.

State your reasons of dissatisfaction?—We have very great difficulty in recovering averages or losses in Lloyd's coffee-house; I have at this moment a risk that the underwriters in Lloyd's coffee-house are refusing to pay, because I cannot bring forward the only witness to prove the loss, who is in a French prison; and though it was understood, at a meeting I had with the underwriters, that they should give certain admissions if we should bring an action, when we brought our action their attorney refused to sign the admissions.

In the general course of your business have you not found the companies more fairly disposed to settle their losses than the private underwriters?—Yes, I certainly have; I have heard others complain, but I never have had any reason to complain of the companies. I always, in doing my insurances, shew them the whole of the information I receive, and I never have had any difficulty in settling any loss or average.

You have stated your disposition to prefer the companies to private underwriters, do the two existing companies underwrite upon principles which enable you to apply to them in consequence of that preference?—In all risks that they will take, they in my opinion are preferable to Lloyd's coffee-house; in the first place, I feel myself perfectly insured; I feel that my property is safely insured; I know also that if a loss takes place I shall receive my loss in Bank notes, deducting the premium, the Thursday after the loss is notified; in Lloyd's coffee-house there are, I believe, very few instances upon a large policy that there are not one or two bankrupts upon it before we can effect a settlement, at least I have been so unfortunate as to meet with that generally; if I may be permitted I will state one case to the Committee which happened to us in recovering a loss at Lloyd's; an action we had to bring against an underwriter, on a policy where only 4,000l. was insured, they cast us upon a point of law, it was a very extraordinary cause to be sure; Lord Kenyon, in giving the decision of the Judges upon the point of law, stated that he was compelled to give a decision in favour of the underwriter, but he hoped there was no man upon the policy so dishonest as not to pay the loss; in consequence of which the next morning we received notice from about thirteen underwriters out of thirty, that they were willing to pay their proportion, and they did pay, but the rest remains unpaid now, and that is fifteen or sixteen years ago.

A. Glennie,
Esq.

Are not the two companies, in consequence of the difficulties they make in sign-ing certain risks, and in their demands being higher than those of private under-writers, but of little service in the general scale of marine insurances?—I do not think that I can state properly that they are of little service on account of the diffe-rence of premiums; I think it is in the amount that they take; they limit themselves to so small an amount that it is impossible to do risks where property is so much enhanced in value; instead of having a sum that they will do on one risk, it is three, four, or five times as much as they will take. I do not think the difference of pre-mium would ever have much influence with me, for there is a material difference of premium at Lloyd's Coffee-house, you may get the same risk done at five or at ten; but I should always prefer giving the highest premium at Lloyd's, because I should conceive myself insured.

Do you not therefore conceive that the establishment of a company, confining itself solely to marine insurances, with an adequate capital, and under proper manage-ment, would be of great benefit to the trade of the country generally?—Yes, I should think so, provided they will take an extensive sum upon one risk; I should think, as a general merchant, it would answer the purposes of trade much better if more than one was established in addition to those that are already established; and I do not conceive it would injure those that are already established if there were one or more, because those who insure would divide the whole of their insurances among them; that question, however, presses more strongly upon me than it does on the general run of merchants, for there are a great many who have more insurances than I have to do, but they have not so much to do on one risk. I have perhaps fifty, sixty, or seventy thousand pounds to do on one risk, and if that were divided into different risks I could get it done easier.

Since what period have your orders for insurances from America been lessened?—I do not know that I can state the precise period, but since the establishment of the companies in America, from 1790 to 1795, I think.

Do you believe that the present rate of premium in England is exorbitant, or more than to afford a fair profit to the Underwriter?—I do not know that I am a proper judge of that; I can only answer that question by comparing it with the premiums that are given in America on American risks; at the time that we were obliged to give from fifteen to twenty per cent on insurances from America to the West Indies and back again, those were done in America at from seven and an half to ten per cent.

Then in point of fact the rate of premiums is higher in England than it is in America?—On American risks certainly; there have been particular periods where, from a knowledge of circumstances in Europe which were not known in America, the premiums at Lloyd's on American risks have been lower than in America, but that only operated till the circumstances on the knowledge of which the underwriters acted reached America.

Have you any reason to believe that the establishment of a new marine insurance company would have the effect of making a considerable reduction in the rate of premium?—I am not prepared to say whether it will or not; I have not given that consideration; I do not know that I am a proper judge of it, for I am not an under-writer; it is reasonable to suppose that by bringing competition into the market it might; but I certainly think it would facilitate the merchant in getting his property insured.

Do you not believe that the establishment of a new marine insurance company would have the effect of withdrawing a great number of individuals who now under-write at Lloyd's?—Yes, I think it would; and it perhaps would be very beneficial for Lloyd's that it should be so.

In point of fact the greater the number of underwriters the greater must be the competition?—Certainly.

You having stated that the rate of premium in America is less than it is in England, have you any reason to suppose that the establishment of a new marine insurance company or companies would remove insurances which are now effected in America to England?—I do not think it would have much effect in that point of view; the companies having been established in America, and having the merchants there as the proprietors of those companies, they will of course keep all the business they can there; in some instances it would; where the American merchant wishes to place his property in England, and to have the facility of drawing upon it, that would procure me orders for insurance, if I could do it upon the same terms they can do it there where I do not receive them; because there are many instances in

A. Glennie,
Esq.

America where a merchant wishing to have the command of funds, as soon as he can load one ship wishes to draw for nearly the value of that shipment, which enables him to proceed in business; and I do not permit them to draw unless they give me orders for insurance.

Do you not believe, whatever might be the rate of premium, or the facilities of effecting insurances in England, that America, growing in prosperity and progressively increasing in its trade, would be desirous of annexing the insurance branch to the general business and commerce of the country?—I think that the Americans will retain the insurance, in all instances where they can, among themselves; but, for the same reasons I gave to the former question, where the desire of possessing funds acts upon them, they would be induced to send orders for insurance here more frequently than they do if the premiums were the same here as they are in America. I need not state that it would be a very desirable thing for me, because the insurance is an additional profit to the British merchant.

What is the largest sum which the two chartered companies ever take?—The policy I have in my pocket is for the largest sum I ever knew them take, that is for 12,750 *l.*; they never took more than 10,000 *l.* on any risk before from me. That is the Royal Assurance.

Do you know what the other chartered company takes?—The other took the same, it was equally divided between them.

So that you effected 25,000 *l.* between the two companies?—Yes, that was the amount ordered by the Admiralty Court, and they took it equally between them.

State whether you think it would be for the general advantage of trade if there was a power to form companies for marine insurances, instead of confining the insurances to individual subscriptions as they are now?—Yes, and I think it would be a very desirable thing that partnerships should be bound upon policies instead of the individual subscribing the policies; there have been many instances, in some of which my house has suffered; where a bankruptcy takes place the assured can prove it only against the party signing the policy; whereas we are obliged, perhaps, to pay the premium to the partnership, and instead of being able to set off the premium we are compelled to pay the premium, and to prove the loss under the single bankruptcy.

Would not the insurance by partnerships give a greater degree of security to the merchant who insured, than he has from the individual insurances as they now exist?— I think so, for the reasons I have just assigned.

Can you state the difference between the dividends paid by the separate estates of the individual underwriters on your policies, and the estates of the firms or houses in which they were partners?—No, I cannot; I do not know that I could by having reference to that; because until very lately none but the principals assured could prove a policy, and we are very much in the habits of doing insurance for correspondents abroad, and therefore are not the principals; there are many policies lying in our house that we never could prove against bankrupts, but which have been a total loss.

Would not the same difficulty have existed if the policies had been written by partnerships, as exist in the present case?—Certainly, in the last respect I have mentioned.

Does not the law, prohibiting insuring against British capture in this country, necessarily induce Americans, shipping produce to the ports of the enemy, to insure elsewhere?—Yes, where they are shipping produce to an interdicted port, I should suppose that is the case; I have not had any practice in it; I give the answer merely from supposition, and what I have heard others say; but our correspondents have fortunately never gone into any illicit trade; generally speaking, the risks we have come in a great measure under our own control into the British Channel, for our direction to a port, and therefore in many instances we have warranted against British capture, and I believe in all instances we might.

Is it not the general wish of the American merchants, when the cargo consists of produce of the enemy's colonies, and is bound to an enemy's port, to insure against British capture?—It is the wish of the merchants in America to be insured against all risks.

Have not many houses in America suffered great inconvenience in consequence of vessels being brought in for adjudication, on suspicion of the property being enemy's property, and not being able to recover of British underwriters?—It is not the house in America that suffers the inconvenience, but myself; for, generally speaking, when we have orders for insurance we make advances on the cargo; and therefore it is the person making the advance of the money suffers the inconvenience and not the proprietor of the cargo, and I very candidly confess I have suffered in that instance more than once.

You have stated that the underwriters refused to pay a loss, on account of the party who alone could prove it being confined in a French prison; is not the cross-examination of that witness thought by the underwriters very material to their interest?— I apprehend it is, although I do not know that it can be of any service to them; for the only evidence he can give is, the proof of the seizure and condemnation of the ship by the French; the captain of the ship is dead, and this is the chief mate.

You have stated that you seldom recover a large policy without one or more insolvent underwriters, can you state what proportion the amount of the losses your house has sustained by insolvent underwriters bears to the amount of the whole sum you have insured at Lloyd's?—No, I cannot say that ever I made any calculation of it; nor do I mean to say that we have suffered very great losses on what we have done ourselves at Lloyd's Coffee-house; we generally prefer giving the most liberal premium, and we have generally very good underwriters upon our policies; but many instances have occurred where I have had so large a sum to do; I have given it away to brokers to do in all such instances; where we have had recoveries of average or loss to make we have met with bankrupts.

Have you ever known policies done at Lloyd's at the same time, at so strange a difference as 5 and 10 guineas?—Yes, I have known it, and have got letters to prove it; on the same ship or ships bound from the Baltic to a port in Scotland I gave 12 guineas; there was another house in London, whether by mistake, or whether they really did the business I do not know; they advised their correspondent in London, who was concerned in half of the cargo, that they had done it at 6 guineas, and the whole of the correspondence was copied and sent to me, as a proof that I could not do business so well as other people.

Were both insurances done at the same time?—Within forty-eight hours of each other.

And no change of circumstances to occasion any variation in the premium?— None; the only change of circumstances which took place was, that within two or three days after it happened; the person who had done it was obliged to give twelve guineas before he could finish the amount that he had to do.

Then, ultimately, the other party gave the same premium as yourself?—For part of it; but I have no doubt that if he had followed up his insurance the day we began it he would have finished it among a certain set of underwriters.

Do you know whether any failure on that policy done at six guineas took place among the underwriters?—No, I do not; the ship arrived, and therefore it was never inquired into.

Are you a subscriber to the petition in favour of the establishment of a new marine insurance company?—I believe I am.

Have you subscribed for any shares in that new company?—I have.

Veneris, 9° die Martii, 1810.

The Honourable WILLIAM BEAUCHAMP LYGON in the Chair.

Thomas Gillespy, Esq. called in, and Examined.

YOU are engaged in the coal trade?—I am a coal-factor.

Do you know of any association in London, other than the Royal Exchange and London Assurance Companies, for the insurance of ships?—There are I believe two in London.

Do you know of any clubs or societies established in other places for the insurance of ships?—In the northern ports, I should suppose, there must be near twenty; namely, at Scarborough, Whitby, Sunderland, Shields and Newcastle.

How many of such clubs may there be in all?—Twenty, or more.

What do you suppose may be the aggregate amount of their capital?—They have fluctuated very much; I should think they might be taken at 50,000 *l.* each, making a million altogether.

Do you know the nature and object of such institutions?—I have never been a member of those institutions, but I have a general knowledge of them from the nature of my line of business.

T. Gillespy, Esq.

Do you know how they carry on their operations?—They have a policy for a twelvemonth, as a common policy for time, the stamp being paid upon it, which they consider legalizes the insurance; but they have other regulations, which govern their mode of settling averages, and restrict the voyage or conduct of the individuals; in the policy that is so given each individual appears to be an underwriter for a specific sum of money, and therefore is liable for his own act and deed only to the extent set against his name, but to no more; a man is not bound for another, but only for himself, that seems to take away the idea of its being a company.

Have any papers respecting any such clubs fallen in your way?—I have paid and received monies for members of clubs, but I have had no papers left with me, not being a member of any club.

Mr. *John Cheap*, Jun. called in, and Examined.

Mr. J. Cheap.

ARE you secretary to a Society called the Friendly Insurance?—Yes.

When was that instituted?—The latter end of the year 1804.

Can you state the cause of its institution?—It arose from several gentlemen thinking it better to insure, as is the practice in the north of England, in clubs, than to go to the coffee-house.

State the nature and object of the institution.—The insuring transport ships only against losses or averages, and against any damage which they might sustain, captures by the enemy excepted.

Of how many members does it consist?—There is no fixed number of members, we have from seventy to eighty at the present time.

How many transports were insured by this society for the last year?—About eighty-two or eighty-three.

What was the amount of the averages and losses paid by each member of the society for the last year?—The account is not made up yet for the last year, but as far as we can ascertain, about one and a quarter per cent.

What would have been the amount of the premium at Lloyd's Coffee-house to cover the risks insured by this society for the last year?—The premium which the underwriters require at Lloyd's for insuring transports for twelve months is nine per cent., but in our policies a clause is inserted which they do not insert; we insure our transports from the damage which they do to other ships, which is equal to about two or three per cent. more.

Have you brought with you any copy of the rules of the society?—I have brought a copy of the rules, and one of the policies.

[*The witness produced them.*]

Do you know of any similar institution in London, or its neighbourhood?—There is only one in London, called the London Union Society.

Do you know when it was instituted?—I do not.

Can you give any particular information with regard to it?—I cannot

Do you know of any similar institution in other parts of the kingdom?—There are several in Whitby, Scarborough, Shields and Blythe, and other ports in the north of England.

Can you give the Committee particular information respecting them?—I cannot.

Do you conceive that the society of which you are secretary, or any similar institution, would have been called for if greater facility was afforded of doing insurance at Lloyd's, and with the two chartered companies?—I cannot say whether they would or not, as I am not in the practice of effecting insurances at Lloyd's, or with the chartered companies.

In what mode are new members admitted into your society?—By a tender; the form of the tender accompanies the rules which I have given in.

Then a person who wishes to be admitted must tender his ships, and describe their qualities?—Yes.

Does the admission of a member depend upon the good or bad qualities of his ships?—Partly. That presented is the form, which is laid before the Committee, and if the ship is a good ship, and the owner who tenders her is a man of respectability, he is admitted.

Do you admit the owner of bad ships to be a member of your society?—Ships of an inferior quality, badly built, and in bad order, we do not admit

Mr. *John George Wilson* called in.; and Examined.

YOU are secretary to the association called the London Union Society?—Yes, I am.

When was this association instituted?—The exact time I cannot state, but it was revived in the year 1803, when I became the secretary. I believe in its first state it was not so extensive as it is at present; there used to be only a few ships insured; probably twenty or thirty.

What were the causes of its institution?—I believe the cause was from the confidence which ship-owners entertained in one another; they connected themselves together to insure each other's property; they conceived that there was a better security, I suppose.

State the nature and object of the institution.—It is established for the protection of each other's ships; and if a loss occurs, that each person individually pays his proportion, according to the sum which stands insured in his name.

Of how many members does it at present consist?—I think, to the best of my recollection, we have, at this moment, from eighty to eighty-four.

What were the number of vessels insured by the society last year?—The number of ships insured last year were one hundred.

What was the amount of the losses and averages paid by each member of the society last year?—The account is not made up; we have only yet paid 15 s. 2 d. per cent. but I should suppose, from the losses that are unsettled, it may amount to 5 l. or 5 l. 10 s. per cent. for the whole of the losses for the year, as far as I can ascertain; the ships may be absent, and we not be aware of their circumstances.

What would have been the premium charged at Lloyd's coffee-house, if the risks covered by this society had been insured there last year?—It depends very much upon the nature of the voyage; I believe transports would have paid 9 guineas per cent. if the ships had been engaged in the coal-trade for the year. I conceive they would have paid from 18 guineas to 20 per cent. on other ships engaged generally; it depends much upon the destination; there are heavy premiums paid according to the risk.

Have you brought with you a copy of the rules of the society?—I have, with a policy annexed.

[The Witness delivered them in.]

Do you know of any other institutions of a similar kind in London and its neighbourhood?—There is a transport-ship insurance; I believe they only insure transports. Mr. Cheap is their secretary.

Do you know of any other in any other part of the kingdom?—I have heard of several.

May not losses on vessels engaged on foreign voyages, of which you have not yet heard, still come against your last year's account?—Yes.

May not averages, which require some time to make up and bring forward the documents for, still come against your account?—I think that I have pretty well ascertained the losses that have happened to us in the amount of 5 l. to 5 l. 10 s per cent. If there are any averages, of course they must be paid.

If parties wish to become members of this club, is it not necessary that they should give a description of the character and qualities of their ships for the examination of your committee?—If any person wishes to have his ship insured, the secretary gives notice to the surveyors, and if they report that the ship is eligible, the committee admit her into the insurance.

If bad ships are offered, they are not accepted by your society?—If they are known to be bad, they are certainly not accepted.

You leave them to be insured at Lloyd's?—They may go where they please.

Lunæ 12° *die Martii,* 1810.

WILLIAM MANNING, Esq. in the Chair.

John Julius Angerstein, Esq. called in; and Examined.

HOW long have you been in the habit of transacting insurance business?—About fifty-four years.

J. J. Angerstein, Esq.

In your opinion, have the increased means of effecting marine insurances in this country kept pace with its increase of trade and commerce?—I think they have.

Have not two additional rooms above the Royal Exchange been added to the subscribers room, and the boxes been enlarged, so as to make them capable of holding six instead of four persons, within these fifteen years, for the accommodation of the subscribers at Lloyd's?—They have.

Are not the subscribers rooms still crowded with underwriters, notwithstanding this increase of accommodation?—They are.

Do not other underwriters, who do not attend at Lloyd's, carry on the business of marine insurance at the Jamaica Coffee-house, the Jerusalem Coffee-house, and the Coal Exchange, as well as a great number write policies at their own counting houses;—Yes.

Do not many merchants and traders interchange policies with each other, who do not consider themselves as professed general underwriters?—I believe they do, but that does not fall within my knowledge; I have reason now and then to find out, when an average happens, that insurance has been done when I do not know where.

Are there not adequate means in this metropolis of effecting marine insurances on any sum that was ever embarked on any one voyage?—Any sum that I have ever heard of; I can quote some very large sums.

Can you state what sum was insured in the year 1807, on the Diana frigate from Vera Cruz to Great Britain;—There was 631,800*l*. done by the private underwriters, and 25,000*l*. with one of the companies.

Did you effect the whole of that insurance done by the private underwriters:—I did, and at the same premium.—I must beg here to clear up one matter on the examinations, by stating, that it has happened in a number of cases where there are large insurances made on ship or ships; the largest sums in general are on ship or ships, and the underwriter is freer to write a larger line on ship or ships than on a ship named, because the property comes divided; it may come in one ship, but it generally comes divided; but in this case, though the policy runs that it is to be on the Diana, Captain Maling, or any other ship or ships of war of 30 guns or upwards, we knew that the whole property to be insured would come in the same ship; which made it more difficult to get so large a sum done, for every underwriter knew it must come in one bottom; ship or ships were put in because in case the Diana did not get out, another ship was to be sent for the property.

Then in point of fact it was understood by the underwriters the whole of this property was to come in the same bottom?—Yes, it was.

Do all the underwriters at Lloyd's write your policies:—No, not one third; I have about 200 accounts; there are a great number of underwriters.

Then there were a great number of underwriters at Lloyd's who had no opportunity of writing upon the Diana frigate:—There certainly were some; I got some sums taken by people that had not taken a policy for years before, but would take a line upon such a risk as that.

Do you recollect the Scaleby Castle, from Bombay to London, being insured by the house of Law and Bruce, in 1799:—Yes.

Should you, or any broker of extensive connections, have found any difficulty in insuring 100,000*l*. upon that ship at Lloyd's?—I certainly should not.

Do you recollect the ship Shah Ardaseer being insured by the house of David Scott and Company, last year?—I recollect the beginning of January, 1810, seeing the policy, and refusing to write it.

What was your reason for refusing to write that policy:—They would not give me premium enough.

Had an adequate premium been given would there have been any difficulty in effecting an insurance upon that ship in a single day at Lloyd's?—I should think not; very large sums may be done in a single day.

Do you think that any difficulty could be found by a merchant, or a broker of extensive connections and established credit at Lloyd's, in insuring fifty or sixty thousand pounds on a British West Indiaman and her cargo?—No, upon a good ship, certainly not.

Can you state any instance in which larger insurances than that have been effected upon West India risks?—I must go back to the ship called the Lascelles, upon which I had an order from a very considerable house for 49,700*l*. in the month of September; it was an old Indiaman, and the owner of the ship might be an honest man, but he had the character of being a bad fitter out of his ships, and an East India ship is not a fit one to bring home a West India cargo in general; I got the order about the middle of September, and the 49,700*l.* was finished by the end of October, the reason of the delay was, that my principal, though a very liberal man and a very considerable house, would not increase the premiums; I begged of them to let me increase the premium when I had got about 40,000*l.* as their orders had come after others had done their insurance, and she must have been worth in all about 90,000*l.* or 100,000*l.* ship and cargo and freight; I told him I had got to the utmost of my tether with my own underwriters, and begged of them to let me increase the premium; they wished me by no means to do it, for others would send away their accounts at twelve guineas, and they desired I would go on with it at the same premium; I told them I must give it to some other broker, who had perhaps other accounts, to help me out in it, and I would give up my commission to them; and they wished me to do it; by which means they got some bad names; there was but one bad name among my underwriters, but the other brokers got me ten bad names; but the whole order was finished, though so large a sum had been insured before upon her; if I had not done this I should have been obliged to wait till other underwriters came to town, but I always could have done it with a small advance.

Was not the difficulty in effecting this insurance owing to the Lascelles being an old Indiaman that had performed her regular voyages in the East India Company's service, coming home in the winter, and the premium being thought inadequate by the underwriters?—It was; she was not at all liked; and she was obliged as it was to put into one of the islands for repair, which came to a considerable average

Had she been a good ship should you have found the same difficulty in effecting that insurance?—No, I should not.

Should you have found any difficulty in insuring 40,000*l.* on a good ship from Tonningen to London, in the month of August, at the regular premium?—No, I should not.

Should you have found any difficulty in doing double on a good ship at such a season?—No, I should not; I have done many times much larger sums to the continent and from it.

Should you find any difficulty in insuring 200,000*l.* on one of the regular fur-ships from Quebec to London?—At an adequate premium I should not; I used to write them, but I left them off, they gave so low a premium upon them; and the enemy know to an hour when the ships will sail: I have for these reasons avoided writing those ships.

May not difficulties in effecting insurances at Lloyd's be found both by merchants and brokers, who have not been long established, or whose connections among the underwriters are not extensive, when such insurances might easily be effected in other hands?—Yes; I know other brokers as well as myself refuse business continually.

Do not you find caution, both as a broker and an underwriter, necessary, in consequence of the greatest part of the commerce between Great Britain and the continent of Europe having got both into new hands and into new channels? Yes, I think there is great reason to be cautious.

Do not you believe that such considerations weigh both with other underwriters and insurance brokers as well as yourself, and frequently prevent their doing business when no other difficulty exists?—I believe so.

Do not many houses employ young men to effect their insurance business at Lloyd's who have not either much property or much experience?—Many persons employ such young men that they do not know the persons of the underwriters, and ask for them.

Is not much of the litigation at Lloyd's occasioned by want of accuracy in the definition of the risks, and by want of skill to make up complex statements of average and partial losses by young men so employed?—I believe so. What I mean is, a man who is young or inexperienced in his business.

Is there a great deal of litigation in consequence of the business done at present at Lloyd's?—There is, perhaps, more than there should be, but there is great reason for litigation—there are a number of places to which we hardly ever pay averages—to others we are always paying averages: I would instance Hamburgh, which is a great port; my house is particularly experienced in the trade to that port upon a great many goods which go up the country; we hardly know an average when there are so many averages continually demanded by the merchants at Hamburgh, and it is the same in Italy. At Pisa you may get any kind of certificate. I used to do business for a considerable house in Yorkshire, whose goods went up the country, and seldom recovered any average upon them, though I hardly ever write to other houses whose goods did not go up the country where there was not a demand for average.

J. J. Angerstein, Esq.

Then you think much of the litigation at Lloyd's is occasioned by improper claims being brought forward in the way you have described?—Yes.

What regulations are adopted by the chartered companies for the payment of their premiums, or the securing the payment of their premiums?—The broker gives a security for the payment of the premium to a certain amount, and if the sum exceeds he must give further security, that is to say, if I have given 5,000 *l.* security for premiums, and my insurances come to 7 or 8,000 *l.* I must give additional security.

Do they accept your own security alone, or are you obliged to have other persons joined with you in that security?—I have been obliged to get other security, it was when I began business; perhaps the companies when they know a person perfectly may not demand it, but I began my business so, and opened my accounts so; they ran no risk at all.

You do not mean to say that you at present give any security besides your own in effecting insurances with the companies?—When I first began I gave securities, and it continues on; Mr. Locke, my security, is still alive, and his security is not withdrawn.

Do you think young houses trading largely upon small capital would be able to furnish securities for the amount of their premiums, if they were under the necessity of doing the whole of them with chartered companies?—If the company require it I should be doubtful whether it would be convenient.

Is not credit given for premiums to a much longer period, as well as obtained with much greater facility, at Lloyd's than in the mode adopted by the chartered companies?—Yes, it is.

What are called regular risks by the underwriters?—Regular risks are from this country direct to a port in America, and different parts of the continent, and from thence back; and regular traders are called regular risks in general.

What are called cross-risks?—From foreign countries to other foreign countries, to different ports in different countries; there is such a variety of them I cannot distinguish them.

Are not neutral vessels trading with licences to and from the ports of the enemy considered as cross-risks?—Yes.

Are not cross-risks insured almost exclusively by the individual underwriters?—I believe they are, in a great degree.

Has your experience taught you to consider regular risks or cross-risks as the most advantageous to the underwriter?—The regular risks; sometimes cross-risks, with some connections where you know any thing of the ship, are very well; but the other is the easiest done thing.

Do you believe the conduct of the chartered companies in declining cross-risks to be founded on the same opinion as arises from your own experience?—I should think so; it takes up a great deal more time in doing cross-risks.

Is it possible for the acting director or secretary of a chartered company to have the same opportunities of judging of the nature and value of those cross-risks, changing, as they do, with every change of political circumstances, as the large body of underwriters who constantly communicate with each other upon those points at Lloyds?—I think not; for if I have a cross-risk to make, if it is from America, I go to a box where there are Americans to give me information; if I have a cross risk from Turkey, I go to another box where I can get information; and so it is from the Baltic, or any other part. I generally go to the box or the people whom I think best conversant, for they are the people who can begin the policy for me better than others, and I by that means get it done; for it is of no use applying to a Baltic merchant on an American risk, he knows nothing at all about it. I always go to those who know most about it, and there I can always get information about it; for there are so many people frequent the coffee-house, if an underwriter does not himself understand it he soon gets information, and makes me master of the subject at the same time.—If a managing director is so clever as to know all parts of the world, that is not what I have met with yet.

Is it reasonable to presume that any new chartered company would long continue to act upon the principle of writing cross-risks, which they must follow under such comparative disadvantage?—I think it would be difficult for them to go through with the quantity there is excepting at a very large premium; you may command any underwriter if you give him premium enough.

If a new Marine Insurance Company were established, possessing within itself nine tenths of the commercial interests of this metropolis, and selecting all the best risks

J. J. Angerstein, Esq.

of which they had the choice, would not the individual underwriters be discouraged from continuing in their present avocation?—Most certainly; people of property in particular.

If a great proportion of all the best risks were withdrawn from Lloyd's by such a company, would any respectable underwriters continue, or think it worth their while to continue, to write the other indifferent risks that would remain?—No, certainly not; unless at a very advanced premium, and then with great difficulty.

Do you think that any additional facility to the present means of effecting marine insurances would be obtained by the establishment of such a company;—I think, on the contrary, there would not.

Is not the rate of premium lower at Lloyd's than with the chartered companies?—Yes, almost always; I have known particular cases where, from a mistake, the company have been lower than at Lloyd's; but as soon as it was found out by the brokers they poured in, and they stopped it immediately. I look upon it the long voyages are generally two per cent higher with the companies than with the private underwriters; the middle voyages about one per cent; and I believe the shorter voyages about a half per cent; perhaps a quarter.

Does not the system of individual competition, on which insurance business is conducted at Lloyd's, produce the effect of reducing the rate of premium lower than it otherwise would be?—Yes, it does.

Can you state what proportion the losses by the insolvency of underwriters bear to the amount of the property you have insured at Lloyd's?—I can, by the account before me. I have had the honour of doing part of the business of a very respectable and honourable house for the last twenty-two years: the amount I insured for them was 8,483,081 *l*. I recovered for them, for losses, averages and returns, 490,323 *l*. 15 *s*. 11 *d*. (the Lascelles, which I have mentioned, was done in this account). In that account I had underwriters who did not prove solvent; I recovered short of what I should 2,130 *l*. 11 *s*. 1 *d*. by bad underwriters in the twenty-two years. I have had an inquiry made what dividends the underwriters who failed have paid, and I have got most of them; some of them paid in full, some five shillings in the pound, some ten shillings, some fifteen shillings, some two; but out of 2,130 *l*. 11 *s*. 1 *d*. the dividends they have already paid amount to 1,010 *l*. 11 *s*. 4 *d*.; so that my principals lose 1,119 *l*. 19 *s*. 1 *d*. If my principals had thought fit to have taken my security, I should have got, at a half per cent upon the eight millions, above forty-two thousand pounds. I generally get half per cent upon long voyages, and a quarter upon short; supposing half to be long and half to be short, I should have got 31,000 *l*. and I should have lost 1,119 *l*. 19 *s*. 1 *d*.; so that they have saved that money by not giving it me. If the merchant stood *del credire* he would charge half per cent, as many do, and he would of course have got 42,000 *l*. and lost 1,119 *l*. 19 *s*. 1 *d*. besides further dividends which are to be paid, some of them in full; but owing to Chancery suits, and estates to be sold, and so on, all are not yet paid. There are a number of clauses the companies will not take, nor will private underwriters, unless paid for them, which are called foreign clauses, to have the goods covered till put into warehouses, and so on, which are introduced in foreign and cross voyages. I do believe that if that sum, I mean the 8,483,401 *l*. was to have been insured at the offices of the chartered companies, it would have cost nearly 100,000 *l*. more than it did.

Then, in point of fact, losses by the insolvency of underwriters on insurances, amounting to nearly eight millions and a half of property, do not much exceed 1,100 *l*. and will be yet further reduced by the payment of dividends?—Yes; not three pence halfpenny per cent.

Does that statement include the insolvent underwriters whose names were got by other brokers whom you found yourself under the necessity of employing to get insurances on the ship Lascelles you have mentioned?—Yes.

You consider this statement of losses by insolvent underwriters as giving a fair average of the general loss by such insolvencies on the business you have effected at Lloyd's?—I am very careful with whom I open accounts; with some litigious people I must do business, but I take all possible care my accounts are not above two hundred. I have other instances where there have been no failures; in the case of the Emperor Paul seizing the ships in Russia; there was a friend of mine for whom we had done 97,000 *l*. (and a very trying time it was) the proof of interest was 77,960 *l*. 8 *s*. 5 *d*. and there was no failure.

Was there any ultimate loss there, or was not the property recovered?—I believe a year or more afterwards very little was lost, but the money was paid; the settlement was made before the recovery.

J. J. Angerstein, Esq.

Then there was no defaulter whatever among the underwriters upon that occasion?—Not one.

Is it not a practice with underwriters to class their risks, in order that they may not engage in those of any particular description beyond the bounds of prudence?—I believe it is; they class them by voyages.

Does not this subdivision of risks tend very much to the general security of the assured, in case of any sudden or general calamity?—Of course.

Have you found underwriters in general disposed to cavil and evade the payment of losses?—There are a great number of claims made which are not allowed; but the underwriters cannot cheat a merchant, except in one way; that is, by being a bankrupt. I do not call the underwriters calling for papers acting a wrong part, for there are so many fraudulent insurances, and, I am sorry to say, I am afraid I have made many through my office, that I do not wonder where proofs are called for; the demands from foreigners particularly are past all belief; but the mode which they generally follow at the coffee-house is to leave it to a reference; for my part I always do; unless it is a question of law I never go into a court.

In cases where the underwriters are not legally responsible, have you found them liberal, or otherwise?—Very liberal; I could produce a number of instances where they are very liberal.

Can you state any cases of that description?—I have known them dispute a point of law when they could not get a certain voucher, which if they had got, the underwriters must have succeeded; but the assured would not produce that voucher, and the solicitor for the underwriter took the advantage of the illegality of the insurance. When the underwriters found that the law suit was got by that means, they would rather be cheated and pay the loss, though the verdict was in their favour, and that to a considerable amount.

To what amount?—Some thousands of pounds.

Have you any other instances?—Yes; I have known them to pay a loss where the merchant has made a mistake, and called it ship instead of goods, or goods instead of ship, and the underwriter, knowing it, took no advantage, and paid the loss; these are facts from my books. I have known a ship insured from one place to Europe, when she came from another, and that has been paid; I have likewise known them refuse to pay when the commodity has been insured, supposing raw silk, and it has proved to be thrown silk, and they could not enforce it; but that has been owing to some personal disputes between the parties. In 1792, before the commencement of the war, I made an insurance of 69,386 *l.*; the ship was taken coming home the next year, and I see that in September, October and November I settled 57,986 *l.*; for the remaining 11,400 *l.* some would not, and others could not, pay, and it never was recovered. On the second of January last, in consequence of our having insured 5,300 *l.* and recovered a loss, I received this letter:

" Gentlemen,

" We have to acknowledge the receipt of the four policies for 200 *l.*, 600 *l.*, 1,000 *l.* and 3,500 *l.*, together 5,300 *l.*, per the Clasnia, Captain J. J. Böhn, from London to the Elbe, Ems, &c. which you have settled at eighty per cent loss, (with the exception of five underwriters, who alone wait for the certificate of condemnation on the ship), and for amount of which we have debited you in account. We are happy, gentlemen, in this opportunity of returning you our sincere thanks, as much for the great exertion of your good selves as for the singular liberality of the assurer in settling the above average, as, from the unfortunate error of one of our clerks, in giving you the indorsement of the insurance, we have been paid nearly twenty per cent more than we had a right to claim; we beg, therefore, you will assure the different gentlemen who have thus handsomely settled the loss *in toto*, of our high sense of their generosity on the occasion. We are, with great regard,

" Sirs,

" Your most obedient humble servants,

Angerstein and Rivas, Esquires.   " WILSON, AGASSIZ & Co."

The underwriters knew the whole of the circumstances at the time they paid, but five will not pay. There is also a case of a gentleman who has been unfortunate, who set up for insurance broker, and he made an insurance, in which he described the goods to be on provisions, valued at so much; when the loss came to be settled it was found to be mahogany, but the loss was paid; the whole was paid.

In the cases you have stated, where the ship has been insured instead of the goods, where one species of goods has been insured instead of another, where the voyage has been insured as being from one port instead of another, would not the Underwriters have been obliged to return the whole premium, if called upon so to do?—Yes; I believe it to be so, and I know it to have been done by one of the companies. All these are accidents; but the private underwriters will settle the loss for a man of character, where they will not for a man whom they suspect; where they see it is a mistake, they will pay a man of character, but where it is for a man they suspect, they will not do it.

Have you found your underwriters very liberal, when they are satisfied with the probity and good intentions of the parties?—Yes, very liberal in general.

Have you ever found the number of underwriters so diminished, by their occasional absence at any period of the year, as to be incapable of effecting your insurances?—I have heard a great deal said of the months of September and October, and I have had my books examined; I was not in town all the while, but my partner was, and he says that every insurance ordered was made, and we insured last September 236,557*l.* and in the month of October 237,087*l.* and one of the insurances was for 38,000*l.*; and if I had had ten times the sum to do upon different ships, I should have done it with great ease.

Do you speak of what you effected as brokers or underwriters?—As brokers.

Do not many of the underwriters who are absent request their friends to write for them till their return?—Their friends or clerks.

Do not the premiums regularly advance as the winter approaches?—Yes.

Is not the season in which the premiums advance a constant scene of disputes between the underwriter and the assured, from the unwillingness of the one to write without an advance of premium, and the unwillingness of every one to be the first to give that advance?—That is too often the case.

Are not the difficulties of effecting insurances at that season of the year rather owing to this cause than to any other?—Yes.

Is not the bulk of the insurances on the Jamaica fleet, which sails the 26th of July, and the Leeward Island fleet, which sails the 1st of August, generally effected on ship or ships by name during the summer months?—Generally; sometimes in August, and a few in September; but mostly in the summer months.

Are not the ships from the Baltic, Newfoundland, and other parts of the world, generally insured as early as possible in the summer, in order to guard against the advance of premiums expected to take place in the autumn?—A great many are.

If policies were underwritten by partnerships instead of individuals, might not the objection of any one of those partners frequently defeat the disposition of others to settle the loss where the payment of it might be legally contested?—It is an action of feeling; and I would rather trust to one man with right feeling than to two or three other partners, for they might persuade him to the contrary; but I have given a proof in the settlement of the 58,000*l.* which was done instantly, so that I have no reason to complain. As it is, I have met with such liberality in settling so large a sum as that, where there was no consultation of partners, but it was done immediately.

Is it not likely that a man's feelings would be rather more acute where he is individually concerned, than where he is only one of a number?—To be sure they are.

Might not, in such cases, the necessity of consulting other partners frequently retard the business, and expose the assured to inconvenience and risk?—It would take up more time certainly: the very taking the papers home to consult would take up a good deal of time, if they were not immediately brought back.

In case of the failure of commercial houses, where one of the partners is an underwriter, is it not generally found that the separate estate of the individual underwriter pays a better dividend than the joint estate of the partnership?—It has not fell to my lot to have many such; but there have been cases within this year or two, where both the parties have paid, or will pay, twenty shillings on their private account, and upon the account of their partnership two shillings has been paid, and two or three more is all that will be paid upon the partnership account.

Is it not natural to expect, that wherever extensive commerce is carried on, insurances for the security of commerce will be effected also?—Yes.

Must not the merchants of every country be desirous of transacting their business themselves, rather than pay a commission for transacting it to others; and do they not prefer holding in their own hands the policies by which their property is secured?—Yes.

Must not many East India voyages, particularly the country trade, as it is called,

J. J. *Angerstein,*
Esq.

be either insured in India, or not at all, for want of opportunities of writing to Europe
—Certainly; there is no time for it.

Does not the same observation apply to cross-voyages in the West Indies?—Yes.

As the British law prohibits the underwriter from paying in case of British capture, is it not necessary for the security of all property, the nature or destination of which renders it liable to suspicion, that it should be insured, not in Great Britain, but in countries where the law is no bar to the immediate recovery of the property?—Yes.

Would any of those objections to insuring foreign property in Great Britain be done away by the establishment of more marine insurance companies?—No.

Have you not made frequent insurances against British capture?—Yes.

Have they not been made with great facility, and to a great extent, in the coffee-house?—Yes; but not expressed upon the policy.

In a separate clause?—It was understood.

No practicable difficulty, therefore, exists to insuring in this country against British capture?—At a very high premium it may be done; but it is not done at the common premium.

But it is done to a great extent?—Not now so much as it was.

Whenever it is desired to be done, it is to be obtained?—Every insurance almost can be done with fair connections, and at a considerable advance of premium.

Is it not always more easy to effect a large insurance on specie in ships of war, than on any merchandise in merchant ships?—Yes.

Is therefore the effecting the insurance of a large sum on ships of war any criterion by which the Committee is to judge of the extent of sum that may be readily insured on merchandise on board a merchantman?—In war-time, yes; but in peace-time underwriters would rather write packets and constant traders than they would even men of war. The Lutine frigate sailed about the same time the packet did; they both carried property I insured; the Lutine was lost, and the packet arrived: the men of war are well manned, but I am afraid sometimes there is great ignorance in the pilots.

You do not mean to state to the Committee, that when a large sum was insured on the Diana frigate, a similar sum could have been insured on merchandise by any merchantman?—No, I do not think there could.

Can you state to the Committee when the policy upon the Diana was begun, and when it was finished?—The order was given, I believe, the 25th of July; it was done very soon, but I have not the precise date; the whole sum was not ordered at once, it was proceeding.

Was there not at least a month's distance of time between the commencement of the insurance and the closing of it?—Very likely, but I cannot state it; the Lascelles was longer, but the whole was effected at the same price; I could have got one gentleman who would have taken 10,000 l. at five per cent, though he was upon it before at four.

Have you accounts with all the underwriters in the coffee-house whom you consider respectable?—I cannot say all; I do not know all, but those that I know are very respectable.

Are there not a great many with whom you refuse to have accounts?—I certainly would not have any accounts with some of them.

How many underwriters are there in the coffee-house altogether?—I cannot say; it is a thing that hardly any body can say, for I call an underwriter a man who takes part of a risk himself or with another: I understand that the clerks of houses, sent by merchants to do the business, get a line from one and a line from another; it is out of my power to speak to that.

When you made this large insurance upon the Diana, did you not take a great many names that you were not in the habit generally of taking?—I got gentlemen to take them for me, giving it up to them; and some merchants that had not written a policy for ten years before took a line there.

Were there not many names upon the policy that you would not have taken, if you had not had so large a sum to do?—Yes.

Your house act as brokers or agents for effecting insurances, do they not?—Yes.

Do you not conceive they would be materially injured by the establishment of this new projected company? Yes, I suppose they would; I am one of those that are against it, but I must open an account with them if they will open one with me, and must give them security if they require it, because I do not do justice to my principals

If I do not give the preference to such a company as that; to a private underwriter they must have the choice; if they will write at the same premium with the best underwriters at the coffee-house, I must give them the preference.

J. J. Angerstein, Esq.

Do you conceive that if such a company were established merchants would prefer it to private underwriters?—I think they would.

Why would they?—From the greater solidity of it. I have had a great deal of practice, and I know that there are frequently merchants who do not choose to act for themselves; they prefer doing it through a broker, though it is done with a company, and that is the way I have made insurances with the companies for merchants in London the same as I should if there was a new company; that was my reason for opening my accounts so many years ago with the company.

Have you done much of your business with the two existing companies?—At times I have.

Does it bear any considerable proportion to the extent of your general business?—It does; I have done large sums with them, but not lately.

Do you not frequently find inconvenience in the settlement of losses from difference of opinion among different underwriters on the same policy, as to the law and equity of the case; and have you not been obliged sometimes to bring more actions than one to settle the same loss; that is, after suing one underwriter, have you not been obliged to sue another?—Whenever I have been present at those disputes, it has been generally offered to be left to arbitration; or if it is a dispute on a point of law, there has been a committee appointed to transact the business, and offers have always been made to try it with one or two underwriters, to save expense and trouble, and that is, I believe, the custom of the coffee-house.

Do you not find it happen that some of the underwriters are ready to settle a loss when others are not inclined?—Yes; I have mentioned two or three cases of that kind; there was one case where 11,000 *l.* was not paid; the other losses we have recovered. There is the case of Wilson and Agassiz, where there are five that will never pay, for they want a paper that cannot be had.

Had you ever a law suit with either of the companies?—I believe there was some years ago. There was a singular case, a dispute with one of the first houses in all London, and it went to a great height with one of the companies; it went so far that he desired me never to make another insurance with the companies.

Did you ever know the companies lose any action?—I think I have.

You cannot recollect any particular case?—No, I cannot.

Are you not aware, that hardly a term passes without actions being brought upon policies into our courts of justice, and that insurance questions are considered as forming the most profitable business to lawyers?—There are always a great many law suits continually; I hear of them, but in general I am not interested in them, only in those in which there are questions of law. I never go to law unless there is a point of law, or an attempt is made to cheat me, which I resist.

Is there not frequently a material difference in the rates of premium demanded for the same risk, by different underwriters?—Yes.

Have you not heard that attornies frequent the coffee-house to seek out business?—Yes, I think I have seen it.

And that they encourage private underwriters to litigation where they would not otherwise be disposed to it?—I never met with that encouragement from them; I generally employ a man of character.

In making insurances, are you not frequently obliged to pay a higher premium in consequence of the sum being large?—No; but for bad ships and at bad seasons we are pressed, and obliged to give higher premiums.

If it is known you have a very large sum to insure, would it not have that effect?—Yes, it would, but we take care not to let it be known; we do immense large sums at the same premium; I can bring you cases of 200,000 *l.* or 300,000 *l.* without any advance of premium.

When it is known in the coffee-house that there is a large sum to be done on one risk, does not that frequently induce the underwriters to ask more than they would if the sum was moderate?—It may induce them, but we generally find we get on with a common fair premium, and fill our policy.

Do you mean to inform the Committee, that there is not a greater difficulty in effecting insurances in the months of August, September, October, and November, than in other parts of the year?—It is always at a time between the two seasons; there are the northern risks; the merchant wants them at the summer premiums, and the underwriter demands the winter premiums, and there is constantly a dispute.

J. J. Angerstein, Esq.

but to do that away we put in returns for sailing at particular fortnights; the first fortnight in September, and the last fortnight in September, and so on, from the Baltic.

Do not many of the underwriters leave the coffee-house at that period of the year?—Yes, some do certainly, for different reasons, but I never returned an order for a house of reputation at a premium that they would allow me to give at any time of the year; it is always to be done at some premium or other.

Is there not a considerable difference in the coffee-house between the premiums taken by some underwriters and by others, upon the same risks?—I believe there is.

To what is that difference owing?—Either to the broker not doing his duty, or his being satisfied with taking men that I should not like to take.

Was there not a proposition some time ago made in the coffee house for the purpose of separating the trust-worthy underwriters from those who were considered as less so, to invest a certain sum in government securities, and that those under-writers so selected should meet in a separate room?—I never heard of that; it was proposed as a good thing, in case they could get underwriters voluntarily to lodge security: I do not think that could have answered. There were some other schemes talked of which were not brought to maturity.

Was it not considered a desirable thing, by the most respectable persons in the coffee-house, to make some distinction of that sort?—I heard a few underwriters mention it; but all that I heard was, that it would be a good scheme to have such a thing brought on, that those who chose to deposit such a sum in the funds should have it known what they had done; but it never came to any thing more.

Do you know what was the cause and object of those intended regulations?—I suppose the general alarm; it has been only since we heard of this company.

Why should they do it since they heard of this company?—Because they think that the company will destroy the whole of Lloyd's Coffee-house; that the men of property must leave it, and will leave it; and from a calculation I have made I am convinced it will be so; and I have heard men of property say they must leave off attending the coffee-house.

Do you mean that the frequenters of the coffee-house wish to purify their character with the public by these means?—I do not know what their plan was; they did talk something of it, but there was no meeting upon it.

Has not the business at Lloyd's increased very much lately?—Yes, last year: I do not think it is so large at this moment.

Has not this increase induced clerks from merchants counting-houses, and other people not trustworthy, to set themselves up as signers of policies?—It is very likely it is so, but I do not know of it. I could not name half of those that are now in the coffee-house.

Have you not heard it complained, that clerks in counting-houses have lately introduced themselves there to sign policies?—I believe there have been some; but I cannot name any of them.

Do you recollect whether, towards the close of the American war, there were many and considerable failures among the underwriters at Lloyd's Coffee-house?—In the year 1780, when Cordova took the East and West India fleet, and the Quebec fleet was dispersed, and a great many lost, I believe that produced some considerable failures.

Since that period have not considerable and contemporary losses by capture been of more rare occurrence?—Since that time there has been the seizure in Russia, which was a complete loss for the time: the underwriters were obliged to pay the loss; the salvage was not paid till a year or two afterwards.

In the case of the Russian seizure, the loss to the underwriters was merely tem-porary—was it not?—It was a complete loss. I bought of some of them at 50 or 60 per cent. their property; they gave it up as a loss; I had an opinion of it, and purchased it.

Has not the protection afforded to our trade during this and the last war, by our naval force, secured the underwriters from any signal and extensive misfortune in any one year?—The only way I can answer that question is by my own conduct; I have never wrote so little as for the last two or three years; I think the premiums are too low. I have not had an opinion of the risks, though the protection has been very good; yet I have thought the premiums have not been adequate. If I had thought the premiums adequate I would have written them.

Although the premiums, in your opinion, have been too low, yet have, in fact, those losses of fleets occurred which are alluded to in the last question?—No, they have not been in fleets; but from one accident or another (I must always go back to what I know myself) I know my office has never had as many losses as in the last year; I cannot tell how they came—from ships miscarrying, or one accident or another.

J. J. Angerstein, Esq.

Has there been any general calamity which might be expected to put to the test the security of the underwriters in the coffee-house during this and the last war?—I think that the Russian business was a test.

Have you that opinion of the solidity of the underwriters at Lloyd's that you think one considerable calamity would overset them?—I do not think it would.

Why then do you consider that the single circumstance of the Russian seizure should expose them to extensive failures, especially as it was merely a temporary seizure, and afterwards little ultimate loss was suffered from it?—At the time it was made it was not thought to be a temporary seizure, for no person could foresee the Emperor Paul's death, and it would have continued if he had lived.

Do not you believe, in point of fact, that there are a great many underwriters in the coffee-house in Lloyd's, though not among those with whom you deal, who have very little capital?—I suppose this may be the fact, but I cannot say; I go into the coffee-house to do my business with those I have business to do with; and I know there are people of very great property I have no concerns with; but I attend to my own concerns—I am as careful as I possibly can be. I can only answer for what I know—I declare that I do not know the names of half of them.

Though you yourself have been cautious, have not other brokers been less fortunate?—I suppose there are some certain cases, because I hear complaints of underwriters; but I will not lay so much upon the brokers, because I think it is more the merchants, by their clerks choosing to do their own business. I believe the regular brokers are as careful as I am.

Do you not believe, that among a class of underwriters whom you yourself do not confide in, such a loss as that which happened when Cordova took nearly the whole of an outward bound fleet, would cause now considerable failures?—No, I do not, because the number of underwriters has so much increased since that time; that was thirty years ago; it might cause some, but not more than that did, and I do not think that was a great deal.

Do you not believe that in particular trades there are admitted a certain number of underwriters that are not really responsible for the sums they underwrite?—I may now and then see a policy of that sort, but if I do not like a man, I do not take his name if I do not know his stability.

Are there not a certain class of underwriters that write more largely upon particular trades than in proportion they write upon others?—When I have been pressed for a large sum, and offered policies (every body has a partiality for their own line), I have offered to Jamaica houses men of war, and they would rather prefer Jamaica-men than those risks. There is a partiality which they feel to do in their own line, and they will not go out of it.

I allude to your general knowledge of the whole of the underwriting business?—My knowledge consists only of what I do myself; I have so much to do when I am there that I do not concern myself with any thing that others do; only I know that you cannot get you a man who writes you a risk from London to Newcastle and back again, which is very dangerous at some times of the year, to write you a man of war.

Do you not conceive that those who give themselves to the practice of writing partially, and particularly upon one trade in preference to others, would be exposed to the chance of failure, supposing a large fleet captured in that particular trade?—The partiality of keeping to particular trades is less at Lloyd's than at any other place, I believe; for the underwriter who comes there sees such a variety of business, and finds it so much his interest to mix the whole, that if there is a storm at one place he is safe at another; that it is more among the merchants who do not come to Lloyd's; but a man who frequently comes to Lloyd's writes American and East India risks, and every risk.

Would not such persons as you have described, being partial to risks in particular trades, be exposed to great risk of failure, supposing a large fleet captured in that particular trade?—Yes; but they are not persons who generally frequent Lloyd's Coffee-house.

You having stated that there were persons frequenting Lloyd's Coffee-house with whom you would not wish to transact business, do you not mean by that, there are persons frequenting that coffee-house who have little or no capital?—That is mere supposition; I cannot speak to it; I do not know their names.

J. J. Angerstein, Esq.

Do you not believe that there are persons frequenting Lloyd's Coffee-house, as underwriters, who have little or no capital?—I dare say there are.

Have you ever known that there have been policies opened at Lloyd's upon the event of a bill passing, or being rejected, in either of the Houses of Parliament?—I never saw such a thing, nor do I remember having heard of such a thing.

Since it has been fully understood that the law prohibits insuring against British capture, do not many underwriters refuse to write that risk on any terms?—Yes, there are some that certainly will not; there are some that never did, there are others that will not.

Were not very heavy sums paid on the Dutch ships detained in the year 1794, by the underwriters, notwithstanding they understood that the law exonerated them from paying those losses?—They do not fall in my line at all.

Was not the insurance on the Diana frigate effected by you without delay, as the orders came to your hands?—Yes, without delay.

Must not a considerable time necessarily elapse in getting the names taken off of slips and put on to policies, before you can complete those policies for your principals?—Yes, it is sometimes a delay to a considerable inconvenience; a gentleman agrees to take 1,000*l.* upon a policy, and goes out of town, and we now put his initials; we cannot send in the policies till they are signed; but the Diana frigate was different from others, there was no hurry for insuring her, as she went away, I believe, only in the month of May or June, so they gave it me by instalments; I did not know the extent of the sum; there are some who will take advantage of that, and there are others will not; I have known the first merchants, where there has been a ship missing from accident, take fifty pounds a-piece to accommodate, and others will take five or ten thousand pounds.

Did you take any names upon the policies by the Diana frigate of whose solidity you had any other reason to doubt than your own want of knowledge of the parties?—No; I am very cautious when I do give out an insurance of that sort; and I am very careful that the brokers that I get to do them shall be very cautious who they take, and I have been very successful.

As you consider yourself bound to give the preference of your business to the new chartered company, if it should be established, do you not suppose that other brokers and merchants would do the same on equal terms?—I should think every regular broker, and indeed merchant, must give a preference to so responsible and so great a company as that; even if he has not an inclination for it he must do it if at the same premium.

If that preference was so given, would it not destroy underwriting by individuals?—Yes, certainly.

Would not the destruction of individual underwriting, and the taking away the competition occasioned by such underwriting, tend to raise the rate of premiums upon the public?—It would upon the worst risks. I have made a calculation of the difference; I think there would be a very great difference: it is from that I think the great mischief will arise, and that the company must gain considerably; at first I thought otherwise, but when I came to hear that one or two very honourable gentlemen, of whom I have a high opinion, declared in the House of Commons, that nine tenths of the principal merchants in London had agreed to belong to this institution, I changed my mind completely; I sent to the Stamp-Office, and inquired what the taxes were upon the policies of the underwriters the last year, and their answer was, that the tax upon private underwriters policies was 312,000*l.* which, calculating at the 5*s.* duty, comes to 124,800,000*l.* and adding the coasting trade makes it 140,000,000*l.* I suppose that mine tenths of the greatest merchants and people of consequence are those that belong to this institution; I add to them such as myself, and many other brokers, who I think will not do their duty as agents unless they make the offer of their insurance to that company; I suppose they will have an offer of 120 millions; out of those 120 millions I suppose that they will take 80 millions, choosing the best risks, and at the best seasons, and which I average, from an account of twenty-two years to which I have before referred, at seven and a half per cent. if you multiply the 8,483,000*l.* by seven and a half, it will come to more than the premium that was paid, which was 658,227*l.* the average rate of premiums for the last twenty-two years having been seven and a half per cent. This Marine Company I suppose will take eighty millions of risk, at seven and a half per cent, their premiums will amount to six millions; the twenty millions that they have not the choice of may go to other companies, or to private underwriters; but there is a sum short, for the eighty and the twenty form one hundred millions; there is still forty millions that consist of risks

that none of the companies will take if they had the choice. I look upon the gains of
the company will be (at fifteen per cent upon the six millions) 900,000*l.* for they
have no bad debts, if they begin so cautiously as the other companies did fifty years
ago, by taking security of the brokers; and I have met with many losses from brokers
as well as merchants; but this is founded on the supposition of their having no bad
debts. There is forty millions, however, left upon bad ships, cross-voyages, long
voyages, what is to become of them? There is the rock that all this must, I think,
split upon; you will no longer have men of property attending the coffee-house to
write policies, for every part of this forty millions will be supposed to have been
shown to the companies, whether it has or not, and they will be done only at a very
exorbitant premium, if at all.

*J. J. Angerstein,
Esq.*

Would not the establishment of such a company, with such a prospect in view,
diminish, instead of increase, the means for marine insurance?—I think so; the
merchant must either run the risk or send them abroad.

In those cases to which you have alluded, where there was a difference of opinion
among the underwriters, and some would pay and others would not, did you allude
to cases in which none of them were obliged to pay?—Yes, I alluded to cases where
they were not obliged to pay.

Do not the changes of our political relations with different countries continually
place the underwriters and the assured in new situations involving questions of law?
—I should think they would.

Are there not many cases in which losses, wherever they fall, either upon the
underwriters or the assured, must be cases of hardship, and which can only be decided upon by a court of justice?—Many; the lawyers differ among themselves in
some instances, and the courts go different ways.

Have the lawyers who are hunting for business at Lloyd's prevailed upon your
underwriters to become litigious or illiberal?—No, I do not know that they have;
they have frequently consulted them upon matters where there has been any thing
irregular, or any suspicion of fraud, they have asked for particular papers, but no
otherwise, that I know of.

May not the difference of premiums required on the same risk to which you have
alluded be owing to difference of opinion in the underwriters, or to their different
degree of knowledge and information, rather than to their different degree of
solvency?—That is a question I cannot well answer.

If merchants did not employ their clerks to effect their insurance business at
Lloyd's could they become underwriters?—No, I should think not.

Was not one of our Mediterranean fleets last war captured by the squadron of
Admiral Richery?—I believe there was.

Did not the same squadron afterwards proceed to Newfoundland, and do great
mischief there?—That is out of my memory; I remember the silk ships being
taken.

Do you remember any failure among the underwriters on that occasion?—I do
not remember any; the great failure among the underwriters was in the beginning
of 1793, the beginning of the war with France.

Are not a great number of separate losses just as injurious to the underwriters as
the capture of a fleet?—Yes.

Is not the rate of premiums reduced as low, in consequence of the increased protection given to our trade, as it ought to be?—I think it is, and I act upon that.

Do not the political changes, and the new circumstances which you have stated to
lead to law contests, apply just as much to policies written by companies as to policies
written at Lloyd's?—I dare say they do; they consult their lawyers as well as the
private underwriters.

Can you conceive that any company managed by discreet directors, having a
capital of five millions, would take eighty millions of risk annually?—Yes, I should
think so.

Then the evils that you foresee from the projected institution go upon the supposition of the new company writing to the amount of eighty millions annually?—
Yes; it is a supposed case.

Does not your idea of the evil that would arise from this new company proceed
also from your persuasion, that they would select so many of the good risks that
individual underwriters would be discouraged from writing the bad risks which
would be left to them?—Certainly.

Mercurii, 14ᵉ die Martii, 1810.

The LORD BINNING in the Chair.

Thomas Reid, Esq. called in ; and Examined.

T. Reid, Esq.

HOW long have you been in the habit of transacting insurance business at Lloyd's Coffee-house ?—Nineteen or twenty years.

In your opinion are the present means of effecting marine insurance fully adequate to every occasion?—I have never found any difficulty myself.

Have you ever returned any orders for insurance because you have been unable to effect them?—No ; I have written to an out-port once in my life.

Do you recollect the Scaleby Castle being insured in the year 1799?—I do.

Can you explain the reason why difficulty was found in effecting the insurance upon that ship?—At that time the business of Messrs. Law and Bruce was not in my management ; not until 1801.

Did they do their own business at Lloyd's, or were they in the habit of employing brokers at Lloyd's Coffee-house ?—They did their own business.

Had they employed a broker of extensive connections at Lloyd's upon that occasion would there have been any difficulty in effecting that insurance?—I should have thought none.

Should you have found any difficulty in insuring the sum ordered to be insured on that ship?—I have never found any difficulty in my life.

You have occasionally effected insurances for larger sums than was then done upon that ship?—Never upon one single ship ; the largest sums are by ship or ships, but not upon any individual ship.

Are not policies upon ship or ships, generally speaking, more difficult to effect, and less acceptable to underwriters, than policies on ships by name?—Most certainly.

To what amount have you effected policies at any one time by ship or ships?—Frequently two or three hundred thousand pounds.

With what number of underwriters have you effected those policies?—It is hardly in my power to say ; but I have got one policy in my pocket now on ship or ships, with only sixteen names, for 50,000*l.*

With what number of underwriters at Lloyd's have you on account opened?—I think I took out from my book the other day two hundred and forty.

With this number of underwriters you have effected policies to the amount of 300,000*l.* without difficulty?—Yes.

Are there many other underwriters at Lloyd's with whom you have no account?—A great many.

Are there not a much greater number with whom you have not accounts than the number with whom you have accounts?—I should think that there were.

Have you ever found difficulties in effecting insurances at any particular time of the year, on account of the absence of underwriters from Lloyd's?—I have not ; my business being in the spring in general heavier than at other times of the year.

What proportion do you imagine the losses by the insolvency of underwriters on policies you have effected bear to the amount you have insured at Lloyd's?—I think I am accurate in stating that the gross amount of policies effected by me within ten years has been between six and seven millions, and the sufferings by bad debts have been 777*l.*

Have you found your underwriters litigious, and difficult to settle with where losses have happened?—I have had no occasion, never having had any dispute at the coffee-house ; never any difficulty in arrangements of that kind.

Have you ever found any want of liberality on the part of the underwriters, in cases where no legal claim could have been made upon them?—Very much the reverse, in several instances.

Can you state any instances of that kind?—I have one instance of a ship of mine lost in the harbour of Bombay ; the underwriters paid me a loss of 26*l.* 15*s.* 8*d.* per cent upon an insurance of 26,000*l.* on a ship called the Hercules, and then they gave me 1,300*l.* being 5*l.* or five guineas per cent as a present to the captain for his exertions. I had an instance the year before the last, in the Baltic, of a friend of mine, Mr. Larkin, whose insurances go through my office : at the time that our fleet was at Copenhagen his captains were afraid and alarmed, and did not know what to do, and they all went into Copenhagen, which circumstance vitiated the insurances entirely ; I had some conversation with the underwriters, who were liberal

enough not to let this circumstance to so large an extent as seventy or eighty thousand pounds fall upon one man, but for the consideration of two guineas per cent.
they took the risk upon themselves, and suffered it to be no abandonment of the
voyage.

T. Reid,
Esq.

Might not the underwriters, if they had pleased, in consequence of the deviation,
have kept the whole premium, and incurred no further risk?—So I understood from
counsel; I had counsel's opinion upon it.

Did the underwriters sustain any ultimate loss upon that concern?—Upon that
circumstance they sustained a loss; and upon the winding up of the concern, from
the inaccuracy of the correspondence of the agents at Russia and Copenhagen, who
had the management of this concern, we were in a situation that we could not
recover a loss of 5,000l. from some circumstance there, and the underwriters divided
that loss with me, and paid me 50 per cent upon two of the cargoes.

If a new marine insurance company, comprising nine tenths of the commercial
interests of this metropolis, were established, what effect do you imagine such an
establishment would have upon the interests of the individual underwriters and insurance brokers?—As far as my humble opinion goes, I conceive there would be no
occasion for us at all; we must turn our talents to something else, if we have any.

Would not any new mode of effecting marine insurances which tended to diminish the number of individual underwriters, diminish the competition, and tend by
that means ultimately to advance the rate of premium?—I should think that it would
prevent a great many insurances being completed, because you must be wholly at
the mercy of the different societies.

Is it not easy to judge of the prudence, or the want of prudence, of every individual
underwriter, in the present open mode of transacting insurance business at Lloyd's?
—I should think every broker would be competent to that, certainly; one can easily
judge whether a man is prudent in his underwriting.

If underwriting was carried on by companies, or partnerships, might they not
engage in risks out of all proportion to the extent of their capital, without any possibility of its being known?—I should think, in the present circumstances of the
commercial world, in the Baltic particularly, that they might.

If underwriting was carried on in partnerships, might not the objection of one
partner prevent other partners from settling a loss who were disposed so to do?—I
should suppose there must be always a chairman to whom the arrangement of that
business should be left; if there were six partners it must be done by a majority, or
some arrangement of that kind.

If one of those partners objected to settling a loss, might not that defeat the
intentions of the others, who felt a disposition to settle it?—It certainly must, if six
were concerned, and if it was necessary to have the sanction of the whole six.

Could insurances be effected with the same despatch if the business was carried on
at various different offices as it now is, where all the underwriters assemble under
one roof at Lloyd's?—My business happens to be so current and so easy to do that
I have never had occasion to go to the offices but once or twice, so that I am not so
competent to speak to that, people are so well disposed to take a part with me.

Have you observed whether the estates of insolvent underwriters with whom you
have accounts have paid better dividends than the firms or partnerships of the
houses with whom they are connected?—I am not competent to speak to that; I have
had so small a proportion of bad debts, only 777 l. within the last ten years; indeed
on some occasions we have hardly thought it worth while to prove the debts, they
have been so inconsiderable.

Is not considerable skill and knowledge necessary to enable a person to transact
business properly as an insurance broker?—Certainly.

Do not many men of capital pursue underwriting as a profession?—A great many
of my friends do, who have no other concerns.

If insurance business were carried on by merchants insuring each other, or taking
it into their own hands, either as companies or as partnerships, instead of its being
conducted, as it now is, by individual underwriters and insurance brokers, would it
not be their interest to keep premiums up rather than to keep them down?—I should
suppose it must be.

Do you consider that the general interests of commerce would be benefited or
injured by such a change of system?—Never having experienced any difficulty myself
in doing insurances to such an extent as I have, I do not see myself how we could
be much benefited by it.

Do you perceive any way in which the interests of commerce, or the interests of

T. Reid,
Esq.

individuals would be injured by such an arrangement?—My individual interest must of course be injured, and every broker or underwriter, I should think, must suffer by it; the generality of brokers at the coffee-house, and underwriters, I should suppose, must be injured.

If those companies, or partnerships possessing the great part of the commercial interest of the city of London were to retain the best risks in their own hands, could it possibly answer to the individual underwriters to continue their avocation by writing such risks as the merchants themselves would then reject?—I should think that if a man had a capital he would not attend it; that he would give the business entirely up if he was to have nothing but the refuse of the business; it is only by the good and bad coming together that we can save ourselves at certain periods of the year from the heavy losses.

Do you recollect prosecutions having been commenced by the Attorney General, in 1808, against merchants for using slips instead of putting their insurances upon policies?—I have heard of that being several times done, but I do not know it of my own knowledge.

Was not a notice stuck up at Lloyd's of the danger to which underwriters exposed themselves by putting their names upon slips?—Certainly; and I have had an interview with the Commissioners of Stamps several times upon the business.

Have they not since in consequence refused to put their names upon slips?—It is perpetually refused to be done; it is understood the slips that are now presented are only till we can get the policy against the next morning; the underwriter does not write his name, but I put down his initials for him; the stamp is taken out the next day.

Do you not believe that the stamp duty on policies was formerly much evaded by the use of slips?—Most undoubtedly.

In policies upon ship or ships, where it is understood that the risk will be divided to a considerable extent, do not the underwriters generally take larger sums than they do upon single ships?—Most certainly.

Your own business is the greatest and heaviest in the spring?—In the winter and the spring.

Have you not found that at the time when the July and winter risks of the West Indies are coming forward, several, or many of the principal and best underwriters, absent themselves from the coffee-house?—I have seen several gentlemen absent themselves for recreation, or what not.

Do not you think some absent themselves with a view of avoiding being asked by persons with whom they generally do business to write those risks?—I should think it very likely, because risks of that kind you cannot refuse for a general broker who offers all his business; you would be induced to accommodate him rather than let his business not be done.

You have stated the amount of your losses within 10 years, is it within your recollection, whether about the year 1793, at the breaking out of the present war, there were considerable failures in Lloyd's Coffee-house?—No, it did not come within my knowledge; I do not recollect any thing particular in the year 1793.

Although by the great command of business you possess you have escaped losses, does it not fall within your knowledge that there were a great many failures of underwriters at the time when losses of fleets, and considerable losses by sea, were more frequent than they are at present?—I do not recollect any period which has particularly impressed itself upon me.

Do you know whether the two chartered companies, although you do not do much business with them yourself, in general have a higher or lower premium than the individual underwriters upon the same risks?—I think from my observation, and what I have heard, that they are in general 1 or 2 per cent higher than Lloyd's Coffee-house; I think brokers when they have shewn me policies, have said that the Royal Exchange Company have taken this at 1 per cent or 2 per cent higher.

To what cause do you impute it that they are able from any class of assured to obtain that additional premium?—I cannot tell, unless it is from the opinion that people have of the solidity being greater; I know no other reason.

You have said that you do not do much business with them yourself, but from your general knowledge you may be able to say whether a West India merchant for instance, having not more than 10 or 12,000 *l.* to do upon any single ship, may not in a few hours have the whole of his risks by one fleet insured by one of the chartered companies?—In a few minutes, I should suppose, if it does not exceed 10,000*l.* I think I have heard that about 10,000*l.* is about the amount the offices wish to take, though they may take something more.

If a merchant should have 5,000*l.* interest in any company of marine insurance, and should have annually from half a million to a million of insurances to effect, could it be his interest for the sake of the gain upon that 5,000*l.* either to pay a higher premium upon the whole of his insurances, or so to dispose of them as to be obliged to pay a much higher premium upon that class of them which are considered to be dangerous and disadvantageous insurances?—I have that opinion of a London merchant that he never would do any thing of that kind.

Suppose the establishment of companies for insurances should have the effect of bringing more insurance to the country at large, would not that counteract the injury done to the single underwriter by the amount insured by those companies?—I am at a loss to conjecture how that could bring greater insurances to the country from any part of Europe.

Supposing it should?—The injury done to the private underwriter never can be compensated, though it be possible that the nation at large may be benefited; but the underwriters at Lloyd's Coffee-house cannot be compensated by that.

Then in your consideration of the injury which one or two of these establishments would cause, you presume that they would monopolize the insurance business of the country?—I should think that they must, if conducted upon that liberal scale upon which offices would be disposed to conduct themselves.

You have stated, that if risks were taken by small bodies of men, the objection of one single person of that concern would create a difficulty to the settlement; does not the objection of one leading underwriter upon a policy often lead to and induce the objections of others, without the others giving much consideration to the question?—We frequently pay respect to a man's opinion in whose judgment we have confidence.

Does not it, in fact, supposing that the first man upon a policy should object to pay, involve and lead to the objections of the others?—I have heard a great deal of that, but I cannot say I have seen it myself; I never held a conversation upon a loss with any man; probably I am not a fit person to answer that question, never having had a difficulty that I did not surmount in a moment; respect would be paid, certainly, to the judgment of a man in whom confidence was placed, that he had examined the papers properly.

You have stated that skill and knowledge are very necessary to an insurance-broker; is not a good deal of that skill and knowledge employed in discriminating the responsibility of the different underwriters?—I should think it must.

Do not you know of instances where the decision of one man, who has underwritten a policy to pay a loss to which by law he was not compellable, has led and induced other subscribers on that policy to do the same, without making any inquiry into the subject?—I should think it perpetually happened; I have even myself, after a verdict in a court of law within these six months, when I thought I was honourable in going into a court of law upon a question, had it decided in my favour, and have paid the loss afterwards.

Are the leading underwriters in the habit of recommending resistance to just demands?—They have never done it to me, and I have never had with them the smallest difficulty in any arrangement of losses, or any thing whatever I have had to put before them.

What is your motive for preferring individual underwriters to the two chartered companies?—Personal friendship, and the wish to do a man good, is one reason, and the great liberality I have always found induces me to do my business with them.

It is not on account of the premium of individuals being cheaper than that of the two chartered companies that you are induced to prefer the former?—In my line of business it would not make much difference whether with the public offices or the private underwriters; my line of business being the India line, in which there is very little difference between the public offices and the private underwriters. I have never had but one instance of doing an Indiaman with them, they were there two per cent. higher.

Is the Committee to understand that the difference of premium between the chartered companies and individuals is very trifling?—Yes, on India risks.

Is the allowance made to brokers by the two chartered companies the same as that made by individual underwriters?—It is so long ago since I had to do with the

T. Reid,
Esq.

chartered companies that I cannot tell: the private underwriters allow 5 per cent upon the premium, and 12 per cent. upon the balances they receive.

Do you know whether the credit allowed in both instances to brokers is the same? —I believe with the offices you make what is called prompt payment, in order to entitle you to the discount which they allow, that is in three months or six months, and if you have credit for a longer time you give security for a year; if you run your account for a year I believe you give security to a certain amount: but with me it is sometimes two or three years that the underwriters do not send down for their money; the account being a large one, they know whenever they send for a large sum of money they are sure to get it.

In point of fact, the facility given to the brokers with respect to payments is greater from individuals than from the two chartered companies?—As far as respects myself, as a broker, I find every degree of indulgence in the world; people send for their accounts of 2 or 3 or 4 years old, some send earlier.

If the allowances and facilities in payment are greater from individuals to brokers than from the two chartered companies, would not that account for the preference given by the brokers to individuals?—I should think it might; but if a broker had a great command of money he would probably be induced to do a great part of his business at an office, because I believe their allowances are greater, as an inducement to bring business there.

Have you never heard of the chartered companies taking on one risk a larger sum than 10,000 l.?—I have heard that 10,000 l. is the sum they prefer, but I think they have taken with me a greater sum than that; and I have heard to the extent of 20 or 30,000 l. lately, but I do not know it of my own knowledge.

If the whole, or a very considerable part, of the insurance business of the country were conducted by joint stock companies, instead of being carried on as it now is in by far the greatest proportion by individuals, would such a change in the system of insurance, in your opinion, tend to raise or to diminish the rate of premium?—I should suppose that the companies might then almost fix their own rate of premium, and that there would be no competition.

Do you not conceive that a general low rate of premium is advantageous to the trade and commerce of the country?—It must make the commodity fall cheaper ultimately to the consumer if the underwriters can live by a low premium consistently with the capital which they have.

Can you state any thing like the amount of insurance annually done at Lloyd's? —indeed I cannot.

You have said that if the projected company were to be established there would be no longer any occasion for Lloyd's Coffee-house; do you think that this company would be able to do all, or any thing like, the insurance now done at Lloyd's? —The bad business they would reject, I suppose, therefore, that must be done somewhere else.

Do you think they could do all the good risks?—I think they would do all the good risks; there is very seldom a ship worth more than 200,000 l. and if there are many public companies they would not hesitate to take 100,000 l. or 50,000 l.

You have said that it would be the interest of companies to keep up the rate of premium, rather than keep it down; if a company was to be established, not upon any speculation of profit, but for the purpose of underwriting each other's risks, would it not be the interest of that company to keep the premium at a reasonable rate?—I take it this is a general body, in which a vast number of persons that have insurances to make, and others who have none, are parties subscribing; a great many persons who have nothing to do with trade would of course embark in a concern of this kind from the prospect of making use of a few thousand pounds to advantage.

Would it not be the interest of a body of merchants, so collected into a company, to keep the premiums at a reasonable rate?—If they did not the other companies would have the advantage of it: the three or four companies must run in some even proportion; one company would not be above one per cent. above another.

Then, in the event of the establishment of a number of companies, there would be in fact a competition?—There would be a competition.

Do you think that if the exclusive privilege was withdrawn from the two existing chartered companies, the consequence of such an enactment would be the institution of a number of new companies?—I have heard that at Liverpool, and at Glasgow and at other places, such things are in agitation, but I do not know the fact.

To what causes do you attribute that ?—A desire to benefit themselves. Those persons who are incorporated in that way at Liverpool and Glasgow must know that it would be advantageous to them, and therefore they are desirous of having that privilege

T. Reid, Esq.

Do you think there would be a general eagerness among merchants to form themselves into such companies, or to deal with such companies, in preference to Lloyd's ?—To form themselves into such companies I conceive they would be anxious.

Is it your opinion that the merchants would be more inclined to deal with such companies than with the individual underwriters at Lloyd's ?—Many of them would not leave their old connections, I should conceive, where their business was well transacted ; but if deaths or things of that kind were to happen, it is probable most of them subscribing to it would, as it would be for their own interest to carry their business there.

You are therefore of opinion that it would be for the interest of the merchants, generally, to have their risks underwritten by companies in preference to the individual underwriters ?—Their interest would clash in two ways : they would benefit their own dividend in the office the more business was done ; and I should suppose the bye-laws of the society would call upon gentlemen to bring their business there, as in most bodies of that kind. I believe the bye-laws do recommend, if not almost compel, them to bring a certain proportion of their business to the office.

Supposing no such bye-law to exist, and that the share given to each merchant in a new company was so moderate as not to amount to any inducement to him to take his business to any other parties than those to whom it would be most for the interest of his business to take it ; in that case do you think the merchant would go to the companies, or to the private individuals ?—I should think, if he is a man of large capital, he will go to the companies, if it suits him to be paying a great many thousand pounds in one month or two months for his premiums ; to smaller merchants, I conceive, it would not so well answer as to do business with a broker.

Supposing each underwriter to become a sharer in a joint stock company, which should take risks in proportion to the whole of its capital, and take that amount in average risks, and at the average premiums, would he not derive the same advantage as he does in his capacity of a single underwriter ?—I should think the hitherto pursuit of that man would be totally done away. I know many men who pursue it for amusement, and at the same time with the prospect of not injuring their fortunes, but making them better : the remainder of their life would be entirely done away ; as to pecuniary advantage, I am not competent to answer that, my mind is not sufficiently great to take it in, because I do not see how a man having 5 or 10,000 *l.* engaged in that shall be able to say I can receive 5000 *l.* a year for my share. I should suppose also, that in the Baltic, in the Russian or the Prussian ports, there might be a stop in one moment, as there was some time ago by the Emperor Paul, of a vast number of ships. We had at one time last year 200 ships in the ports of Sweden, and I believe there were some doubts whether Sweden would not declare against us ; and if so, the whole of those 200 ships would have been gone, and the amount of that would have been enormous. When we come to take the average amount of the cargoes from the Baltic last year, I think it amounted to seven or eight-and-twenty millions, in sixteen or seventeen hundred ships; if two hundred ships are at one time taken, and you reckon them to be of nearly equal value, there is a great amount gone in one moment.

Upon the question stated, it is supposed that the company was to take the amount of its risks, of average risks ; is not the individual underwriter liable to his proportion of that contingency which you have just stated, as much as he would be if he was a sharer in a joint stock company that underwrote with such discretion ?—I should think not, for this reason, a prudent underwriter would not venture more into the Baltic at one time, he sees the money he has there, supposing it all to be lost ; therefore he may say I will go to the extent of fifty or one hundred thousand in the Baltic, and no farther.

In the last question, by average risks was meant that the companies should take no more of any one kind of risk, in proportion to its capital, than a discreet single underwriter would do in proportion to his capital ?—Then we should be both on the same footing, the company and the underwriter.

Do the present existing companies monopolize any great share of the underwriting business, to the injury of the coffee-house ?—No, I do not think they do.

Is not the business of the companies generally conducted with less zeal and activity than that of separate individuals ?—I should think that an individual, who has nothing but his own head, and his own ability and talent, to forward his interest, would adhere as much to it as possible; his whole mind and time is given up to it.

If therefore any branch of business is thrown open to fair competition between individuals of all classes and companies, do you think that it is natural for the companies to get the better of individuals?—I should think that they would, if we had a great many of them so formed, because every man belonging to it would carry his business entirely to it. If I belonged to a company, and I had 100,000 l. to insure, I should naturally offer them the refusal of it.

It is not found at present that companies, even with exclusive privileges, monopolize any great extent of underwriting to the injury of the coffee-house?—Their proceedings are so formal; if we have any little difficulty to overcome we can do it with individuals, but their conduct is so uniform and so strict that we are obliged to give up losses rather than make difficulties and be supposed litigious; but they have a committee to regulate their proceedings, and we have no appeal from their decisions; losses are frequently paid by private underwriters which the Royal Exchange company have not paid, I believe.

Do you mean to represent that the companies would be more litigious than the private underwriters?—No; but only that they cannot act with so great facility as private underwriters.

Do you act as an underwriter and as a broker?—Yes; but I underwrite for another person's account, not my own.

You have stated, that the profit to the broker consists in five per cent. on the premiums, and twelve per cent. on the ultimate profit of the underwriter: in your situation as a broker can you state to the Committee which of these items is the most profitable—the five per cent. upon the premiums, or the twelve per cent. upon the ultimate profits?—To a general broker, I should think the five per cent., but I am not a general broker, but in the India line: it is to us the twelve per cent. to some houses I could name, who are general brokers during war; I should think the five per cent. were better than the twelve.

Do you think considerably better?—I cannot answer that.

Supposing the five per cent. upon the premium to be exactly equal in value to the broker to the twelve per cent. upon the profits, would it not follow that the broker derives nearly one quarter of the profit of the underwriter for his agency?—Yes.

Do you not think that a brokerage which amounts to one quarter of the whole profits of the underwriter is higher upon the whole than it should be?—The labour, the agitation of mind, the perpetual vexation, is not to be described; I would rather begin the world again and pursue any other line; it is painful to a degree; the inconveniencies that arise are not to be calculated; we can hardly ever satisfy our principal; I see that, though I do not feel it.

You are of opinion, therefore, that the great trouble attending the business of a broker, under the actual system of effecting insurances, is so great that you think a brokerage amounting to one fourth of the whole profits of the underwriter, not too great a compensation for it?—A broker in a moderate line of business certainly is not overpaid by it; but if men get their twenty or thirty thousand a year, the trouble is not too great for the compensation they receive.

Supposing the whole of the insurance business that can be commanded by the directors and proprietors of the Royal Exchange and London Assurance Companies to be given to those companies, would it, in your opinion, form any considerable proportion of the whole insurance business of the country at large?—No, I think not.

Do you believe that nine tenths of all the insurances made in London consist of risks not exceeding 50,000 l. on any one ship?—I think nine tenths of the insurances are on ships not exceeding 50,000 l.

If a new joint stock company were formed, comprising nine tenths of the mercantile houses in London, is it not probable that all insurances under the control of the members of such a company, not exceeding 50,000 l. on any one ship, would be given to such new company?—I should suppose that they would; and as I stated before, I should suppose that the bye-laws and regulations of the society would induce the proprietors to take their business there.

Would not the effect of this be to secure to such new joint stock company nine tenths of the whole insurance business of the country?—It must secure the greater share of the insurance business.

Would it not, in your opinion, ensure considerably more than one half of the insurance business of the country?--I should think it might; but it would take only the best.

T. Reid,
Esq.

and Lloyd's Coffee-house would not take the worst.   I do not know where that is to go to.

Might not a merchant insure all his risks by one fleet, not exceeding ten or twelve thousand pounds in one ship, in a very few hours among the underwriters at Lloyd's?—It happens to me to do very large sums; I cannot say in hours, for it does not take me hours about it, but in a very few minutes in the course of one morning.

The larger the profits of the insurance broker are, does it not become a more important object to the merchants to keep those profits or emoluments in their own hands?—Certainly.

Would not the effect of the establishment of the intended new marine insurance company, be to keep both those profits and the profits of the underwriters in the hands of the subscribers to the new concern?—There can be no doubt of it; there would be no occasion for a broker.

You have said that the establishment of companies, in your opinion, would tend to raise the premiums of insurance, do you think that the result of such a rise in the premiums would be to bring any additional quantity of insurance business into this country?—I do not see where the insurance business is to come from.

Do not the underwriters prefer leaving a balance in the hands of the brokers, to set off against losses that may happen, lest after allowing them the discount of twelve per cent upon the balance, they may be called upon to pay losses in full?—Most undoubtedly; the balances in my hands are enormous belonging to the coffee-house.

Is not the facility given in the payment of premiums by individual underwriters a great accommodation to many houses?—Most undoubtedly.

Would not many houses find it difficult, if not impossible, to pay their premiums within the time required by the chartered companies?—I should think none but merchants of great capital could do it; a new established merchant, I should think, could not do it, unless he had an enormous capital to begin trade with.

If the great bulk of the insurance business were thrown into the hands of a new marine insurance company, would not the directors of that company have a great controul over the commercial operations of other houses, by the system on which they might be pleased to regulate the giving or refusing credit for premiums of insurance?—I should suppose they must; they would be acquainted also with all the speculations and undertakings they made, and with their correspondence and other things, having their letters exhibited to them.

Would that power be very acceptable to commercial houses in general?—I should think not.

If the merchants found any inconvenience arise from such a disclosure to any public company, would not that inconvenience be very much aggravated by its disclosure to all the different underwriters who might sign their policies?—We have nothing of that kind; we rely a great deal upon the honour and character of the broker with whom we have to do; and if a man tells you this is a fair, honourable, and just average, many people settle upon that; they do not want to see all the commercial concerns of a gentleman's house, and I am a stranger to such a proceeding. In foreign losses upon the continent, in Holland and Tonningen, and Denmark at this time, the underwriters do require a little more, on account of the peculiar circumstances, than they would if we were at peace, or had not the kind of warfare which is now carrying on.

Should you, as a broker, carry your best business to people who did not help you out with what you considered the worst?—At Lloyd's Coffee-house I should not, we give and we take, the good and the bad together; and if I cannot do a thousand pound line upon a bad risk, I can do two hundred; or if not two hundred, I can do one; therefore by having one good and another bad we are able to get on.

If any inconveniencies arose on the establishment of a new company, would they not fall upon the merchants generally?—I should suppose that they would; but that is only matter of opinion.

If the merchants generally are in favour of the establishment of such a company, is it not a proof that they are not very apprehensive of such inconveniencies?— I believe a great many people have embarked in it from complaisance, and from wishing to get into something new; a great many have told me, they did it without weighing in their minds the extent to which it went, they have done it for the sake of appropriating as much money, and that it might be profitable so to lay it out.

If it would be inconvenient to many merchants, on account of the narrowness of

T. Reid,
Esq

their capital, to deal with a company, on account of the small credit which it gives, would not that of course check the monopoly of such a company, and throw a great deal of average business into the hands of the private underwriters?—As they must be insured, it must throw a portion of it into our hands.

Do you not understand that the motive of securing the emoluments now made by the brokers and underwriters to themselves, has been the principal object with many of the subscribers in taking shares in this new marine insurance company?— I should think it must.

If the individual underwriters were discouraged from pursuing their avocations, by the establishment of these new marine insurance companies, would not many inconveniencies arise before individual underwriting could be so re-established by a new set of men as to carry on the insurance business of this country, in case objections were found to arise to the continuance of a new chartered company?—I have always thought that underwriters who had property would begin to wind up their concerns immediately, considering their business at an end, and would never write another policy.

Are the evils which you predict in your last answer, upon a supposition that the projected company would take to the amount of one half of the good business of the port of London, or any thing near it?—They would take an enormous deal; I cannot speak of the proportion to one half.

Do you conceive the evils you have predicted, and which you have supposed would happen upon the establishment of such a company, would take place if that company did not upon the whole write more than twenty millions a year, the whole business of the port being one hundred and forty millions?—If the company takes only twenty millions out of one hundred and forty, and the other one hundred and twenty is to be done with the other companies, or at Lloyds, I should think the evil could not be so great as we are taught to believe.

If this company is established, do you not apprehend, that other applications will be made for the establishment of other companies also?—We have heard of applications from Glasgow, Liverpool, and other places.

As the broker receives a principal part of his compensation from the profits of the underwriter, is it not for his interest to protect the underwriter against the claims of the merchant; is it not for his interest to encourage the underwriter to resist the claims of the merchant?—I should think not; and for this reason, that he must lose the confidence and the business of the merchant; he would be unworthy in future to be entrusted, and the loss of every thing that is to turn to making his fortune must result from his losing the confidence of his principal.

Veneris, 16° die Martii, 1810.

The Honourable WILLIAM BEAUCHAMP LYGON in the Chair

George Browne, Esq. called in; and Examined.

G. Browne.
Esq

WHAT is your line of business?—The house with which I am connected are merchants, we do our own insurance business, and the insurance business of our correspondents as insurance brokers, and my partner and myself are underwriters on our own separate accounts.

Do you make your insurances with the two chartered companies, or at Lloyd's Coffee-house principally?—At Lloyd's Coffee-house.

Entirely at Lloyd's Coffee-house?—Yes.

You make no insurance with the two chartered companies?—We have not for a great number of years.

State your reasons for preferring Lloyd's to the two chartered companies?—We never found any difficulty in doing our business at Lloyd's Coffee-house, and being underwriters, we generally find by giving our business to others we have a share of theirs.

It is not then any difference of premium, or any want of facility afforded by the company which you experience at Lloyds, that has induced you to prefer individuals to those two companies?—No, it is not.

Do you conceive that there may be many other persons who underwrite at Lloyd's, and who may be influenced by the same motives in the preference which they give to Lloyd's coffee-house?—Yes, I should think a very great number.

G. Browne, Esq.

Is not this a reason why the companies should be deprived of a great share of insurance business?—Yes, I should think it is.

Do you believe that nine-tenths of the whole insurance business of London consists of risks not exceeding 50,000 *l.* upon any one ship?—I should think fully nine-tenths.

Supposing a new marine insurance company to be established, do not you believe that the members of such company would make their insurances with their own company rather than at Lloyd's, or with the two existing chartered companies, the premium, credit and allowances being the same?—I should think as merchants they certainly would; whether being underwriters likewise they might not feel more their interest to do it at Lloyd's Coffee-house than with the company, is a matter that would be for their consideration.

Do you think it likely that underwriters, whose interest it might be to make their insurances at Lloyd's Coffee-house, are likely to become members of such company?—I know that a good many at Lloyd's Coffee-house have proposed themselves as members of the intended marine insurance company, and have signed the petition.

Supposing such new marine insurance company to comprise nine-tenths of the mercantile houses in London, is it not probable that all insurances not exceeding 50,000 *l*, on any one ship,' which members of such new company would have to effect, would by preference be given to that company?—I think a very great proportion of them, provided that company mean to take to the extent of 50,000 *l.* on one risk.

Would not the effect of this be to secure to such new company by far the greatest proportion of the whole insurance business of the country?—In my opinion it would.

Do you believe that there is any difficulty, under the present system of underwriting, in effecting insurances to any amount which the trade and commerce of the country now requires?—I never experienced or heard of any, where an adequate premium was offered.

You have stated, that your reason for preferring Lloyd's is, that giving your business to some of the gentlemen at Lloyd's, you found that it generally produced to you a return of part of theirs; does that reasoning apply to any description of persons except those who are both brokers and underwriters?—No, it does not.

Have you found your underwriters ready to settle fair demands upon them when they have been made, or have you found them litigious?—I have always found them very ready to settle all fair demands upon them, and never but in one case found them litigious; which was a case that we were told by our own solicitors we were wrong in; we would have given up had we not been prevented doing it by our correspondent, who insisted upon our bringing an action.

What was the result of that action?—We were cast.

You mean that a verdict was given in favour of the underwriters?—Yes, it was.

What proportion may the losses on the business which you have done among the underwriters at Lloyd's bear to the amount of the sums insured?—A very small proportion indeed; we once recovered a loss of thirty-two thousand odd hundred pounds upon an Indiaman, twelve months after her insurance had been effected, without any bankruptcy.

Can you answer the last question more particularly than you have now done?—About two years ago we recovered a loss of 26,300 *l.* upon a ship, fifteen months after the insurance was effected, in which, in consequence of failures of two houses, three of the underwriters to the extent of 700 *l.* became bankrupts; that was the case of the Garland, for Rio Plata; we have since received of dividends upon that 700 *l.* 368 *l.* and expect to receive near 200 *l.* more; so that I do not conceive the ultimate loss will be much above 150 *l.* eventually.

Have you met with any other losses of late by the insolvency of underwriters?—No; we lately recovered a loss of eighty per cent upon 7,000 *l.* upon which there were no bankrupt underwriters.

Are the losses you have mentioned by insolvent underwriters the only losses of that description you have lately met with in the course of your business?—I think,

O. Browne.
Esq.

in one case, we had a loss of 100 *l.* by a failure, upon which there has already been six shillings paid, and that is the whole in the course of a number of years.

Have you ever found any difficulty in effecting your insurances at Lloyd's, on account of the absence of underwriters at any particular period of the year?—No; in those months in which it is generally supposed the underwriters are absent, we have done to the extent of between thirty and forty thousand pounds, upon risks which are not generally supposed favourite risks; we could have done more if we had had it to do.

Were you offered any shares in the intended new marine insurance company?—I was.

Did you accept any of those shares?—No, I did not.

What was your motive for declining?—Because I considered that a new marine insurance company would be contrary to the interest of the brokers and under-writers at Lloyd's Coffee-house, and therefore I determined to sign the petition at Lloyd's Coffee-house; and I did not think I could, consistently with propriety, accept of them after having done so.

You mean the petition against the Bill?—Yes.

Have many of your friends at Lloyd's accepted shares in that company?—A good many.

Have you heard them assign their reasons for accepting such shares?—Because if the company obtained a charter they considered that it would be a profitable concern, and on that account they wished to have a share in it.

Did they express to you that their acceptance of such shares was founded upon their approbation of the intended new establishment?—Quite the contrary.

What effect, in your opinion, would the establishment of this intended new marine insurance company, comprehending so very large a proportion of the mercantile interests of this metropolis, produce upon the interests of the individual under-writers?—I think that it would absorb so great a part of the best risks that there would very little remain for the underwriters at Lloyd's Coffee-house; except the surplus upon the large risks which the offices could not take, or risks of that hazardous nature that they would not take at all; that the consequence would be, there would not be sufficient business to make it an object for the underwriters at Lloyd's Coffee-house, and that they would give up the business there.

If the number of underwriters was diminished, would not the present competition be diminished, and the rate of premiums probably be advanced upon the public?—I think that would very probably be the consequence of it.

If merchants received consignments of produce, and instead of employing brokers to dispose of that produce, were to take it to themselves without the intervention of a broker, would such conduct be thought strictly mercantile or justifiable?—Certainly not.

Does not the same principle apply to effecting their own insurances without the intervention of an insurance broker?—Yes, with this difference, that the premiums of insurance are more generally known than the prices of produce.

If the competition of individual underwriters were destroyed by the establishment of such a large company, would there then be the same open market for regulating the prices of insurance by competition as now exists?—Certainly not.

Then would not the merchants who kept the insurance business in their own hands, either in one or more companies, have the means of regulating the rate of premium as they pleased?—Yes, to a great degree.

Is it not easy, in the present mode of transacting underwriting business at Lloyd's, to judge of the prudence or the rashness with which every individual underwriter conducts his business?—Very easy; in fact it is very generally known among the brokers at Lloyd's Coffee-house.

If insurance business was carried on by companies would you have the same means of judging of the conduct of those companies?—I do not see how you could.

If underwriting was carried on by firms or partnerships, would it not be necessary in case of loss, if one of the partners thought proper to absent himself by going to a foreign country, or even by crossing the Tweed, to outlaw that partner before you could recover from the rest of the firm?—I understand that to be a necessary process in the law.

Would that difficulty occur in any greater degree in the case of a policy of insurance than it occurs in any mercantile question whatever?—I believe not.

Is not the recovery of losses much expedited by underwriting being carried on by individual underwriters, with whom no such process can be necessary?—I think it is.

C. Browne, Esq.

Have you found that the estates of the insolvent underwriters with whom you have had accounts, and who have been partners in commercial houses, have paid greater or smaller dividends than the joint estate of those firms?—In the few instances I have mentioned in the former part of my evidence, the dividends upon the estates of the individual partners as underwriters were greater than the dividends paid by the house.

If the insurance business was carried on by companies, and the regulations adopted by the present chartered companies with respect to the payment of premiums were continued, would it be convenient or perhaps practicable to many houses to pay their premiums within the short time required by the existing companies?—I am not so well acquainted with the mode in which business is carried on by the public offices as to be able to answer that question correctly.

In the case of such an establishment, conducted by the leading merchants of this metropolis, would it be a satisfactory circumstance to other merchants to be obliged to expose their correspondence and the nature of their concerns in the way they must necessarily do by effecting their insurances with such companies?—I think not.

Are not insurance brokers subject to be under very considerable advances of money in case of losses?—Yes.

Explain how that arises?—In case of loss, the underwriter deducts from the amount of the loss all the premiums which are due to him by the broker; and in many cases the broker has nothing at all to receive from the underwriter, while he may be under the necessity of paying to the assured the whole loss, deducting only the premium that may have been paid upon that loss.

Are not insurance brokers responsible also to the underwriters for the payment of their premiums, and subject to heavy losses in case of the insolvency of houses for which they transact business?—They are.

Are not the profits of the insurance broker calculated with a view to these considerations, as well as to the immediate trouble in carrying on their branch of business?—That part of the profit of the insurance broker that arises from discount upon the net balance paid to the underwriters, I conceive to be the consideration for the advance of the money in case of loss, and the risk they run in being guarantee for the assured.

What effect, in your opinion, would the establishment of this intended new marine insurance company have upon the interests of the insurance brokers?—I think a very material one; because it is probable that the merchants would do their own insurances without the intervention of an insurance broker, from the facility with which it would be done, having only to open one account in place of forty or fifty, perhaps, with the underwriters at Lloyd's Coffee-house.

If the merchant was to effectuate his insurances in the way that is supposed in that answer, would not that be a considerable saving to the merchant?—I think that must depend upon what allowances the office would give to the merchant; because I believe, although I am not quite certain, that the two public offices give a larger allowance to the broker than they do at present to the merchant.

Would not he save at least that sum which he pays to the broker in the shape of discount upon losses?—There can be no doubt, that if the merchant does his own business as an insurance-broker he would derive all the benefit the insurance broker does, if the office allows the same discount to the merchant that it does to the insurance broker.

Would it not be a great convenience to the merchant to open one account instead of opening forty or fifty, as you have stated in your answer to a former question?—Yes.

Are you of opinion that partnerships in mercantile concerns add to the security of those with whom they contract?—Yes, in mercantile concerns.

Why does not that same principle apply to the case of underwriting as it does to the case of any other mercantile arrangement?—Because I have generally found that the failure of underwriters has been occasioned by the failure of the houses in which they were concerned as merchants; and that their own individual estates, which are kept separate from the general concern, have paid better than the estates of the company as merchants.

You have stated that in your own practice you have known few losses happen from the failure of underwriters; in the practice of others have not you known of a great many failures?—I have heard, certainly, of a good many failures amongst underwriters, but I think, in general, as I stated before, it was in consequence of connections in business separate from their underwriting concerns.

You mean by that, that underwriting has been in general a gaining trade?—I think, with prudence, it has.

You have stated as your opinion, that the practice of merchants effecting their own insurances without the intervention of a broker, is not strictly mercantile; do you not know that many of the most respectable merchants do in fact at present effect their insurances in that manner?—Yes.

Do you not know that many of those merchants attend the coffee-house themselves for that purpose, and that some send their clerks there?—Yes.

Can you state to the Committee what the profits of the broker consist in?—Yes; in the first instance the broker is allowed about five per cent upon the premium, he is then allowed by the underwriter a discount of twelve per cent upon the net balance which he pays the underwriter upon the settlement of the account.

By which you mean twelve per cent upon the net profits of the underwriter upon the account?—Upon the net balance paid by the broker to the underwriter.

Can you, from your experience as a broker, state to the Committee whether the five per cent upon the premium is more or less profitable to the broker than the twelve per cent upon the ultimate settlement?—A good deal of that must depend upon the nature of the risks; the five per cent is always the surest, and I should think generally the best.

Supposing the five per cent upon the premium to be equal to the twelve per cent. upon the ultimate profit, would not the whole of the profit of the broker amount to twenty-four per cent or nearly one-fourth part of the whole profit of the underwriter?—Yes, I think it might very nearly do so.

You have stated, that the broker is drawn into advances in consequence of the underwriter's deducting from any losses they may pay, out of premiums they may owe to him; does not the broker, in paying to the assured, also deduct from them any balance they may owe to him?—Yes.

Is it not therefore to be supposed that this payment of the assured to the broker must generally compensate the payment the broker must owe to the underwriter?—No, very seldom; because the broker doing business for a great number of houses, owes the underwriter a much larger sum in premiums than what is due to him generally from any one house.

Supposing a man to act merely as broker, how can he owe any thing to the underwriter which he has not a corresponding debtor to him for?—Because he may have done that insurance for a house that owes him only a very small sum in premiums, perhaps only the premium upon that single risk; in which case he must pay the whole sum less that premium to the assured, although he may receive a very small sum, if any thing, from the underwriters; which we have frequently experienced in our own case.

May not the reverse be the case, and the broker have a large sum to claim from the assured, in consequence of which he may not have to pay him the amount of the loss he may recover?—Certainly, he may have a sum due by the assured to set off against the amount of the loss recovered.

If the broker gives a credit to the merchant, does not he also receive an equal credit from the underwriter?—Certainly; he does not pay the underwriter at the time of underwriting.

Have not most of the principal brokers a considerable balance belonging to underwriters in their hands?—Yes, they owe them considerable balances.

Do they give the underwriters any interest for that money in their hands?—No; because the premiums are supposed to be due to the underwriters at a certain period, and generally about or soon after that time the brokers pay it to the underwriters when they call for it.

Is it not also a reason why the underwriter leaves a considerable sum in the hands of the broker, that when he takes it out he must pay the twelve per cent upon it?—Yes; because in the event of loss he would have to pay the money again.

Do not you know that in point of fact, many of the underwriters do leave the coffee-house in the autumn months: have you not frequently heard that it has been a subject of complaint?—Yes, I know that many of them do so.

With how many brokers at Lloyd's have you an account?—From 150 to 200 I should think.

Do you not confine your connection to those of whose character you have a good opinion?—Certainly.

Are there not a great many of an opposite character?—There are a considerable number; in so large a society there must be some of a contrary description.

When you transact business as an insurance broker for a number of mercantile houses, do you not give them credit for their premiums till after the end of the year?—Yes, for a considerable time after the end of the year.

If before the accustomed period of your calling upon the merchants for the payment of the premiums, losses happen in the business of any one of these merchants to a much larger amount than they are indebted to you for premiums, must you not, and do you not, advance to them the difference due to them out of your own funds?—Yes, always.

Do not the profits of an insurance broker increase with the increase of premiums; and consequently are they not much higher in time of war than in time of peace?—Yes.

Is not the hazard incurred by insurance brokers, of being brought under large advances by losses, greater in time of war than in time of peace?—Yes.

Is not the hazard incurred by insurance brokers, of the insolvency of their principals, greater in time of war than in time of peace, from the vicissitudes to which commercial establishments are then liable?—Yes; and also from the premiums being so much larger in time of war than in time of peace, the risk is increased.

Do not then the profits of an insurance broker bear a fair proportion to the increase of his risks under different circumstances?—Yes; but not more, I conceive.

Thomas Halliday, Esq. called in; and Examined.

IN what line of business are you engaged?—I have been in the Russia trade, and an insurance broker and underwriter.

Have you found the present means of effecting marine insurances fully adequate to the business you have had to transact?—Yes.

Have you ever been obliged to return any orders for want of being able to execute them?—No.

What proportion have the losses you have sustained by the insolvency of underwriters borne to the amount of the business you have transacted at Lloyd's?—For the last seven years I have insured 4,980,000*l.* as an insurance broker and merchant; the failures in that time have been to the amount of 799*l.* upon which, of course, there are dividends, but I have not calculated what they were upon that sum.

Have you found the underwriters litigious when losses have happened, or disposed to settle demands without difficulty?—I have never found any difficulty in settling losses.

Have you ever been obliged to bring actions against any of your underwriters?—Never.

If a new marine insurance company were established, comprising nine-tenths of the commercial interests of this metropolis, what effect, in your opinion, would such an establishment have upon the individual underwriters?—I think it would diminish the individual underwriters greatly; other societies would rise up, and the best business would go to the societies, and the principal individual underwriters would give it up, in my opinion.

If individual underwriters were discouraged from pursuing their avocation, would the premiums, in your opinion, be as low as they are now?—If the individual underwriters were driven from that kind of business I think that they would not be lower than they are generally now.

Do you not think they would be higher than they now are; that is, that the premiums would increase in proportion as the competition was diminished?—Yes.

Have you made any observation as to dividends paid by individual underwriters who were partners in mercantile houses, and the dividends paid by the firms of those houses, in case of insolvency?—I have not had any opportunity of ascertaining that except from hearsay, not from my own experience.

Is it not easy to form a judgment of the prudence or want of prudence with which every individual underwriter transacts his business at Lloyd's Coffee-house?—Yes.

T. Halliday, Esq.

Would there be the same possibility of forming a judgment as to the prudence or want of prudence with which companies might carry on their concerns?—No, I think not.

Do you recollect prosecutions having been brought in the year 1808, by the attorney general, against merchants, for using slips and not paying the stamp duty on policies?—I heard of such a thing.

Was not a notice stuck up at Lloyd's, warning the underwriters of the danger to which they exposed themselves by putting their names on slips, and cautioning them not to continue such practice?—Yes.

Has not that practice been discontinued in consequence?—The slips are still offered, but the broker generally puts the name of the underwriter down.

On former occasions, did not the underwriter put down his own name?—Yes.

Was not that considered as binding upon him as a policy?—Yes.

At present the underwriter gives no signature and comes under no obligation, and the memorandum is merely the act of the broker, and is considered as a memorandum till the policy can be procured from the office?—The broker being a man of credit, if he says that I promised to write such a risk, I am bound to pay it if it is a loss.

Would you think yourself bound to pay it unless he put it upon a policy stamp?—No.

If the means of insurance were much injured by the establishment of any new company, would not the merchants generally be the principal sufferers by it?—I think I stated that the individual underwriters at present would be greatly injured by any societies.

Would not the merchants also be much injured by it?—The merchants, I conceive, would not be injured if they were all upon a footing with regard to premiums, whether they were high or low.

Luna, 19° die Martii, 1810.

ALEXANDER BARING, Esq. in the Chair.

Moses Getting, Esq. called in; and Examined.

M. Getting, Esq.

WHAT line of business do you follow?—I am an insurance broker.

How long have you been in the habit of doing insurance business at Lloyd's?—Between eleven and twelve years.

Have you ever been under the necessity of returning orders for insurance for want of being able to effect them?—Never.

That has never happened to you at any period whatever of the year?—Never.

Should you have found any difficulty in effecting an insurance from Tonningen to London, in the month of September or October, to the amount of 40,000 l.?—No.

Have you effected any such insurance?—I have effected, from the month of September till December inclusive, about 114,000 l.; in December I effected one insurance alone of 40,000 l.

Was the whole of that insurance effected on one and the same ship?—It was effected on the same ship in the space of about two hours.

What was the name of that ship on which you effected the insurance for 40,000 l.?—The Richmond; Bartlett, master.

Have you made many bad debts among the underwriters with whom you have transacted business at Lloyd's?—I do not think my merchants have lost through me 1,000 l. nor 700 l. nor 600 l. in the whole course of my business.

To what amount do you imagine you have insured property in the course of the last year?—I have done some millions.

In the whole of your transactions as an insurance broker, the losses by the insolvency of underwriters have not exceeded the sums you have mentioned?—No, I think they have not.

Have you found the underwriters disposed to be litigious, or otherwise?—I do not think I ever had a law suit in the house on policies, which came effected through my hands; there have been policies transferred to me, done by other brokers, where there were some deficiencies in wording the policies; where there was some litigation; but not on my own policies.

Have you frequently found the underwriters disposed to settle losses without such documents as they were in fact legally entitled to require?—In 1809, when the insurances to the continent became very dangerous, I had some losses, and they settled to the amount of about 110,000*l.* and I never had even a protest; it was settled on the letters only of the different merchants, and on the confidence the underwriters placed in me.

Have you been offered, or have you accepted, any shares in the intended new marine insurance company?—I hold no shares.

Did you ever apply for any?—No.

What was your reason for not applying?—I am a broker, and I find friends at Lloyd's, and I do not like to offend my friends.

Would, in your opinion, the establishment of such a company be injurious to the interests of the individual underwriters at Lloyd's?—No doubt of it; to brokers and to underwriters.

In cases of insolvent underwriters, where they have been partners in commercial houses, have you found the estate of the individual underwriter, or of the partnership, pay the best dividend?—It is understood that where there is a partnership, and the underwriting is only in any one name, the dividend of the underwriter is always better than that of the firm of the house.

Is not the underwriter bound to pay his losses within a month after they happen?—Yes.

Does not he give the brokers and merchants to whom he underwrites, twelve months credit for his premiums?—Yes, and more too; I know some of the underwriters who do not call for their premiums for two or three years.

Is not an underwriter, on first entering into that line of business, obliged to come under considerable advances to pay his losses before he can begin to collect his premiums?—It depends upon the underwriter calling in his accounts; he certainly is under great advance.

In cases where an underwriter stops payment, does it not generally happen that the premiums due to him for the risks that are run off, as well as for the risks still pending, will form a fund adequate to the payment of the losses which may happen on his outstanding risks?—It has generally done so by experience; there may be a few exceptions.

Would, in your opinion, the public security be increased by underwriting being carried on by firms or partnerships, instead of being, as it now is, carried on by individuals?—I always find that the individual underwriter pays better than the firm of the house does.

Does not the competition which subsists among the insurance brokers keep down the premiums to the lowest possible rate?—The merchants desire us to do it as low as we can; and it is the duty of a broker, if he can find good underwriters, to do it for the good of his employer as low as he can.

Unless a broker makes his insurances at the lowest possible premiums, will he not lose his connections and lose the employment of his principals?—It depends upon the merchants; some do not care whose names they have upon the policies, and some require good names.

Does not the business of an underwriter depend also on his writing at the lowest current premiums; and if he does not do so, would not the merchant open accounts with other underwriters, instead of continuing to transact business with him?—A good underwriter asks his premium, and tries to get it, and he certainly will not write too low; there is business daily done at Lloyd's at lower premiums than are effected by some of the brokers in the room, but who the underwriters are I do not know.

Does not this competition produce the effect of obliging underwriters to accept as low premiums as they think are adequate to the risk?—The first underwriters are obliged to give way when they see that they cannot get what they ask at first.

Would equal competition exist and premiums be kept down to the same low rate if the same set of men, the merchants, were both merchants, underwriters, and brokers, as they would be by forming themselves into a new marine insurance company?—I do not think it would; because they would act against their own interests; they would certainly try to get the best profits out of the concern.

M. Getting,
Esq.

M. *Gatting, Esq.*

In your experience as a broker have you not found that you have more difficulty to effect your insurances in the autumn months than in any others?—In 1809 particularly, there was a great deal of business done in those months.

Do you not find greater difficulty in those months than in any other months?—I do not; I never find it; the old standards at Lloyd's always remain in their places, and whenever they can get their premium they will write.

Do you mean to inform the Committee that you do not as a broker find greater difficulty in effecting your insurances in the autumn months than in the other months of the year?—I certainly have not found great difficulty; some underwriters certainly take a little pleasure, and go out of town.

Some of the underwriters do go out of town?—Yes; but the old underwriters who are known to the first respectable houses always remain in the room, or have a substitute who will write for them.

With how many persons in the coffee-house have you an account?—About two hundred and forty.

There are of course a great many who underwrite, with whom you have no account?—I have no doubt there are.

Are there not a great many with whom you would not have an account, from your opinion of their security not being good?—Lloyd's is the room just over the Royal Exchange; there is a mixture there as well as below, certainly.

The Richmond you insured in December?—Yes.

What was her voyage?—From Tonningen to London. I have insured from Hamburgh, in September or October, about 24,000l. and from the Elbe, which is a similar risk, and have had the best names in the house.

Do you make your insurances with the Royal Exchange Company, or at Lloyd's?—I do my business at Lloyd's. I had the honour to open an account with the Royal Exchange Company last week.

You have hitherto preferred Lloyd's to the Royal Exchange Company?—There is a little difficulty at the Royal Exchange; the broker has not it always in his power to pay premiums every three months; I have given Lloyd's the preference.

You gave the preference to Lloyd's because you had some advantages in point of credit which are not allowed by the Royal Exchange Company?—That is one of my reasons; and as to the continental business, the Baltic and Tonningen, and so on, I do not think the Royal Exchange Company would write with the clauses I introduce into my policies.

Do you believe that nine tenths of all the insurances made in London consist of risks not exceeding fifty thousand pounds upon any one ship?—I have done on one ship, freight and cargo, from the Baltic, to the amount of about 60,000l.

Do you believe that more than one merchant ship in ten has property on board of a greater value than 50,000l.?—No, certainly not.

You have stated to the Committee that you do very little business with the public companies, in consequence of their giving but short credit; is that your only reason for preferring Lloyd's?—No, that is not my only reason; they would not agree to those clauses which we are obliged to introduce into our continental policies.

Is the Committee to understand that you find the regulations by which the companies are guided are such that you cannot do many of your insurances with them?—By experience of the companies I cannot judge, because I only made a beginning the last week; I only judge from hearsay.

How comes it that having been so long a broker at Lloyd's, and doing business to so considerable extent as you do, you should not before now have opened an account with the companies?—As long as I can find good names and facility in the room, I think it is more pleasing to all parties to stay there.

Do you underwrite yourself?—No, I do not; I am quite an impartial man in my business.

John Fisher Throckmorton, Esq. called in ; and Examined.

WHAT line of business do you pursue ?—I am an underwriter.

Are you an underwriter only ?—Principally so.

Do not many men of capital besides yourself make underwriting their sole or principal pursuit ?—Yes, I am pretty well assured they do.

Have you had offered to you, or have you accepted, any shares in the intended new marine insurance company?—When I first heard of it a gentleman belonging to that establishment offered me a couple of shares, which I requested might be kept for me, but on further consideration I altered my opinion upon it, and when I got the letter to attend and sign the petition to Parliament, I wrote back a letter requesting them to tender my resignation of those shares, which I suppose was done.

By what motives were you influenced in accepting those shares in the first instance ?—At first I thought I would take them like any stock or loan, or any thing of that kind by which something might be got ; afterwards, having altered my opinion, and thinking it would do material injury to Lloyd's Coffee-house, where I was more interested than I could be in that small matter, I gave them up.

Have many other of your friends and acquaintance at Lloyd's accepted shares in the new company ?—I know of several that have done it, and that have not gone the length of signing the petition ; whether they totally withdrew, or gave up their shares as I did, I do not know.

Have you heard them express the motives by which they were actuated in taking those shares ?—Yes ; the motives by which those with whom I conversed were actuated, were similar to my own, that they hoped to get something by it in case it was carried.

If such an establishment was formed, possessing so large a proportion of the commercial interests of the metropolis, and of course having the choice of a great proportion of the best risks, would it in your opinion discourage individual underwriters from pursuing their present avocation at Lloyd's?—Certainly ; I should think very much so indeed.

If individual underwriting was discouraged would not the present competition be diminished, and would not that circumstance tend ultimately to raise the premiums upon the, public?—I should think that would be the natural consequence.

If this company was formed would not other companies be probably formed both here and in the out-ports?—I am pretty well assured of that ; in fact I had an application from one of the out-ports. requesting I would make interest to name a person there as an agent for this company, should it take place ; he wished me first to apply for a share for him, but as I told him I had no concern in it, he said they would of course want agents at the out-ports, and requested me to apply for that situation for him at Bristol.

Is not an underwriter bound to pay his losses within a month from the time of the adjustment ?—Yes, and he is invariably called upon at that time.

Does not he give twelve months credit for his premiums?—Generally longer.

Is not an underwriter when he first engages in that line of business under the necessity of advancing the sums necessary to pay his losses, before he can begin to collect his premiums ?—Certainly.

Are not the advances so made a sort of capital which he is obliged to advance, and which contributes in fact to the security of the assured ?—Yes, I think it does ; it operates to that effect.

Does it not generally happen, if an underwriter is obliged to suspend his payments, that the premiums due to him upon the risks run off, as well as for those which are still outstanding, are sufficient to pay the losses which happen upon his account ?—In most cases they will, unless his account is a very desperate one indeed.

Is not that the reason why in cases of bankruptcy the estate of the individual underwriter so frequently pays in full, when the house in which he is a partner pays only a small dividend ? - I believe it to be so.

Would, in your opinion, the security of the assured be increased by the in-

John Fisher Throckmorton, Esq..

surance business, being carried on in firms, or partnerships?—I do not think it would; and unless the law of the land should be altered respecting partnerships, a serious objection to the security might occur in the case of one or more of the partners going abroad, or even into Scotland, a suit could not be carried on but through the long process of outlawing the absent partner, which would do away the object of all indemnity for loss by the delay.

Are not frauds frequently practised, or attempted to be practised, upon underwriters?—I have known a great many.

Can you state instances of that sort which have happened to yourself as an underwriter?—I have got a list of a considerable number of them, which have happened since I have first been an underwriter: the first was a ship called the Eagle; an order came to have her insured; we proved it afterwards to have been fully known to the party wishing to be insured, who lived at Philadelphia, that the ship was lost when he writes his order for insurance.

Was that fact established in a court of justice?—It did not come to that; they did not go so far: the next was that of the noted captain Codling, ship Adventure, and Messieurs Easterby and Macfarlane, the ship was destroyed and the captain hanged; the next was a ship or sloop from Dieppe in France to a place on the coast of England, with a great quantity of specie on board; they went to sea in the evening, and the ship was destroyed before morning, and the captain and crew on shore on the coast of France to breakfast; the captain appeared before the underwriters in London, and on a suggestion made in the committee-room, where the business was spoken of by me, to have the man taken into custody, he set off about his business, and it turned out to be a complete fraud, and not a farthing of it was recovered, because there never was any money shipped: the next was the case of a ship from Leghorn; an insurance was made for a large amount on silks, but she was only loaded with brimstone; she was insured against sea-risk only, went to sea on a fine morning and was destroyed in the evening, and the captain and crew went on shore in their boats; she had been insured at a number of places, London, Liverpool, Marseilles, and I believe Manchester; the witnesses were even brought here to substantiate their loss, but they took wing the day before the trial was to come on. There was another insurance by the same parties, at nearly the same time, on another risk of the same kind, against capture only; she was taken and carried into Corsica in the course of a few hours after she left Leghorn; the fraud of that not coming out in time, she was paid for: a ship from Boston, called the Hannah and Mary, was sunk by design; she was insured at Lloyd's, at Bristol, and at Liverpool, to a very considerable amount.

How did that fact appear?—We had the man in custody, the principal run away at Liverpool; we had the acting man up here, and he acknowledged that he had forged the bills of lading, the invoices, and every thing necessary to substantiate the interest, and on American stamps, which he had also procured, and sent them out to Boston, by order of his principal, with the plot ready made out to be acted upon: the next in which I happened to be concerned, and which I had a hand in detecting, was a ship going from Gibraltar to Lisbon; she was seen to be captured in Gibraltar bay as she went out of the bay; couriers were despatched by different roads to Lisbon and elsewhere with four or five duplicate orders for insurance; which orders found their way to London, and the insurances were effected, but the fraud was discovered, and the loss was not paid: a ship called the Aurora was said to be burned by design in Madeira roads, bound to the Brazils from Lisbon, insured to a very large amount, which never has been paid; I was not an underwriter on that myself, but I know the facts. There was a ship from New York to Belfast, which went to sea and was destroyed; she had been a noted ship in the Barbadoes trade, called the Philippa Harben; the assured came to London, and there was a respectable meeting of the underwriters held, and who would have given him any thing they thought he was entitled to; but the matter was so gross that he went off about his business, and did not even ask for the premium. There was a ship in the year 1803, called the Merry Andrew, sunk in King's Road at Bristol by design; the captain was hanged for it, and the owner absconded. I wrote a ship that had sailed from Portsmouth, on a Saturday morning, she was called the Bourdeaux Trader; she was captured immediately outside the Isle of Wight; the captain came back, and was with the owner at Portsmouth when he wrote his letter of order for insurance on the Sunday afternoon; this was discovered, and being a fraud it was not paid. There was a man of the name of Smythies, at Hull, made an insurance which has been described at Lloyd's as the tenfold insurance; it was merely done in order to get averages upon it; there was a complete set of average papers brought over; the ship had been insured at Hull, Manchester, Liverpool, Bristol, and, in short, almost every place where insurances are done, and he thought to have got an average of 40 per cent at each place on the same documents; however, the matter, by some means or other, was detected, and the man absconded at first, but he was afterwards taken; but in the end, I believe, escaped justice. I have frequently seen cases of very great suspicion, that letters were antedated, and that other frauds were practised, such as telling the truth, but not the whole truth, in their letters and orders for insurance from abroad; which makes it necessary the underwriters should be wary, and see that they are properly dealt with.

Are not insolvent persons frequently employed by merchants, to whom they owe money, to do insurance business for them at Lloyd's, in order to shift a bad debt off their own shoulders on to that of the underwriters?—I have known it done several times.

Are you not assignee to the estate of an insurance broker, where such transactions were brought to light?—To a very great amount.

State the particulars of that transaction?—It appears that on the 1st of July 1808 this broker's assets were 14,285*l.*; the debts due from him were to the amount of 28,338*l.*; there was, therefore, a deficiency, on the 1st of July 1808, to the amount of 14,052*l.* 9*s.* 9*d.*; this arose from settlements of losses, which he as a broker had taken upon himself to be the underwriter for, to a very considerable amount.

Did it not also arise in part from the failure of a house at Poole for which he had done business?—Not the failure of the house; but he had played the same trick on the Poole house, on a risk of 5,000*l.* and had it to account for; which pressure on him made him insolvent; that was one reason; by this means he became indebted to a house to the amount of 10 or 11,000*l.* or more; that house had an interview (a very private one) with him on the 24th of August, and finding he was not able to pay them their debt, they furnished him with policies, and sent him into Lloyd's Coffee-house, where he made insurances, between that and the 16th of October, the premiums upon which amounted to 11,600*l.*; by which operation this 11,000*l.* of bad debt was diffused among the underwriters, and transferred to them.

Were actions brought by that house against any of the underwriters for return of premium upon those policies?—There was one tried a few days ago.

What was the result of that trial?—A verdict for the underwriters, upon a very strong charge from Lord Ellenborough.

Explain the nature of that charge?—His lordship stated, that it was a case of common honesty, and there was nothing of law in it; that the jury were as good judges as he; and if they believed that it was done in good faith and honesty they would find for the plaintiff; if on the contrary, then they would find for the defendant. I here wish to add, that actions were about to be commenced against the house for the premiums due upon those insurances so effected, and which never have been paid, one of the partners in the house being out of the kingdom. The firm refuse to appear for him; it must therefore go through the long process of making the absent partner an outlaw before the actions can be proceeded in.

Are there not many merchants, having insurances to effect, who are also underwriters?—Yes, certainly.

Is it not for the interest of persons of that description to make their insurances at Lloyd's Coffee-house rather than with the two chartered companies, even at equal premiums, because by giving their insurances to individual underwriters they may thereby obtain business for themselves in return?—Yes, certainly.

Does not this circumstance account for the small proportion of insurance business done by the two chartered companies, compared with the business effected at Lloyd's Coffee-house?—I think that is one of the great reasons, perhaps.

In point of fact, the proportion effected by the two companies is very little, compared with the business done at Lloyd's?—Yes, I believe it is very trifling indeed, compared with that.

Are you sufficiently acquainted with the directors and proprietors of the two chartered companies to be able to say whether you think they can command any considerable proportion of the insurances effected in London?—I cannot well answer that question: I believe that the directors who own India ships carry their own

John Fisher Throckmorton, Esq.

John Fisher
Throckmorton,
Esq.

ships there, and there is business carried to the chartered companies by that means.

You do not believe that such directors and proprietors of the two companies can influence any great proportion of the insurance business effected in London?—Not at present; it is so very large that it would be more than they could effect, perhaps.

Do you not think that the members of any new marine insurance company would make the insurances with their own company rather than at Lloyd's, or with the two chartered companies, the premium, credit and allowances being equal?—It is very likely that merchants concerned in the new company would go to their own company to do it in preference.

Do you believe that more than one ship in ten that is insured exceeds in value (that is, ship and cargo) 50,000 *l.*?—No; if you take them all together, I do not think they do.

Do you believe that nine tenths of all the insurances made in London consist of risks not exceeding 50,000*l.* on any one ship?—Perhaps nine tenths might be a little more, because there are a great many ships that are very valuable; but it would be very much in that proportion, I should think.

Do you think four fifths are on risks not exceeding 50,000*l.* on any one ship?—Yes, I should think they are.

Supposing a new marine insurance company to be formed that would take 50,000*l.* on any one risk, and supposing that company to comprise nine tenths of the mercantile interest of London, is it not probable that all the insurances to be effected by members of such company, not exceeding 50,000*l.* on any one ship, would be given exclusively to such new company?—A very great majority, I should think, would.

Then would not the effect of this be to secure to such new marine company a very large proportion of the whole insurance business of London?—Undoubtedly it would, in my opinion.

Would not that induce a large proportion of the present underwriters at Lloyd's to give up altogether the underwriting business?—I should think it certainly would have that effect, because they could not live by the bad risks if the good ones were taken away.

In the transactions of the insurance broker which you have related, did he put his own name upon the policies on which there stood such very large sums?—I saw some of those policies, and I cannot tell whose names they were; they were so completely obliterated, blotted out, erased, and such pains taken that the names should not be visible, that I cannot possibly say whose they were; but he had taken the responsibility upon himself.

Did the whole amount of his premiums go into his own insurance account in his own books?—Yes.

Then it appeared that he was the real underwriter, though other names were put upon the policies?—Yes.

Did those names appear to you to be the names of known regular underwriters at Lloyd's?—Certainly not; there was only one or two of those I could make out in any way that I knew, but others certainly not; he took from 2,600*l.* up to 4,200*l.* on one single risk, and that upon a number of different vessels, hazardous bad risks.

Was not much discredit brought upon the underwriters at Lloyd's by this transaction, in consequence of so great a proportion of the sums insured upon those policies not being paid?—I have heard them spoken of as furnishing one of the reasons of throwing discredit generally upon Lloyd's Coffee-house.

When you underwrite a policy, do you consider that you have no legal claim upon the house who are principals in the transaction, and that you have only a claim upon the broker?—In no case, except such a one as I have been speaking of, where it was not done *bonâ fide*; in such a case, where it was done with the knowledge of the broker being insolvent, and where we could prove it, but not otherwise; and it requires a very strong case to get over it, because premium received is thought quite sufficient, unless we can prove any thing to the contrary; it is a case which has not been often tried, but I am afraid too often practised.

Do you think that any considerable merchants, supposing they could only have five shares in this new intended company, would be tempted by so small an interest to carry their business to that company, unless it were by an opinion that their business would be well done there?—It is hard for me to say that; they may perhaps be tied by a clause in their agreement to carry their business there.

John Fisher
Throckmorton, Esq.

Do you think they would if they were not so tied; or do you think that any merchant could or would tie himself down to any such condition?—I really cannot say.

Have you found the competition of the present existing companies injurious to the underwriters at Lloyd's?—Their competition is so very small in proportion to the business done at Lloyd's, that I cannot say that it has yet had that effect; if it was to come upon so great a scale as this spoken of, that might materially alter it.

Is not it found, from general experience, that companies cannot long maintain any serious competition with individuals where no exclusive privileges exist?— A great company like this might perhaps destroy all the individual competition we have at present.

You have stated that a principal motive for merchants to bring their business into the coffee-house, instead of carrying it to the companies, is that where they are themselves underwriters; they get other risks in return offered to them; would not that inducement continue if another company were added to those now existing?— If it was worth while for underwriters to remain at Lloyd's, having nine tenths of their business taken away, perhaps it would still remain, more or less.

With how many brokers do you keep an account?—I should think I may have accounts with from 150 to 200 brokers and merchants.

When you underwrite to any person, not a broker, of course you make no compensation to him for brokerage?—We put him upon the exact footing of a broker.

You give him the twelve per cent upon the profits, and the five per cent upon the premium?—Yes.

What proportion of your business do you suppose passes through brokers, and what proportion through those who are not brokers?—I cannot exactly say; perhaps it may be a little more than half passes through brokers.

Do you mean to say, that nearly one half of your business that you do as an underwriter does not come through brokers? I should think perhaps it may be two thirds through brokers, and one third through merchants, ship-owners, and other persons with whom I have accounts opened.

Do you not consider the compensation to the broker, or the difference between what the underwriter receives and the assured pays, as too great?—It is great when it turns out a good account; but the broker at the same time is subject to many inconveniencies; there is a great advance of money for which he should be paid; sometimes such heavy advances as require a great capital to stand it, and put him to great shifts.

Have you for several years past had occasion to pay any considerable sum to your insurance brokers?—Yes; a man who has much business at Lloyd's must have advances now and then, sometimes more, sometimes less.

You have stated that partnerships in underwriting would afford no additional security, because individual underwriters, when they fail, are found to have money with the broker, which goes towards the payment of their underwriting creditors, and that therefore they pay more than the houses of which they are partners; but if partnerships were to exist, would not those partnerships also have money in the hands of their brokers in the same manner as individuals?—That would depend upon whether those partnerships gave the same kind of credit, or demanded their premiums at shorter date, or not.

If they acted upon the same principles upon which the individual underwriters now act, they would then equally have funds in the hands of their brokers to pay their underwriting losses, in the same manner that individuals have?--It would operate in the same way.

In that case, how do you make out the opinion you have stated to the Committee, that partnerships would give no additional security to the merchant who has his policy underwritten?—Because those partners who write policies in general are the best part of the house, as far as I can see; where there is a partnership at present, the head of the house, for respectability, sends his name into the world as an underwriter, and the junior partner, if he attends Lloyd's, writes for the other partner, or the principal man in the house; that is generally the case

John Fisher
Throckmorton,
Esq.

Would not the business of the broker be much facilitated, if instead of being obliged to apply to different individuals for every line upon his policy, one individual was empowered to sign as much as two or three do at present?—I do not think it would be good for the general business of the merchants; certainly, the larger the lines the faster the broker will get on; but the competition there is at present is one means of keeping down the premiums, where he can go from one to another, and see what different mens ideas are.

Why would not the competition of ten partners, each signing 1,500 *l.* be of equal advantage with the competition of thirty individuals signing each 500 *l.*?— They might get their business done as fast, but they would not get it so well done, in my opinion.

Why not?—In the kind of open competition there is at Lloyd's Coffee-house the broker can go from one underwriter to another, who are conversant with different trades, and know how things are as to India risks; as to West India risks, and as to Baltic risks; he knows where to find each of those men, and he can form a pretty good judgment by the time he has been round what he can do his risk for; and if it is respectably begun, he will find no difficulty in getting through it; perhaps less than in going to seven or eight offices, for there he must go through the whole history in each of their counting-houses, which would take him up much longer time than he is now employed at Lloyd's.

Were any of the frauds which you have mentioned to have been practised upon the underwriters detected in courts of justice in consequence of actions brought by the assured, or did not the parties give up their claim without coming into court?— They went to the threshold of the court, in general, and there dropped it: they carried on their actions till they came almost to the day of trial, in some instances; others were so glaring they durst not do it.

Do you recollect whether any one of the cases you have mentioned actually came into court?—The Leghorn case came into court; it was not tried, for the witnesses took wing after being brought all the way from Italy here: an action was brought upon the Eagle; an action was brought upon the ship from Gibraltar, called the Nostra Signora del Rosaria.

Do you mean to state that any one of those cases was actually tried in a court of justice, and a verdict pronounced by a jury?—Most of them did not proceed to a jury; the case of the Bourdeaux Trader went to a jury, and I had a verdict.

The case of the Bourdeaux Trader is the only one which in your recollection went to a jury?—Yes; the others were in such preparation that nothing hindered their going to a jury but the parties declining to come there: in the case of the Gibraltar risk a commission was sent out to examine witnesses, the answer to which put an end to the case.

If this new-intended marine insurance company was established, would not merchants who had shares in it be disposed to give that company the preference on equal terms?—Certainly, I think so.

Would not that preference ensure them the choice of all the best risks? — Undoubtedly.

If commercial firms or partnerships were permitted by law to underwrite, would not their underwriting accounts be subject to the losses arising from their mercantile transactions?—They certainly would be quite blended.

Are not the accounts of individual underwriters at present exempted from such losses?—Yes.

Does not the extent of competition, in your opinion, depend upon the number of competitors?—Yes.

John Mavor, Esq. called in; and Examined.

John Mavor,
Esq.

IN what line of business are you engaged?—As a merchant and underwriter.

How long have you been in the habit of doing business as an underwriter at Lloyd's Coffee-house?—About twenty-three years.

Were you offered, or did you accept, any shares in the intended new marine insurance company?—I applied for them.

Did you obtain any?—I did.

Did you sign the petition to parliament for the incorporation of that company?—
I did.

Do you still retain those shares?—I do.

What was your motive in accepting shares in that company?—My motive for applying for them was my apprehension that this insurance company would occupy the principal part of the business of the city, and of course exclude every description of risks from Lloyd's Coffee-house worth looking at; I therefore thought it worth my while to apply; and my idea of the extended foundation of the company was such, that I applied upon the ground of having two East Indiamen, besides other matters, and on which I thought I had some claim to be admitted.

Have many of your friends at Lloyd's also accepted shares in this new company?
—Several, with whom I have had conversation.

Have they expressed their motives for so doing to be the same as your own?—
Precisely the same.

What effect, in your opinion, would the establishment of this new company have upon the individual underwriters?—I conceive it would render the individual under-writers unnecessary, in a great measure.

On what grounds do you form that conclusion?—I thought, in the first instance, this company would afford a great deal of facility; but having heard a great many things said *pro* and *con*, I took some pains to analyze the existing state of shipping in this country, in order to satisfy myself. The shipping employed in this country is registered alphabetically in a book, which is kept at the expense of Lloyd's Coffee-house; and at a very considerable expense, by means of proper surveyors competent to the task, and who make returns of the state of shipping from the various places where they have an opportunity of seeing them; this is kept extremely correct. It occurred to me, that to enable me to judge how far this company might or might not have a bad effect on the insurance trade of the country, I would by means of this book analyze the quality of the risks comprised in the shipping of Great Britain. There are 13,220 ships in the trade of this country, as appears by this book; I took the letter A, for it was too hard a labour to go through the whole; indeed the letter A cost me six hours labour; I found that the letter A contains 1,252 ships, the tonnage of which amounts to 216,940; this register classes the value of the ships, or rather the nature of the risks; they are distinguished into three classes, first, second and third; the first A, the second E, and the third I; there are some lesser shades of difference in these classes, but of little importance. I found that in the first class, in the alphabetical letter A, there is a tonnage of 112,191; in the second class, 94,597; in the third class, 10,152; making together the tons 216,940. I then took all the other letters of the alphabet in order, and I found they contained ships amounting in number to 11,968, and the average of letter A, being at the rate of 173½ tons each vessel, it gives for the 11,968 a tonnage of 2,073,456; to which adding the 216,940 in letter A, there is a total of 2,290,396; to that 2,290,396 I add the East India shipping, which is all of the first class, say 90,000 tons, the aggregate forms a tonnage of 2,380,396; which tonnage will class in the same proportion as letter A; viz. of the first class of risks there are 1,280,000 tons, of the second class 1,000,000, of the third class 100,000; my inference is this, that if it requires risks of the first class to the amount of more than half the tonnage of the British trade, say 1,280,000 tons, to protect at the present low rates of insurance, the other two classes, amounting to 1,100,000 tons, and if the proposed corporate body, founded as it is said to be, on nine tenths of the commercial interests, and professing its intentions to act on the most liberal scale, shall in conjunction with the other two corporate bodies absorb not nine tenths, but even only two thirds of the first class of risks, one third only of that first class of risks will then remain to protect the indifferent and bad risks; that is, that in-stead of there being 1,280,000 tons of good risks to protect 1,100,000 tons of the more hazardous, there will be only 426,000 tons of the first class of risks remaining in the hands of the general underwriter, to enable him to protect 1,100,000 indifferent and bad risks; that is one quarter good to protect three quarters indifferent and bad. In order that he may do that and exist at all, it will be incumbent on him to charge a much higher premium upon those indifferent risks, if he can take them at all. I much question whether he could take them at all; but supposing that it were practicable to take them, and that he were to charge, as he must do, a higher premium upon those indifferent risks, it would inevitably follow that the first class of risks would be drawn after them, and that the premiums upon that class would likewise rise in great pro-

J. Mavor,
Esq.

portion. The general trade of the country of course would suffer by being so much burthened; and by the competition being destroyed, the foreign underwriter would snatch from Great Britain the beneficial trade she has held for so many years. Should this company be established, and should they act up to their present professions, the London and Royal must follow their example; and in the contest the underwriters would be compelled to quit the field, leaving the insurance trade in the committee-rooms of the three chartered companies; and it is presumed, as they would enjoy the monopoly, they would enrich themselves at the expense of the public.

At present are not ships of all classes, whether good or bad, if engaged at the same voyage, underwritten at the same premium?—Yes, they are nearly so.

Does not the underwriter make a point of taking the good and bad ships together for the parties for whom he has accounts?—Yes, he does, generally speaking; the good and the more indifferent.

Was not an action lately brought against you as an underwriter, by a mercantile house in the city, for a return of premium on a policy written to an insurance broker who became a bankrupt?—The action was not brought against me, but I was second on the policy, and I understand the next will be against me if they proceed.

On what ground did you and the other underwriters contest the payment of that return of premiums?—I do not wish to implicate the name of the firm in giving my answer; and without naming the parties, I answer, on the score of fraud.

Was the verdict on the action tried given in favour of the merchant, or of the underwriter?—Of the underwriter.

Are there not many merchants, who have insurances to effect, who are underwriters also?—There are many.

Is it not for the interest of persons of that description to make their insurances at Lloyd's Coffee-house rather than with the two chartered companies, even at equal premiums, because by giving their insurances to other underwriters they often obtain business for themselves in return?—Certainly.

Does not this of itself account for the small proportion of insurance business done by the two chartered companies, compared with the business effected at Lloyd's Coffee-house?—No, I believe it arises from a different cause; I believe the facility given at Lloyd's Coffee-house in effecting insurances on risks of an inferior description, brings to it the insurances of a better description; for it appears by the investigation of the shipping of the country that above one half of that shipping is of the first description of risks; and we know that without the protection of good risks at Lloyd's Coffee-house the indifferent risks would not be effected; a broker in general, when he has an indifferent risk to effect, will, if he can, produce at the same time a good one, for the purpose of getting the indifferent one effected; the offices will not do that, at least in all the transactions I have heard of with them; I believe this is the cause from which the preference to Lloyd's Coffee-house arises.

When you signed the petition to the House of Commons, in favour of the company seeking to establish itself, were not you at that time of opinion that it was for the benefit of the trade of the country such a company should be established?—I was of opinion at that time that it would give facility, but beyond that I thought the reasons given in the petition were frivolous; at least that they ought not to have been brought forward; and it was in consequence of hearing so much said on both sides that I sat down to the investigation I have stated, to satisfy myself whether it would or would not give facility; the result of that has been my conviction that instead of giving facility it will embarrass the trade of the country.

Is the Committee to understand you were of opinion that the grounds upon which the petition was founded were frivolous at the time you signed it?—Two of them, certainly; the term frivolous may be too strong; they ought not to have been advanced, but it was not for me, as an individual, to correct a general petition; I thought the principal one, namely, the facility which might be given to trade, was the only one on which a merchant ought to sign it; but of that facility I now think differently.

But you thought, upon the whole, you were petitioning for what would be a benefit to the trade of the country?—In regard to the facility to be given to trade I then conceived it was.

Is the Committee to understand that the alteration in your opinion has arisen from the reasonings you have stated to the Committee?—From nothing else; I sat down to it perfectly unprejudiced, and was surprised at the result.

Do you mean to state to the Committee that no distinction is made at Lloyd's Coffee-house, in consequence of the quality of different ships in the same voyage?—I mean, that if there is a risk of the first class, and one of the second class, going upon any voyage, I will suppose to any of our colonies, the one would be as readily done as the other, by underwriters who are in the habit of writing generally, and for brokers who are generally in the habit of showing all their risks to them.

In that case what advantage is there in this classification of the different ships?—An evident advantage to the underwriter, showing the nature of the risk he takes, so far as regards the ship; circumstances may alter a risk completely from the best to the worst, or otherwise.

Though he makes no difference in his premium?—He is enabled to judge of that from seeing the class in which the risk stands, and from combining in his mind the attending circumstances. If a broker were to come to me in Lloyd's Coffee-house, who was not in the habit of transacting business with me, and were to show me a risk of the second class, I should naturally look suspicious upon it, and unless he could say to me he wished to continue, and meant to continue the account, I should not take a second-class risk unless he gave me a second-class premium for it. If I have an account with that broker, and he shows me his risk generally, I take it from him at the same premium as risks of the first class on the same voyage bear, but this is presumed the voyage to be direct and otherwise unobjectionable as to season, &c.

Do you not think that if Parliament were not to grant any charter to any new company, but the exclusive charter of the existing companies were repealed, so that underwriters might act in partnerships in the same manner as other trades are carried on, such an arrangement would be productive of considerable facility to the trading interests of this country?—I certainly do not think it would give facility, but I rather think that facility would be destroyed by the competition being narrowed; there would be fewer underwriters in that case.

In what way do you suppose the competition would be narrowed by such an arrangement?—There would be fewer underwriters; for though my partner and I write individually now, we write with interests approved to each other, and our separate estates are responsible for our separate undertakings; but if a house were to be allowed by law to write, the partner of that house would act on a combined interest, and on certain regulations, and as they would take a large amount upon one risk, they would sooner absorb the best risks, and by that means narrow the competition by combining three or more interests in one.

Is there any reason why the scale of competition would be different in the business of insurance from what it is in any other business conducted in a similar manner?—I should think insurance is rather of a more limited nature than the general business of the country; it is not every person who would readily enter into the insurance trade; it is not so generally understood as probably the particular branches of trade are by different people, it is a trade peculiar to itself; were the present restrictions removed, it is indeed not impossible it might generate a very destructive spirit of speculation in the country, every village might have its insurance company.

Would not the association of individual underwriters together obviate the complaint now made by merchants, of underwriters absenting themselves in the autumn months?—Probably I may be allowed to question the propriety of that complaint, because I happen to know that many gentlemen do attend Lloyd's particularly at that season; and there are many that will even write in the winter months in preference, in some measure. That there are fewer underwriters at that periods in the coffee-house there is no doubt; and I have no doubt many absent themselves to avoid the risks which are current at that season of the year; but they are limited in their number, and I cannot think that on that account there is any increased difficulty.

What proportion of the business that you underwrite comes to you through a broker, and what proportion through other merchants or underwriters?—I think at least three fifths comes through a broker.

If individual underwriters absent themselves from Lloyd's in autumn from motives of interest, would not the same motives operate upon partnerships, and prevent their writing risks at the same period?—I should think so, the motives being prudential.

Claes Grill, Esq. called in ; and Examined.

HOW long have you been established as a merchant in this country ? Since the year 1769, about 40 years.

In the insurances you have effected in this country, have you found the underwriters disposed to be litigious?—I never found them so.

How many actions have you been under the necessity of bringing against underwriters in the course of your business?—I never had one.

What losses have you sustained by the insolvency of underwriters?—I do not suppose that, during the forty years, I have proved under ten commissions.

Are you acquainted with the estimation in which the underwriters at Lloyd's are generally considered on the Continent of Europe?—I can only speak from the insurances and averages of losses I have had myself; and as I have never had a law suit, the clear consequence must be, my employers cannot be otherwise than satisfied with Lloyd's.

Are you acquainted with the state of insurances on the Continent of Europe, whether it is carried on principally by companies, or by individuals?—In Stockholm there is a public insurance company ; but their business cannot be of great extent, because the risks being generally of the same nature, they dare not go so deeply into the insurances as in this country, being central, and having insurances from all parts of the world, and of all sorts. In Copenhagen the insurances have been upon a large scale, inasmuch as they have had a pretty extensive East and West India trade of their own.

Do you know the number of insurance offices there are established at Hamburgh? —Some years ago, perhaps six or eight years ago, the number was upwards of thirty ; but I have been informed that there are not above five or six of them remaining, some of them have closed their accounts, because they found it was not worth while to go on, and have paid in full; others again have, from heavy losses, been obliged to declare their incapacity of paying in full, and I am told they have paid from four up to fifteen shillings in the pound; and now I believe there remain about five or six of them.

Although your own correspondents have made no complaint against the English underwriters, from your general intercourse with foreigners, have you ever heard that the English underwriters are in bad estimation on the Continent?—No, never; there are some certain modes of settlement with the underwriters in this country which differ from those on the Continent, for instance, one : if a ship puts into a port and repairs, and those repairs take the time of two or three months, the underwriters in this country do not allow the wages and victualling of the crew during the time of the repairs; but in Hamburgh and Amsterdam it is one of those charges which the underwriters allow, and that is the only material difference that I know of.

In point of fact, from your intercourse with foreigners, do you not believe that the character of the English underwriters, both for probity and solidity, is in higher estimation than that of any underwriters or insurance companies throughout the rest of the world?—I should have no doubt in my mind that an English underwriter stands in very high estimation upon the Continent, both in point of honour and character.

Is not your business chiefly confined to Sweden?—Chiefly to Sweden, and likewise to the Baltic in general.

Have the insurances you have made for the last two or three years been considerable ?—They have not ; because of late years, being advanced in life, I have rather curtailed my business than otherwise.

Can you state to the Committee the amount of premiums which you have paid within the last year?—The premiums of last year were, generally speaking, very high to and from the Baltic; indeed I am sorry I have not looked into my book to speak with more precision ; but I should suppose my premiums at this moment might be about ten, twelve, or fourteen thousand pounds, at the same time my business is now small ; I have not sought for much business lately.

Mercurii, 21° die Martii, 1810.

The Honourable WILLIAM BEAUCHAMP LYGON in the Chair.

George Shedden, Esq. called in; and Examined.

HOW long have you been an underwriter at Lloyd's?—For myself, thirteen years; I underwrote for my father about 7 or 8 years prior.

Had not your father, for many years previous to that period, made underwriting his principal pursuit?—For the first 5 or 6 years I underwrote for my father, he did not do much business but underwriting.

Do not many persons make underwriting their sole or principal pursuit?—Several do.

Had not the underwriters very heavy losses brought upon them in the course of the last war by various events, such as the detention and condemnation of the Dutch ships in 1794, previous to hostilities breaking out between this country and Holland?—There were very large claims upon the underwriters about that time; in 1794 and 1795, upon my father's underwriting account we paid about 190,000 l. in the two years, arising in part from the detention of the Dutch ships in British ports.

Was not a very considerable part of one of our outward-bound fleets from the Mediterranean, also captured by the squadron under Admiral Richery?—I do not recollect the particular year, but there was a very heavy loss in consequence of that capture.

Were not very heavy losses also sustained by the capture and condemnation of American vessels by France and Spain, on the pretence of their not being navigated with the *roll d'equipage*, required by treaty?—There were losses to a considerable amount paid on American vessels during the last war; I do not recollect exactly the year.

Were not heavy losses also sustained by the seizure of British shipping in the ports of Russia, by the late Emperor Paul?—To the best of my recollection, our losses paid upon the seizure of vessels by the Emperor of Russia were about 20,000 l., and I believe it applied generally to underwriters who underwrote at Lloyd's upon the same scale that my father did.

Were not the vessels trading on the coast of Africa swept off more than once by French squadrons during the course of the last war?—There were several sweeps on the coast of Africa during the last war; I think three.

Do you not think that those various events, put the solidity of the underwriters at Lloyd's to the test?—I can only judge of that from the business I have to do as a merchant at Lloyd's; the underwriters who underwrote policies done for our house proved good.

What losses have you sustained by the insolvency of underwriters, upon the business your house has done at Lloyd's?—During the last war, from the year 1792 to 1802, we had occasion to insure a great number of vessels on cross-voyages, from the British provinces to the West Indies, to Jamaica, and *vice versa*, and from America to St. Domingo; it proved a very bad account, from the number of privateers out in the West Indies, and from the number that rendezvoused in American ports, where their prizes were carried in; in consequence of which, during the war, the underwriters at Lloyd's paid our house more than their whole premiums; during the war, the sum of 17,326 l. 7 s. 2 d. I had occasion to make up the account correctly, from a correspondent, in the year 1802, during the peace, complaining of the premiums we had given. The premium upon a single voyage was at first five; in consequence of the captures it increased to eight, ten, fifteen, twenty; and as high as twenty-five was given. In answer to the complaint of our correspondent, I had an account taken correctly of the whole premiums we had paid, and the whole losses, and I found the sum in cash received of the underwriters at Lloyd's, exceeded the sum they had received by that amount, 17,326 l. 7 s. 2 d. We had recovered in all 106,776 l. 7 s. 5 d.

Did you not pay considerable sums to some of your underwriters, and receive very considerable sums from others?—Surely; some would make money by us, and others would lose.

Did any of those from whom you had sums to recover prove insolvent?—In the whole of that nine years, from the premiums varying at times, we were obliged

G. Shedden,
Esq.

occasionally to put some of the policies into the hands of brokers, to complete. The only deficiency that we ever had, in consequence of an underwriter being a bankrupt, was in the case of one ship that had been insured, the ship, cargo and freight, at 15 guineas; there remained a small sum to complete it, which could have been done certainly for 18, but I gave it to a broker to finish it at the same rate, 15 guineas; the vessel was captured, and one of those underwriters was deficient in the sum of 49 *l.* 3 *s.* I am not certain as to the sum he underwrote upon the vessel, but I suppose 100 *l.*; and that the broker set off the sum he owed the underwriter against the amount he had to pay, which reduced the claim on him to 49 *l.* 3 *s.*

Is that the only loss you sustained during that period, by the insolvency of underwriters?—Yes; and I have since received a dividend of three shillings upon it, so that the loss was reduced to 36 *l.* 17 *s.* 3 *d.*

Are not British underwriters exonerated from paying in case of British capture? —We understood that the law was formerly that we were to pay for British capture, and in consequence of that understanding we wrote French and Dutch vessels, prior to the war taking place with those powers, and paid for them; now the law is understood to be, decidedly, that an underwriter in England is not liable to pay for the British capture of a vessel he underwrote, which was a neutral vessel when he underwrote her.

Did you, notwithstanding that decision of our courts of law, continue to pay all the losses on vessels you had underwritten under those circumstances?—All that we had underwritten prior to its being known that that was the law we considered ourselves bound in honour to pay, and I believe it was generally done; there were some persons that disputed it. In consequence of the law being ascertained, there was a law-suit with a gentleman, now dead, who underwrote at Lloyd's at that time. But every thing we underwrote prior to that we paid; and since that decision we have paid losses we wrote prior to that decision taking place.

Have you not paid very considerable sums which you were under no legal obligation to pay, since that decision was known?—We have.

Have you had frequent law-suits with your underwriters?—As merchants, in the course of the business done for us at Lloyd's, we never had a single law-suit; the underwriters always paid every claim we brought forward.

As underwriters, you and your father have of course had several litigations?— Many; in the nature of an underwriter's business it is absolutely necessary for law-suits to occur sometimes, to settle points; but we seldom have law-suits with the old established mercantile houses, or with the regular brokers, it is chiefly either with new houses, or upon speculative voyages, unless it is to settle some specific point; for instance, it was a disputed point some years ago whether an average was to be paid on the gross proceeds or the nett proceeds, which we carried through all the courts.

Is it not of importance to the interest of the mercantile world that such points should be definitively settled by the decision of a court of law?—Most certainly.

Is not much litigation ultimately prevented by procuring such decisions?—I conclude so; there have been no law-suits since, about that point to which I have referred.

Have you any shares in this intended new marine insurance company?—I have five.

Have any other branches of your family any shares in that concern?—My brothers, who are concerned in business, have each of them five shares.

Has your father any shares in that company?—He was also to have five, I understood.

Have many of your friends at Lloyd's taken shares in that company?—Some have.

What was your motive in accepting shares in that company?—It was offered to me to take five shares, and I accepted them, without having any particular motive for it; I certainly did not suppose it would be a bad thing: at the same time, the shares are so small it could not be productive of any great advantage.

Did you accept shares in that concern from an approbation of the principle on which it was intended to be established?—I had not investigated the principle; I merely accepted the shares that were offered me.

If a company were established, comprehending nine tenths of the mercantile interest of this metropolis, what effect would it have, in your opinion, upon the insurance-brokers and the individual underwriters at Lloyd's?—That is merely matter of opinion: from my knowledge of Lloyd's Coffee-house, I conceive it would materially affect the private underwriters; whether it would affect the brokers would depend upon the merchants; if the brokers are employed in the same way they are now by the merchants, of course it could not affect them.

Do you not conceive the object of this institution to be in part to save the emoluments which are now made by the insurance-brokers, by the merchants doing their own business with this company, in which they are to be partners?—That will depend upon the plan which may be pursued by the merchants; a great many merchants now are their own brokers at Lloyd's, and save their brokerage; all the business done by our house at Lloyd's is done by ourselves as brokers.

If this company was established should you be disposed to give the profits of your insurance business to a broker, or would you do your own insurance business with that company?—I have always done our own insurance business at Lloyd's as a broker, therefore if I did anything with that company, of course I should do the same.

Do you not believe that merchants in general, having the facility of effecting their whole insurance in one line with that company, would effect it themselves rather than employ an insurance-broker?—I should rather think they would.

Would not the members of that company naturally give the preference of their risks to that company on equal terms?—I should suppose so, upon equal terms, certainly.

Would not that preference secure them the choice of all the good risks?—No doubt it would secure to them the preference of the business of those merchants who are interested in the company.

If nine tenths of the best risks were first offered to this new company, do you think that individual underwriters would find it worth their while to pursue their present occupation?—I have stated before, that I thought the establishment of such a company would materially affect private underwriters.

If this intended new company were established, would not other companies probably be formed, both here and in the out-ports?—That would depend upon the charter they got.

Would not all other parties have the same pretensions to form companies as the members of the present intended new company?—I should think so.

In the open manner in which insurance business is at present carried on at Lloyd's, have not persons who do business with an underwriter an opportunity of judging of the prudence or want of prudence with which he acts?—Surely they have.

Is it possible to form such a judgment of the conduct of any public company; and might not they speculate to an unwarrantable extent, without the possibility of its being known?—I conceive no merchants in the city of London could know the risks that were taken by public companies, further than those they offer them themselves.

When you absent yourself from Lloyd's, does not some person write for you during your absence?—In the twenty odd years my father has been an underwriter at Lloyd's, it has been our custom always for some one to be there when he is absent; and if I am absent, some one for me. It has occurred, in the case of a family misfortune, we might be absent for a day or so; but in general we always have some person there.

In those cases, does not the party who remains write for those who are absent?—Yes.

If partnerships were permitted to underwrite instead of individuals, might not the necessity of consulting an absent partner frequently occasion much delay and inconvenience, both in writing policies and settling losses?—I should conceive, if a partnership underwrote, one partner would be the managing partner of that business, who would conduct it.

If one of those persons objected to the payment of a loss, do you think the other partner or partners would hold themselves justified in settling it contrary to his consent?—I should suppose the managing partner, who managed that part of the business, would have the control.

Might not the absence of one partner make it necessary to go through the process of outlawry against him, before it would be possible for the assured to recover the loss against the other partners?—That is a law question, to which I am not competent to give any answer.

Is not at present the individual partner who underwrites generally the head of the house?—I believe it is so.

G. Shedden,
Esq.

Is it not generally found that the estate of the individual underwriter pays a better dividend than the estate of the partnership, in cases of insolvency?—I have certainly found that to be the case where I have had to prove debts due to me as an underwriter from a company; and where one of the company underwrote, that his estate has turned out better than the estate of the company. This I have found to be the case in more instances than one.

Would then, in your opinion, the security of the assured be increased by underwriting being carried on in partnerships instead of being in individual names?—Not having had experience of the effect of writing in partnerships I really cannot give an answer to that, to the satisfaction of my own mind.

If the merchants of this metropolis, by forming themselves into one or more companies or partnerships, were to take the insurance business into their own hands, and be at the same time insurance-brokers and underwriters, would they not have an interest opposite to that of the correspondents for whom they underwrite?—As far as my experience goes of the effect upon my own mind, it has rather had a contrary tendency with me; as an underwriter, I have generally been more partial to those risks which have come to our house to be insured, than probably others not so well acquainted with them; and instead of the interest of our correspondent being affected by my being an underwriter, I am confident it has been much benefited.

Is at present a regular rate of premium fixed by the competition between the different underwriters and brokers?— Some of the underwriters at Lloyd's differ in respect of the premium which they require on a particular risk; very often it happens some underwriters think it worth a certain rate, others think it worth less; and although those who consider it worth more do not immediately write at a lower premium, they generally are brought down to do it at what others write at.

If individual underwriting was destroyed by the establishment of this new system, would the competition exist, in your opinion, to the same degree?—Not, certainly, to the same degree; if there were half a dozen or a dozen companies, it would exist to a certain degree, but not to the same degree as where there are fifty or a hundred individual underwriters, who regulate and guide the premium at Lloyd's.

If the competition were diminished, would not the directors of those companies have considerable influence in regulating the rate of premiums?—If there were no private underwriters at Lloyd's the directors of the different companies would certainly have great influence in regulating the premiums.

Would it not be the interest of the proprietors of those companies to raise the premiums rather than lower them; and would not their profits be the greater the higher those premiums were advanced?—From the small share now held by each individual, the profits would be so very trifling that the directors could have no great interest in making the premiums either larger or smaller.

Would they not have an interest in so doing in proportion to the number of shares they hold?—Certainly; but that number is so small it could not have much influence upon them.

Does not the business of every insurance-broker depend upon his effecting insurances for his employers at the lowest possible rate?—In a great degree it does.

If he gives a higher premium than other brokers give will he not necessarily lose his business?—I presume he would lose his business.

Does not the competition for business among the insurance-brokers, acting upon the competition for business among the underwriters, produce the effect of depressing premiums of insurance to their fair rate between the parties?—I believe so.

Do you think the same competition would exist to the same extent if any change of system respecting the mode of effecting marine insurances were adopted?—Not to the extent that it now exists.

You are a merchant as well as an underwriter?—I am.

Is it not for your interest to make your insurances at Lloyd's Coffee-house rather than with the two chartered companies, even at equal premiums; because, by giving your insurances to individual underwriters you thereby often obtain business from them in return?—The business I have to do as a merchant is chiefly confined to those risks which are termed cross-risks, from the British provinces to the West Indies, and *vice versa*, risks that the offices I believe never underwrite: I once went to the offices when the premiums rose to twenty or twenty-five guineas on those risks, and they declined writing them; that was the only time I ever made them the offer of any business from our house, except once I made an insurance on an Indiaman, which we were directed to do at the office.

You have no other insurances to make, as a merchant, except those you make on cross-risks?—Certainly we have other insurances to make, but the chief part of our business is in those risks.

Having insurances to do not of the description which you say the two chartered companies would not take, would it not be for your interest to prefer the underwriters, for the reason referred to in the former question?—Certainly it would.

The same cause must no doubt operate in the same way with other underwriters who are merchants?—Certainly.

Would not this of itself account for the small proportion of insurance business done with the two chartered companies, compared with the whole amount of the insurance business effected at Lloyd's Coffee-house?—That reason could influence only those who are underwriters at Lloyd's; it could not influence those who are not underwriters there.

Would it in fact influence those who are both merchants and underwriters at Lloyd's Coffee-house?—Certainly.

Do you not believe that by far the greatest proportion of insurance business done at Lloyd's is effected without its having ever been offered to the two chartered companies?—I believe the greater part is; underwriters generally are very cautious of writing risks that have first been offered to the companies and refused.

If those merchants who are underwriters are induced to have their risks insured in the coffee-house, in preference to having them done with the companies, because they get in return risks offered to them, would not that inducement continue to exist even if any additional companies were established?—I should think that would depend upon the effect it produced upon the underwriters at Lloyd's; if there were a sufficient number remaining of responsibility, the same reason would influence them.

Do you find that at present the two existing companies combine together for the purpose of settling premiums at all?—I never did any insurances with the companies but once, and really am not competent to answer that question.

Did you ever hear it complained of that they did so combine?—No, I never did.

Do not you know from your experience that a great many merchants now do a great deal of their business directly with the underwriters, either by themselves, or through their clerks?—A great many.

Can you state what proportion of the business passes through brokers, and what proportion is done immediately with the principals?—That would be mere supposition; I could not exactly say.

Do you think one half passes in that way?—I should think not quite so much; from one third to an half, probably; fifteen years ago, there was scarcely any business done but through the means of brokers; it is only within the last fifteen years that the merchants have done their business either themselves, or through the means of their clerks.

What do you suppose induces the merchants to do their insurances so?—To have the emolument of the brokerage.

Do not you consider the rate of brokerage, or the difference between what the insurer gets and the insured pays, to be extravagant?—I do not think it is; the broker has the risk of the premium, which he is always liable to pay the underwriter, whether he gets paid or not; and in addition to that, it often occurs, that if in doing an insurance for a particular merchant a heavy loss happens, he is obliged to advance the whole of that money to that merchant, when probably he owes the underwriters the whole amount, being premiums due to him from other merchants from whom it will not be payable till the end of the year.

Do not you think that in the general course of the business of a broker he is oftener in cash than in advance?—That depends upon the casualty of his business; it may be sometimes one way and sometimes the other.

Is not also the trouble of the broker very much increased by the great number of underwriters with whom he has to deal?—The broker, of course, has a great deal of trouble in going to fifty or a hundred underwriters; at the same time that gives him a facility, when he has a large sum to do, to have accounts with many.

You have stated, that you paid large sums in 1794 and 1795, in consequence of the detention of the Dutch ships in our harbours; was that ultimately a loss, or was it restored?—It was a loss, as not one shilling was ever got back for the Dutch detained ships.

Was any part of the 20,000 l. paid for property detained in Russia got back?—I believe from about one half to two thirds was afterwards returned, but we paid the whole in the first instance.

G. Shedden,
Esq.

Do you think that the small amount which you understand the individual merchants to hold in the new intended company would be an inducement to them to carry their business to that company if it were not well done, or would induce them to injure Lloyd's coffee-house, if they thought their insurance business would not be better conducted?—I conceive the share that each individual merchant is to hold in the company is so small that it could have very little influence upon him in that respect; at least, I judge of others by myself.

Has not your family been very extensively concerned as underwriters in the coffee-house?—For about twenty-five years my father has been a considerable underwriter at Lloyd's.

Do you think they would concur in giving support to any plan which, in their opinion, would be a very serious injury to the underwriters generally?—Our family differ in opinion upon that subject; some think one way and some another.

You have stated, that you never heard of the two existing chartered companies consulting together, or combining for the purpose of settling the premium; supposing one or two more new insurance companies to be established, and that the present system of individual underwriting were thereby to be destroyed; do you not believe that in such a state of things such companies would combine and settle together the rate of premium?—They certainly would have it in their power, if private under-writing was at an end.

Do you not believe there is now a great deal of business done at Lloyd's, which would be taken by the chartered companies, and at the same premium, if the offer of it had been made to those companies?—I believe there is a proportion that would be taken by one chartered company at least, if offered to them; I have understood one wrote more freely than the other.

Thomas Nicholson, Esq. called in; and Examined.

T. Nicholson,
Esq.

WHAT is your line of business?—An insurance-broker and underwriter.

Have you always been able to effect the insurances which you have received orders to do, at all seasons of the year?—Always.

Have you found your underwriters litigious, or found them ready in general to pay just demands?—I have never found them litigious; I have always found them very ready, and particularly so in many cases where we have had averages to be settled that probably would not have been settled by any company, or even in a court of justice we could not legally have recovered.

Have you ever been obliged to enforce demands upon your underwriters by law?—Nothing further than by letters of abandonment; but I never had a policy which has been tried in any court of law from the commencement of my business.

Letters of abandonment are sent when the party assured wishes to recover the sum insured on his policies, and to oblige the underwriter to take to himself the property insured?—Certainly.

What losses have there been by the insolvency of underwriters on the business you have transacted at Lloyd's?—I think it would not amount to 200 l. but, I am perfectly clear, not to 300 l. and those have been on cases of averages; not one on the case of a total loss.

Have you taken any shares in this intended new marine insurance company?—Yes, I have.

What was your motive in taking those shares?—I considered that if it did take place, I might as well be in the boat, and that it might stand against any thing I might lose from my business as a broker being taken from me.

Did you accept those shares from any approbation of the principle of this new institution?—Certainly not; I had hardly given it a consideration at the time.

What effect, in your opinion, would the establishment of this new marine insurance company have upon the interest of the insurance-brokers?—I think it would be a national evil, myself.

Explain in what respects?—In the first place, though it might not immediately have the appearance of a monopoly, yet I think it would grow into it in the end; I have not a doubt of that.

Does not the business of an insurance-broker depend upon his effecting the business of his principals on the lowest possible terms?—Certainly.

Does he not, therefore, for his own sake, use his utmost exertions with the underwriters to induce them to write at the lowest premiums possible?—Yes, or he would lose his business. There is such a competition at Lloyd's, that unless a broker can get his business done upon equal terms, or lower than his neighbour, he will lose his business.

T. Nicholson, Esq.

Are not the premiums of insurance reduced to as low a rate as the underwriter can afford to accept by this competition?—Much lower; many risks are now doing under peace price, and most of them at peace premiums: ships to Quebec are now doing at the peace premium; ships from the West Indies have been done at or under the peace premium.

If the merchants of this metropolis form themselves into one or more companies, for the purpose of taking the insurance business into their own hands, would not they have an interest contrary to the interest of those for whom they act?—Certainly they would have an interest; because if they got a complete monopoly, they might fix any premium, and there would be no competition with them.

Do you think that the interest of the assured would be equally consulted if this intended new company were to be established, instead of the present mode of effecting marine insurances by individual competition?—It would not.

Do you live in the city?—I live in the city three months in the year, I reside in Yorkshire principally.

Are you ever called upon to serve on juries at Guildhall?—No.

You do not know, then, that a great proportion of the actions brought there are on policies of insurance?—I know that a great many of them are on policies of insurance.

You are of opinion that the establishment of a new company would ultimately be a great injury to the interests of the merchants and the trade of the country?—I have no doubt of it.

You must think, therefore, that the merchants of the city are much mistaken in their opinion that it would be of great service?—I think that the subscribers to Lloyd's are men of that property that they are equal to any insurances that can be brought into the country, or have been. I have no hesitation in saying, any sum might be done at Lloyd's, provided they will give a proper premium; a premium that may be considered proper for the risk.

You must think, therefore, that the merchants of the city are much mistaken in their opinion, that it would be of great service?—I do.

You only attend the coffee-house two or three months in the year?—On account of my health, for the last two or three years I have resided principally in Yorkshire, where I have property.

Your business, then, is not extensive?—I have a brother, who is in connection with me in business.

James Barnes, Esq. called in; and Examined.

WHAT line of business do you follow?—That of an insurance-broker.

How long have you been in that line of business?—For myself seventeen years; some years before that I was a clerk, and part of the time to Andrew French and Company, who were insurance-brokers also.

J. Barnes, Esq.

Have you always been able to effect such insurances as you have received orders to do?—When the premium has not been limited, I have.

At all seasons of the year?—Yes, at all seasons of the year.

Do you imagine that the present or any new companies would have taken the risks which were refused at Lloyd's Coffee-house, because the underwriters thought the limited premium inadequate?—I should think certainly not. I never could do insurance at the companies, because they are always higher than the individual underwriters. I have tried them very often.

Have you had difficulty in recovering losses and averages with the underwriters at Lloyd's?—I never found any myself.

Have you been obliged to have recourse to legal means of recovery?—No policy effected by me ever went into the hands of an attorney but one, on a question that was tried mutually by consent, upon admissions on a policy per the Chiswick, and two others belonging to the estate of Mr. Bent, in which, I believe, an honourable member of this Committee is co-assignee with myself.

Were the verdicts upon those policies in favour of the underwriters or the

J. Barnes,
Esq.

assured?—The assured per Chiswick had no demand whatever against the under-writers, and he consequently lost the cause, which was tried in the Court of King's Bench. One, of Mr. Bent's policies never came to a verdict, because Lord Ellenborough and the legal men had given so decided an opinion what must have been the result, that we thought it right to withdraw the record, and pay our underwriters costs and our own. Previously to that, about 17,000 *l.* had been recovered upon Mr. Bent's policies from Lloyd's. The other policy of Mr. Bent's is now before the Court of Common Pleas, undecided.

Were the underwriters at all bound to pay that 17,000 *l.*?—Not one shilling of it, I believe.

Was it not paid from considerations of fairness and liberality?—It was paid from a variety of motives, fairness and liberality, and that kind of influence which exists between man and man; that kind of influence which we have when we have individual access to each man.

Do you imagine such a demand would have been paid by any chartered company?—I think I may say it would not: it is impossible for me to say positively what a chartered company would do, but I should think not; and I am sure, if I had the management or direction of a chartered company, no part of it would have been paid.

What bad debts have you made by the failure of underwriters at Lloyd's, in the course of your insurance business?—I have looked very carefully with my book-keeper over the last six years, and it is under 300 *l.* for that time; I have not examined further back.

Are not insurance-brokers liable to losses in case of the insolvency of the principals for whom they transact business?—I know to my cost that they are.

Are not insurance-brokers liable to very heavy advances of money in case of losses?—Very heavy; I am at this moment, I believe, in advance, to the amount of upwards of 20,000 *l.* for losses.

If losses arise, in consequence of a mistake or error of the broker in transacting his business, is not he responsible to his principal for the consequences?—I should conceive he would be.

Are not the emoluments of the broker calculated with a view to all those considerations, as well as with a view merely to his trouble in effecting his business?—I should presume that must be the original ground of the broker's commission; I do not know how it came originally to be five per cent. and a discount.

Does not the length of credit given by the underwriters to the brokers enable them to give longer credit to the merchants than they otherwise could do?—Surely; I could not pay the premiums in ready money; if the underwriters did not give us credit, it would be quite impossible we could give the merchants credit.

Do you not frequently extend the credit to your merchants beyond the usual time, being enabled to do so by the underwriters not calling upon you immediately for their money?—Very frequently.

Then in point of fact, is not the length of credit given by the underwriter to the broker an advantage in that way to the merchant?—Many of the merchants that I am connected with in the out-ports could not carry on their business without it.

If a new marine insurance company, comprising a very great proportion of the mercantile houses of this metropolis, were established, what effect in your opinion would it have upon individual underwriters and insurance-brokers?—I should presume it must take away a very large proportion of their business, if not the whole; if they had nine tenths, it would take away nine tenths, I presume: I do not know what other effect it could have.

Would not the members of that company make a point of giving that company the preference of all their risks upon equal terms?—I should think they would.

If that company were to select the good risks and reject the bad risks, would it be possible for individual underwriters to continue their present avocation?—I should think it quite impossible.

Do not underwriters at present with whom you have accounts take the good and the bad risks together?—They do.

If you had only such risks to offer to them as had been rejected by the companies, do you imagine they would keep open such an account?—I do not imagine I could do any business whatever, unless I had the good to mix with the bad; it would be quite impossible.

Do not many merchants employ young men without sufficient knowledge or experience to effect their insurance business at Lloyd's, in order to save the expense of the brokerage?—A great many, I believe, do, though brokerage is no expense to the merchant, it being wholly paid by the underwriters; but many merchants do this for the purpose of benefit to themselves, for such brokerage they never, I believe, give to their correspondents.

Is not much litigation occasioned by want of accuracy in filling up policies, and in stating demands, by young men so employed?—No doubt there is a great deal.

Do not such young men frequently avail themselves of their situation to become underwriters, by exchanging lines on the policies they are intrusted to effect, with other young men employed on the same business by other houses?—Yes.

Does not much discredit sometimes attach on the regular underwriter and broker by such practices, arising from the misplaced confidence of the merchants?—Most undoubtedly.

If the present intended new marine insurance company were established, would not other companies be formed, both here and in the out-ports?—I should think it extremely likely.

Are you enabled to form a pretty correct judgment of the prudence with which the individual underwriters at Lloyd's carry on their business?—If I had not the means of judging, it would be quite impossible I could have recovered so much money, about 280,000 *l.* in six years, with so little loss. Every broker of care and prudence can judge of persons that are constantly there.

If insurance business were carried on by companies would it be possible to form the same judgment of the prudence, or want of prudence, of their conduct?—It would be impossible, because no person could see what they did in their offices; whereas we can see every day what individuals do in the public room at Lloyd's Coffee-house.

If business was carried on by one or more companies, would not much delay probably arise from the acting directors or secretaries of those companies not being exactly acquainted with the nature of the risks offered them, and finding it necessary to consult absent persons before they determined whether they would or not write the policies shown them?—Most likely that would be the case; it would be quite impossible for me to go round to twenty insurance companies in the time I go to twenty underwriters, sitting in the same room; I have frequently done large insurances that have pressed for time, with many names, sooner than I could go to one company.

Among the number of underwriters at Lloyd's are not men always to be found conversant with risks of every description; and will not other underwriters, who see a policy begun by a person in whose judgment they have confidence, follow his example?—Constantly so.

Must not the same comparative facility and despatch always exist while individual underwriting is kept up at Lloyd's?—It will necessarily be so.

If partnerships were permitted to underwrite instead of individuals, might not the necessity of consulting an absent partner frequently occasion much delay and inconvenience, both in writing policies and settling losses?—I should think it would.

Might not the absence of one partner render it necessary to outlaw him, before it could be possible for the assured to recover his loss from the others?—No doubt it would.

Is not that process frequently resorted to in order to gain time?—Too often, I fear. I am at this moment in the situation of suing a man in Liverpool, and because I cannot prove the partnership, as it applies to the particular bill of exchange upon which the process is issued, when I come into court I am non-suited; I am then obliged to sue him (because it is A. B. and company upon the Bills) as A. B. alone, and then he pleads in abatement a partnership, setting forth a partner abroad; I am then obliged to outlaw that partner before I can even support an action against the resident partner at home, and bring it to issue; which occasions great loss of time and serious inconveniences, and which might and would, I have little doubt, be the case with insurances, if policies were subscribed in partnership, as every bad and litigious man at Lloyd's would take care to have an absent partner.

Can such delays be pleaded by an individual underwriter?—Certainly not.

Is not the underwriting partner in a house generally the head of the house?—He is generally selected as the richest man, the man who has most influence in every respect; all that I know are so.

Is it not generally found that the separate estate of the individual underwriter pays a better dividend than the joint estate of the partnership does, in cases of insolvency?—In the several insolvencies which I have known they have always done so but in one

J. Barnes,
Esq.

case; and that private estate would have been more than solvent, with a surplus, but for the circumstance of some legal effect, which threw a heavy debt upon that estate, which did not belong to it, and caused a very great insolvency, and he paid only 7 s. in the pound; he may pay another shilling, perhaps.

Is that the only exception you have found to the estate of the individual underwriter paying a better dividend than the estate of the partnership?—It is the only one; I have known three or four to the contrary.

Would then, in your opinion, the security of the assured be increased by underwriting being carried on in partnerships instead of individually?—No, I think the security would be very materially diminished.

If the merchants were to become also insurance brokers and underwriters, would they not have an interest opposite to that of the foreign correspondents for whom they acted?—The higher the premium the more their profit, of course, if they united in themselves the different characters of broker and underwriter.

Do you think that the same justice would be done to the interest of the assured by any new system, as is done at present in the open mode of competition in which insurance business is carried on at Lloyd's?—In my humble opinion nothing can be more for their advantage than it is, so far as I am able to judge.

You have stated, that by underwriters writing in partnerships the security of the assured would be diminished; state to the Committee upon what you found that opinion.—The very circumstance I have stated, the impossibility of suing different partners, where you do not know who those different partners are; and very often when they are even resident in the country, it would be impossible to sue them; and therefore as it is impossible to sue them, I take the security to be less.

Is the Committee to understand, that the only reason you have for thinking that the security would be diminished is in consequence of this legal difficulty of getting at the partners?—In my opinion, that is one great reason; but I think another reason is, that a man is never so secure as when he knows the parties he is trusting, and it would be quite impossible he should know the parties he gives credit to if underwriting were carried on in partnerships. By the present mode of underwriting it very frequently happens the private fortune of the individual (he being usually the richest man of the firm) is more than equal to pay all the demands against him as an underwriter, when the firm itself, of which he is a partner, is insolvent; and this material advantage would be taken away from the assured if policies were subscribed in partnerships.

From what could arise the great difficulty you apprehend, in knowing whom you are trusting in cases of partnership; are you not aware that business of every other description is carried on by partnerships, and that no such difficulty exists?—Yes; but any other business is different from the business of underwriting, in which, as you make a contract with a man in one minute, there are no means of knowing who are the partners, and you must take it upon the credit of the man with whom you are conversing; it would be impossible you should have the means of knowing who his partners are, and his partners might be persons whom you would not give credit to. In the general transactions of trade we usually inquire who a man's partners are.

As a broker, are you upon the whole in advance, or in cash?—I should think constantly in advance; I am sure I am constantly in advance, and at this moment in very heavy advance, for Lloyd's Coffee-house will lose 20,000 l. or 25,000 l. by me last year.

In your business as a broker, you find you are constantly in advance?—Yes.

And that it requires a capital of your own to carry on your business?—Yes; and a very heavy one.

Are you not not aware that most of the brokers at Lloyd's are in an opposite situation?—I believe there are many in an opposite situation.

Veneris, 23° die Martii, 1810.

The LORD BINNING in the Chair.

James Meyer, Esq. called in ; and Examined.

HOW long have you carried on business as a merchant in this metropolis ?—Eight-and-twenty years ; thirty-five years in the house, and twenty-eight years as a principal.

To what parts of the world has the business of your house chiefly been carried on?—Chiefly to Germany and Holland, and different parts of the Mediterranean.

Have your connections in Holland and Germany been very extensive ?—They have.

Are there many houses in this city who have carried on business to a greater extent than your house has done ?—I question if any house has carried on business in the commission line (which mine has chiefly been) to a larger extent, and but few to so large a one.

Where have the insurances of your house been effected?—At Lloyd's Coffee-house.

Did you effect them by means of a broker ?—Always by means of a broker.

Have you found the underwriters at Lloyd's litigious, or have they been ready to settle just demands?—I never found them litigious, but I think they have always settled their policies in a very honourable way.

Have you made many bad debts by the insolvency of underwriters at Lloyd's ?—The bad debts which I have made either on insurances on my own account, or those of my friends abroad, have been very few, not worth mentioning ; and for the last few years I may say none at all.

Have your correspondents on the continent of Europe expressed any dissatisfaction with the mode in which the insurance business has been effected at Lloyd's, either as to the rate of premiums, or the solvency of the underwriters ?—With respect to the solvency of the underwriters they have not found any fault, because they have had none, nor, that I know of, with respect to the rate of the premium ; we have often been limited and had premiums mentioned to us, but they have been satisfied with the premiums at which I have effected them.

Has a great part of the business you have done, and of the goods you have shipped, been upon account of foreign houses?—Almost all ; I have done very little or nothing on my own account.

Has that property been insured at Lloyd's by the request of those foreign houses?—A part of it, and a considerable part of it ; but of course not all.

Mr. *John Bennett*, Junior, called in ; and Examined.

IS not your father one of the masters of Lloyd's, and do not you keep the accounts of that establishment ?—Yes.

Are not you also secretary to the committee for managing the affairs of Lloyd's?—Yes.

What number of subscribers does there appear from your books to have been at Lloyd's in the year 1771 ?—Seventy-nine.

What number is there at present ?—Between fourteen and fifteen hundred.

Do you mean to convey that those fourteen or fifteen hundred subscribers are underwriters?—Certainly they are not all underwriters.

What proportion of them are ?—Probably two-thirds of them.

Can any person be admitted as a subscriber to Lloyd's without being first recommended as a proper person by six subscribers, and his nomination being subsequently approved of by the Committee?—No, he cannot.

Is that regulation ever dispensed with in favour of any person whatever?—It has not since the year 1800, when new regulations took place.

For what number of underwriters are there accommodations provided at Lloyd's?—Between four and five hundred take their seats every day, and there are many who have not their fixed seats, but walk about and take seats as may be convenient.

J. Bennett, Jun.

Are those seats in general fully occupied?—Completely so ; in fact, there is not sufficient room.

Do not many persons stand in the room at Lloyd's and write policies, without having an opportunity of sitting down, for want of greater accommodation ?—Yes.

Are not surveyors appointed by the committee at Lloyd's in almost every port of the United Kingdom to examine into and report upon the age and equipment of every merchant vessel employed in the trade of this country?—Not by the committee to which I am secretary, but by another committee ; I believe some of the house-committee are members of it.

Are not the reports of those surveyors posted up weekly into a register printed for the use of each subscriber?—Yes.

Are not returns regularly received at Lloyd's of all the vessels that arrived at or have sailed from every port in these kingdoms, together with information of every description, on maritime affairs?—Yes, speaking generally, every port ; there may, probably, be some few ports from which returns are not received.

Are not correspondents established in every part of the world, who constantly transmit similar returns to Lloyd's ?—I will not say every part of the world, but most ports, certainly.

Is not the whole of the intelligence thus received, as far as the interests of commerce are concerned, immediately, and without reserve, copied into books, placed in various parts of the room at Lloyd's, and communicated not only to the subscribers but to the public at large ?—Yes, according to one of the resolutions that passed in the year 1800, at a general meeting of the subscribers, "that the books of arrivals " and losses in the other rooms, known by the name of Lloyd's Coffee-house, be " regularly posted up, and the several port-letters be likewise daily copied, for the " due and speedy information of the public at large."

Is not much important intelligence relative to the maritime interests of the country frequently transmitted exclusively to Lloyd's ; and in such case, is it not immediately communicated to His Majesty's government?—Yes, I have brought some recent instances of communications with the Admiralty.

Are you not in the frequent habit of making communications of that sort to the Admiralty, and receiving the thanks of their Lordships for those communications?—Yes, I have letters to that effect here.

Has not this system been matured and brought to its present state of perfection, by the most unremitting attention, for a great number of years?—Certainly.

Is it not maintained at a very heavy expense?—Yes.

If the subscribers to Lloyd's were discouraged from keeping up this establishment, could it be put upon the same footing by any other set of men without a great loss of time ?—No, I should conceive not.

Would not the want of such a system of intelligence be injurious to the public interest, as well as to the commercial world ?—I conceive so.

Has not a provision been made by the subscribers to Lloyd's by a large donation to the London Hospital for the receipt of seamen employed in the merchant service into that hospital, in case of sickness or of casualty ?—Yes.

Are not innumerable cases of distress among individuals engaged in the seafaring line, and their families, which never come to the knowledge of the public, constantly relieved at Lloyd's, to an extent unprecedented in the annals of any other institution ?—There are very frequent subscriptions for such purpose.

Has not a petition been prepared to be presented to the House of Commons against the incorporation of the intended new marine insurance company, in case a bill for that purpose should be brought into parliament ?—Yes

By what number of subscribers to Lloyd's has that petition been signed?—About 800.

Is there not an annual subscription to Lloyd's, paid by underwriters and other persons frequenting it, independent of a life-subscription?—Yes.

What number of persons paid that annual subscription in the course of the last year ?—I think about thirteen hundred, probably more.

Have you not observed in an American newspaper, very recently received, an advertisement, inviting the re-establishment of underwriting by individuals in that country ?—Yes, I have.

Have you any knowledge from what cause those invitations originated ? — No, I have not ; it was a singular advertisement, and I cut it out, thinking it worthy of notice, in consequence of the application to Parliament for a new marine insurance company.

You do not know whether it was the speculation of an individual?—No, it appeared to be a meeting called by the merchants of New York.

J. Bennett, Jun.

Peter Warren, Esq. called in; and Examined.

HOW long were you in business as an insurance broker?—I was originally apprentice to Mr. Wiling, fifty years ago, and I have followed no other practice from that time.

P. Warren, Esq.

How long is it since you quitted that line of business?—Ten years and a half; when my health rendered it necessary.

Were you always able to effect such insurances as you received orders to do from your friends?—I never had occasion to return any order whatever, that I chose to trust the principal with effecting; if it was a person of respectability that I chose to do his business I never felt any difficulty in completely effecting it.

Did you find the underwriters at Lloyd's in general disposed to settle fair and just demands?—Always very ready to settle all fair and just demands.

Have you been able to effect very large insurances there in a very short space of time?—Yes, I have; I think I could mention one that was acknowledged to be so: A gentleman accustomed to foreign insurances, an agent for one of the first houses in Europe, gave me an order for 50,000*l.* to do on a very short voyage, from L'Orient to London, which required despatch; he gave it me in the morning when the business was over. At three o'clock he came up and inquired what progress I had made; I told him his insurance was done, and he might take the policy home with him, upon which he exclaimed with a strong asseveration, "it would have taken me a week at Amsterdam!" It was a matter of no exertion, I had done it without any difficulty.

Are not insurance-brokers subject to great losses through the insolvency of the houses for which they transact business?—Very great; I could mention one house in particular, whose annual balance for a few years was constantly fluctuating between 50 and 80,000*l.*

Do you mean the balance due to your house as insurance-brokers?—Yes; it was constantly fluctuating; sometimes it was diminished in the course of the month by returns of losses, and then increased by additional insurances, so that it was fluctuating from 50 to 80,000*l.*; ultimately the house failed, and it appeared by the examination of their accounts, that they were insolvent the whole time; and had they failed at first, as they afterwards did, they could never have paid more than a shilling in the pound, and we must have paid the underwriters.

How many instances have come within your knowledge in the course of these last fifty years of insurance-brokers having retired upon a competency?—Very few indeed; I think I do not recollect any having made large fortunes, not one certainly, and very few with a competency: the utmost that I recollect do not live beyond this establishment; two maids and a man servant; some others, two maids, and many with only a single servant, of whom I am one instance. I recollect a great many houses that have failed as insurance-brokers.

Has the number of those who have retired upon a competency, or the number of those who have failed, been the greatest?—I can recollect more who have failed than who have retired with a competency, as far as my own recollection goes.

To what cause have those failures been owing?—To the insufficiency of their employers the merchants, and failures in the payment of their insurances.

What, in your opinion, would be the effect of establishing a new marine insurance company in this metropolis, comprising nine tenths of the commercial interests in it?—I think the consequence would be the utter ruin of Lloyd's Coffee-house as an insurance market.

When you say that you have never had an insurance to do which you have not effected at the coffee-house, do you mean to inform the Committee that you have never been unable to effect an insurance at what the assured have considered a fair premium?—I have sometimes been under the necessity of leaving my insurance undone if limited; but I have always been able to do my business at some price, unless checked by my principal.

You mean then, that you have always been able to do it provided you have agreed to give what the underwriters wanted?—When I could have free liberty to do it upon the best terms I could, I have always been able to execute my orders.

P. Warren,
Esq.

Were not you for many years a partner of Mr. Angerstein's?—Yes, fourteen years.

You do not mean to include your partner among those who retire from business with such very moderate fortunes?—No, I do not; but his immense fortune does not arise from his commissions as an insurance-broker, it in a great measure arises from a long-continued attention as an underwriter, and a very successful one, with many other circumstances that have assisted in raising his fortune; by no means by commissions only.

Have you found the underwriters in general exact extravagant or unreasonable premiums?—I rather think the competition with the common underwriters has lowered the premiums so much, that the best underwriters have been obliged to discontinue the business they lower the premiums upon one another so much.

Supposing that by the establishment of any new system the credit of Lloyd's should be materially affected, would not that be in your opinion of great detriment to the public interest?—My opinion is, that it would ruin Lloyd's Coffee-house as an insurance market; and I beg leave to observe, it is well worth the serious consideration of the Committee how materially it might affect the commercial interests of this country were the credit of Lloyd's to be shaken in the opinion of foreigners, which to the present time has been looked up to by the commercial world as an inexhaustible source of security and universal mercantile information.

Christopher Idle, Esq. called in; and Examined.

C. Idle,
Esq.

IN what line of business are you?—We are general merchants; our principal lines are wine and spirits.

In the course of your business do you make considerable insurances on marine risks?—Yes, we do.

Do you find any difficulty in effecting insurances to the amount which your engagements require?—No, none at all; we never had occasion to go out of London to effect them, that I recollect.

Do you effect those insurances with private underwriters, or with the two chartered companies, or with both?—With both.

With both the chartered companies, or only one?—What we do with the companies is principally with the Royal Exchange Assurance Company.

Do you find any objection on the part of the Royal Exchange Company to cover the risks which you generally offer, and are your insurances with that company to a considerable amount?—We find very great accommodation with that company in general, and our insurances are to a very considerable amount with them.

Can you effect the whole sum you have to do on any one ship without the intervention of private underwriters?—The cargoes in our ships generally do not amount to a very large sum; we have done whole cargoes at the Royal Exchange, but in general are divided.

Has your house, for some years past, had very extensive engagements for the importation of goods into this country?—Yes, very large for many years.

Should you think it good to enter into such prospective engagements to the extent you do, if you were doubtful of being able to cover yourselves by insurance?—We find from experience so little difficulty that we never contemplate it.

In point of fact, you never have experienced any such difficulty?—No, we never have.

To what amount have you in any one year insured with the Royal Exchange Company?—We have insured in one year to the extent of 500,000 l.

From your experience does it appear to you, that notwithstanding the great increase of the commerce of the country, the underwriters have also so greatly increased, that with the aid of the two existing companies they are sufficient to cover every probable risk, in point of sum, by one ship, or by ship or ships?—If the question is confined to those branches of commerce I am connected with, I certainly think they are perfectly adequate.

Have you ever heard any complaints stated in your branch of commerce of the insufficiency of the present means of effecting marine insurances?—No, I cannot say that I have.

Is it your opinion that the two chartered companies are hurtful or inconvenient to the public?—That is partly a speculative question, on which I can hardly give an answer; it is a subject I have not much considered.

Have you not, in your own line of business, found them advantageous and convenient to you?—I have found a particular convenience in them, and the greatest accommodation, certainly; the greatest consideration to our business I have always found in the Royal Exchange Company.

Have you any reason to believe that they are not equally advantageous and convenient to persons carrying on other branches of trade?—I have no doubt whatever of it.

Have you been great sufferers by the insolvency or litigious spirit of underwriters?—By no means; while I have been in business, which embraces a period of twenty-four years, I find the whole of our bad debts from underwriters amount only to 860 *L*, and, with respect to litigation, we never had during the whole course of that time any litigation, to the best of my recollection, but upon one policy to a small amount, and another now pending.

What are generally the nature of the risks you have to insure?—Our risks are as general as they can possibly be conceived to be; they are direct risks, and indirect risks, and cross-risks, and from almost every part of the world, and to every part of the world nearly; from Canada, from the West Indies, to and from the Western Islands, the Canary Islands, and from all those places I have mentioned with each other; they are also from every part of Europe and the Mediterranean.

They are always in British ships, are they not?—No; very much indeed in neutral ships; in British ships from Canada and the West Indies, and the Western Islands; the Canary Islands in neutral ships while they were at war with us; and to and from the Mediterranean and many parts of Europe, in neutral ships.

Do you insure any of the risks by neutral ships with the chartered companies?—Yes, we do at the Royal Exchange very largely, and without names also, that is by ship or ships; I think we have frequently done it.

Do you also insure with those companies the risks from Canada; for instance, to the West Indies?—Yes, that is called a cross-risk; I do not think it comes within their general scope, but they have done it for us, and therefore I say they have given us great accommodation.

Are you aware that the companies, in insuring those risks for you gave you a particular accommodation, and that it is not their general practice to cover what are called cross-risks?—I have understood that such had been their practice, but that feeling that consideration arising out of the circumstances of the times, and probably the circumstances of our business, which is on a large scale, they have yielded to the representations we have made.

You understand, therefore, that the company, in consequence of your being a good customer, does insure to you those risks which they are not in the general habit of covering?—I do not understand they do that because we are good customers, but on account of the nature of our business, and yielding to the representations we have made of the circumstances of the times.

You do understand it is not their general custom to insure those risks?—I have so understood.

What proportion of your insurance business do you do with the companies, and what proportion with Lloyd's?—Last year we did with the Royal Exchange Company, 327,000*l.*, and with Lloyd's, 510,000*l.*; the year before we did with the Royal Exchange Company, 517,000 *l.*, and with Lloyd's, 280,000 *l.*

Do you think you do with the London Assurance Company a fourth part of what you do with the Royal Exchange Company?—No, we do very little with the London, scarcely any thing to speak of.

Do you generally pay the companies a higher premium than you pay in the coffeehouse?—In some cases we do; there are considerations which make it perhaps relatively as cheap.

What are those considerations?—Their manner of paying is different, and their allowances are different.

What is the difference upon the average amount, between the premiums of the company and those of the coffee-house?—Some things are done cheaper at the Royal Exchange, and others cheaper at Lloyd's; I do not know that the thing is susceptible of being reduced to an average: they have particular tastes on the subject that govern their prices.

You find the company generally higher?—Nominally higher, but it is according

C. Idle, Esq.

to the price that we are governed, as will be seen by our having done so little with the company last year, and so much in proportion with Lloyd's.

Do you give no preference to the companies on account of their peculiar security, and the facility with which business is done with them?—Yes, that is one of the considerations.

And an important one, is it not?—It certainly is an important one for every body to be secure, and to feel secure; but our experience does not warrant any disconfidence in Lloyd's Coffee-house, but the contrary.

Do you do your business at Lloyd's Coffee-house through a broker or yourselves?—Almost entirely ourselves; we select our own people, and know them very well.

In that case you get at the coffee-house the profit that would otherwise go to the broker?—Entirely.

Do you or any of your partners underwrite yourselves?—Not at all; we have not for twelve years.

From what you have just said, does it not follow in consequence of the mode of payment and allowances made by the chartered companies, that though the premiums with the companies may be nominally higher, it may be equally or more to your advantage to insure with the companies than with the private underwriters?—Yes, in all cases, where we give them a preference at a higher premium, we consider that we receive equivalents in those considerations to which I have alluded for the difference.

Have you found any difficulties in effecting with the chartered companies your insurances upon neutral ships, and on cross-risks, such as you have described in your former answer?—Unquestionably there is not the same currency for risks of that description with the companies that there is for risks in British bottoms; at the same time we have done very large insurances upon such risks with the Royal Exchange Company.

Have you ever done any cross-risks with the London Assurance Company?—I do not recollect that we have.

What is the greatest amount you ever effected at the Royal Exchange Assurance upon any one ship?—We effected upwards of 10,000 *l.* upon the same bottom; the amount is 10,200 *l.*

Is that the whole amount you had to effect upon that ship?—No.

With whom did you effect the remainder?—At Lloyd's.

Could you have effected a larger sum than the 10,200 *l,* with the Royal Exchange, had you been desirous of doing so?—I rather think not.

You have stated that the allowances from the companies, and their mode of payment, are more favourable than those in the coffee-house; be so good as to state what those allowances are, and in what the mode of payment is different?—I believe the allowance is, in the first instance, five per cent. upon the premium, as at Lloyd's; and that finally an allowance is made of ten per cent. upon the net profit of the year's account.

You say that the company allows five per cent. upon the premium, as at Lloyd's, and ten per cent. upon the net profit; do not the underwriters at Lloyd's allow twelve per cent. upon the net profit?—No; their net profit is not made up in that kind of way.

Is it not in the mode of its payment equivalent to twelve per cent. upon its net profit?—I should think so, and more.

Are there any allowances which are more favourable with the companies than in the coffee-house?—At the Royal Exchange they allow for prompt payment of the premium, fifteen per cent. besides the first five per cent. and this without reference to the contingencies of the risk insured, except the returns of premium reserved in the policy.

When merchants insure with the coffee-house, what credit do they upon the average get for their premiums?—I believe the premiums are paid yearly, unless in cases of loss, when the premiums are set off against the loss.

Do they not, one case taken with another, get a full twelve months credit?—It is so understood; the mode of payment to which I adverted in a former answer operating as a consideration with us in giving a higher nominal premium to the Royal Exchange Company, was, that when a loss happens, the Royal Exchange insulates that loss, deducting only from the amount of the loss the premium upon that individual risk, leaving the merchant still debtor for the premium upon other risks, running on to the end of the year, if he pleases.

'Does that practice prevail also at Lloyd's Coffee-house ;—No, I believe not.; at Lloyd's, before a loss is adjusted, the whole of the premiums up to the period of its adjustment are set off against the loss.

C Idle, Esq.

So that in case of a loss of 1,900*l.* the premium upon which may have been 50*l.* and supposing the amount of premiums for other risks due from the merchant amount to 950*l.* at the Royal Exchange a merchant would receive 950*l.* in money, whereas at Lloyd's he would receive nothing, the whole amount of such loss being applicable to the payment of premiums due upon other risks ?—Precisely so.

Do you ever act in the coffee-house as an agent for any insurances but those of your own house ?—Very seldom ; scarcely ever.

Do you think that if underwriters were enabled to associate together as merchants do, and by that means were enabled to take larger sums, it would be a facility to those who have insurances to make there ?—That is a very speculative question ; it might operate to facilitate insurances, or it might not ; persons acting in association with others are sometimes not so prompt in their determinations as when they act alone, and persons acting as we find the gentlemen of Lloyd's Coffee-house, with great promptitude, might then reserve themselves by a reference to partners, so that it is impossible to say whether it would give facility or not ; I think it involves questions as to whether it would afford great facilities or not.

Should not you think your security better by having several names to each line on the policy instead of single names ?—I understand that in point of law you cannot prosecute against a partnership unless all are in England ; now, as in firms, you cannot be sure all are in England, there would be that inconvenience ; whereas an underwriter must be at Lloyd's.

Does that inconvenience exist in a greater degree in insurance business than in any other operations of trade ?—In other operations of trade the credit is more limited ; in insurances, the point of security to which we look may be drawn out to an indefinite period, and requires, therefore, a more circumscribed limit in point of personal responsibility.

Are not your credits in business much more extended in amount than your credit to underwriters ?—Unquestionably so.

Did you ever, in the course of your business, experience any inconvenience from the circumstance you have mentioned, of being obliged to outlaw partners ?—Never ; very fortunately we have scarcely had any thing to do with law.

Is it not an inconvenience in having a single name to an engagement of any sort, that when that individual dies the means of settlement are often rendered more difficult ?—It certainly is ; in general cases I consider a firm safer than an individual.

Would not that apply in a still greater degree to engagements, the final extinction of which is (as in cases of marine insurance) frequently much protracted ?—I have already stated what our experience is as to bad debts, that with such contingencies they have never exceeded 860*l.*

John Rogers, Esq. called in ; and Examined,

I BELIEVE you are a broker ?—I am.

J Rogers, Esq.

How long have you acted as a broker ?—Seventeen years.

Are you in the habit of making considerable marine insurances ?—I am.

Do you effect those insurances with the private underwriters, or with the two chartered companies, or with both ?—With both ; more considerably at Lloyd's Coffee-house.

Do you find any objection on the part of the chartered companies to cover risks which you offer them, and are your insurances with those companies to a large amount ?—They are to a considerable amount ; the only difficulty I find is the quantum of premium ; I do not know that I have had any refusal to take the risks, provided that with the risk what they deemed an adequate premium was given.

You effect the insurances for the house of Messrs. Isaac Solly and Sons ?—I do.

In the very extensive engagements which those gentlemen and other principals of yours undertake, do you think they would enter into such engagements if they did not feel perfectly satisfied that they could cover their risks by means of the present existing companies and respectable underwriters at Lloyd's ?—I should think not.

J. Rogers,
Esq.

In the course of your practice, have you found any great difficulty in effecting insurances in the months of August, September, October, November and December, and at what period do the chartered companies decline the Baltic risks?—There is always more difficulty in effecting insurances in the fall of the year; but the chartered companies expect a greater increase of premium than individual underwriters do at the latter end of the year. I can state the amount of insurances I have effected during the months of last August, September and October; in August, to the amount of 476,000 *l.*; in September, 314,000 *l.*; in October, 282,000 *l.*

At any period of the year, have you found that the chartered companies absolutely decline the Baltic risks?—The London Assurance Company have declined the latter end of the last year to write them at any premium whatever from the Baltic.

Has this been the case with the Royal Exchange Company also?—The Royal Exchange have been willing to take them, but at the latter end of the year they required a larger premium than I could effect them for at Lloyd's Coffee-house, and therefore I did not give it.

Were the insurances which you state to have been effected in the months of August, September and October last, chiefly risks from the Baltic?—By far the majority.

In the course of your practice at Lloyd's Coffee-house, have you found the underwriters litigious, and have you suffered considerably by their insolvency?—I do not know in the course of seventeen years of more than one, or at most two law suits having been commenced by my principals against the underwriters.

Have you suffered considerably by the insolvency of underwriters?—Very little; within the last three or four years not one shilling: previously to that a very trifle.

Had you any considerable losses on Baltic risks in the autumn of the year 1808?—Yes, in the month of January 1809, losses were known to have taken place to a considerable amount.

Can you state the amount of losses from the Baltic that you had upon your own policies, within the period referred to?—I should think 200,000 *l.* loss; this includes what was insured at the companies as well as Lloyd's Coffee-house.

Upon that loss of 200,000 *l.* was there any loss from the insolvency of underwriters?—Not any.

The whole 200,000 *l.* was paid by the insurers?—It was.

Did you ever guarantee for your merchants the solvency of the underwriters?—But seldom.

When the guarantee is allowed, what is the rate charged for it?—An half per cent. for risks of long duration; a quarter per cent. for short risks.

If it had been your invariable practice to guarantee the solvency of underwriters, during the whole time you have been in business, would not that guarantee have produced a very considerable sum of profit?—A very large one indeed.

Do you consider the two chartered companies as hurtful, or inconvenient to the public?—No, I do not.

Do you conceive they are convenient and advantageous to the public?—I conceive them as affording a competition with Lloyd's Coffee-house.

And in that point of view advantageous and convenient?—Yes, certainly.

Is it your opinion, that the increased commerce of the country requires one or more companies in addition to the two existing ones; and are you of opinion that the establishment of the proposed new marine insurance company would be beneficial to the public?—I have never found any difficulty in effecting all the insurances I have had occasion for, and I therefore see no necessity for an increase of means.

Are there not a variety of risks in the present state of the commerce of the country which the chartered companies do not take?—There are a great many risks, and parts of risks, which they will not take upon the insurances to and from the Baltic; the companies will not take the risk of capture in port.

Do you know the reasons which prevent the chartered companies taking risks of this description?—I presume from their being incompetent judges of the value of those risks; individual underwriters are many of them merchants in those lines of trade, and are therefore more competent to decide upon the risk they run; but the companies, I believe, refuse them altogether, at least they have invariably done so to me.

What, in your opinion, would be the effect of the establishment of a new Marine Insurance Company, comprehending a considerable proportion of the great mercantile risks of London?—I should suppose a company comprising the leading mercantile interests in the city must engross the insurances from Lloyd's Coffee-house, excepting those sort of risks which companies never will take, which I should suppose would then remain for the underwriters; and there would be a considerable difficulty in getting those done if other risks were not offered at the same time.

Would not the establishment of such a company narrow competition?—If it lessened the number of underwriters, it unquestionably must; because the company would be as one voice only, their secretary choosing whether he would take the risks or not.

Are you a subscriber to the proposed new marine insurance company?—I am.

Viewing such an establishment as you appear to do, what were your motives for becoming a subscriber to it?—Considering the great interest that was to support this company, I expected it would be profitable.

J. Rogers, Esq.

Mr. *James Holland*, called in; and Examined.

WHAT situation do you hold in the Royal Exchange Assurance Company?— Chief clerk in the committee-room.

The committee-room is the room where all the marine insurance business is effected?—Yes, I am chief clerk in the marine insurance department.

In consequence of your situation, are you acquainted with the nature of marine insurance?—I am.

Is it your opinion that the company would do more business than they do, if it were offered to them?—Most undoubtedly.

To what extent do the company generally insure any one risk?—Up to 25, 30, or 40,000 *l.*

State to the Committee some of those instances?—On the Juno frigate we insured 30,000 *l.* the Amethyst, 20,000 *l.* the Lutine frigate, 22,000 *l.* on which we paid a total loss; on the Nile cutter, we insured 22,500 *l.* the Andromeda frigate, 25,000 *l.* the Inspector sloop, 25,000 *l.* the Hyæna frigate, 25,000 *l.* the Pretty Lass, an armed ship, 25,000 *l.* with a variety of others which I have not put down.

The ships you have described appear to be ships of war; is the Committee to understand that sums to that amount are taken only on ships of that description?— By no means; we have taken very large sums on private ships as well; 20 and 25,000 *l.* on packets, and on East India ships.

Have you it in your recollection, that sums to a great amount have been taken by the Royal Exchange Insurance Office on ship or ships?—Frequently very large sums, particularly from the Baltic, from the Mediterranean, from the Western Islands to the West Indies, we have insured from 20 to 40 or 45,000 *l.*

Explain to the Committee what is meant by insuring on ship or ships?--When a merchant abroad has a large property to ship he may have a good many vessels in the port and not know on what vessels he may ship it; he sends therefore a direction to insure upon such ships as may come from the port, without naming them, and in course a specific sum is insured by any ships that may come from the port, probably to be named as soon as the bill of lading comes, so that a very large sum may happen to be taken on one ship. I recollect making at the office a large insurance in the course of last summer for a West India House; the sum of 80,000 *l.* was offered us from the island of St. Croix, and we probably should have taken the whole, but that some difference arose between our sitting director and the gentleman who offered it, on account of some average clause; we therefore took 40,000 *l.* and the London Assurance Company took the other 40,000 *l.* without any limitation as to any ship; we might therefore have had the whole come upon one ship.

In how many ships did that interest come forward?—I really do not charge my memory, but I believe in five or six; as far as related to us, I do not know that the whole sum was declared to us by what ships it came.

It having been stated that the two companies decline taking Baltic risks at a certain period of the year, can you inform the Committee at what period the Royal Exchange Assurance declines those risks?—I do not know that the Royal Exchange Company refuses them at any period of the year, provided the broker agrees to pay

Mr. J. Holland.

Mr.
J. Holland.

the premium demanded by the sitting director; so far from it, the last four months of the last year we insured to the extent of 228,000 *l.* even to the month of December, upon those risks.

You have stated it as your belief that the company would do more business if more were offered to them.—Certainly, I think so.

Do you not know that the gentleman who has the conducting of the marine business rejects a great number of risks which are proposed to him?—Yes, and I think very properly so, acting prudentially; a great many cases may arise to induce a person to reject a ship, as a private underwriter may do; it may be, a bad ship, or a stranger bringing a risk, we do not take. If insurances were tendered fairly I think many insurances rejected would be taken.

What do you mean by insurances being tendered fairly?—There are a great many persons come about the office whom we may designate as sea-gulls, who only come when there is an appearance of stormy weather; if gentlemen came all the year round we might take them, but when they come only in the winter, we feel it necessary to decline them from prudential motives.

Does it not invariably happen that only a small proportion in a number of ships in the West India or Baltic fleets are offered to the Royal Exchange Insurance Company?—I think generally so; the fleets are sometimes very numerous.

What proportion do you suppose the ships so offered bear to the number in the whole fleet?—It must depend upon the number; fleets are various, from fifty to two hundred, but I should suppose that a tenth part is as many as are generally offered to us of any fleet; of the very large fleets we sometimes have more.

Supposing, instead of one tenth part, the whole, or nearly the whole, of the ships in such fleets were offered to the company, would not the company in that case be disposed to increase very much the sum taken on each ship?—Very much, I should suppose, because it would be playing a more equal game; we are in the habit of taking from 5 to 8 or 10,000 *l.* upon ships, if we know they are good ships, but if the whole fleet were offered I think the company would have no hesitation in taking from 20 to 25,000 *l.* upon a ship.

Is not the number of East India ships offered to the company trifling, compared with the whole number of ships employed in our East India trade?—I believe that the East India fleets generally consist of from 40 to 50 ships; we have insurances offered to us, perhaps upon 10 or 12, some of them larger and some of them smaller sums; we insure to the amount of 20,000 *l.* upon any Indiaman that is offered; were they all to come we should, perhaps, be inclined to take much more.

Do the company confine themselves generally to what are called the best risks?—The company uniformly decline taking risks of ships that are known to be any thing below the first and second class, because they consider them as not sea-worthy.

Do they not take what may be called the second and third class of risks from all persons who give them a fair share of their whole business?—They take second class, but they will not take the third class of ships, at least it is very seldom indeed that the company take them; they are generally deficient in their tackle, cables and anchors, or in the materials of their hulls; they are not well built or good ships.

Are there not amongst the governors and directors of the company a large proportion of merchants and others who have practical knowledge of the trade of the East and West Indies, the Baltic, the Mediterranean, and almost every country with which Great Britain carries on its commerce?—Our direction is composed generally of merchants and captains of vessels in the East and West India trades, and of course they have a general knowledge of those matters; there are some gentlemen among them who have been in the habit of underwriting, and who of course have a knowledge of that business also.

Do you not conceive those directors capable of judging of, and anxious to promote, whatever may be advantageous to the company?—Most assuredly, and I conceive that they are bound by their oath to give every assistance to the company.

If in their judgment it were advantageous to increase the sums now generally taken on any one ship, or to take risks which they now reject, do you not believe that their judgment and advice would be acted upon?—Certainly; when any difficult matter or any risk has been offered which has not been usual, the committee or the governors have been applied to generally by the sitting director for their advice and opinion.

Do you not believe it to be the duty of such directors, as well as their interest, to recommend and to act upon that system which in their judgment may best conduce to the permanent advantage of the corporation?—Certainly; and I believe they do so.

Can you state to the Committee any instance of the company having taken 40,000*l.* on a single ship?—I do not know that I can state any instance of their having taken that sum on a single ship, but it might happen when they had insured on ship or ships.

When you say that the company have insured as high as 40,000*l.* upon one risk, do you mean in any other way than upon ship or ships?—I mean on ship or ships only; I have not known any instance of a risk to that amount on one ship.

To what extent do the company generally take on merchantmen?—On West Indiamen from 8 to 12,000*l.*; 14,000*l.* I have known on one ship to the Brazils.

You have stated, that if the company could underwrite all the ships in any Baltic convoy, you think they would in that case take from 20 to 25,000*l.*?—I have said on a general risk; but I should apprehend, if such risks were offered on a Baltic convoy, they would do them on that as well as another.

Are you aware that a Baltic convoy consists sometimes of 2 or 300 vessels?—Yes.

Are you not aware that in war time whole convoys have been taken?—Not to that amount; I never knew an instance of three hundred ships being taken, or any thing like it.

If you have known no instance of three hundred ships being taken, have you not heard of instances of convoys of 150 ships being taken?—Not in my experience.

Is not such a thing very possible?—It is possible no doubt, but not under present circumstances I should conceive; nor under any circumstances that have happened since I have been in the office.

Would not the possibility of such a circumstance make it extremely imprudent for any company to take to the extent you mention upon any one convoy?—I should think no more imprudent than it would be for the general business to be done through the country by private underwriters, if we got the whole insurance, as we now have only our proportion of the losses; if it was the whole loss, we should, at the same time, have the whole premium.

Are not convoys exposed to danger in a mass?—Not so much as individual ships certainly, from the protection they receive from men of war.

Is not underwriting reduced to a much less degree of hazard by taking small sums on many ships, than by taking large sums on few ships?—Most undoubtedly.

Supposing a fleet of 200 sail of vessels was coming to this country, would you not think it quite consistent with prudence to insure 400,000*l.* upon that fleet, by taking 2,000*l.* on each of those ships, when you would consider it highly imprudent to insure that 400,000*l.* by taking 40,000*l.* on ten of those ships?—Most undoubtedly; I should not take those risks if I had the management of it.

Is not this the system on which you believe the directors of the chartered companies, as well as individual underwriters, generally act?—It is so; and it is upon that ground I stated that I thought the company would take so much, having the whole convoy offered to them.

Mr. *Timothy Greathead,* called in; and Examined.

WHAT is the situation you hold under the corporation of the London Assurance Company?—Chief clerk in the shipping department.

Have you an opportunity of observing the marine insurances effected by the company?—They all pass under my inspection; they are generally taken by me under the sanction of the managing director, and the committee in waiting.

Do you understand 10,000*l.* is the highest sum taken by the company on any interest proposed to be insured there?—By no means; I have several instances in my hand where we have exceeded that sum; I have selected numerous instances since the year 1800.

See Appendix,
No. 8.
Mr. T.
Greathead.

P. Grenfell,
Esq.

[The witness delivered in the account, which was read.]

Are you enabled to state what sums to the amount of 10,000*l.* or upwards, have been insured by the company within the last ten years on ship or ships?—We have made several insurances on ship or ships far beyond 10,000*l.*; to the extent of 50,000*l.* on one policy.

Have you ever observed any unwillingness on the part of the company to take a larger sum than 10,000*l.* on a fair risk, and at a fair premium?—They seldom have an opportunity of taking so much as 10,000*l.*; but the instances which I have referred to will shew, that where they have been offered, the company have not refused to take a larger sum.

Do you apprehend, that if fair risks, with adequate premiums, were offered, the company would gradually extend the scale of their insurances?—The company would be very ready to extend their business.

Have you observed, that at the fall of the year brokers and strangers apply more frequently for insurances than in the earlier months?—Yes, I think they do.

Does the company, upon those occasions, accept the risks offered or not?—They always take them at a fair premium.

Were the autumn insurances of last year to a greater or less amount, in the whole, than the insurances for an equal number of months in the year preceding?—I have not that particular account; I have selected the insurances for June 1809, which were to the amount of 128,343*l.*; in July 197,963*l.*; in September 214,267*l.*; in October 134,297*l.*; in November 294,546*l.*

It appears from this statement, that the amount of insurances in the autumn months exceeded greatly that of the summer months?—Yes, that was the fact.

Are not insurances frequently refused at the office of the London Assurance Company?—When we cannot agree upon the premium, or there are circumstances in the risk which we do not consider as favourable, and they will not give a premium for it accordingly.

Does it not frequently happen you do disagree with the persons desiring to have insurances effected?—Occasionally.

In what manner do you account for the circumstance of the whole insurances effected by your office amounting to much less than what is done by a single under-writer in the coffee-house, if your office is always disposed to take the risks that are offered at a reasonable premium?—We cannot insure if the parties do not apply to us; it is for want of application, I presume.

Pascoe Grenfell, Esq. a Member of the Committee; Examined.

ARE you not a director of the Royal Exchange Assurance Company?—I am.

Can you state to the Committee what was the original capital of that company at the time of its institution, and what changes have taken place in the amount of that capital since?—I really cannot state what the original capital was, without reference to the books of the office; but the present capital, that is, capital stock, is 680,000*l.* which is worth, at the present market price, very nearly two millions of money: I beg to add, that the present stock-holders are liable to a call, whenever wanted, that would carry the capital stock to any sum not exceeding a million and a half, and, by reference to the charter, it will be found that the responsibility of the proprietors is not confined to the capital stock respectively held by them, but that they are further individually liable to any demands beyond the amount of such capital stock which the exigencies of the company may require.

Do you mean to state that the proprietors of the stock of the Royal Exchange Assurance Company are responsible, in their individual capacities, for any engage-ments of that company?—For any pecuniary engagements of that company beyond the amount of their capital stock they are.

When you say that the capital of that company, at its present price in the market, would be worth two millions, is not that in consequence of the speculative price people give for a share in what is considered a profitable concern?—It is precisely the same sort of speculation by which bank stock is, at this moment, said to be worth 270*l.*

Can you state to the Committee what the capital, if realized to-morrow, would be really worth?—It is impossible for me to answer that question till I know what will be the event of the risks now running, and to which the Company will be ultimately liable.

Supposing the outstanding risks to be compensated by the premiums paid for them, what, in your opinion, would then be the capital stock of the company, if immediately realized?—I cannot answer that question, without referring to the amount of bank stock and public funds possessed by the Company, and of that I have at present no accurate recollection ; and I also beg leave to add, that I do not conceive it could at all answer the purposes of this investigation to demand of the Royal Exchange Assurance Company a statement of their property, such as I have now described.

The Committee is then to understand that 680,000 *l.* is the extent of what may be properly called their capital?—580,000 *l.* is what is called their capital stock, in addition to which, as I have before stated, the proprietors are liable to an immediate call that would increase the capital stock from 680,000 *l.* to one million and a half; the capital stock of 680,000 *l.* is that upon which a dividend is now made of ten per cent.

In that case, is the Committee to understand that one million and a half would be the security to the public for their insurances with that company, supposing no responsibility to attach to the individual members of it?—I have already stated, that such a responsibility does attach upon the individual members of the corporation.

Do not the company conduct their affairs with a view to the extent of their capital, and in such a manner as not to put them under the necessity, as far as caution can go, of calling upon their proprietors for any thing beyond the nominal amount of their capital?—That is a state of things that has never entered into my contemplation.

Can you state to the Committee the extent of the outstanding risks by the company on lives, and on policies for fire?—I have no distinct knowledge whatever of any claims of that description.

Are not the fire insurances very considerable?—They certainly are.

Is not that the principal branch of the business of the company?—I have not made any such comparison of the several branches of the business of the company, as to be able to give any satisfactory answer to that question.

Do you not know that the life insurances and the fire insurances are each much more considerable than the marine insurances?—If by more considerable is meant greater in amount assured, I should certainly consider that those two branches, namely, the life and fire, exceed that of marine insurances, but to what extent I really cannot positively answer.

OBSERVATIONS,

&c.

—————

MARINE INSURANCE being the main spring of
the great and complicated machinery of commerce, is now well understood to be, especially,
so necessary to foreign trade, as to be justly
considered the vital principle which gives
strength and vigour to its existence, without
whose continual influence it would soon lan-
guish into a decay, that would speedily terminate in its utter destruction.

The investigation of the nature and establishment of the laws which govern so important a
concern, cannot but be well worth the serious
attention of every commercial state.

In England, where foreign trade is interwoven, in a manner, with her political greatness,

B

these must be subjects of superlative importance.

They have, at the present moment, been
brought under the consideration of her legislature, by as bold an attempt at a monopoly, in
favour of the petitioners for the establishment
of a new Marine Insurance Company, as ever
distinguished the reign of monopolies, in earlier
and less enlightened times.

Their petition has been followed by one from
the Globe Fire Insurance Company, for similar
purposes; and both having been referred to a
select Committee of the House of Commons,
appointed to take the state of Marine Insurance into consideration; their report, accompanied by minutes of the evidence which they
have collected, concludes with the following
resolutions.

Resolved, That it is the opinion of this
Committee, that property requiring to be insured against sea and enemies risks, should have
all the security that can be found for it, whether that security exists in chartered companies,
in other companies, or through individuals.

Resolved, That it is the opinion of this
Committee that the exclusive privilege for Marine Insurance of the two chartered companies
should be repealed, saving their charters, and
their powers and privileges, in all other re-

spects, and that leave should be given to bring in a bill for this purpose.

RESOLVED, That it is the opinion of this Committee, that, with respect to the two petitions which have been referred to them, it should be left to the discretion of the petitioners, to bring their respective cases under the consideration of the House, by bills for carrying into effect the prayer of their petitions, if they shall think proper so to do.

These resolutions leave nearly the whole subject to the wisdom of the House.

They encourage, rather than discourage, the object of the petitioners; since a decided opinion is given in the report, in favour of large companies for Marine Insurance, and no other objection is stated, even to their being invested with chartered rights, which must always be, more or less, exclusive rights, than that no one company should have any privileges or exemptions, from which any other company should be excluded.

The first resolution is made, therefore, with a view to legalize companies for Marine Insurance, at present prohibited by the two existing charters.

Should that resolution be adopted by the House, and passed unlimited and unrestrained into a law; it will be attempted to be shewn, that the petitioners will be able to attain the monopoly sought for, almost as effectually as if it had been given to them with all the formality of the charter, with which they hoped to be invested.

The effect of the exclusive privilege of the two existing companies, as it extends only to other companies, has been to throw nearly the whole *legal* business of Marine Insurance into the hands of individuals ; for what appears by the evidence taken by the Committee, to be insured by both these companies together, is so inconsiderable a proportion of the Marine Insurances of the country, as, in a general consideration, to be unworthy of any notice.

These charters have, however, contrary indeed to their intention when granted by the legislature, not only thrown the *legal* business of Marine Insurance into the hands of individuals; but, by precluding them from *legally* insuring in partnership, have thereby produced other important advantages in that business, which were as unforeseen, as they were unintended, when these charters were made into a law.

These advantages, it is proposed briefly to contrast with the disadvantages which must have followed, if the monopoly intended, at the time of their formation, had been secured to the two existing companies, and which must now follow, should the present petitioners be able to carry their plans into effect.

What has been said of many important interests of commerce, "they flourish, not in consequence of the laws made to encourage, to regulate, and support them, but in spite of those laws," may aptly be applied to this subject; for though, indeed, the law, in so far as it intended to give greater security to Marine Insurance, has accomplished its end; yet it has been by means exactly opposite to the expectations of the legislators: while intending to give, to the two existing chartered companies, a great monopoly, it has, in effect, in that branch of trade, utterly destroyed monopoly, to which, as will be shewn, it is in its own nature but too much exposed; and thereby mainly promoted its present flourishing condition.

How far the present petitioners aimed at the erection of a new and more effectual monopoly, by the establishment of *their* new Marine Insurance Company, those who are acquainted with the motives and objects of the framers of the scheme, can have no hesitation in deciding.

They themselves have loudly proclaimed, *as is usual on such occasions,* that their views are directed only to the public good; but when the good of the commonwealth is to be advanced, only along with the private advantage of its promoters, there must always be room for much well-grounded suspicion, whether the ostensible be the real object.

Exclusive privileges in trade, ought to preclude no individual from the equal pursuit of its advantages, in a well regulated state, and, as infringements of natural liberty, must be viewed, by every enlightened statesman of a free one, with peculiar jealousy. The establishment of such, at this day, will naturally, therefore, require to be justified by some very powerful and preponderating considerations,

The exclusive privileges demanded in their petition, it is generally understood, the new Marine Insurance Company have abandoned their unjust pretensions to be openly invested with. Maturer consideration has shewn them, what their over eagerness at first prevented them from seeing, the inconsistency, and even the absurdity, of asking in one breath, exclusive privileges to be taken from two existing companies, and, in the next, to be conferred upon themselves. It has not escaped the sagacity of these petitioners, however, that if the second resolution of the Committee shall obtain the force of law, it will remove the insurmountable barrier which the existing law opposes to them; and, by breaking it down, will enable them, almost as effectually to accomplish their scheme, as if they had been formally erected into a chartered company for the purposes of it: not indeed, by means of exclusive privileges, sanctioned by public law, but by a combination, which would then no longer be unlawful; that will enable them effectually to monopolize a half, or three-fourths, and to forestall nearly the whole of the Marine Insurances of Great Britain, and consequently to destroy the whole of the present system, and all its advantages to the state, together with the capital, and multitude of individuals embarked in it.

What are the facilities that would enable them to accomplish such a scheme will be shewn hereafter.

These petitioners are, therefore, straining every nerve without the doors of the House of Commons, to influence those within, to give the Resolution of the Committee, that force.

How great, soever, may be the probable benefits of such a law, which, with due limitation, may, in some degree, promote the security, facility, and economy of Marine Insurance, the only objects the legislature *can* have in view; all its consequences ought cautiously to be weighed, and deeply investigated, when its enactment is so eagerly supported, by men, who may be more than suspected of indirect views, from their sudden abandonment of pretensions so lately insisted upon.

Though, as it is generally understood, the petitioners have withdrawn, or do intend silently and prudently to withdraw, their unjust pretensions from the scrutinizing eye of the legislature; it may yet fairly be concluded, from their anxiety to have the resolution of the Committee, which has been the result of their application, passed into a law, that they have not abandoned their designs.

The Report of the Committee is, certainly, very favorable to their views : a few observations will hereafter be made on it, that may materially alter the complexion it gives to the subject. In the first place, as the Committee have been entirely silent, as to any probable dangers there might be in granting the prayer of the petitions, it may not be thought improper to make a slight inquiry into some of them, and to endeavour to ascertain, how much or how little nearer, the petitioners will be able to reach the accomplishment of their ends by the repeal of the law, recommended by the Committee, for which they so industriously seek support.

The general reasoning against monopolies is become trite, and is so well understood, that a word need not be wasted on the subject.

It is a nicer and more undecided question, whether there may not be some branches of trade, which, from their very nature require, that those who embark in them should be invested with extraordinary privileges.

These are all, more or less, monopolies, because, extraordinary privileges must always be, more or less, *exclusive privileges.* It is against the danger of their becoming entirely such, that the legislature have anxiously to guard in granting them.

What are the branches of trade that require such aid, it would be useless here to investigate farther, than as Marine Insurance may or may not be one of those branches.

The Committee having in their Report quoted the opinion of Dr. Smith, in favor of joint stock companies, for Marine Insurance, and accused the learned author of mistake, it may not be improper, or unacceptable to the reader, to have his memory refreshed by a few extracts, as short as the sense and connection will permit, from the chapter from which the quotation is taken.

The subject cannot be better elucidated, and the reader will be able to decide with what fairness the learned author is accused of error.

The article will be found in the 1st chap. of the 3d. volume of the Wealth of Nations, and is,

Of the public Works and Institutions which are necessary for facilitating particular Branches of Commerce.

In the beginning of the article the author remarks, that, '' in order to facilitate some par-

ticular branches of commerce, particular institutions are necessary.   The protection of trade in
general has always been considered as essential
to the defence of the commonwealth, and upon
that account a necessary part of the duty of the
executive power.   The protection of any particular branch is a part of the general protection
of trade ; a part, therefore, of the duty of that
power." He then proceeds to observe, that in
the greater part of the commercial states of Europe, particular companies of merchants have
had the address to persuade the legislature, not
only to invest them with exclusive privileges,
but even to entrust them with the duty of the
sovereign, and all the powers which are necessarily connected with it.—"These companies,"
he continues, "though they may, perhaps, have
been useful for the first introduction of some
branches of commerce, by making, at their own
expence, an experiment, which the state might
not think it prudent to make, have in the long
run proved universally either burdensome or
useless, and have either mismanaged or confined
the trade."

The learned author next describes particularly
several different companies of merchants that
now exist, or have existed, in Great Britain, dividing them into two classes, "Regulated Companies, and Joint Stock Companies. " These

companies, he says, sometimes have, and sometimes have not, exclusive privileges.

What is said of regulated companies is here omitted, as inapplicable to the present subject.

"Joint Stock Companies, established either by royal charter, or by act of parliament, differ in several respects, not only from regulated companies, but from private copartneries.

"First. In a private copartnery, no partner without the consent of the company, can transfer his share to another person, or introduce a new member into the company : each member, however, may, upon proper warning, withdraw from the copartnery, and demand payment from them of his share of the common stock. In a joint stock company, on the contrary, no member can demand payment of his share from the company ; but each member can, without their consent, transfer his share to another person, and thereby introduce a new member. The value of a share in a joint stock is always the price which it will bring in the market; and this may be either greater or less, in any proportion, than the sum which its owner stands credited for in the stock of the company.

"Secondly. In a private copartnery, each partner is bound for the debts contracted by the company to the whole extent of his fortune.

"In a joint stock company, on the contrary,

3

each partner is bound only to the extent of his share.

"The trade of a joint stock company is always managed by a court of directors. This court, indeed, is frequently subject, in many respects, to the control of a general court of proprietors.

"But the greater part of these proprietors seldom pretend to understand any thing of the business of the company; and when the spirit of faction does not happen to prevail among them, give themselves no trouble about it, but receive contentedly such half yearly or yearly dividend, as the directors think proper to make to them. This total exemption from trouble and from risk, beyond a limited sum, encourages many people to become adventurers in joint stock companies, who would, upon no account, hazard their fortunes in any private copartnery. Such companies, therefore, commonly draw to themselves much greater stocks than any private copartnery can boast of. The trading stock of the South Sea Company, at one time, amounted to upwards of thirty-three millions eight hundred thousand pounds. The divided capital of the Bank of England amounts, at present, to ten millions seven hundred and eighty thousand pounds. The directors of such companies, however, being the managers rather of other peoples' money than their own, it cannot well be expected, that they should watch over it with the same anxious vigilance, with which the partners in a private copartnery frequently watch over their own. Like the stewards of a rich man, they are apt to consider attention to small matters as not for their master's honor, and very easily give themselves a dispensation from having it. Negligence and profusion, therefore, must always prevail, more or less, in the management of the affairs of such companies. It is upon this account that joint stock companies for foreign trade have seldom been able to maintain the competion against private adventurers. They have, accordingly, very seldom succeeded without an exclusive privilege; and frequently have not succeeded with one. Without an exclusive privilege they have commonly mismanaged the trade, with an exclusive privilege, they have both mismanaged and confined it.

The only trades which it seems possible for a joint stock company to carry on successfully, without an exclusive privilege, are those of which all the operations are capable of being reduced to what is called a routine, or to such a uniformity of method as admits of little or no variation.

"Of this kind is, first, the banking trade; secondly, the trade of insurance from fire, and from sea risk and capture in time of war; thirdly, the trade of making and maintaining a navigable cut or canal; and fourthly, the similar trade of bringing water for the supply of a great city.

The value of the risk, either from fire, or from loss by sea, or by capture, though, it cannot, perhaps, be calculated very exactly, admits, however, of such a gross estimation as renders it, in some degree, reducible to strict rule and method. The trade of insurance, therefore, may be carried on successfully by a joint stock company, without any exclusive privilege.

" Neither the London Assurance, nor the Royal Exchange Assurance, Companies, have any such privileges."

"*To establish a joint stock company, however, for any undertaking, merely because such a company might be capable of managing it successfully, or to exempt a particular set of dealers from some of the general laws which take place among all their neighbours, merely because they might be capable of thriving, if they had such an exemption, would certainly not be reasonable.* To render such an establishment perfectly reasonable, with the circumstance of being reducible to strict rule and method, two other circumstances ought to concur. First, it ought to appear with the clearest evidence, that the undertaking is of greater and of more general utility than the greater part of common trades;

and secondly, that it requires a greater capital than can easily be collected in a private copartnery. If a moderate capital were sufficient, the great utility of the undertaking would not be a sufficient reason for establishing a joint stock company; because, in this case, the demand for what it was to produce would readily and easily be supplied by private adventurers. In the four trades above-mentioned both these circumstances concur.

"The trade of insurance gives great security to the fortunes of private people, and by dividing among a great many, that loss that would ruin an individual, makes it fall light and easy upon the whole society. In order to give this security, however, it is necessary that the insurers should have a very large capital. Before the establishment of the two joint stock companies for insurance, in London, a list, it is said, was laid before the attorney-general, of one hundred and fifty private insurers who had failed in the course of a few years."

The term joint stock company, as used by Dr. Smith, it must be observed, means always a company whose members, by some charter, or act of incorporation, having the force of public law, are secured from being liable for their debts beyond the share of each in the joint stock; by far the most important privilege of such companies where they have none that are exclusive.

Without an express provision to the contrary, sanctioned by law, the whole fortune of the members of every mercantile copartnery, is liable for the transactions and debts of the partnership.

Except in the trade of a banker, any number of individuals may unite in private copartnery; although it is not an uncommon mistake among merchants, that the Bank Act, passed in the year 1720, which prescribed to bankers a limitation of partners to the number of six, in order to secure a great monopoly to the Bank of England, extends also to other branches of commerce.

In all other common or lawful trades, any number of individuals may associate in a partnership; they may agree to set apart each only a portion of his fortune for the purposes of the concern, and may, if they think proper, commit the management of it to a court of directors; they may also agree to allow any proprietor, with the consent of tnat court, to sell or transfer his share of the joint stock, and thereby introduce a new member without consulting with the rest, but in all such associations every individual member is liable in all respects as in a common private copartnery.

Such joint stock companies, unsanctioned, and therefore unprotected, by any public law, have greatly multiplied in the present day: of these some farther notice shall be taken hereafter, as bubbles affording no permanent security to the public, and fraught with great danger to the fortunes of their constituents.

The law, when it authorizes the formation of any joint stock company, may, or may not, invest the members of it with the privilege of excluding all other individuals or companies from dealing in the same branch of trade. Such exclusive privilege is now enjoyed by the East India Company, and was, as Dr. Smith observes, formerly enjoyed by the South Sea, Royal African, and Hudson's Bay Companies. Such exclusive privilege has also been conferred on the East and West India Dock and other companies of modern creation.

With what fairness the Committee of the House of Commons accuse the learned author of having fallen into an error, in stating that the London and Royal Exchange Assurance Companies have no *such* exclusive privilege, may be left to the candid reader to determine. It is somewhat odd, however, that by a singular inconsistency, the report of the Committee should itself afford the best proof of the accuracy of the learned author, by shewing nearly the whole business of

c

the Marine Insurances of Great Britain to be; in fact, transacted *exclusive of those companies.*

They have, indeed, an exclusive privilege against other *companies* for Marine Insurance, which is but one branch of their trade; but this circumstance, since their general business was open like all other trades, and even this branch was open to every individual in the nation, Dr. Smith, in treating of insurance in general did not, perhaps, think worthy of particular notice.

When exclusive privileges are demanded of the legislature by any joint stock company, however speciously the grounds of such demands may be stated, they are almost universally, in truth, mere pretexts for securing to themselves some exorbitant power or profit. In granting exclusive privileges, it is, perhaps, impossible to prevent an undue exercise of power; but in later years, when it has been deemed expedient to grant such, as in the case of the East and West India Dock and many other companies, the profits have been limited not to exceed some reasonable fixed rate upon the capital embarked by the company, to prevent the evil inseparable from leaving profits which must be paid by the public, to be measured only by the reasonableness and moderation of those who are to receive them.

All that ought, perhaps, to be done by the legislature in sanctioning a joint stock company, is on behalf of the company, to indemnify the members from being liable for the debts farther than each for his share of the joint stock, and on behalf both of the company and of the public, to enable them to sue and be sued in the name of their governor, or other officer, or some small number of directors.

Though the legislature, in granting such to any joint stock company, does not apparently grant any exclusive privileges, either against individuals, private copartneries, or other joint stock companies; yet in conferring such privileges only, it gives great and manifest advantages to the members of the company, both over individuals and private copartneries, by exempting them from some important general laws which govern the commonwealth.

It is of the utmost importance, therefore, not only that all the circumstances which can alone render the establishment of joint stock companies in any particular branch of trade at all reasonable should concur; but also that the legislature, in giving its sanction to their formation, should anxiously guard against the danger of the extraordinary privileges which it may be proper or necessary to grant to any of them, becoming altogether exclusive privileges, although such may not be inserted in their act of

incorporation, and may even be quite contrary
to the intention of the legislature.

The particular branches of trade for the management of which joint stock companies can
reasonably be established, are of necessity in
their nature such as to be very ill-suited to the
enterprize of individuals or private copartneries.

As the joint stock companies that might
be incorporated in such branches of trade,
would naturally, all together, enjoy the exclusive privilege or monopoly of them, the number to be established in each branch would,
therefore, be a consideration of the highest importance.

If, for example, an act of incorporation
should be granted to a Marine Insurance Company, whose members should be composed of
three-fourths of the principal merchants of
London ; or if these merchants could legally
form themselves into a joint stock partnership
without any act of incorporation, the remaining
one-fourth would, as individuals or private copartneries, labour under so great disadvantages,
compared with such a company, as to be altogether unable to maintain the unequal contest
against capital and influence. To enable
them to insure on the same terms for their
foreign correspondents, they would themselves be obliged to have recourse to the

company, who would soon thus obtain the monopoly of London, which will be shewn hereafter to be the monopoly of the whole country.

Of the four trades mentioned by Dr. Smith as the only ones for the management of which the establishment of joint stock companies can be reasonable, the third and fourth, the making and maintaining a navigable cut or canal, and the supply of a large city with water, are evidently trades peculiarly suited to joint stock companies: they are, however, of local importance, and can be carried on only to a limited extent. It is evident, that when a canal is once cut, or a town once supplied with water, the joint stock companies to which these concerns belong must virtually enjoy a monopoly of them. The legislature accordingly, of late years, since canals and towns have so multiplied and improved, have almost invariably found it expedient to fix some limitation of profits on the capital embarked in such undertakings.

The first and second trades; those of bankers and insurers, are of general, and therefore of much higher, importance.

The trade of bankers has flourished without the aid of joint stock companies, and though restrained by the limitation of partners to the number of six, has reached a high degree of perfection throughout the whole country.

Six partners are rather more than any prudent man cares to be engaged with in ordinary trades, and accordingly very few private copartneries consist of more than three or four. Whether the limitation of six partners in the trade of bankers, by increasing their number, and thereby the competition among them, has been of advantage or disadvantage to that trade, and to the public; or whether the establishment of a number of well-regulated joint stock companies would carry it to a still higher degree of perfection, is foreign to the present subject to inquire.

In the trade of insurance, the remaining one mentioned by Dr. Smith, as possessing the requisite of being reducible to a routine, to fit it for the *successful management* of a joint stock company, and in which the circumstances of being of greater utility than the greater part of common trades, and of requiring a greater capital than can easily be collected into a private copartnery, concur to make the establishment of such a company in that trade *reasonable,* he includes Marine Insurance under the head of 'Insurance in general.'

The vast increase of the commerce of this country since the learned author's work was published, has given a practical knowledge of, and thrown lights upon the trade of, Marine Insurance, as well as upon commerce in general, which it cannot be too deeply regretted that great man has not lived to receive. It requires all these to overcome the reverence due to the least of his opinions, and the weight of his authority even in a matter so slightly touched upon in his enlightened "Inquiry."

It has, however, been practically demonstrated, that in the trade of Marine Insurance, with the circumstance of being certainly of greater utility than, perhaps, any other trade, the other circumstance of requiring a larger capital than can easily be collected into a private copartnery, which the learned author says should appear with the *clearest evidence* to make the establishment of a joint stock company in any trade *reasonable*, does not concur. By the evidence taken by the Committee, it appears in the clearest manner, that the trade of Marine Insurance has been carried, with the commerce of the country, to the unparalleled extent it has now reached, not only without the aid of the capital of joint stock companies, but without even the *legal* aid of that of private copartneries. It may be safely averred too, that it is now carried on at the lowest expence consistent with a reasonable profit for the labour and risk of those who are engaged in it, and with the maintenance of the capital set apart, in the general distribntion of stock, for the support of this branch of trade.

In the midst of a destructive and protracted war, the premiums of insurance, on all established and regular trades, very little exceed the rate of them in times of the most profound peace, and seem, indeed, by the great competition among the present insurers, to be incapable of any further reduction.

The New Marine Insurance Company may, at the same time, boldly be challenged to produce to the Attorney General, instead of a list of 150 names, any list of names, of private insurers, worthy of consideration, who have failed within the last few years.

If practical experience, since Dr. Smith lived, has demonstrated the absence of the most material circumstance necessary to make the establishment of a Joint Stock Company for Marine Insurance at all *reasonable*, so a little reflection will shew, that, in times of war especially, and yet more particularly in the wars against commerce that are now waged, it is not reducible to such a routine, or uniformity of method, as he states to be the first and indispensible requisite to adapt any branch of trade, even to the *successful management* of a Joint Stock Company.

In times of such war, all the activity, vigi-

lance, and sagacity of a great number of the
most observing and inquiring individuals, all
anxious for their several interests, has not been
found more than is requisite for the successful
management of the business of Marine Insurance; the premiums whereof vary from day to
day, not only with the seasons, but with all the
varying relations between Great Britain and
foreign powers, and between foreign powers
with each other; with the disposition and success of fleets and armies, and with the greater
or less protection afforded to commerce, they
vary with the force, quality, and nation of the
ship. An insurer duly weighs all the shades
of difference in the risk between a ship built of
English oak, or of American cedar or pine;—
between a ship navigated by the hardy, bold,
and skilful British seaman; by the Portuguese
or Italian; or by the feeble and helpless Las-
car. The body of insurers in London, accordingly have established a correspondence with all
the nations, and almost every principal maritime
place in the world, which they daily expose to
public view in rooms set apart for that purpose,
at their own expence. They maintain an
active correspondence with the Admiralty,
both to receive and give information, when
and where protection is wanted for our own
or for the trade of friendly powers, and

upon the general state of relations at sea.
They have established, in all the principal sea-
ports of the kingdom, surveyors, who examine
into, and report the age, state, and condition
of every ship at each time of entry or departure.

Where all this vigilance and activity are necessary in any business, it seems little capable of
being reduced to a routine, and accordingly
the existing chartered companies have, in a manner, abandoned the pursuit of it. Whether such
vigilance and activity could or would be equally
exerted, by one, or a small number of joint
stock companies; or whether, if equally exerted, their results might not, instead of being
fairly brought forward to the public view, and
used for its benefit, be converted to the private
advantage of such companies, may easily be
conjectured. The number of insurers interested
who contribute to this sort of information alone,
secures its publicity; but as almost every considerable merchant, in order to obtain access
to such a body of information, subscribes to the
establishment of the insurers at Lloyds, that
publicity is further insured even beyond
the possibility of concealment.

Premiums of insurance, not only vary with all
these, and many other varying circumstances,
they vary also with the profit afforded by them
upon the whole from year to year. If the profits of

insurers be insufficient to yield a reasonable recompence for their skill and labor, and to maintain the capital set apart for that branch of trade
in any particular year; or should the business of
two or three years together, as it sometimes
happens, terminate in loss, premiums upon every
description of risk rise, so as to afford them that
reasonable and necessary recompence.

The trade of insurance, as mentioned by Dr.
Smith, naturally divides itself into two parts;—
Marine Insurance and Insurance of Houses and
other fixed property from fire. There is another
sort of insurance not mentioned by the learned
author, the Insurance of Lives, and a trade similar to it, the Purchase and Sale of Annuities.

In the trade of Insurance of Houses from fire,
and these other last mentioned trades, besides
their having all the requisites which fit them for
the successful management of joint stock companies, and that render the establishment of
such companies, for the business of them, perfectly reasonable. There is another important
circumstance also not noticed by the learned
author, and that is the length of their contracts
—of the time necessary for the accomplishment
of each single transaction. This circumstance
operates in two ways.

First. By so delaying the issue, and consequently
the ascertainment of the profit and loss of their

undertakings, as altogether to unfit them for the enterprise of individuals, or common private copartneries, and accordingly none have embarked in them.

And secondly, By so prolonging the credit necessary to be given, as to preclude individuals, owing to the great uncertainty of the continuance of their security, from dealing with one another, or with common private copartneries, in those trades.

They are, however, all of great importance and utility, and since they cannot be undertaken, or the dealers in them safely relied on, except when conducted by larger associations than ordinary private copartneries, it seems extremely desirable that joint stock companies should be authorized for the necessary and excellent objects of them.

These joint stock companies, though they need by no means be invested with any exclusive privileges, require the attention of the legislature to their regulation and security.

It is evident that the nature of things precludes individuals from dealing with one another in all these trades. No prudent man, for example, would insure a hundred pounds, on a house against fire, for a year, for two shillings, which is the common premium, because he could not, by his individual influence, procure a sufficient number of insurances to pay for a single loss: neither would any judicious person accept his security, because, the uncertainty alone of finding an individual insurer, who may be removed by a thousand accidents, or death itself, would give great insecurity to such a contract.

Well constituted joint stock companies alone, therefore, whose security is unaffected by the uncertainty of the affairs of individuals, and whose permanence prevails against the certainty of their deaths, seem calculated to answer the purposes of those trades.

All that need be required of the legislature, however, is not a decree of monopoly, or any *exclusive* privilege, to any one or any number of these companies, but a power to combine in larger copartneries than would otherwise be prudent, freed from the risk of loss beyond the share of each individual member in the joint stock. The very nature of these trades will give to all the joint stock companies together, engaged in any one of them, a monopoly, since the business is unsuited to the enterprise of individuals, or private copartneries. The points of greatest importance for the consideration of the legislature in establishing such companies, are

First, That no one company should be permitted to be so large as to prevent a sufficient number of them being appointed, so as to produce a com-

petition among them, that should insure their
accepting the lowest rate of profit consistent
with a reasonable advantage on their respective
capitals ; and

Secondly, That their security and stability
should be so ascertained, as to insure to the public, the objects for which they may have been
created.

The best proof of such security would be the
deposit of their capital under legislative inspection.   Without a protection to the members that
they should not be liable, farther than each for
his share of the joint stock, no prudent man
would embark in such a company, for as
only a few can be directors and managers,
though he might, in the hope of profit risk
some part, he never would consent to risk the
whole of his fortune being taken out of his own
immediate control.   In the event of some great
national calamities, moreover, such as pestilence,
against a Life Insurance, or the conflagration of
a great town against a Fire Insurance Company,
the weight of the calamity would be highly aggravated by the ruin of all the members of these
companies, which would probably ensue if the
whole property of the individuals embarked
in them were liable.

The internal regulation of such Joint Stock
Companies might, perhaps, be very safely left

to themselves. How far it might be expedient, to have these regulations embodied in the act of the legislature authorizing their formation, is unnecessary here to be inquired into.

For insurance against fire, every great town might have a joint stock company for itself and the surrounding villages and country, and for the insurance of lives and purchase and sale of annuities every considerable county.

The case is widely different with respect to Marine Insurances, though of vital importance to a country, where, as in England, foreign commerce has become in a manner necessary to her political existence; and though the trade in *them*, therefore, must be more deeply interesting than in fire or life assurance, to every member of the state, it cannot be equally diffused amongst them; it must be confined to few principal maritime cities. In York, Manchester, Birmingham, or Nottingham, a Marine Insurance probably never was effected. These, though some of the chief cities of the empire, furnishing an immense quantity of the most important exports, and working from the raw material, and otherwise consuming, a no less important quantity of imports are, by their situation in the interior of the country, precluded from dealing in Marine Insurances, which require to be conducted in sea-ports, where the earliest intelligence of nautical adventures naturally arrives.

Owners of ships, residing in sea-ports, prefer to insure on the scene of their business.

The maritime cities, which possess the advantages of situation and of access, naturally obtain a superiority in foreign trade.

London, above all, from its peculiar advantages in these respects, being the metropolis of the empire, the residence of the court and nobility, one of the largest and most populous cities in Europe; but particularly from the operation of public commercial regulations and revenue laws, which draw to it *exclusively* the whole of the East India, and a great proportion of many other important branches of foreign trade, possesses such a pre-eminence over all the other maritime cities of Great Britain, that her market for Marine Insurance regulates that of the whole country: London, together with a very few other maritime cities, effects the whole of the Marine Insurances of the British Empire. These places, therefore, by the nature of things, and the force of commercial laws and regulations, enjoy a monopoly of that trade against all the rest of the country.

The impolicy of increasing this natural monopoly by the erection of joint stock companies in all, or any of these cities, but especially in London, whose market governs all the rest must therefore be apparent. That London does govern

all the market, and in effect, herself alone enjoy a monopoly of Marine Insurance, is demonstrated by the Report of the Committee,
which shews that nearly the whole duty on the
policies of Marine Insurance, collected in Great
Britain, is paid by London alone.*

In this situation of things, amid such facility
and temptation, it is surprising that the merchants of London, who are well aware of the
opportunity afforded them, have not made
more frequent attempts to obtain charters from
the legislature, for securing this natural monopoly
to their own body. That they have not so attempted oftener, and that they have perceived
all their address would have been insufficient
to persuade the legislature, to confirm to them
directly the monopoly aimed at by the late scheme,
is one of the unforeseen benefits for which
we are indebted to those charters themselves;
by prohibiting all partnership in the trade
of Marine Iñsurance, though they have not
in effect, as will be shewn, been able to
prevent private copartneries, they have effec-

---

* The exact proportion cannot be stated as the distributors
of stamps in the country, do not distinguish the amount of
policy duty in their remittances. In 1809, £.317,290, was
collected at the office in Lombard Street, established for the
convenience of Lloyd's Coffee-House, and in all Great
Britain as far as the account can be made up, £.348,592.

D

tually kept down and prevented such associations, or friendly societies of merchants, for the
purpose of openly carrying on that trade, as have
sprung up in the trades of insurance of lives,
and from fire, and the purchase and sale of annuities. A society of that sort, established for
Marine Insurance, would be so notoriously illegal, that no person would publicly deal with
it, even if the existing companies should not
oppose such an infringement of their privileges.
The charters, besides, having thrown the whole
legal business into the hands of individuals, they
have become so numerous, that the merchants
have seen little hopes of prevailing against the
natural opposition of so formidable and respectable a body, who have to contend against such
attempts for their very existence in the state.

The charter of the Royal Exchange and London Assurance Companies, though it gives them
by law an exclusive privilege against other
companies for Marine Insurance, does not confer any such privilege for the insurance of lives
or from fire, or for the purchase and sale of
annuities. To have granted an exclusive privilege only against other *companies*, in those which
are the chief branches of their trade, since it has
been shewn they are unsuited to the enterprise
of individuals or private copartneries, would

have alone secured to them the monopoly of the whole country.

The great utility of those trades have, however, made them practically necessary, though the attention of the legislature has not been excited by any attempts to obtain exclusive privileges for the exercise of them. The project would be too bold and the object too manifest, to give such a scheme any chance of success. Their very great utility, however, has given rise to a great number of associations larger than private co-partneries; in London, especially, these have of late years wonderfully increased. These, as they are almost universally formed without any legislative sanction, and, therefore, without any legislative scrutiny, afford a very different sort of security to the public, from what would be given by a number of well-regulated joint stock companies, having that sanction, established throughout the country.

Such associations being subject to no legislative supervision, make rules and regulations for themselves, and having erected themselves into a sort of mock joint stock company, delude the public with splendid descriptions of their capital and security, though these are in fact, in most cases, of the most diminutive and slender description.

One thousand shares are arranged on a list

of £.1000 each, making an amount of one million; these are taken in greater or less numbers by, perhaps, five hundred persons, who set forth that they have established a company for insurance of lives, or against fire, or for the purchase and sale of annuities, with a capital of ONE MILLION.

This capital, however, is never set apart for the security of the public, sometimes one per cent., scarcely ever more than ten per cent., is so set apart and invested in the funds, or some public security for the payment of directors and clerks, and for the general purposes of the business. Taking five per cent. or one-twentieth part of each share, as the sum set apart, at that rate, upon a million, would amount to £.50,000. Each subscriber pays his five per cent. on his share or shares, and is held liable, for the remaining ninety five per cent. or nineteen twentieths in case they may be wanted.

How much, or how little, such a company differs from one with a capital of £.50,000, must depend, not only upon the ability of each subscriber to pay the whole of his subscription, which may almost universally be questioned; but, also, upon the continuance of his ability to pay the remaining nineteen-twentieths, for which he is only *held liable:* this ability the public have no means of ascertaining. It is sufficiently evident, however, that they remain in his possession, subject to all the fluctuations of circumstances, and reverses of fortune, to which mercantile men, who form the chief part of these associations, are liable. It is equally evi-. dent that many of these subscribers do become bankrupts, or fail, without ever making good the remainder of their subscriptions.

But besides that important consideration, when, by the death alone of the original subscribers, their property becomes divided among their heirs or successors; the security of the association must be very much impaired, and when the whole property has once changed hands, which, in the very nature of things, must, in no very long period of time, be the case, the original security is altogether lost.

The sum paid for the purchase of any of these shares will, of course, be only the same as the deposit, made by the original proprietor, with, perhaps, some premium or deduction, according to the more or less flourishing condition of the concern; but as the premium, if any, goes into the pocket of the first proprietor, or his representative, not to the funds of the association; when such a transfer has taken place, there ceases to be the shadow of security that the new proprietors possess one shilling beyond what they have each paid for their shares.

Finally, then, such an association is changed

into a company, whose boasted million has
dwindled to one-tenth, or one-twentieth, or
one-hundredth part of the sum.

Thus, however magnificent these schemes may
at first be made to appear, it is quite plain they
partake very much of the nature of bubbles of
a very empty kind, affording no permanent security in the estimation of any man accustomed to take a large and extensive view of
things.

As such associations cannot be sued in any
corporate capacity, the public have no sufficient
legal hold upon their members; when the original shares have all been once sold, it would
not be a very easy matter to prove the partnership of any individual; for though these societies do open books, and transfer their shares, as
if they were legal joint stock companies, the
public are, perhaps, little aware that every such
transfer, by the introduction of a new member,
creates a new partnership. The directors and
clerks have only to withdraw with the books and
lists when such an association comes to be ruined, and leave the public the possession of their
gaudy, but empty office, as the sole indemnity
for the losses entailed upon it.

Insufficient and unsatisfactory as those associations are, when a large and extensive view of
them is taken, their first formation being gen-

erally supported by opulent and creditable mer-, chants, whose honourable intentions may be unquestionable, they have drawn to themselves a very considerable trade. Even those who are aware of their insecurity, prefer the chance of their honour and stability to being altogether without the benefit of their trade.

How much more beneficial and solid would be joint stock companies, protected by the legislature, and having given security by public deposit of their capital, is a subject well worthy of its attention. It is foreign to the business in hand to inquire how far it would be conducive to the public advantage, to bring the associations, now existing, under the eye of the legislature; and to suppress, by law, such as are unwilling, or in other words, unable to give such security.

How magnificently soever the new proposed Marine Insurance Company have vaunted their boasted capital of FIVE MILLIONS, every mercantile man in London knows it was intended to be no other than just such a bubble as has been described. If the legislature had compelled them, could it have been possible it should have granted them a charter, to make a public deposit of their capital? any one acquainted with the names which fill the scheme lists of this proposed company, will smile when he observes

those that now grace these lists, which such
an enactment would cause to vanish from
their pages.

The trades of insurance of lives against fire,
and of the purchase and sale of annuities, have
been enlarged upon as having a certain affinity
to the trade of Marine Insurance.

If it has been successfully shewn that this last
trade does not possess the requisite of being reducible to a routine, to fit it for the *successful
management* of a joint stock company; and that
the circumstance of requiring a greater capital
than can be easily collected in a private copartnery is also wanting, to render the establishment
of such a company in that trade *reasonable:* so
it will, on examination, be seen that the other
circumstance, not mentioned by Dr. Smith, the
time occupied in each separate transaction,
which renders these other trades unfit for the
enterprise of individuals or private copartneries,
is not of a length to have such disqualifying
effects upon the trade of Marine Insurance.

The duration of the *risk,* or of each separate
adventure of an insurer, and the length of time
the assured incurs the hazard of his stability, are
both shorter than in the greater part of ordinary
trades.

The bodies of ships are seldom insured for
time, during war; and when they are, the law,
imposing the stamp duty on insurances, prohi-

bits their being insured for longer than a year to secure the renewal of that duty. In time of war, when premiums are high, the bodies of ships, or the freight money, are seldom insured for double voyages; that is, out and home. The assured must give, for a double voyage, a double premium, the whole of which would be lost to him should the ship perish, or be taken, on the outward voyage; he naturally, therefore, prefers to insure for a single voyage.

Goods, from their nature, can very seldom be insured but for a single voyage, from some one country or quarter of the world to some other.

The voyage to the Baltic; the bottom of the Mediterranean; the West Indies; South and North America; the Newfoundland Fishery; Africa, as far as the Cape of Good Hope; does not out and home, on an average, exceed, at the longest, 6 or 8 months; and the termination of the outward voyage is generally heard of in little more than half that time. The voyage to ports in the Mediterranean nearer the Streights of Gibraltar; to France and Spain without them; to Portugal; to Holland, and ports of the North Sea without the Baltic; does not exceed half the period of 6 or 8 months. It is on these voyages that almost the whole insurances of private merchants have to be made.

The longest voyages which are insured are those to the East Indies and back; but, as the

East India Company never insures, these bear but a small proportion to the whole insurances of the country: even on these, the duration of the risk, or the length of time the merchant runs the risk of the stability of the underwriter, does not exceed 18 months, or at the most 20 months, for the double, and half that time for the single voyage.

The longest of these times does not exceed the length of the credit the merchant receives, from his clothier, his ironmonger, or any other of his tradesmen; as the credit he receives for the very merchandize insured. Taking the average length of the voyages altogether, it does not exceed one-half, or one-third, of the usual length of that credit. Practically, moreover, the merchant is often indebted to the underwriter, on which debt he has a lien for any loss. The underwriter too, though he does not receive his premium often for years, invariably pays his loss within one month after adjustment, in ready money, whereby his stability is almost daily put to a very strict test.

The duration of the risk, therefore, as it does not preclude individuals from ascertaining the issue of each transaction as soon, or rather sooner, than in the greater number of ordinary trades, cannot be a circumstance to render the establishment of a joint stock company for Ma-

rine Insurance *necessary*; and the length of the
risk, of the stability of the underwriter, not
exceeding one-half, or one-third, of the usual
length of mercantile credit, cannot be a circumstance to render the establishment of such a
company *reasonable.*

The tradesman or manufacturer, besides,
gives an absolute credit to the amount of the
goods supplied to the merchant, while the merchant to the underwriter only gives credit for a
probable loss; the chances against which must
obviously be greatly in favor of the merchant,
if the average of premiums be 5 per cent. it must
be a hundred to five in his favor.

The credit for this probable debt must be very
unreasonably objected to by the merchant, for
3, 6, or 8 months, who is himself taking an absolute credit for the very thing insured for 12 or 18
months; at the same time he exacts from the
underwriter payment of his losses at the end of
a month after adjustment, while, if there be no
loss, he seldom pays him the premium for 18
months, or even longer.

If there are, sometimes, failures among underwriters, as in other trades, no one will hesitate
to conclude, when their mode of dealing is
considered, that they must be much fewer, and
of less calamitous extent, than among merchants,
who are not subjected to such tests, and who,

by the longer credit they obtain from the tradesman and manufacturer, and even from the underwriter, are enabled to, and generally do, carry on their trade for a long period after they are absolutely ruined.

The existing charters, besides by limiting the *legal* trade of underwriting to individuals only, have produced another very important effect. They have precluded those persons who devote their whole time and capital to underwriting, the benefit of the statute of bankruptcy. The merchant has thus the advantage of holding liable the property an underwriter may, after having failed, acquire in all his future life. If underwriters are involved in bankruptcy, therefore, their bankruptcy must be the effect of their dealings as *merchants*, and not as *underwriters*.

From this circumstance, no judgment can be formed of the comparative failures among merchants and underwriters; but it is said, by persons conversant with the subject, and partly appears by the evidence taken by the Committee, that, whenever an underwriter has been involved as a partner in the bankruptcy of a mercantile firm, his estate has always given a better dividend to his separate creditors, than any of the mercantile partners; from which it may fairly be inferred, that the underwriting partner's transactions was not the occasion of their mercantile destruction.

Persons, who have taken some pains to inquire into the matter, have asserted, that on investigation, it appears, that for the last 15 years, the failures, even among bankers, who fail much seldomer than merchants, have been 1 in 7, and among underwriters 1 in 101.

No stress, however, can be laid upon a statement the truth of which cannot be ascertained. Whatever may have been the necessity at the time of granting them for the charters to the existing companies, on account of the failure of underwriters, there cannot be the least foundation for a new charter upon that ground now; for whatever may be the exact proportion of failures of underwriters compared to merchants, there cannot be the smallest doubt, that, upon the whole, the comparison is very much in favor of the underwriters; these last cannot too loudly call upon the merchants of the New Marine Insurance Company, who talk rather at large in their evidence on that head, for *a list of names*, like the 150 produced to the Attorney General, when these existing charters were granted.

To erect, in the trade of a Marine Insurance, a joint stock company of merchants, who would so be exempted from the general laws which take place with respect to other insurers, would be more unjust than to erect a joint stock company in any of the branches of the trade of merchants; because, insurers being already prevented from legally associating in private copartneries, and from the benefit of the statute of bankruptcy, are already thereby excluded from these important privileges of their neighbours.

If the duration of the risk, and consequent length of time the assured incurs the hazard of the stability of the assurer, afford no *reasonable* ground for establishing joint stock companies, in the trade of Marine Assurance, as little does the value of the things to be insured.

The value of ship, freight, and cargo of a West Indiaman, or vessel engaged in the South American trade, does not exceed from £20,000 to £60,000; these are of much greater value than ships engaged in the European or North American, or any other, except the East India trade. As the East India Company never insures; the ship, freight, and private trade of an East Indiaman, which are obly to be insured, does not exceed the value of from £50,000 to £100,000. Let the largest of these sums be divided among, only, five hundred underwriters, probably not near half of the number at Lloyd's (many underwriters insuring by procuration for two or three other persons'), and it would not furnish a risk of

£200 each on an average. Few judicious underwriters of the first rate, for practical prudential reasons, exceed £1000 on one vessel on the best risk, £1500, perhaps £2000, on an Indiaman; and on such a risk a small underwriter seldom exceeds £100, or £200, or £300, or £400, on an Indiaman.

The value of the things to be insured, therefore is evidently quite suitable to the power of the individual insurers, which the demand of the market of insurance has provided ; and quite consistent with the perfect security of the merchant.

If, indeed, there were practically much less facility than exists; of insuring sums of £150,000, or £200,000, it might, in sound policy, be wiser to diminish that facility, than to increase it by the establishment of a joint stock company, supposing it would have that effect. Facility in insuring such vast sums on one ship, encourages the building and use of large vessels, which is politically unsafe, diminishes the number of seamen, incurs greater danger in the narrow seas around England, occasions a heavier misfortune in case of loss, and enables merchants to make, at one operation, an adventure to one market of such magnitude, as that a loss of only ten, or fifteen per cent. upon it may at once ruin them, besides spoiling the market for

merchants of more prudence. It is the opinion
of many sensible persons, that it would be a
wise law which prohibited the building of any
merchant vessel above the size of 400, or 500
tons.

As the matter now stands for £.20,000, or
£.50,000, on a capital West India, or Brazil ship,
sufficient insurers may be found in, perhaps, less
than as many minutes. If the ship be indifferent,
it may take a longer time, because underwriters insure less sums upon such ships; but, if the ship be
even very indifferent or old, the business, though
a work of more time and labour to the broker,
is still always to be done. It may be remarked,
that large sums are, or at least *ought*, only to be
insured on fine ships ; and on these, brokers
will almost never permit underwriters to insure
any excessive sum, because they are anxious to
divide such a risk among all their underwriters,
to encourage them, and support their accounts
against risks of a more indifferent nature.

If half the underwriters at Lloyd's, who it
must be remembered are *necessarily* the insurers
of the whole country, be sufficient to insure at a
risk of only £.200 each, £.100,000; nearly
double the value of the richest West Indian, or
South American trader, which are by far the
most valuable of any merchant ships, except
East India, that go to sea; the security of that

insurance is greatly enhanced by this circumstance; that the law does, by the charters of the existing companies, prohibit private copartneries in the trade of Marine Insurance; yet, as that law never is or can be enforced (except in cases of bankruptcy, when partnership ceases to be of much consequence) that underwriters do unite in private copartneries, and insure upon the capital of, and share the profit with such copartneries, is a fact so notorious, that to every merchant in London, the bare mention of it suffices for its proof. Two thirds, perhaps three fourths, of the underwriters at Lloyd's, insure upon the capital of some private copartnery.

Instead of the trade of Marine Insurance being supported then, as the report of the Committee would make it appear, by 1400, or 1500, individuals at Lloyd's, considering that some of them insure by procuration for two or three others, and those connected in private copartneries, it is in fact supported by, perhaps, four or five times that number: they form quite as respectable a body as the Exchange adjoining to them exhibits; and that they carry on their branch of trade, with all the economy consistent with its maintenance and security, is sufficiently demonstrated by the rate of premiums of insurance, which, in the midst of the implacable war now waged against the commerce of the country, does not,

in all regular and established trades, much exceed what it is in times of profound peace.

These observations may, perhaps, be thought
by the impartial reader, conclusive proofs of
the sufficiency of the present system of Marine
Insurance, and of the injustice and impolicy of
erecting in that trade a joint stock company;
for though (in the words of the learned author
quoted by the Committee) it might be capable of thriving, to except one particular set of
dealers from the general laws which take place
with regard to their neighbours, merely because
they would be *capable of thriving*, would certainly not be reasonable.

Among the brokers at Lloyd's, there are few
whose business does not run in some particular
trade, such as, the West India, North or
South American, the Baltic, &c. &c.

Should a large Marine Insurance Company
be established, there can be little doubt that it
would soon be divided into departments; there
would be a magnificent building, with halls
and anti-rooms, with offices, superscribed in
letters of gold, The Mediterranean, The West
Indies, The Baltic, &c. In each of these might be
seen a little oligarchy of merchants, engaged in
every one of those different branches of trade,
(since they would be the best judges of these several risks) for directors and managers. Is it not

obvious how inconsistent all this would be with the enterprise of individuals? As, in insurance, all questions in explanation of the risk must be answered, if a merchant have a new scheme or adventure, he must declare it to this little oligarchy in his own branch of trade, who might obstruct his insurance, and hasten to the market of his enterprise and discovery before him.

This consideration would alone be an insuperable objection to a joint stock company of merchant insurers, even were equal or greater security and facility afforded by it.

London, as has been already shewn, enjoys from its natural advantages, public laws, and commercial regulations, a monopoly of the trade of Marine Insurance; to grant then a charter of incorporation to its merchants, through whose hands all orders for insurance *must* pass, would be infallibly to secure to them one of the most perfect monopolies that can easily be imagined.

As to the security that would be afforded by such a company, when contrasted with what is afforded under the present system, the superiority of the latter is apparent.

The capital of an underwriter is of two sorts ; his capital of money, or property convertible into money, and his capital of premiums.

Although the underwriter when he subscribes

the policy, gives a receipt for the premium, the law so requiring, he does not, in point of fact, then receive that premium; he charges it in an account against the broker, and is, by usage, not entitled to demand any of the premiums he has insured for, till the end of the year. He is then only to receive the difference between the amount of them, and the losses, averages, and returns he may have settled to the broker in the course of that year. The broker gives a similar credit to the merchant, for whom he is responsible. These credits are, however, merely nominal; in point of fact, the underwriter seldom or never calls upon the broker, for reasons that will be explained hereafter, for a year and a half, often not for two years, which enables the broker to give a proportionable credit to the merchant.

If an underwriter meets with a loss, his account is balanced with the broker upon the day the loss is publicly known at Lloyd's, and he pays in ready money, *one month after adjustment*, whatever may be due for the loss. The solvency of an underwriter is, therefore, put to the test upon every loss which brings a balance against him: this may happen to a principal underwriter once in a week, and subjects him to sudden and unexpected calls for money. His money capital, therefore, he invests in public, or other available securities, to be ready to meet such calls; his capital of premiums remains in the hands of the merchant, and is drawn upon through the broker, for the expences and management of his business, the maintenance of his family, or the increase of his money capital, when his insurances are successful.

An estimate of the money capital of the underwriters and brokers (who must also be able to command capital) at Lloyd's, would be as difficult, uncertain, and probably as fallacious, as an estimate of the money capital of the merchants on the Exchange which it overlooks. Their capitals are besides a good deal intermixed; many of the merchants on the exchange, however illegal the practice may be, while they are negociating their business in the square below, have a partner or agent assiduously engaged for them in the rooms of the insurers above.

To become an extensive underwriter requires, as may be seen from the manner the business is conducted, an extensive capital. Underwriters and insurance brokers, like merchants and other brokers are, however, as often those, who from small beginnings advance themselves, by the aid of industry and frugality, those ancient handmaids of fortune, to wealth and prosperity, as those who have commenced with great capitals; but great fortunes among underwriters and brokers are less frequently amassed, and are seldom so exaggerated as among merchants; a proof, that in their trades, the profit is not so immoderate as in the trade of a merchant.

The capital of premiums, may more easily be estimated. If the number of underwriters be taken at 600, whose capital of premiums is £30,000 each (sinking all the number above 600, this will, by practical men, be known to be rather an under than over estimate) that will give a capital of 18 millions. Besides this capital of premiums, there is to support it, the money capital of all the underwriters, and to support the machinery of the business, the money capital of all the brokers. Sinking the number of underwriters and brokers above 1000, it must be a calculation much below the truth, when the actual aid of private copartneries is considered, to take that capital at £6000 each, that will give a money capital of 6 millions. With respect to security then, how great must be the difference between the magnificent, but airy, 5 millions of the proposed New Marine Insurance Company, and the real substantial capital of the Insurers of Lloyd's, who, be it always remembered, are, by the monopoly of London, the insurers of the empire, and almost of the world.

What must have been the difference between this real and substantial capital; the stock set apart in the general distribution of commercial stock for the maintenance of this branch of business, and the 5 or 10 per cent. upon those airy 5 millions.

The more that the system of Marine Insurance of England is examined, it will afford to the patriot the greater satisfaction, and inspire the legislator with a salutary caution in giving sanction to new laws, whose enactment is urged by those who wished to overthrow this system for their private emolument.

If the merchants of London, by the passing of the 2d Resolution of the Committee, unlimited and unrestrained, into a law, should be enabled to form themselves into a large joint stock association, such as has been described, they would soon monopolize the whole Marine Insurances of that city.

It is more than probable that they would then manage the business ill, and finally destroy it. Besides extinguishing from the state two important classes of individuals, with the stock it is their business to set apart, in the general distribution of commercial stock, for the maintenance of this, by far the most important of all trades, they would probably so lower the premiums as to destroy themselves.

If, after a few successful years, such an association should have so lowered the rate of premiums, as to afford only the interest of their
capital (which in the New Marine Insurance
scheme would have required no great amount)
and the payment of their directors and clerks;
and *then*, such a calamity as the capture of a
whole fleet, or the seizure of all the ships of one
nation, in the ports of another, become hostile,
a loss, perhaps, of three or four millions of
money should be incurred, it is plain that that
loss must be drawn from their *mercantile capital:*
for the capital set apart for such an accident,
which it has been shewn, now remains, practically, in the hands of the merchants themselves,
being extinguished, with the thousands of individuals whose business it was to maintain it—
recourse can no more be had to its aid.

What would be the difference of a company
with even 20 per cent. upon 5 millions, or
1 million of capital, drawing upon *their* funds
for the loss of a fleet of West Indiamen of only
200 sail, at only £20,000 each, or 4 millions;
and the insurers of London drawing that loss on
18 millions of capital in premiums, in the hands
of the merchants, and 6 millions of capital in
money, in their own hands, need not be enlarged upon.

That such a company would be likely to make

such an end, is much more than probable. The Committee in their Report, indeed, themselves say, that if merchants were allowed to be their own insurers the premium would, probably, not *much* exceed the aggregate value of the losses on each class of risks. It will hereafter be shewn, that it does not exceed that value at present, more than is barely sufficient to maintain the capital set apart for the trade, and to afford a reasonable profit to the maintenance of the individuals who wield it. If that shall be successfully shewn, it will remain for the merchants to shew the justice and policy of a law that would enable them to take that profit from those individuals, in order to bestow it on themselves.

With respect to facility in effecting Marine Insurances, in all probability it would be much lessened by such a company. There is no likelihood that in three or four directors would be found all the variety of opinion of risks, and competition for premiums, that is found among eight hundred or a thousand contending insurers at Lloyd's. There is as little probability that there would be equal facility of settlement of average or loss, where, perhaps, one mind is to judge of the justice or reasonableness of the demand, as where many are judges; or, if recourse to law be necessary, where the wealth of a company, as where the purses of a few private and divided underwriters, are to be engaged in the contest, from which much cost is inseparable. As to *usage*, that could only arise and prevail according to the pleasure of the company ; it would, therefore, be always in their favour.

The effect of the existing law having, by the charters, prevented the merchants from securing the natural monopoly of London to their own body, and, having thrown the business into the hands of individuals, has been then, to occasion a three-fold division of labour in the trade of Marine Insurance;—the merchant, the insurer or underwriter, and the insurance broker.

It is the province of the merchant, to supply the demands of all the known markets of the world, and to discover new ones ;—to maintain the exchange of the surplus, produce, and manufactures of his own, with that of other countries;—to establish factories abroad;—to manage his correspondence ;—to watch his credit;—to husband his resourses and to furnish to the grower and manufacturer new schemes of improvement and invention: by these, and a thousand other important considerations, his whole mind is occupied.

It is the province of the underwriter, to relieve him from the perils of the policy of insurance, to which his whole attention is directed : he has to watch the voyage, the quality of the ship, the more or less perishable nature of the goods, the perils of the seasons in all the regions, and the political relations of all the nations of the earth.

From all these, and many other important considerations, the mind of the merchant is almost entirely relieved; for though he has to consider the political relations of his own country, with the nations wherewith he trades; yet, these receive from him a much slighter consideration than from the underwriter. By the policy, his merchandize is conducted, free from all perils, across the ocean, and until safely landed in its port of destination.

Where goods may be safely landed, they are likely to remain safe. A strong practical proof, how little merchants embarrass their thoughts with this most important consideration, is given by their having, almost universally, insisted, since trade has become so insecure on the continent of Europe from the dominion of arbitrary power, on having their policies of insurance extended to the peril of seizure, during the passage of their merchandize from the ship to the warehouse of the consignee, where, once deposited, what little remains of law and usage on that Continent serves, even yet, almost uniformly to secure it from any farther risk of confiscation. The merchant has only to find markets for his trade; the underwriter conveys it through the channels to them.

It is the province of the broker, to arrange and settle between these two parties, the price of these perils; he frequents the counting-house of the merchant, and the market of the insurer; and he maintains the contest between them, which cánnot be so conveniently done by the merchant himself. It is the business of the broker too, to have all the knowledge of the underwriter; he is acquainted with all the minutiæ of the trade; the ship, the goods, and all the perils of the voyage; these he can discuss in detail, with a readiness and facility unattainable by a merchant, whose thoughts must be directed to his general undertakings; the broker ascertains for him, in an open market full of insurers, all anxious for business, the lowest rate at which the perils of his policy can be undertaken. He is thus more necessary to the merchant than to the insurer; being the agent of the former, it is *his* interest which he maintains, and for him he makes himself responsible to the underwriter, for the amount of his premiums. The merchant ought, therefore, to be the pay-master of the broker; but how the compensation for his skill, capital, and labour, is practically ascertained, shall be shewn hereafter.

Two sets of labourers, besides the merchant,

are thus employed and supported. The merchant is obliged, for his own advantage, to furnish them with the profits of their trade, and thus to increase the industrious population, the commercial prosperity, and the wealth of the country.

It has been already observed, that London, from the local advantages of her situation, and from existing laws and commercial regulations, enjoys an almost exclusive monopoly of the Marine Insurances of Great Britain, in other words, almost of the whole world. In this metropolis, therefore, these two classes of insurers have grown into consideration, and some of them into wealth and importance; with their clerks, connexions in partnership, and dependents, they form a commercial body of many thousand individuals.

Her merchants, through whose hands all orders for insurances must pass, perceiving that in order to carry on their trade, they must necessarily, set apart in the general distribution of mercantile profit, which flows from the public, the fountain of all profit, first, *always*, through their hands, a portion for the maintenance of insurers, would be glad, though they do not complain of the insufficiency of their present share in that general distribution, to increase it by appropriating to themselves the profit of insurers also. To be insurers, they have themselves, individually, neither spare capital, time, nor, under the existing laws, ability; but the monopoly enjoyed by the metropolis, has already brought the business of Marine Insurance into so narrow a compass, that her merchants see it would be easy to secure the whole profits of that trade to themselves, if they could by address, persuade the legislature, to invest them, or allow them to invest themselves, with the exclusive privilege of dealing in it. They would then be able to overcome the present insurmountable obstacles, to such views, and, by appointing a committee of a few, to secure these profits to their own body.

The legislature is too enlightened, not to know how prejudicial the success of such an attempt would be to the general interests of commerce, and consequently to our national prosperity; and could merchants see with the impartial eyes of statesmen, it would not be difficult for them to perceive, that its success would not be consistent even with their own interest.

The cause, notwithstanding, of the anxiety of the late petitioners for The New Marine Insurance Company to influence the legislature to pass the seemingly just, equitable, and reasonable law, founded on the resolution of the Committee, and now under consideration of Parliament, in place of the proposed chartered monopoly, which has been so silently withdrawn from its scrutinizing eye, *may arise* from the opportunity, they cannot but have the penetration to perceive will thereby be afforded to them, of carrying their intended monopoly almost as completely into effect, by means of a *mock* joint stock company, as if they had obtained the direct sanction of the legislature to the formation of a *real* one.

Should such a company, then, by the abrogation of the present law, become legal, there is every reason, from that very anxiety, to expect it would be formed. It would be widely different in its effects from the mock joint stock companies already described as existing, for insurance against fire or of lives. These companies have no more employment than the public may be induced to give them, from a confidence in their security and honour, or, than they can draw to themselves by the magnificent promise of their advertisements, the number of their hand-bills, and the style of their placards; but, with respect to Marine Insurances, as the members of such an association would be the very persons, the *only persons*, who have insurances to effect, and through whose hands all orders for insurance must pass, the case is widely different.

Whatever may be the expediency of leaving
all things relating to trade in their free and natural state, a point on which all enlightened
statesmen are agreed, there can be no doubt that
when, by the operation of laws and of commercial regulations, trade has been diverted from its
natural channels, and directed or accumulated,
by the force of those laws and regulations, in
any particular manner, or in any particular
place, that other laws and other regulations
must be made, to counteract the evils that must
inevitably follow the first disturbance of that
natural freedom.

The law of the charters of the two existing
companies, though they themselves have sunk
into utter insignificance, has existed nearly
a hundred years undisturbed; has produced,
and is the corner stone of the present system
of Marine Insurance, upon which a great
fabric of commercial laws and usages relating to
that important branch of trade, has been raised.

The passing of the law now under the consideration of parliament, without limitation or
restriction, must be at the risk of shaking that
fabric to its very foundation.

The framers of the law of these charters, indeed, did not foresee its effects. Like the famous Act of Navigation, which, though passed
merely from a spirit of hostility to the Dutch,

has yet, in its effects, been one of the chief means of our naval superiority, of our dominion over the seas, and of our commercial prosperity: so these charters, though intending only to give a monopoly, have in effect, prevented that monopoly of Marine Insurances, which natural circumstances, heightened by commercial laws and regulations, would have enabled the merchants of London to secure to themselves.

If the legislature shall think fit, and that it would be for the advancement of the security, facility, and economy of Marine Insurances, to bring to their aid the *legal* support of private copartneries, by giving its sanction to a division of profits and loss, which does, in point of fact, take place, and which might be attended with some other practical advantages; it will in its wisdom, doubtless, at the same time, guard against the danger of opening the door to a monopoly, that would destroy the whole system, which it has required the experience of a century to bring to its present state of perfection, together with the capital or store, set apart in the general distribution of commercial stock, for its business; and the thousands of individuals that wield and depend upon that capital, who, since they manage a business, without which the foreign commerce of the country could not

F

exist for a year, must form an important member of the body of the state.

The Committee of the House of Commons have taken a very different view of the state of Marine Insurances, from what has been given in the preceding pages. If some of the members of the New Marine Insurance Company had been permitted to draw a report to promote the scheme of a mock joint stock company, it could not have been more favourable to their views, nor could they have better exerted their mercantile address to prevail upon the other members of the Committee to coincide in their deductions.

The facts stated in this hasty tract, and its very opposite reasoning from that of the Committee, renders it unnecessary to follow their Report very closely in the observations to be made upon it.

The first division of it, "On the nature of the exclusive privilege conferred on the Royal Exchange and London Assurance Companies, and the manner and extent of its exercise," may shortly be summed up in this.

That they have an exclusive privilege, against other *companies*, for Marine Insurance; but, having themselves sunk into utter insignificance in that branch of trade, the manner of their exercising it is utterly unworthy of any notice.

That their exclusive privilege, though of little value to themselves, has had a most important effect, in preventing the monopoly of Marine Insurance, enjoyed by the city of London, from being converted by its merchants to their own purposes, at great hazard to themselves, and the risk of preventing the growth of that branch of trade.

That by that important and salutary effect, it has raised and fostered two classes of industrious and thriving individuals, who would otherwise never have existed in the commercial state, and an immense capital for the maintenance of this branch of trade, *itself the foundation of foreign trade*, which would otherwise never have been accumulated for its support, and been equally without existence in the commercial capital of the country.

That they have, therefore, produced, though unforeseen by the legislature, those very effects which its wisdom would have been exerted to produce, by other apparently more direct, but perhaps less effectual, means.

The real motives which induced the legislature to pass the law confirming these charters, no longer exist.

By the improvements of practice, merchant do not now *pay* insurers, " the consideration monies for insurances," until the risks are de-

termined, and often have large securities consisting of such consideration monies in their
hands, to indemnify them in case of the failure
of underwriters.

"Failures" are now so rare, that no list of
names can be produced of any that have happened of late years, worthy of consideration;
and no instance can be produced of any merchant who has been "ruined or impoverished,"
by such failure of insurers.

The Committee, though they treat of the
nature and exercise, do not inquire into the
origin of these charters, though they say, "the
intention of the legislature in granting them has
been defeated." The time of granting them
was during the reign of the South Sea Bubble,
when a sort of infatuation for schemes prevailed
throughout England. The following account,
taken from a description of that Bubble, may
not prove unacceptable to the reader.

"It appeared, by an inquiry of the House of
Commons, in February preceding, that this hu-
mour of new projects or bubbles had been on
foot for about two years past; as also appeared
by a petition in January 1718, for a charter for
insuring ships and merchandize, signed by near
three hundred merchants and gentlemen, and
that a million of money had been previously
subscribed for it. That another petition about

the same time, for a grand fishery company was signed by seven peers of the realm, and many merchants and gentlemen. A third petition was, in May, 1719, by the societies of the city of London for the mines royal, the mineral and battery works, under certain obsolete charters of queen Elizabeth and James I. for mines, &c. for a like patent to insure ships and merchandize, for which £1,152,000 had been subscribed. These were, in reality, the same persons as those in the first petition : they petitioned a third time, on the 8th of January, 1720, only as so many private gentlemen and merchants, dropping their claim by the obsolete charters, and were in the end successful by their present name of the Royal Exchange Assuránce Company; its capital consisting of £500,000. That same day another body of petitioners applied for a patent for insuring ships and merchandize, with a subscription of two millions, and were incorporated by the name of the London Assurance Company. The act for incorporation was accompanied by a proclamation, strictly forbidding all such schemes or projects for raising money, in consequence of which it might have been expected that they would all have ceased. For a few days, indeed, some check was given to them; yet, in the face of all authority it soon revived, and even increased more than ever. From morning till evening the dealers in them, as well as in South Sea stock, appeared in continual crowds all over Exchange-Alley, so as to choak up the passage through it. Not a day passed without fresh projects recommended by pompous advertisments in all the newspapers, directing where to subscribe to them. On some, sixpence per cent. was paid down; on others, one shilling per cent., and some came so low as one shilling per thousand, at the time of subscribing. Some of the obscure keepers of those books of subscription, contenting themselves with what they had got in the forenoon by the subscriptions of one or two millions, were not to be found in the afternoon of the same day, the room they had hired being shut up, and they and their subscription-books never heard of more. On others of those projects, 2s. 6d. per cent. was paid down; and on some few 10s. per cent. was deposited; being such as had some person of known credit to usher them into the alley. Some were divided into shares, instead of hundreds and thousands, upon each of which so much was paid down, and for them there were printed receipts signed by persons utterly unknown.

" Persons of quality of both sexes were deeply engaged in these bubbles, avarice prevailing over all considerations of either dignity or equity; the males coming to taverns and coffee-houses to meet their brokers, and the

ladies to the shops of milliners and haberdash-
ers for the same ends. Any impudent imposter
whilst the delusion was at its height, needed
only to hire a room at some coffee-house, or
other house near the Alley, for a few hours, and
open a subscription-book, for somewhat relative
to commerce, manufacture, plantation, or of some
supposed invention, having first advertised it in
the newspapers the preceding day, and he might
in a few hours find subscribers for one or two
millions of imaginary stock.

" The infatuation was at length so strong,
that one project was in the newspapers, advertised thus : ' For subscribing two millions to a
certain promising or profitable design which will
be hereafter promulgated.' The very advertisments of these bubbles, were so many as to fill
up two or three sheets of paper in the daily
newspapers for some months. Yet, all men
were not infatuated: and one advertisment in a
weekly newspaper well enough burlesqued the
prevailing madness of men in the following
strain: ' At a certain (sham) place, on Tues-
day next, books will be opened for a subscription of two millions, for the invention of melt-
ing down saw-dust and chips, and casting them
into clean deal boards, without cracks or
knots !"

Whether a like infatuation now prevails in the
minds of any of the late petitioners for the New

Marine Insurance Company, need not be inquired into; but if, from this description, it appears, that it was an attempt to cure the mania which then prevailed, as well with respect to insurance, as other schemes, which induced the legislature of those days to confirm the charters of the existing companies it may, perhaps, however contrary to the opinion of the Committee, be safely asserted, that, with the aid of other important laws since made relative to the trade of insurance, the intentions of the legislature *have* been fulfilled.

Long subsequent to that time, wager policies were lawful, and so ill-governed was the practice of Insurers, that a broker would sometimes insure a ship without any order or interest, and when the merchant wanted a real insurance, would sell him the policy for a profit; but by the important Act of 14 Geo. II. prohibiting and rendering void insurances where there is not a real interest; by the law prohibiting the insurance of enemies' property; and by the prevalence of a great body of commercial law, as applied to Marine Insurances; that business may now be truly said to be as respectably conducted as, perhaps, the nature of things will admit in any business, and that instances of fraud in Lloyd's Coffee House are full as rare, in proportion, as among merchants.

The calculation of the Committee of sums

that *might* have been insured last year, is very fanciful. No doubt those sums *might* have been insured, *had there been orders for so doing.*

As the calculation is quite an imaginary one, no time need be wasted on its consideration. If the Committee mean, that a proportion of all but half of the property required to be insured in the last year, went uninsured, the evidence proves directly the contrary; for all the insurances that were ordered were effected, excepting a stray order or two, unworthy of notice.

On the second division of the Report, "The effect of the exclusive privilege upon Marine Insurance, and the state and means of effecting Marine Insurances in this country," much has been already said. The Committee observe, that Lloyd's Coffee House has a monopoly of the trade of insurance; but it has so no more than the Exchange has a monopoly of the trade of merchants.

London has the monopoly of Marine Insurances, and her insurers must assemble somewhere. The only difference between their assembly, and that of the merchants, is, that as *their* business cannot be transacted in the open air, they are obliged to pay the "Gresham Committee," for the use of part of the same structure, which, by the munificence of its founder, the merchants frequent free of any expence; and that they do not admit within its walls any person without a certificate of character—a precaution which merchants cannot take with respect to their own body. Any respectable merchant, and all the partners of a firm, may be insurers, and may by one partner, or a deputy, having a procuration, insure at Lloyd's, (which is as open to such as the Exchange,) as much as they please, or as much as their capital and connection can procure them.

They can only insure by deputy in a *company*.

"The first merchants," says the Report, "do not and *cannot* attend Lloyd's Coffee House." *If* they cannot attend the Exchange of Insurance, which only a flight of steps separates from their own, it may be asked, how these "first merchants" can or will be able to attend a *company* where its office can be more conveniently situated? or how it is to diminish the MONOPOLY of Lloyd's, except by transferring it to itself.

Though individuals are prevented from *legally* associating in partnership in the trade of insurance, it has been frequently observed, that they do in fact associate, and that, perhaps, the greater number of the insurers of London have partners with whom they divide the risk and profit of the business. That circumstance, and the conveniences mentioned by the Committee, may be sufficient reasons for rendering legal a division of profits, that does in point of fact take place. The effects of doing so without limitation or restriction, need not be farther dwelt upon.

The circumstance of some underwriters absenting themselves from their market during the autumn months, is dwelt on by the Committee as occasioning a necessity of giving an extravagant premium to those who remain. Not to dwell *here,* upon the improbability of men absenting themselves at a time when extravagant premiums, in other words, extravagant profits, are to be had: or on the discolouration given by the Report to the length of these occasional absences; the fact is, that in the autumn months premiums begin to rise, till they double and treble, or increase yet more, from the change of the season. It may very safely be asserted, that if all the underwriters were brought back at that season, premiums would not be a shade lower. The principal underwriters too, generally leave a deputy to insure for them. The contest between merchants and insurers then runs high, but ends, almost uniformly, in favour of the merchant; for it is a common remark among underwriters, that the business of the autumn months is generally attended with loss. Insurances are then, as at

other times, always to be done, an assertion
completely confirmed by the evidence taken
by the Committee.

The value of the things to be insured in these
months, the Committee may be thought, by
practical men, to have over-rated. All ships
sailing from the West Indies before the first of
August, may be insured, without exception, to
any amount a ship can carry, at a regular premium of 3 per cent. with convoy ; from Jamaica
4 per cent. Ships that sail before the 1st. of
August are four-fifths of the trade. Any ship to
any amount she can carry may he insured *out* to
those colonies, at all seasons, for a regular premium of 3 per cent. with convoy. East India
risks, in regular ships, do not vary at all.
These instances may suffice to shew the height-
ening of the Report.

It is easy to prove, that in the last five months
of the last year, the *whole business* of the country,
as may be seen by the account of exports and
imports, increased suddenly in a much greater
proportion than was ever known. On the
fairness of the Committee's, having produced
the accounts of a single underwriter, as a proof
of their statement, and as a light to the House
of Commons, it may be remarked ; that there is
no purpose which the particular accounts of
some one underwriter might not be found to

suit. The increase of the general trade of the country would be more than sufficient to account for the increase the account exhibited, which, like all other underwriters' accounts, is governed by the judgment, or even by the caprice of the individual.

As London enjoys the monopoly of the insurances of the kingdom, the laws which are wholesome for her, ought to govern the outports.

The Committee observe, that a Company consisting of the owners of 83 transports, insured the sea risk for each other, and that their averages and *losses* came *last year* to one and one-quarter per cent. The Committee do not give an average of several years. It must be pretty plain, however, that, if there were many averages, there could not be *one loss*, since one and one-quarter per cent. on 83, would little more than pay for one loss. It seems not a little partial to state the charge for *one* year, and that too before the accounts were made up, or the averages could be ascertained. It may be asked too, what would be the consequence if these 83 transports, *the property of* 70 *or* 80 *individuals,* had been gathered together in one fleet and lost, other than the probable ruin of the whole of their owners? Or where such a number of ownres of transports can be collected, except in *London !*

The same observation applies to the other society of 80 to 84 members, insuring 100 ships,
which must also be a *London* society. The
Committee state, that these persons insured each
other, at *an expence*, for last year of five and a
half per cent. : but the person who gives evidence, states, that the *losses* were not yet half
ascertained; and it is very ambiguous from his
evidence, whether he does not mean that the
losses alone, came to five and a half per cent.
Every person acquainted with the business of
insurance, knows, that averages are, upon the
whole, full as heavy a charge as losses against
insurers, if not heavier.

From the manner the evidence is stated by
the person, who furnishes the Committee with
evidence of the existence of clubs in the country, it seems very uncertain whether these clubs
be any thing more than *The Lloyd's* of the
place. For he says each member puts his name
on the policy, and is liable for no more than
the amount set against it.

These statements of the Committee are such
leaps to conclusions, from such evidence, that
it cannot but seem a little strange how they
have come to be made.

The third and last division of the Report,
" Of the Importance of a better System to the
Commerce and Revenue of the Empire, and to

the Parties concerned," contains a still more extraordinary partiality of statement. Indeed, if the Report be meant to be a summary of the evidence and to guide the House of Commons, there is a downright suppression of a fact. In this division the Committee state the superiority in their opinion, of *Companies* for Marine Iusurance. They state there were 36 companies at Hambro' two at Stockholm, one at Gottenburg, and five at Copenhagen, and enumerate a great many in America.

Of the nature of these Companies there is no account· The consul of the Swedish nation, however, states in his evidence to the Committee, that there is but one company at Stockholm, whose business cannot be of great extent; and that of the 36 at Hambro', there are not above five or six remaining; *some have not found it worth while to go on, and others have failed and have paid from four to fifteen shillings in the pound*. Whatever may have been the cause of these failures, the suppression of the fact in the Report gives a very different feature to the case. To have inserted it would have, indeed, been rather an *odd ground,* for the favour entertained towards *companies* by the Committee.

The Report states, that " what gives the *best* insurance at the cheapest rate is the enabling

merchants to insure one another." In which
case, the *Assured* becomes the *Assurer*. It may,
however, by parliament, be thought a wiser
and better mode of insurance, to separate these
two characters, which the monopoly of London
already too much confounds, as much as the
operation of laws can produce that effect : and
to make insurance a division of labour, with a
separate capital set apart by the labourers in it,
for the maintenance of their branch of trade.

By that policy, existence must be given to
a larger industrious population, and to a larger
commercial capital, than would otherwise arise;
than if the merchants of London enjoying the
monopoly almost of the world, were to insure
one another, and extinguish that division of
labour, merely to engross profits, of which
their present share, already, too much inclines
to excess.

It has been the business of these pages to
shew, that the law of the two existing charters,
impotent of producing a monopoly to the persons who possess them, has corrected the monopoly, in this branch of trade, enjoyed by London, to the utmost; by prohibiting the association of the merchants who enjoy that monopoly, even to the number of two; and has produced that division of labour and accumulation

of capital, which, most probably, would otherwise never have been engaged in that branch of
trade, and the enactment of the law, recommended by the Committee, *may* pull down that
system, and dry up a great fountain of our
national wealth and prosperity.

If merchants were to insure one another; as
their connexions, acquaintances, and their mercantile knowledge too, are generally confined to
their own branch of trade; they would, if permitted, naturally form companies in each branch
What would, it may be asked then, be the effect
of a company of West India or Jamaica Merchants, insuring fleets of ships in their own
trade, insuring their own goods and ships, which
very much resembles no insurance at all? If one
of those fleets should be lost or taken, instead
of having, as now, recourse to insurers, and the
capital, it is their business to set apart for the
maintenance of their trade, and being fully indemnified for such a loss, which *has* happened,
they would, in all probability, be utterly ruined,
and involve a numerous body of industrious
creditors in their general destruction.

With respect to the cheapness of Marine Insurances;—it is brought by the present system
with all its machinery, at least, as far as respects
the underwriter, to as great economy, as perhaps it is capable of. It is an assertion that

G

may easily be proved, that underwriters do not receive for gross profit, taking an average of successful and unsuccessful years, more than fifteen shillings per cent. upon all the sums insured by them; or, in the language of the Committee, " the price paid for insurance does not exceed the aggregate value of all the losses, and averages" by more than fifteen shillings per cent. By that profit all the insurers, their clerks, and dependants, and the capital set apart for the maintenance of the trade, are to be supported.   If the eighty-three transports, the sea risk of which costs 1 ½ per cent. and the ninety coasters, whose insurance cost as far as the account could be made up 5 ¼ per cent, and all the insurances of all the clubs in Great Britain were to. be thrown in, at the usual premiums, it would not alter this general rate of profit, one penny, perhaps not one farthing, in the hundred pounds.

A merchant, for handing an order for insurance to his broker, receives a *profit* of ten shillings in the £100; the broker, who merely sells the goods when arrived, receives always ten shillings, sometimes twenty shillings, in the £100, for selling them; and the merchant receives fifty shillings per cent. more for his management.   If it be true then, that after all the perils of seas, fire, thieves, and the enemy, no more than fifteen shillings per cent. remain to the underwriter for all his risk, capital, and anxiety; it is not very easy to suppose how HIS trade can be farther economized. It would not be difficult, however, to point out where, if greater economy in foreign trade is necessary, it might be more successfully practised.

The Committee state, as a proof of the difficulty in effecting of Marine Insurance, that the *brokers* receive one fourth part of the total profits on *underwriting*. This is rather a confusion of terms, but the meaning of the Committee may be gathered more distinctly, when, as a proof of the want of economy in the present system, they state, that the brokerage is *equal* to one fourth of the underwriter's profits. If the rate of these has been truly stated, at fifteen shillings in the £100, one fourth of that rate may not be thought exorbitant for the brokers. But the Committee do not state, that the *profits* of the broker, are equal to one fourth of the profits of the underwriter; though they seem rather to insinuate that meaning. Out of the *brokerage,* which in the gross, may exceed one fourth of the profits of underwriting, the broker has to maintain his counting-house establishment, and to indemnify himself for the losses he sustains by the failure of merchants, and for the advances which he is obliged to make to them, which are both often and very considerable.

Insurance brokers, different from all other brokers, must, by making themselves liable for the merchant, be *dealers in insurances*; their brokerage, therefore, which in the gross, may be, on an average, equal to eight or even ten shillings in the £100), can by no means be accounted as their profit, which is, in fact, greatly under that proportion.   A broker who *sells* goods, receives sometimes twenty, never less than ten shillings in the £100, without any risk of the solvency of the merchant; but, whatever may be the rate of insurance brokers' profits, it is a rate fixed by the merchants themselves, and settled in a manner, that gives colour to the ingenious, but not, on the part of the *mercantile* members of the Committee, very ingenuous statement of the report.

It has been already shewn, that the merchant ought to be the pay master of his agent the broker; but how that matter is really arranged, shall now be described.—

When a merchant receives an order for insurance, he hands it over to his broker, and charges 10*s*. per cent. to his correspondent abroad, for "effecting" it. It is then agreed between the merchant and broker, that whatever be the rate of premium, the latter shall have one shilling in the pound on it, for his skill and trouble, and for being answerable for the merchant: his brokerage thus increases with the risk of that reponsibility.

In order to enable the merchant to retain the whole of these ten shillings per cent. which is the proper fund from which the broker *ought* to be paid, it is agreed between the merchant and him, that the underwriter shall not be permitted to charge, in his account against the broker, the whole premium inserted in the policy, but a sum less by one shilling in the pound. If the premium, for instance, be ten guineas, the underwriter charges the broker with ten pounds, but gives a receipt in the policy for ten guineas, which the broker charges in full to the merchant, and the merchant, increased by the ten shillings for "effecting," to his foreign correspondent, at whose expence the broker's commission is thus arranged.

When a broker pays an underwriter any balance that may be due to him, he deducts 12 per cent. from the amount. Underwriters, therefore, delay calling upon brokers till a great many risks are expired, almost never sooner than for a year and a half, often two years, in order to save that discount, which they do not have to pay should losses turn the balance in favour

of the broker. The fear of the loss of this 12
per cent. on the balances, keeps them longer
due to the underwriters, in the hands, apparently of the broker, but in fact, of the merchant.

It is evident, however, that in settling the
premium *to be inserted in the policy*, the underwriter must, though nominally with respect to
himself, raise it by the amount of these deductions to be made from it for the merchant and
broker. The Committee, in their report, describe these as the fourth of the profits of *underwriting*; they are, however, mere contrivances of the merchant to conceal the real
amount of *his own* profits; for to his foreign
correspondent, or any person unversed in the
trade, it is thus made to appear that the underwriter receives the whole premium in the policy, and that the merchant receives no more
than the 10 shillings per cent. for his own and
the broker's trouble and responsibility in "effecting" the insurance. To the Committee of the
House of Commons it would seem to appear,
that all this is a mere contrivance of the *under-
derwriter and broker* against the *merchant*, whose
charge of the ten shillings for "effecting" is
not even mentioned in the report.

Though the profits of underwriters cannot,

perhaps, be further economized, it does not seem so clear that those of the bróker might not. It is a delicate matter for merchants, however, to propose economy in that branch of the business, it touching too closely upon their own profits; for it is a very common prac‑ tice among merchants, who employ brokers, to receive six-pence out of the broker's shil- lings, and an equally common one to be their own brokers, by means of a clerk at Lloyd's Coffee-House, whereby the whole of these pro- fits, however *undue*, are secured entirely to themselves.

When the great risk of insurance brokers, and the large advances they are sometimes obliged to make, are considered, they may not perhaps be overpaid. However that may be, there is something so unfair in the report, in stating the manner in which the details of the business are arranged, as a conspiracy of the broker and underwriter against the innocent merchants, as causes of "diminution of their profits," or as "clogs upon their trade," that this explanation seems due to justice.

The monopoly enjoyed by London, of the Marine Insurances of the country, it may be thought, therefore, notwithstanding the pow‑ erful law of the charters, gives her merchants at

ready too much power to secure to themselves
undue profits in this branch of trade. How
that would be amended by their being allowed
to form themselves for the purposes of carrying
it on, in to large associations, must now be left
to the candid reader to determine.

May 31, 1810.

OBSERVATIONS,

&c. &c.

———

THE Report of the Committee on Marine Insurance, has been followed up with that rapidity which usually marks the conduct of those whose proceedings are quickened by a sense of interest, and which in the present case has scarcely allowed time for deliberate investigation and cool reflection. While the sheets of that Report, and of the voluminous mass of evidence annexed to it, were yet wet from the press, notice was given of a motion for leave to bring a Bill into Parliament, with a view of commencing that revolution in our present system of effecting Marine Insurances, which the Report recommends. In the course of the debate on that motion, the Chancellor of the Exchequer observed, that the Act of the 6th of George the First, appeared to have vested the power of annulling the exclusive privileges of the two

B

chartered companies in the King, and that therefore he doubted whether, if leave were given to
bring in a Bill for that purpose, it could be proceeded upon. On this declaration, the opposition
to the motion was withdrawn; and the delay in
obtaining legal opinions upon this point, and in
adopting the new course of proceedings which
those opinions may suggest, will probably give
an opportunity, before any final decision can
take place, of counteracting the prepossession
which the authority of a Report of a Special
Committee of the House of Commons may be
expected to create, by examining how far the
principles laid down in that Report, and the deductions drawn from them, are justly founded.

It would be doing injustice to the Gentleman
by whom the Report was framed, not to admit
that it has great claims to praise as a very ingenious essay on marine insurance; and if a chapter
upon that subject were wanting for a new work
upon political economy, by any writer whose
opinions coincided with those of the author,
he would find it admirably suited to his purpose. But considering it as the Report of a Committee of the House of Commons, it is not entitled to the same commendation. The Committee
were directed to enquire into, and report upon, the
Act of the 6th of George the First, together
with the present state of, and the means of effect-

ing marine insurances in Great Britain; and farther, to report upon the two petitions referred to
their consideration. In order to enable them to
form their judgment upon these subjects, they
examined a great number of witnesses; but instead of taking the evidence of those witnesses
as the basis of their Report, and keeping it constantly in view, they frequently lose sight of it
altogether, and quit the straight path of practical utility, to wander in the mazes of conjecture and speculation. Nor is this the full extent of
the complaint that may be urged against this Report; for it not only decides without evidence, but
in many most important points, contrary to evidence; and contrary to the fair and obvious in-
terpretation of the documents referred to the
consideration of the Committee.

In the first place this Report assumes, that the
intention of the legislature in framing the Act of
the 6th of George the First, was to throw the
whole insurance business of these kingdoms into
the hands of the two chartered companies; and
states, that in consequence of the small proportion
the insurances effected by them bear to the whole
insurance business of the country, the intention
of the legislature was wholly disappointed, and that
the merchants continue exposed to all the consequences of the insolvency of individual underwriters, from which the Act meant to relieve

them. It appears on the contrary, that though the legislature, under the pressure of a great national calamity which had occasioned the failure of many individuals, established the existing chartered companies; conceiving, to use the language of the Act, that " several merchants and traders " who adventure their estates in ships, goods, and " merchandizes, at sea or going to sea, especially in " remote or hazardous voyages, would think it much " safer to depend on the policies or assurances of " either of those two corporations so to be created " and established, than on the policies or assurances " of private or particular persons;" still they limited the number of those companies, and reserved the right of redeeming their charters at any time, if they proved hurtful and inconvenient to the public: a caution that evidently shewed the distrust the legislature entertained of the utility of such establishments. So far from admitting as a general principle that marine insurances are best done by companies, they express their disapprobation of them in the strongest language; for this very Act declares, " that all joint stock companies manifestly " tend to the common grievance, prejudice, and " inconvenience of many of his Majesty's sub- " jects, in their trade and commerce and other " affairs;" describes them by the odious term of " nuisances;" and it is under this Act that all parties concerned in them are subject to prosecution. What the motives of our ancestors were in imposing the restrictions contained in this Act, against underwriting in societies or partnerships, the Act itself does not explain; but it may be fairly presumed that this measure was adopted, from a conviction of the greater security which the assured would derive, from their policies of insurance being exempted from the consequences of mercantile speculations, of the ruinous effects of which so many lamentable examples were then before their eyes: a security most effectually provided by the restrictions in question, as the evidence given before this Committee, which will hereafter be adverted to, completely demonstrates. Such a conviction would naturally turn the attention of our ancestors to restrictions against insuring in partnerships, and lead them to confine that branch of business, either to well regulated companies or to individual underwriters, as was done by this Act; which established two companies for this purpose, " with " a competent joint stock to each of them belong- " ing, and under proper conditions, restrictions, " and regulations," leaving the increase of individual competition free and unrestrained.

The Report, speaking of the time when the Act of the 6th of George the First was passed, says, "That in those times political economy was imper- " fectly understood." Those times, when referred to on other occasions, are generally spoken of as the good old times; and indeed it was in those times,

or even prior to those times, that the founda-
tions of all our present prosperity were laid: that
the navigation laws, to which we owe both our
naval and commercial greatness, were enacted;
that the revolutions to which we owe our liberties
were accomplished; and that the British constitution was perfected. For us to decry the knowledge and understanding of our ancestors, is to re-
semble modern spendthrifts, who ridicule the wise
and frugal conduct of their forefathers, to which
they owe the goodly inheritance they are wasting.
We may indeed have more theoretical and speculative knowledge than our ancestors, but in the useful science of practical legislation, in the art of
making a nation great and happy, it will be well
if we act up to the bright example they have left
us: and this aspersion upon their memory is only
hazarded, in order to reconcile us to the great object of this Report, the subversion of that system
of marine insurance, which they in their wisdom
established,

After this dissertation the Report presents us with
estimates of the insured and insurable property of
Great Britain. Such estimates are perhaps vague
at best; but this is in the highest degree fallacious. The policy duty paid in London alone,
for the year 1809, according to the official returns, covers property actually insured to the
amount of more than one hundred and forty mil-

Jions. The business of the rest of the kingdom is generally considered as equal to at least one fourth of that done in London, and the Honourable Member who moved for leave to bring in the Bill, described some of the out-ports as almost rivalling the metropolis; yet only 22 millions is allowed for the whole of them in this estimate, making the total of property actually insured in Great Britain 162 millions. In calculating the amount of the property that might have been insured, fifty per cent. is added to the amount of the official value, both of the imports and exports, as the criterion of their real value; although Mr. Irwin, inspector-general of imports and exports, in his examination before the Secret Committee of the House of Lords in 1797, declared, " that taking all circumstances " with respect to the rates and values into conside- " ration, he was of opinion that an advance of near " thirty per cent. might be added to the ancient " estimates; and that in stating the general com- " mercial balance of the kingdom, he should adopt " this principle." The value of the British vessels is estimated upon the whole tonnage entered inwards and outwards, as if every ship was insured on each separate voyage out or home; whereas it is well known, and indeed proved by the evidence given before this Committee, that transports, colliers, and coasters, however frequently they may enter inwards and outwards, are generally insured for the whole year on one policy.

East Indiamen are uniformly insured for the double
voyage out and home; West Indiamen, and indeed ships employed in every other branch of commerce, are frequently insured in the same manner. This item, therefore, is evidently much over-
rated. The same observations apply to foreign
vessels employed in the commerce of Great Britain, with the farther remark, that it must be
presumed many of these vessels are insured in
those countries to which they belong, and where
their owners reside. In the estimate of the property actually insured, the amount of the coasting trade insured in London, is stated from the
official return of the 2s. 6d. duty, which dis-
tinguishes that trade from the foreign trade, at
15,763,600l.; the coasting trade of Scotland, at
992,000l.; and that of the out-ports of England, at
1,985,800l.; making together 18,741,400l. But in
the estimate of the property that might be insured, the coasting trade is stated at 60,531,622l.
Such is the different mode of stating the very
same item on the different sides of this account---
a mode, which if a man were to adopt in private
life, he would be considered either as having committed a very great error, or as having attempted
a very great imposition. Arithmetic has hitherto
had the reputation of being the most certain of all
the sciences; but it must resign every pretension to
that characteristic, if these contradictory statements can be maintained, and the coasting trade

can be proved at one and the same time, to amount to no more than 18,741,400*l.* and yet to amount to 60,531,622*l.* just as it suits the purpose of the calculator. The same spirit-of exaggeration appears in the next item, the value of foreign adventures upon British capital, estimated at 50 millions; for in the present annihilated state of the commerce of Europe, that with this country excepted, and the suspended state of the commerce of the United States of America, sources of insurable property to such an extent, or even to one-fifth part of such an extent, in which British capital can be employed, are not to be found in foreign commerce, throughout the whole surface of the navigable globe.

A reference may be traced, in many passages of this Report, to a pamphlet recently published, and entitled " a Letter to Jasper Vaux, Esq." The letter writer seems to have acted as a sort of pioneer, to have gone before and to have cleared the ground, as it were, for the reporter. He too has given similar estimates; but in stating the annual amount of the policy duty, as varying between 190,000*l.* and 210,000*l.* he has committed too egregious an error for the reporter to copy, while the official return of the amount paid last year in London, having exceeded 330,000*l.* was before him. Instead therefore of ninety-six millions, which the letter writer asserts is the sum

total of property actually insured in Great Britain,
he admits it to be 162 millions; but then contrives
to swell his calculation of the property that might
be insured, so as to keep up precisely the same
relative proportion of uninsured property as the
letter writer: for as 96 millions insured is to 94
millions uninsured, according to the statement of
the letter writer, so is 162 millions insured to 158
millions uninsured, according to the statement of
the reporter. This is truly a most wonderful coin-
cidence! These calculators, although they differ nearly 100 millions in their estimates, agree
precisely in their result; and both contend that
the charters of the two existing companies ought
to be abrogated, to make room for the new marine
insurance company.

Enough has been said to prove the excessive
exaggeration of the estimate of the insurable
property in this Report. When it is considered
that his Majesty's government never insure, that
the East India Company never insure, and that individuals in general remain voluntarily uninsured,
for a considerable proportion of the ships, freights,
and goods, in which they are interested, it will appear on a just estimate, that all the property meant
to be insured, or that can be expected to be insured, is actually insured in Great Britain.

If any confirmation of those positive proofs

which have already been adduced to shew the fallacy of this estimate were necessary, negative proof, equally convincing, still remains; for if this estimate were correct, if property to the amount of one hundred and fifty-eight millions per annum were really left uninsured, for want of means to insure it, would not thousands of witnesses have come forward to establish this fact? Would not the evidence given before the Committee, have abounded with proofs of this alledged deficiency in our present means of effecting marine insurances? with instances of ships being obliged to go out and return home, without the possibility of their cargoes being insured? and of others being lost or captured, under these circumstances, to the ruin of the unfortunate individuals whose property was embarked in them?—Were any such facts brought forward, either by any of the eminent merchants who were members of this Committee, and also subscribers to the intended new marine insurance company, and therefore well disposed to prove such facts had they really existed, or by any other persons? No, not one. On the contrary, after London had been ransacked for evidence, all that could be adduced on this point was as follows. The first witness called, a Gentleman who came over from Hamburgh to this country five or six years ago, declared that he had been unable, though the brokers whom he employed, to insure more than

18,000*l.* on a good ship from Tonningen to London in the month of August last; and that he
had found great difficulty in insuring from 20 to
25,000 *l.* on a homeward-bound West Indiaman.
In answer to these assertions, a broker produced a
policy for 40,000 *l.* on a ship from Tonningen to London, which he had effected at Lloyd's, in less than
two hours, and that not in the month of August,
but in the very depth of winter, the month of
December last; and a number of witnesses declared, that no difficulty could possibly be found
in effecting either of the insurances mentioned, by
any man of established responsibility and extensive
connections among the underwriters at Lloyd's.
The second witness, another Hamburgh Gentleman, alledged that he had not been able to complete an insurance of 8000 *l.* on a ship to the Baltic
in the month of September last, at the same premium at which it had been begun; but admitted
that no additional premium was offered: and premiums upon ships trading to an enemy's port, including the risk of capture and seizure while
there, perpetually change with every change of political circumstances. The evidence of this witness, therefore, only proves that some change of
this sort had taken place, at least in the estimation of the underwriters, between the time that he
began, and that he attempted to complete the insurance in question. The third witness stated, that
his house had been able to insure only 148,600*l.* out

of 161,000*l.* on a ship from India to London; but
he too acknowledged that no additional premium
was offered; and it appeared that the ship was an
India built ship, manned with Lascars, which many
underwriters refused to write without an advanced
premium, on account of that circumstance. These
are the only cases brought forward of insurances
having been left undone. Indeed to such distress
were the petitioners driven for evidence on this
point, that they actually called a merchant to complain, not of his being unable to insure, but of the
difficulty he had found in insuring 128,000*l.* on two
ships engaged in a contraband adventure to the Spanish provinces in South America, which exposed
them to confiscation the whole time they were trading there; though the premium he had paid was
no more than the current premium given for the same
voyage on ships engaged in the legitimate occupation of the South Sea fishery. Complaints were
made by some other witnesses of difficulties which
they had experienced in effecting insurances at
Lloyd's, and their being obliged to complete them
at the out-ports, rather than pay a premium which
they considered as disproportionate to the risk;
but these differences as to the rate of premium, are only such as take place between the
parties concerned in bargains of every other description. Many of the witnesses called by the
petitioners, whose commercial engagements were
of the first magnitude, had not only been able to

effect their insurances at all times, but even without the necessity of ever applying in the whole course of their business to either of the existing chartered companies. Such is the evidence adduced to satisfy Parliament of the inadequacy of our present means of effecting marine insurances, and of the necessity of establishing new companies; and this in opposition to the testimony of men, who have transacted business at Lloyd's on the most extensive scale, and for a great number of years, who not only never received an order for insurance which they were unable to complete at a fair and adequate premium, but declared that our present means of effecting marine insurances are equal to every possible occasion that the increased commerce of the country can require.

The Report then enters upon the consideration of the effect of the exclusive privilege upon marine insurance, and the state of, and means of effecting marine insurances in this country; and commences this branch of the subject with a most extraordinary complaint on the part of the first merchants of the City of London, " that they " do not and cannot attend Lloyd's;" and that therefore the exclusive privilege granted, and the restrictions imposed by the Act of the 6th of George the 1st, operate as a monopoly, not merely to the companies, but to the underwriters at Lloyd's. The first merchants in London are certainly not prohibited from attending at Lloyd's by any clause in that Act. Those therefore who do not attend, only stay away because they imagine they can employ their time to more advantage in pursuing other avocations; and it would puzzle them to explain how they would have, possessed the faculty of earning money in all manner of ways, and in all manner of places, at the same time, if the Act of the 6th of George the First had never been passed. We have heard sometimes of the omnipotence of Parliament, and it seems intended in this case to call that omnipotence into exercise. Parliament, indeed, have not the power to endow these first merchants of the City of London with the gift of ubiquity, in the full sense of the word: but Parliament can endow them with this gift, as far as relates to the particular object they have in view, by granting them an act of incorporation for their intended new marine insurance company, which will enable them to divide amongst themselves the profits of underwriting, without the necessity of giving their personal attendance at Lloyd's.

Perhaps it is under this impression, that the first merchants of the City of London do not and cannot attend Lloyd's, that the letter writer says, " it appears evident to him, from circumstances " he meets with every day, that the underwriters " at Lloyd's have reached their ne plus ultra, as

" to extent, both in their numbers and the quan-
" tity of insurance effected." What these every
day circumstances are, as he does not condescend
to state, it is impossible to divine. Some every
day circumstances, such as the frequent additions
made to the rooms, and the recent enlargement of
the boxes, in order to provide the necessary accommodation for the increased number of subscribers, might have induced a contrary belief,
because they prove that the number of underwriters continues to increase in proportion to the
extent of our commerce.

As a plea for not entering into any particular
detail of the evidence given on the great point referred to the consideration of the Committee, the
present state of, and means of effecting marine
insurances in Great Britain, the Report then states,
" that it will appear from the evidence, that
" the merchants pretty generally complain of the
" mode of transacting business at Lloyd's, which,
" on the other hand, is as generally defended by
" the underwriters and brokers; and that, without
" pretending positively to decide between such
" contradictory opinions, your Committee, in form-
" ing theirs, think it most prudent to confine
" themselves to obvious deductions from general
" principles, and from such facts as appear well
" established." It certainly was the duty of the
Committee to ascertain the truth between these

conflicting testimonies. the great object for which
they were appointed, being to report or the state
of, and the present means of effecting marine insurances in Great Britain. Obvious deductions
might have been drawn from general principles, or
from such facts as appear well established, without
the appointment of any Select Committee whatever. But the truth is, that much of the evidence
given did not suit the purpose of the author of
this Report, and therefore he found it convenient
to keep it in the back ground; instead of facts, to
give opinions; and instead of practical inferences
from evidence, what he calls obvious deductions
from general principles.

But how is the fact alledged borne out, that the
merchants pretty generally complain of the manner of transacting business at Lloyd's? It is complained of by two Hamburgh merchants, and some
of the subscribers to the intended new marine insurance company. Reasons may be given, why it is
hardly fair to call merchants born and bred in Hamburgh, a city where, according to, the testimony
of Mr. Angerstein, the art of making averages
is carried to greater perfection than in any other
place on the known globe, to give evidence against
the underwriters. For many years, the under-
derwriters at Lloyd's submitted to pay most enormous averages on goods shipped to Hamburgh and
Bremen. Frequently, when goods arrived to a

falling market, certificates were procured that they
were all damaged more or less, and according to
the courteous phraseology used on those occasions,
they were immediately sold at public sale for the
benefit of the underwriters, but in point of fact at
a loss of 40 or 50 per cent.   This practice was carried
to such an intolerable height, that at length the
underwriters determined to make a stand; and the
stand was made against a correspondent of one of
the very gentlemen who was called by the members of the intended new marine insurance company, to give evidence before this Committee. A
claim was brought forward against the underwriters of nearly 40 per cent. for an average upon
sugar; and was supported with all the accustomed
documents in due form.   On examining the papers,
it appeared that the invoice weights of the sugars
when shipped here, and the weights when landed
abroad, very nearly corresponded; though the
survey stated, they had all been damaged by salt
water, to the extent of the demand made upon the
underwriters.   Now it is obvious that water will
melt sugar; and these sugars not having been
melted, it was equally obvious that they could not
have come into contact with salt water, as was pretended.   On this ground, the underwriters refused
to pay the demand: but the infallibility of the
Hahs-Town certificates was too valuable to be sur-
rendered to reason and common sense. The law
therefore was called in to their aid, and an action

was brought against the underwriters. On the trial, a crowd of witnesses proved, that it was the property of water to melt sugar; that when sugars arrived in this country damaged by salt water, a diminution of weight uniformly took place, in proportion to the extent of the damage sustained; and that frequently the casks were landed entirely empty. After a long trial, both the judge and the jury being of opinion, that positive facts were entitled to more credit than positive oaths, and to borrow an expression from the writer of this Report, drawing " obvious deductions from general " principles," found a verdict for the defendants. This decision created as much consternation among many of the merchants at Hamburgh and Bremen, as ever was occasioned by the approach of a French army to their gates; for they had been in the habit of levying as heavy contributions upon the underwriters at Lloyd's, as were ever imposed upon them by any of Bonaparte's generals.

The foregoing anecdote will explain the soreness with which these Hamburgh Gentlemen give their testimony; a testimony refuted in its most material parts, by Mr. Grill and Mr. Meyer, merchants of the first respectability, and most mature experience; who were carrying on extensive business in London, before these Hamburgh young Gentlemen were born, and who being neither bro-

kers nor underwriters, cannot be supposed to have
any undue bias on their minds, in favour of the
present system.

When it is considered that the subscribers to
this intended new marine insurance company com-
prize 9-10ths of the commercial interest of the City
of London, and that they naturally feel every disposition to promote their own views, by procuring
the incorporation for which they have petitioned
Parliament, the very lame and defective evidence
given in support of their allegations can only be
accounted for, by presuming that a conviction was
very generally impressed upon their minds that
they had no real cause of complaint against the
underwriters at Lloyd's. As however the Report
asserts; " that it will appear from the evidence that
" the merchants pretty generally complain of the
" mode of transacting business at Lloyd's;" it is
fair to examine how far this assertion is justly
founded, and who the parties are by whom such
complaints are made.

The first of these complainants, Mr. J. D. Rucker,
is a young Gentleman who came over from Hamburgh only 5 or 6 years ago; and who can hardly
have had time, therefore, to wear off the rust of his
native partialities, much less to have very eminently
qualified himself by experience, to sit in judgment
upon the established commercial systems of this

country. The second complainant, Mr. F. Molling, jun. is another young Gentleman from Hamburgh, taken into the house of Spitta, Molling, and Co. as a partner, within these few years; and to whom the same observations are applicable. Mr. Simpson is a Gentleman of unquestionable intelligence and respectability; but he merely states the difficulty his house experienced in insuring an India built ship, manned with Lascars, at the same premium as was given on the regular ships in the service of the East India Company: a charge which the underwriters are by no means solicitous to repel, being satisfied to be found guilty of duly appreciating the superiority of British seamen. But not a single complaint against the present system of effecting marine insurances at Lloyd's, is to be found throughout the whole evidence of Mr. Simpson. Mr. Lyndsey is another young Gentleman, who like Mr. Molling, has very recently been taken as a partner into the house of Messrs. Greg and Co. He admits that he never was unable to complete any insurance he received orders to effect, and gives no opinion whatever as to the advantages that would be derived from any change in the present system. Mr. J. Milford is as silent upon this subject as Mr. Lyndsey. He never found any difficulty in effecting insurances, but on one occasion; and that difficulty, though of no common description, he at last surmounted, by actually completing the insurance of his vessels

engaged in a contraband traffic, at as low a premium as if they had been employed in a legal trade.
The next witnesses are three clerks, and a junior
partner, in three East India houses; not one of
whose leading partners thought proper to come
forward. Mr. Bridgman says, that the establishment of any new marine insurance companies in
Great Britain, would afford no additional facilities
to the effecting of India insurances here, unless
additional means of communication were also furnished. Mr. Barr always effected all the insurances
of the house for which he acted at Lloyd's, without ever applying to the chartered companies already existing. Mr. Lumley gave the same testimony as to the house in which he is a partner,
that they "never had occasion to trouble the
"public companies;" and Mr. Russell only speaks
to a difficulty similar to that stated by Mr. Simpson,
of ensuring a ship manned with Lascars without
any additional premium; which however was
accomplished before the account of her loss arrived.
Mr. Williams, an American merchant, was then
called, who stated, totidem verbis, in direct contradiction to the evidence afterwards given by Mr.
Glennie, " that he never heard the mode of doing
" insurance business at Lloyd's had been the sub-
" ject of any complaint with the merchants in
" America." Mr. Jones, travelling secretary to the
Phœnix Fire Office, hazards many opinions; but
states few facts from his own knowledge. With all

his partiality to companies, he admits them " to be " a dearer resort for insurances ;" and observes that in consequence of their being established in America, private underwriters have nearly disappeared there. This Gentleman, be it known, was the original projector of the intended new marine insurance company. Mr. Forsyth is an underwriter, and a member of the committee of the new marine insurance company, which he " considers " would draw a great deal of business to London." Mr. Inglis states, that in his opinion greater facilities in making marine insurances are wanting ; but admits that though his house has occasionally completed insurances at the out-ports, he has never been obliged to leave any insurances undone, for want of means to effect them. The evidence of Mr. Inglis, where he speaks of facts, is certainly entitled to the utmost respect; but his opinions, like those of other men, may be fallible; and while allowed their due weight, can be allowed no more, where they differ from those of other persons of experience and respectability. Mr. Glennie, one of the partners in a very considerable house, trading chiefly to the United States of America, complains very strongly of the present system of effecting marine insurances in this country. Mr. Glennie was one of the witnesses examined at the bar of the House of Commons respecting the orders in council: he then said, that " in ordi-

nary times his house accepted " bills when they
received bills of lading;" he now says, that "he
" does not permit his correspondents to draw,
" unless they give him orders for insurance." The
orders in council were then the sole subject of his
complaint, and not one word was said about the deficiency in our means of effecting marine insurances,
though the subject of insurance formed a very
prominent part of his testimony. Now, the deficiency in our means of effecting marine insurances
is the sole subject of his complaint, and not one
word is said about the orders in council. If the diminution of his American business was owing in part
to the defects in our system of effecting marine
insurances, why on his former examination was the
whole blame thrown on the orders in council? Or
has some new light broken in upon his mind, respecting the defects in our present system of effecting marine insurances, since he became a subscriber
to this intended new company? Mr. Gillespie, a coal
factor, Mr. Wilson and Mr. Cheap, two secretaries
to two clubs of ship owners, bring up the rear of
the witnesses examined on the part of the petitioners; but confine their testimony solely to the
history of these clubs or societies.

On perusing this recital, where is the unanimous
voice of the great and respectable body of merchants of which the Report speaks? Every mer-

chant called, who expressed an opinion unfavourable to the present system of effecting marine insurances, with the exception of Mr. J. D. Rucker, has a direct interest in the question, as holding shares in the intended new marine insurance company; and therefore is as much exposed to the suspicion of partiality, as any of the merchants examined who are underwriters or insurance brokers. If the testimony of the one of these classes is set against that of the other, there will remain only Mr. Rucker who complains, against Mr. Grill, Mr. Meyer, and Mr. Idle, who approve. With what justice then can it be asserted in the Report, that it will appear from the evidence the merchants pretty generally " complain of the present system?" when in point of fact the weight of evidence preponderates in favour of the present system, and not in favour of the intended new marine insurance company.

The profits of the insurance brokers are described in the Report as being singularly high; and are mentioned as a proof of the great difficulty and trouble in effecting insurances. Whereas, on the contrary, the remuneration that the brokers receive, is a compensation, not merely for their trouble, but for the risk they run of losses by the insolvency of their principals, and for the heavy advances they are frequently obliged to make in the course of their business. These facts are fully explained in the evidence, and are essential to an impartial statement; but nevertheless are wholly suppressed by the author of this Report.

Great fault is found with the underwriters, for absenting themselves from Lloyd's in the autumnal months; and as a proof of the consequences of this practice, a statement is given of the sums insured by an underwriter who attended there every month of the last year. This statement shews, that the premiums of the Gentleman in question, during the last five months in the year, amounted to 30,411*l.*; and those during the first seven months to only 15,990*l.*; a plain proof, that when some underwriters are absent, those who remain write the more, and that thus the inconvenience complained of is obviated. He admits, too, that he underwrites on a more extensive scale during the autumnal months, because he conceives that he then does so to the greatest advantage; and thus contradicts, by his practice, the very point he is called upon to establish. It appears that on the approach of winter, contests always take place about the advance of premiums; and the Report should have shewn, that the intended new marine insurance company, or persons who wish to underwrite in partnership, would be more disposed to write winter risks at summer premiums, than individual underwriters; for unless this can be proved, the grievance complained of would not be remedied by the proposed change of system.

An entire new and pleasant contrivance for remedying this evil, is then suggested, of forming partnerships, for the alternate purposes of underwriting and recreation, so that the firm should at no time be absent from Lloyd's. But unfortunately experience has shewn, that every attempt to unite business and pleasure proves abortive; that underwriting, like other pursuits, is not to be trifled with; and that it must be attended to with regular and unremitting assiduity, to be carried on to any advantage.

In order to shew the necessity of companies, the Report then introduces the history of certain clubs or societies of ship owners, formed for the purpose of insuring each other's vessels. From the evidence of the secretary to one of these establishments, It appears that by selecting the good ships, and rejecting the bad, the society in which he is employed, insured each other last year at an expence of about 5 l. 10s. per cent.; whereas, if the same insurances had been made at Lloyd's, where the underwriters take the good and bad ships together, they would have cost, if transports 9 l.; and if colliers from 18 l. to 20 l. per cent. From this statement, some idea may be formed of the immense profit that would be made by this intended new marine insurance company, acting on the same system, and possessing nine-tenths of the whole commercial interest of the City of London. It is proved, by the official return of the policy duty, that property to the amount of 140 millions was insured in London last year. It is given in evidence, as the opinion of witnesses of great experience in the business of underwriting, that out of the nine-tenths of risks to the amount of the 140 millions, of which the subscribers to the new company would, of course, give their own company the preference, they would select 80 millions of good risks, and reject the rest as bad. The premium on 80 millions of property insured, would not amount to less than six millions; and supposing the company, by acting on the same system as the clubs, to realize the same proportion of their premiums, their annual profit would be four millions. This profit would be made at the expence of thousands of individuals, who would either find no means whatever of insuring the risks which had been rejected by the company, or only be able to insure them at an extravagant rate of premium; for the evidence given before the Committee proves, that few, if any underwriters, would remain at Lloyd's, to write the bad risks, if nine-tenths of the good ones were monopolized by this intended new marine-insurance company.

The Report then asserts that the defects in the present mode of transacting marine insurances are sufficiently manifest, although no evidence whatever to prove those defects has been adduced. If the statement of the insured and the insurable property, was meant to shew that insurances to a greater amount would be effected, if they could be effected at Lloyd's, the answer is, that the estimate itself is fallacious, and, of course, the inferences drawn from it must be equally so; and farther, that a number of witnesses have deposed, from practical knowledge, that the present means of effecting insurances are equal to every possible occasion. Mr. Forsyth's account of his premiums for the different months of the last year, makes against the argument it was intended to support; and the history of the clubs or societies, only proves the great emoluments which the subscribers to the intended new marine insurance company may promise themselves, if they succeed in obtaining an act of incorporation. Yet these are the only references to the evidence taken before the Committee, hitherto given in the Report; and consequently, the only proofs by which the assertion, that " the defects in the " present mode of transacting marine insurances " are sufficiently manifest," can possibly be supported.

Having, however, thus attempted to establish

the defects in the present system of effecting marine insurances, the writer of the Report proceeds to consider ": the importance of a better system to ": the commerce and revenue of the empire, and " to the parties concerned." This discussion is introduced by a position which no person will venture to dispute , that the best system is that which gives the best security at the cheapest' rate; But two others of a more disputable nature immediately follow: that this mode is the enabling merchants to insure each other; and that " the advantage to the merchant from a "cheap rate of good insurance is so great, that " no profit he could make from a participation " of premium in any association he might enter " into for the purpose would over-balance it; and " his interest would therefore lead him to keep " the premium of insurance always as low as pos-' " sible."

It must be remembered, that the British merchant insures not so much for himself as for others; and that, therefore, if he becomes an underwriter, his interest will evidently lead him to keep the premium of insurance, not as low, but on the contrary, as high as possible. The truth of this assertion may be proved by example. The regular outward-bound West-Indiamen that sail with convoy, are favourite risks, and therefore are chiefly kept by the merchants themselves. They are

favourite risks, because they go out completely
fitted, and well manned; being seldom fully laden,
they are in good sailing trim, and have the certainty of a fair wind, and fine weather, as soon
as they come into the latitude of the trade
winds, or for at least two-thirds of the voyage.
Ships homeward-bound from the West Indies,
on the contrary, are liable to have received
injury both from accident and from the cli-
mate, which they have very imperfect means of
repairing in many of those islands. Their crews
are frequently diminished by the impress, by de-
sertion, and by disease. They come home so
deeply laden, that they suffer much if they en-
counter bad weather; and if they separate from
their convoy, and fall in with an enemy, they are
not in a state either to fight or to run away. The
books of every underwriter will shew, that the
number of outward-bound West Indiamen he
writes, is very trifling compared to the number of
those homeward-bound. This certainly arises in
part from the cargoes of the former being less valuable than those of the latter, the convoy ships
taking out scarcely any thing but plantation stores;
the more valuable goods shipped for the merchants
being generally sent in running ships, to avoid the
delay of waiting for convoy. But it arises also, and
in a much greater degree, from the merchants insuring a very large proportion of these risks themselves.
If, then, the position advanced in the Report be

just, the premiums on the outward-bound West-Indiamen are always kept as low as possible. But the fact is just the reverse; for the premiums on them are higher in proportion than on other descriptions of risks. They are kept up, at this very moment, to the same rate as is paid on the homeward-bound ships from the Leeward Islands. Nay, more, the very same premium is charged on ships going with convoy, as is paid on ships going without convoy, three guineas per cent.; and it surely will not be contended, that this could be the case, if proper exertions were used to reduce the premium on these risks, by putting them up to fair and open competition at Lloyd's. This example shews what would be the result of the merchants taking the whole insurance business into their own hands; as would be the case, if they were permitted to form themselves into this intended new marine insurance company.

But it may be said that this company would be directed by men of such high respectability and liberal principles, that no considerations of interest could possibly influence their conduct. If, however, we look to the example of other public companies, under the direction of men of equal respectability and liberality in private life, we shall find them in their public character, contracting a certain esprit du corps, and preferring the interest of the establishments they superintend, either to those of individuals or of the public. Have we already forgotten the complaints so recently made in the House of Commons, of the litigious and rapacious disposition shewn by the directors of the West India and the London Dock Companies? Have we already forgotten the resolution of the House of Commons, that the directors of the West India Dock Company had exceeded the extreme rate of interest allowed them by law? and is it not a notorious fact, that not satisfied with the liberal dividend of 10 per cent. which they may legally divide upon their capital, they have paid the property-tax upon that dividend for many years past, out of a fund appropriated by the legislature to the reduction of the rates on those commodities, which are compulsatively lodged in their warehouses? The pleas urged by the directors for the continuance of this exaction, the great pains they had taken, and the great risk they had ran in the formation of that establishment, would apply just as well in vindication of a high rate of premiums, as of a high rate of charges, on the commodities of their correspondents; and we must trust not so much to the professions of men as to their practices. Have we also forgot that a Bill is now pending in Parliament, in order to remedy the evils that have arisen from the directors of most of the fire-offices in this metropolis having acted on the same principle, of preferring their own inte-

D

rests to the security of the public, the object for
which they were established.   Numerous as these
offices are, it might have been expected that property of every description could easily be insured
against fire, and at a moderate premium.   But,
on the contrary, almost the whole of these offices for some time past have refused to insure
against fire in any foreign country, and even in
our own West India colonies.   In consequence of
this resolution, out of property to the amount of
a million of money, that was destroyed the year
before last, in the conflagration of Port D'Espagne,
the metropolis of Trinidad, not one-tenth part
was insured; and this heavy loss fell upon the
unfortunate sufferers, or on their correspondents
here to whom they were indebted, although the
law gave these public companies the exclusive
privilege of effecting this description of insurances.   In consequence of the remonstrances of
the parties concerned, a Bill is now before Parliament, permitting individuals to insure against the
risk of fire in the West Indies.   All these facts
shew the true character of corporate bodies, and
demonstrate how little confidence can be placed in
their paying a just regard to the interests of the
public, when they come in competition with those
of their own proprietors.

The advantages to be derived by the subscribers to
the intended new company, have been much under-

rated; and some of the parties concerned have given themselves great credit for their disinterestedness and moderation, in limiting the number of shares that can be held by any individual, to five. Five shares, out of five thousand, or one thousandth part of nine-tenths of the underwriting business of this metropolis, is more than the average share that falls to the lot of the individual underwriter, who regularly devotes his time and attention to that pursuit; for the number of underwriters in this metropolis, is estimated at 1500. It farther appears, from the evidence given before the Committee, that each partner in a firm, or each member of a family, may hold five shares; 20 shares being held by the family of a witness who gave this testimony: and the history of the clubs or societies proves, that the system on which the company will have an opportunity of acting, of selecting all the good risks, will enable them to divide infinitely larger profits on the same scale of business, than can possibly be made by any individual underwriter, who necessarily takes the good and bad risks together. Let us hear no more then of the disinterestedness of these Gentlemen; or let them make good their pretensions to that characteristic, by offering to appropriate their surplus profits, after dividing a reasonable interest on their capital, to the relief of the public burthens.

Many of the subscribers, however, who were exa-

mined before the Committee, very candidly re-
nounced all claim to disinterestedness in this undertaking. Some declared that they never considered
the probable effects of it at all; and others, that
though they disapproved of it, they subscribed as
they would have done to a loan, or to any thing
else which held out a prospect of advantage. It
is much to be apprehended, therefore, that if the
position laid down in the Report, " that if such a
" system shall be established, it is probable that
" the price paid for insurance, will not much ex-
" ceed the aggregate value of the losses sustained
" on each class of risks insured," were taken for
gospel, most of the subscribers would withdraw
their names, and the intended new company fall to
the ground. As soon as the day was fixed for
taking this Report into consideration in the House
of Commons, the following circular letter was
sent to each subscriber:—

PROPOSED MARINE INSURANCE COMPANY.
" Sir,
" I beg leave to inform you that the Report of the Select
" Committee upon the subject of Marine Insurance, is to
" be taken into consideration by the House of Commons,
" upon Thursday the 17th day of May ; when, as a share-
" holder in the proposed marine insurance institution, you
" will no doubt use your influence with your friends to
" attend. I am, Sir,
" Your most obedient humble servant,
" ALEX. MUNDELL.
" 45, Parliament-street, May 10, 1810."

In writing this letter, Mr. Mundell acted without doubt under the orders of the committee who superintend the interests of this intended institution; and in so doing, he calls upon the parties to use their influence with their friends to attend, not as merchants interested in the commercial prosperity of the empire, but as share holders in the proposed marine institution: pretty plainly designating, that in the opinion of the Committee, this was the most forcible call that could be made upon the exertions of the subscribers, this the chord to which their feelings would vibrate in the most perfect unison.

In the subsequent paragraph the Report asserts the superiority of companies for facility, security, and cheapness; as appearing from the concurring testimony of all the merchants examined. A reference to the evidence will shew that this opinion is not supported by the concurring testimony of all the merchants examined; but on the contrary, is expressedly contradicted by many of them, as well as by the brokers and underwriters.

With respect to the superiority of companies in the facility of doing business, it will hardly be disputed, but that those who actually do it, are better judges than those who merely order it to be done; and the brokers uniformly agree, that though larger sums are taken by companies than by individual underwriters, yet that so much time is spent in going about from one company to another, and waiting for the answers of the acting secretaries, who perhaps refer again to the sitting directors, that they dispatch their business with more facility among a large number of underwriters, all assembled in the same room.

This testimony is a complete answer to the allegations in the Report, respecting the inconvenience which arises to the brokers, from the necessity of applying to so many persons, either for signing a policy or settling a loss. A passage towards the conclusion of the Report observes, that "the trouble " of brokers would be much diminished by dealing " with partnerships, which are always at hand, in- " stead of a great number of individuals, frequently " scattered about the country." If those partners transacted their business at home, the same inconvenience would be felt by the brokers in going about to them, that is felt in going about to companies; and if they attended at Lloyd's alternately, things would be precisely in the same state they now are; for the evidence proves, that when any of the leading underwriters are occasionally absent, they are represented by other persons.

With respect to the superiority of companies in point of security, the evidence furnishes the example of Hamburgh; where, out of 36 companies that existed seven years ago, only five or six now remain. Some of them did indeed pay in full; but the greater number only paid from four to fifteen shillings in the pound. The events that occasioned the ruin of these companies, produced no sensation among the underwriters at Lloyd's, although a very great proportion of the commerce of Hamburgh is at all times insured in London, because the universality of the insurance business guarantees the security of the general underwriter: his premiums on the commerce carrying on to and from every quarter of the globe, enable him to bear the brunt of a disaster that may happen to any particular branch of commerce; but companies or societies on a small scale, generally consist of persons engaged in the same line of business; their underwriting is in consequence principally confined to that particular line of business, and if that receives a shock, they have not the same resources as general underwriters. These observations apply to the companies in India, where 3 out 13, it is stated in the evidence, " have ceased to act,' though from what cause is not explained. When, however, the circumstance of their agents in this country having refused to pay losses for them, because they had not funds in hand, is coupled with the great number of captures lately made by the enemy in the Indian seas, the cause of their having ceased to act does not seem very doubtful. It is unnecessary, therefore, to travel out of the re-

cord of the evidence before the Committee, to
shew the instability of companies; or the Abbé
Morellet's list of 55 joint stock companies, which
have been established in Europe since 1600, and
have failed, might be appealed to.   Dr. Adam Smith
indeed says, the Abbé has been misinformed with respect to two or three of them which have not failed;
but that in compensation several others have failed,
which he has omitted.   It is no irrelevant nor un-
important observation on this point, that the
failure of a company with whom a large sum is insured, may bring total ruin on the party interested
in the property, by whom the failure of a single
underwriter on a policy would scarcely be felt.

With respect to the superiority of companies as
to cheapness, the evidence proves that premiums
are generally lower in Great Britain than in any
other part of the world; and this appears to be
the natural result of the present system of effecting marine insurances here by individual underwriters: for the extent of competition depends
upon the number of competitors.   Competition
therefore is indisputably increased in proportion as
underwriting is carried on by individuals, and diminished in proportion as it is carried on by companies. All the witnesses admit that the two
chartered companies charge a higher rate of premium than the underwriters at Lloyd's; and this
is a fair criterion to prove the different effects of

the two systems, both being carried on in the same country, and under the same circumstances. Even Mr. Jones, secretary to an insurance company, and who has travelled almost all the world over to enquire into the nature of companies, admits that companies are a dearer resort for insurance; and the letter writer himself admits the fact, of every species of marine risk being assurable at a cheaper rate here than elsewhere. It is proved, too, in evidence, that some risks are now actually insured at Lloyd's, at, and some even under peace premium. This may be produced by competition, but would never be the result of choice, nor happen again if the insurance business were monopolized by a few great companies.

The letter writer states the comparison between corporate bodies and individuals, in precisely the same manner as the writer of the Report; but places both on an equality as to cheapness, and only gives corporate bodies the preference as to facility and security, a distinction in which the Reporter has not followed him. His discussion on these points, is somewhat inconsistent with what is said of England in a former part of his work, that " establishing for the protection and advance-
" ment of her early commerce, a variety of corpo-.
" rate bodies, she encouraged with the gradual
" developement of wealth and enterprize, that
" progressive display of individual effort, which

" has at length raised her to an eminence unri-
" valled in commercial history." This admission
oversets the whole theory his book is meant to
establish ; and after observing " that public bodies
" have gradually disappeared whenever the in-
" crease of private resources enables individual
" members of the community to transact concerns
" more advantageously than a company," it is with
rather an ill grace, that in this very state of things,
he recommends the retrograde movement of establishing a new chartered company here, to super-
cede the exertions of individuals.

Both the letter writer and the Reporter labour
this point, of the superiority of companies over
individual underwriters, with more than common
care. The latter presses poor Dr. Adam Smith
into the service, with the view of supporting this
doctrine by his authority; and it is really most un-
merciful usage of the poor Doctor, whose work is
replete with so much profound knowledge and valuable information, to bring up in judgment against
him, one of the very few instances of inadvertence
that can be laid to his charge. The Doctor, in
enumerating the only trades " which it seems pos-
" sible for a joint stock company to carry on with-
" out an exclusive privilege," as being those of
which all the " operations are capable of being re-
" duced to what is called a routine, or to such an
" uniformity of method as admits of little or no

" variation," specifies among others, insurance from sea-risk, and capture in time of war. Now unfortunately it does so happen, that scarcely any thing in nature admits of more variation, than the risk of capture in time of war. Every change in the political system of any country, every new decree issued by Buonaparte, or every fresh order to carry any old decree into more rigorous effect, every alteration in the non-intercourse or embargo laws of the United States of America, every change in the destination of the enemy's cruizers, every change in the destination of our own squadrons, every enterprize which either augments or diminishes the number of ports in possession of the enemy, necessarily occasions a variation in the risk of capture in time of war; and some of these vicissitudes are incessantly happening; so that unless Dr. Adam Smith had applied this characteristic of being subject to little or no variation to the wind, he scarcely could have applied it more unluckily than to the risk of capture in time of war: and this the framer of the Report must have well known; but system-mongers sacrifice every consideration, even the characters of their most respected friends, to the hope of establishing their favourite dogmas.

Still labouring to maintain this great point of the superiority of companies, the Report then remarks, " That wherever there are no restric-
" tions, that is every where but in Great Bri-

" tain, insurances are invariably done by com-
" panies;" and reciting the number of those companies in foreign countries, states, " that there
" were thirty-six in Hamburgh." Why had not
the Reporter the candour to state how many
insurance companies there are now at Hamburgh?
Because the fact did not suit his purpose. The
Hamburgh Gentlemen who were called to give
evidence before the Committee, also concealed the
circumstance of their number being reduced to five
or six. Nay, one of them declared that losses were
more easily settled there than here; and that he
had never heard any complaints of those companies. Charity would induce a belief, which it is
rather difficult to reconcile to probability, that a
Gentleman in constant habits of commercial correspondence with that City, knew nothing of
those failures, in which commercial men are so
peculiarly interested; for it is the bounden duty of
a witness to speak not only the truth, but the
whole truth.

The following transaction, which came under the
cognizance of the writer of these pages, as assignee to the estate of a foreign house in this City,
will shew whether losses are more easily settled
at Hamburgh than at Lloyd's. A ship was chartered at Hamburgh early in the year 1802, on a
voyage to St. Domingo; and in order to guard
against the risk of British capture, the insurance

was effected at Hamburgh, partly with the companies there, and partly with individual underwriters. This ship was carried into Jamaica by a
British cruizer, and together with her cargo, condemned and sold; but on an appeal, restitution
was decreed to the claimants. The property sold
to so much disadvantage, and the law charges as
well as other charges, were so heavy, that a very
large deficit remained to be made good by the assurers. One of the parties interested in this adventure, who was, at the head of a mercantile
house at Hamburgh, conducted the negociation
with them; and so persuaded was he of their ca-
villing and litigious disposition, that in his very
first letter on the subject, dated August 3d, 1802,
he writes thus: " We are almost certain that our
" assurers will not pay in full; and that we shall
" be obliged either to go to law, or settle with
" them by compromise." In his next letter he
gives the following account of the mode of recovering demands there upon policies of insurance:
" By the laws and usages of this City, the ac-
" counts must be examined and made up by the
" dispacheur public, who when papers get into his
" desk, generally keeps them a year before they see
" day-light; and therefore we propose having the
" account settled by a sworn insurance broker."
In December he advised, " that the demand of the
" assured, as stated by the sworn Insurance broker.

" amounted to 94,800 banco marcs; and that the
" assurers, after consulting together, had offered to
" pay only one half of the demand, an offer which
" he had not thought proper to accept." In February, 1803, he wrote again, " that nothing could be
" done till the dispacheur public, who was always
" five or six hundred accounts in arrear, had made
" up the account; that if the assurers refused to
" settle upon his statement, the claim must be re-
" ferred to arbitrators; and that if the assurers
" again refused to pay upon their award, the next
" step was to commence proceedings in a court of
" law; an experiment which he by no means re-
" commended," thinking, according to the French
proverb, that " un mauvais accommodement vaut
" mieux qu'un bon procés." Finally, on the 3d of
January, 1804, he advised that the dispacheur public had made up the account; and that the assurers
had agreed to pay it on being allowed a deduction
of about 10 per cent. which he thought it more
advisable to make, than to run the risk of litiga-
,tion, or of further failures by delay. On finally
closing the account he remitted 36,295 banco marcs,
instead of 66,000, the proportion due to the estate
of the house in London; the difference being lost
by the insolvency of two of the companies, and
some of the underwriters with whom the insurance
had been effected. This recital will shew without
any comment, how far the claim made for the

Hamburghers, to superiority over the underwriters at Lloyd's, both for facility in settling losses and solidity in paying them, is well founded.

The history of the clubs or societies of ship owners is then again referred to, as an additional proof of the great want of companies for the purpose of effecting marine insurances : but the history of these clubs only shews, that different persons pursue the same end by different means; that those who possess but little influence, as for example the members of these clubs, evade that law which they cannot hope to alter; and that those who possess great influence, as for example, the members of the new marine insurance company, instead of evading, try to alter the law, when prompted by their interest so to do.

It is mentioned as matter of complaint in two different passages of the Report, that the assured are obliged to resort to individual security; and from the speech of Mr. Manning, in the House of Commons, it might have been expected, that the evidence given of the heavy losses sustained by the insolvency of the underwriters at Lloyd's, would have formed the leading ground of the application to Parliament for the establishment of the intended new marine insurance company ; for he stated, that on an insurance of 36,000*l*. effected at Lloyd's by a house in this City, there had been defaulters to the

amount of 12,000*l*. No merchant came forward
before the Committee to give any evidence respecting this transaction ; but the underwriters thought
it necessary to state it in their defence, and the
history may be found in the evidence of Mr. Throckmorton ; shewing, that a merchant in this City,
to whom an insolvent broker was largely indebted,
gave him insurances to effect at Lloyd's, in order
to shift a bad debt off his own shoulders, and
throw it on those of the underwriters ; that the
broker imposed upon the merchant, by putting
fictitious names upon his policies, when in fact he
was himself the underwriter, and that in this affair,
disgraceful indeed to the other parties concerned,
the underwriters were intended to be made dupes,
but were not accomplices. The evidence given
before the Committee places both the solidity
and the liberality of the underwriters on very high
ground ; and it is doing them injustice, not
only to suppress all mention of that part of the
evidence in the Report, but to complain of the
" very great hardships to which the merchants in
" this kingdom are exposed, because they can
" have no joint security to their insurances."

A fair judgment may be formed of the comparative advantages of individual and joint security,
by the following statement. In the course of
twenty years' business at Lloyd's, ninety-four
mercantile houses have failed in debt to the writer

of these remarks for premiums; and only seven underwriters for losses on policies. The dividends paid by the merchants average between 4*s.* and 5*s.* in the pound; those paid by the underwriters between 13*s.* and 14*s.* If then the system of underwriting in firms had been adopted twenty years ago, his foreign correspondents would have made bad debts with 94 houses, paying dividends of between 4*s.* and 5*s.* instead of having made bad debts with only seven underwriters, paying dividends of between 13*s.* to 14*s.*: and this is the improved security that is offered to the assured, by repealing the restrictions imposed by the Act of the 6th of George the First, against underwriting in partnerships. In the list of these insolvent houses are to be found members of Parliament, directors of the great corporate bodies, and individuals who were known to be possessed of immense property; but speculation is a whirlpool, in which the largest fortunes are soon swallowed up, when once they are drawn within its vortex. Houses of the greatest opulence are the most exposed to its influence, from having the largest capitals at command. Hence it is, that vicissitudes so frequently happen among commercial men of the highest distinction; as those who are nearest the top of the pinnacle, are in the greatest danger of falling. Wisely, therefore, did our ancestors guard the assured against the baneful consequences of mercantile speculation.

B

By the restrictions against underwriting in partnership, imposed by the Act of the 6th of George the First, and which this Report recommends to remove, the assured are exempted as far as possible from the effects of all mercantile speculations, the account of the underwriter, in case of failure, being kept totally distinct from the concerns of the house in which he is a partner; all demands against him for losses being proved against his separate estate, and all sums due to him for premiums being appropriated to the payment of the debts due by his separate estate; the surplus only being responsible to the creditors of the partnership, after the creditors of the separate estate have been paid in full. The evidence given before the Committee proves, that the separate estate of the underwriter very frequently pays in full, when the joint estate of the partnership pays little or nothing; and a reference to the present mode of carrying on insurance business, will shew that an underwriter, except in case of some very extraordinary misfortune, cannot but have funds sufficient, or nearly sufficient, to pay his losses. An underwriter must pay his losses within a month after they happen, but cannot collect his premiums till after the expiration of the year. He may expect total losses to the amount of 50 per cent. on his premiums; his returns for convoy and averages will be about 40 per cent. more; and then a profit of 10 per cent. will remain, subject to the usual deduction of the discounts allowed the brokers, and to bad debts. By the 1st of March in the year following, 4-5ths of his risks of the year preceding will have run off: and consequently 4-5ths of his losses be ascertained, Supposing his premiums to have been 50,000*l.* the amount of the losses for which he will have been called upon, is 20.000*l.* one half of which, or 10,000*l.* he will probably have set off against premiums due to him from the parties claiming them, and the other half he will have paid in cash. This 10,000*l.* in addition to his profits, he will ultimately have to receive from those parties on whose accounts no losses have taken place. The customary period of collecting premiums commences in May, and ends in September; before therefore the balances of the last year can be received, fresh payments must be made in cash for the losses on the underwriting account of the current year; and thus the underwriter, from one year to another, has always a capital advanced, which it is out of his power to dispose of in any possible way. This capital, so locked up, serves as a deposit made for the security of the assured, because it is responsible for none of the engagements of the house in which the underwriter is a partner; and independent of any other property, is generally sufficient to pay the amount of his losses, unless they exceed all reasonable proportion to his premiums. This security was given to the assured by the Act of the

6th of George the First, passed at a period when speculations in the South Sea Company, and many other companies, all bubbles alike, had occasioned failures among mercantile men, altogether unprecedented in the annals of British commerce. If indeed the merchants engaged in the intended new marine insurance company had alledged, that it was unreasonable so much better security should be given by this Act to the holders of policies of insurance, than is given by law to any other description of mercantile creditors, they might with more plausibility have moved for a repeal of the restrictions in question on that ground : but to move for it on the ground they have taken, is to choose the most untenable position that any set of men ever attempted to maintain.

After the writer of the Report has pointed out the necessity of getting rid of the present system of marine insurance, he recommends to Parliament " not to enforce any other system by law ; " but, on the contrary, having released this " branch of business from the restraints now " existing, to leave it to shape itself, as it then " infallibly would do, in conformity with the true " interests of the public." This is reviving the Epicurean doctrine of the fortuitous concourse of atoms : on the same principle, the Report might recommend the destruction of this world, and all that therein is, in order to take the chance of a better world being formed by a fresh jumble. Common sense dictates, that before we destroy existing establishments, we should be sure that we can replace them with better; for it is much more easy to pull down than to build up, and as Dr. Johnson has observed, "the hand that cannot build a hovel, "may demolish a temple." By the laws of society, as well as those of nature, every thing is of progressive growth. Man advances from infancy to youth, and from youth to manhood: the tree is long planted before it brings forth fruit. France indeed attempted to plant her trees of liberty full grown; but they took no root, they afforded no kindly shade, they produced no grateful fruit; they presented to the eye fit emblems of the works of those who planted them— withered sticks painted with a gaudy exterior, and decorated with flaunting ribbons, to hide the rottenness and want of vital sap within. Let us beware how we suffer ourselves to be persuaded to become disciples of this new school; to discard all our reverence for established institutions; to quit the steady light of reason and experience, and follow the ignis fatuus of modern philosophy, that lures to destruction. Not only has the system of marine insurance at Lloyd's kept pace with the increase of our commerce, grown with its growth, and strengthened with its strength; but a system of commercial intelligence has also been established there, by the labour of half a century,

and has at length been brought to a degree of
perfection, which renders it of the utmost importance to the mercantile world.   This intelligence,
though procured at a very heavy expence to the
individual underwriters, is gratuitously communicated, both to the existing chartered companies,
and to the public.   If the insurance business were
transferred from Lloyd's to the intended new
marine insurance company, the directors of that
company could no more supply the same intelligence, than those who transplanted the French trees
of liberty, could continue to display them in the same
verdant foliage, as adorned them in the place of their
native growth, before they had been uprooted and
transplanted by the hand of violence.

The Report then pretends that this change of system will be productive of general benefit to all parties
concerned. Here the Report and the Evidence
are directly at issue; for the underwriters and brokers
uniformly state, that nine-tenths of their good
business would be taken away from them by the
establishment of this new company, and that then
the remaining one-tenth would not be worth
pursuing.   How such an event can be productive
of general benefit to their interests, or how this
assertion can be reconciled to their declarations,
it is not very easy to conceive.

As a final argument, the Report brings forward

the unanimous voice of the great and respectable body of general merchants, on this occasion. But, in point of fact, no voice whatever has been heard on this occasion, except the voice of the very merchants who are desirous of engrossing to themselves the profits of the insurance brokers and underwriters; and when men's interests agree, as Puff says in the Critic, " their unanimity is " wonderful."

To accomplish the scheme of this great and respectable body, the Report recommends, that the exclusive privileges "of the two chartered " companies should be repealed ; and that it " should be left to the discretion of the petitioners " to bring their respective cases under the consi- " deration of Parliament, by bills for carrying into " effect the prayer of their petitions, if they shall " think proper so to do." Thus no distinct opinion is given on the merits of the petitions which led to the appointment of the Committee ; but Parliament having referred them to the Committee, the Committee refer them back again to Parliament. Oh, most lame and impotent conclusion!

The writer of this Report has treated the evidence, which should have formed the basis of his observations, much in the same manner as the Edinburgh Reviewers frequently treat those productions which they profess to review. After giving the title page of the work, and the name

of the author, they present their readers with a very
clever Essay upon the same subject as that which
the author in question undertakes to discuss; but
take no more notice of him, or of his work, than if
neither the one nor the other had ever existed.
So, in this Report, the evidence is scarcely adverted
to, or where occasionally introduced, is misquoted
and misrepresented, by partial extracts; for from
the beginning to the end, not one syllable is to be
found of the testimony of a single witness called
on the part of the underwriters or insurance
brokers. Instead of inferences drawn from evidence, the author gives what he terms, "obvious
"deductions from general principles;" a very pretty
phrase indeed, but by no means appropriate
to the observations to which it is applied: for
many of them, so far from being obvious deductions from general principles, are mere assumptions,
without either principle or proof to support them;
and consequently, however ingenious, neither
convincing nor conclusive.

This Report, in opposition to the sense of the
legislature, as declared in repeated Acts of Parliament, in opposition to the dictates of experience,
and to every sound principle of political economy,
recommends the exploded system of joint stock
companies. The true principle respecting the
establishment of companies is, that they should
only be permitted to do that which cannot be done
by individuals. This applies to several cases; such as

wet docks and canals, because these undertakings are beyond the reach of individual capital; to insurances against fire, because an extensive apparatus of engines and firemen is necessary.for the public safety, and can only be maintained by companies. But it is not so with marine insurances, for they can be, and indeed are effected, more to the public advantage by individuals, than by companies; and if companies are sanctioned, individual underwriting must cease, as has been proved by the example of all other countries, more particularly by the recent example of America. The slightest consideration of the subject will shew, that this consequence must inevitably ensue; for companies act with the advantage of an overwhelming capital, against which no individual capital can stand in competition; and with the farther advantage of being able to perform that by the labour of a very few individuals, to which, on the other system, every individual concerned must necessarily devote his time and attention. It is just as impossible for individuals to withstand the competition of companies, as for manual labour to withstand that of machinery. The reduction of expence at which business is carried on, is the same in both cases; but with this important difference to the public, that the substitution of machinery for manual labour, lowers the price of every commodity to which it is applied; but the substitution of marine insurance companies for individual underwriters, advances the rate of premiums by dimi-

nishing the number of competitors; and as all
charges on commodities are added to their price,
this advance falls ultimately upon the consumer.

It is really derogatory to that liberality which
ought to characterize the great and opulent body
of English merchants, not to be content with their
own legitimate and ample emoluments, but to be
grasping at those of the underwriters and insurance
brokers, whose business they do not understand,
and whose duties they never intend to perform.
To grant their application, would be to drive the
industrious bees from the hive, and give the honey to
the drones. Besides, if these over-grown capitalists
are permitted to erect themselves into joint stock
companies, the example must be acted upon in
other cases ; all individual enterprise and exertion
will be destroyed, and the same consequences will
ensue from the same system, as took place in the
reign of James the First; when, we are told by
great historical authority, and find it confirmed
by the journals of Parliament, that the trade of
these kingdoms fell into great decay, " being
" brought into the hands of a few rapacious
" engrossers."

The promoters of this intended new marine
insurance company have contrived to give popu-
larity to their proceedings, by proposing in the
first instance merely to repeal the exclusive privileges granted to the two existing chartered

companies, and the restrictions imposed by the Act of the 6th of George the First: It should however be considered, that the experience of near a century has proved, these privileges to be at least harmless in the hands of the chartered companies, on account of tho limited extent of commercial influence possessed by their directors and proprietors; and that these privileges serve as a barrier against that formidable intended company, whose immense influence would establish a system of monopoly and combination, instead of the present system of fair and open competition. Before we join any set of men, we should consider the ultimate object they have in view. We ought not to go even to Hounslow, with those who we know mean to lead us on to Windsor; we ought not to engage even in a reform, with those who meditate a revolution.

No necessity for any reform in the present system of marine insurance has been proved by the evidence given before the Committee : on the contrary; it has been shewn that our present means of effecting marine insurances are equal to every possible occasion that the increased commerce of the country can require; and the solidity of the individual underwriters at Lloyd's has been most satisfactorily established. The allegations on which the petitioners rested their case are therefore unfounded, and legislative interference is unnecessary.

The subscribers to the new marine insurance
company have mistaken their road: instead of
addressing themselves to the House of Commons,
they should have addressed themselves to his
Majesty; who, if they made out their case, and
proved the chartered companies to be hurtful
or inconvenient to the public, would, with the
advice of his privy council, and the law officers
of the crown, determine these corporations by
his letters patent, as the Act of the 6th of George
the First directs. But the House of Commons
would be wanting in due respect to his Majesty, if, after having delegated a power to
him, they were to resume and exercise it themselves; and the House is not yet so reformed,
(to use an expression quoted in   late debate) as
" to make the King but as dust in the balance."

This argument appears in itself conclusive
against the bill now pending; but other cogent
reasons may be given, why it ought not to be
entertained. This bill is framed upon the principle repeatedly laid down in the Report of the
Committee of Marine Insurance, and expressed
in the various phrases, of "unfettering the system
" from all restrictions;" " releasing it from the re-
" straints now existing;" "leaving it to shape itself,
" as it then infallibly would do, in conformity
" with the true interests of the public;" and
" removing the restraints of law;" or as the
Honourable Member who brought in the bill ex-

pressed it in his speech, " throwing the business
" entirely open." To adopt the latter metaphor:
if this Honorable Gentleman would try the system
of throwing things entirely open, upon one of his
own estates, he probably would not be so well
satisfied with the success of the experiment in
agriculture, as again to recommend it in legislation. The cases seem very analogous, for as plau-
sible objections might be urged against fences on an
estate, as against the restrictions in the Act of the
6th of George the First. Fences harbour vermin ;
they occupy ground that might be employed in
cultivation; and they obstruct vegetation, by
keeping the sun and air from the adjacent land.
But would the interests of agriculture, or of the
owner, be benefitted by taking them away, and
exposing the fields to the inroads of all kinds of
animals? The Act of the 6th of George the First,
has set up certain fences and restrictions round the
system of marine insurance, and the result of
throwing it open to all manner of innovations and
speculations, as is proposed by the present bill,
would be, as in the other case, that all the fair
fruits of honest industry and patient labour would
be laid waste and destroyed. The exclusive privileges of the chartered companies, and the restrictions against underwriting in partnership, are the
great fences against the inroads of mercantile speculations; but by this bill, underwriting in partnership is to be permitted, and instead of two
joint stock companies, " with a competent capital

" to each belonging, and under proper conditions,
" restrictions, and regulations," as provided by the
Act of the 6th of George the First, companies are to
be formed, ad libitum, with or without capital, and
without any conditions, restrictions, or regulations
whatever.

One of the witnesses examined before the
Marine Insurance Committee declared, that with
the disposition to speculation that now exists,
fifty companies would soon be filled up; and his
opinion is probably correct. A few men desirous
of making their fortunes by one bold stroke, and
many such men are certainly to be found, might
form themselves into a marine insurance company. By lowering the premiums upon the Baltic
risks from 30 to 25 guineas per cent. they might
soon insure them to the amount of many millions.
If the vessels escaped capture and seizure in the
ports of the enemy, their fortunes would be made;
or if that event took place, their fortunes would
still b made; for instead of paying the losses, they
might decamp with the premiums, which the
system adop'ed by companies, of allowing a large
discount for prompt payment, would enable them
to receive. Then, in a foreign clime, they might
enjoy the fruits of their ill-gotten gains; laugh at
the unfortunate dupes who had been ruined by
their credulity, and thank the legislature, for
having opened to them this new road to riches. If
this bill were to pass, such impositions would be

perpetually practised, such bubbles would be constantly bursting, and all the evils of the memorable year 1720, against which the Act of the 6th of George the First was intended to guard, would again be renewed.

Admitting, for the sake of argument, that new regulations in the present system of marine insurance were really necessary, and that the establishment of more companies were thought advisable; these companies ought to be so constituted, as to secure the public against monopoly on the one hand, and against imposition on the other. No company possessing within its own members such immense influence as the intended new marine insurance company, ought to be permitted to act in one body; nor any company, without a competent capital invested in government securities, and never to be trenched upon but with the full knowledge of the public, who have a right to require such a deposit as a security for their engagements. These and many other arrangements, requiring grave and mature deliberation, should be introduced into any bill which interferes with the Act of the 6th of George the First, if any such bill were necessary; but a crude, hasty, indigested bill, like the present, founded on those disorganizing principles, laid down in the Report of the Committee for Marine Insurance, ought not, for a moment, to be tolerated. The Report upon which this bill is founded is a reflection upon the legislature; for, by calling upon them to remove the restraints of law, it implies legislation to be not only useless, but mischievous; by asserting, that this branch of business, if left to shape itself, will infallibly do so in conformity to the true interests of the public, it preaches a doctrine of disorganization and revolution; takes it for granted that a new creation will spring out of chaos, and that order will arise out of confusion. Whether, therefore, the House of Commons consider the respect due to his Majesty, the respect due to themselves, or the duty they owe to the public, they cannot but reject this bill.

The writer of these observations, proposed in the Committee of Marine Insurance, the annexed Report, which has at least the merit of being founded on evidence; and contains, in the margin of each sentence, a reference to the testimonies by which it is supported. He requests it may be carefully compared with the evidence, and doubts not that those who impartially investigate this subject, will agree with him in his conclusion, that the present application to Parliament, however laudable may be the intention of some individuals by whom it is supported, is in its nature and consequences as dangerous and reprehensible, as any application that ever was prompted by private interest, under the pretence of public good.

COPY OF A REPORT

PROPOSED

AS AN AMENDMENT

TO THE

REPORT ADOPTED BY THE COMMITTEE

ON

MARINE INSURANCE.

REPORT.

—

THE COMMITTEE appointed to consider an Act made in
the 6th year of King George the First, intituled,
" An Act for better securing certain powers and
" privileges intended to be granted by his Ma-
" jesty, by two charters, for assurance of ships
" and merchandizes at sea, and for lending money
" upon bottomry, and for restraining certain ex-
" travagant and unwarrantable practices therein.
" mentioned;" and also to consider the state of,
and means of effecting marine insurances in Great
Britain, and to report the same, with their observations and opinions thereon, from time to time, to
the House; and to whom two petitions, one from
various merchants and others in the City of Lon-

don, and the other from the Globe Insurance Company, both praying that the parties may be permitted to effect marine insurances as companies, were also referred ;—have, pursuant to the Order of the House, examined the matters referred to them, and have agreed upon the following

REPORT.

Your Committee, the better to enable them to form their opinion of the effects of the Act of the 6th of George the First, thought it expedient in the first instance, to enquire into and ascertain the present state of, and means of effecting marine insurances in Great Britain. They therefore commenced their proceedings by hearing evidence on the part of the petitioners; and then proceeded to hear evidence also on the part of the two chartered companies, and the underwriters and insurance brokers at Lloyd's, the parties whose interests would be affected by any alteration in the present mode of effecting marine insurances.

This evidence may be classed under the following distinct heads; the necessity of an enquiry into each of which appears to your Committee to result from the reference under which they act, and the allegations contained in the petitions referred to their consideration.

1. The present means of effecting marine insurances with the two existing chartered companies.

2. The present means of effecting marine insurances with individual underwriters.

3. The causes of the establishment of foreign insurance companies; and the practicability of bringing any part of the marine insurance business now effected abroad, to Great Britain.

4. The expediency of granting the additional incorporations prayed for by the petitioners; or of annulling those already granted, and throwing the marine insurance business entirely open, either to joint stock companies, or partnerships of every description, by repealing the restrictions imposed by the Act of the 6th of George the First.

It appears that the confined scale upon which the existing chartered companies transact the business of marine insurance, is matter of complaint among many merchants, who are disposed to give them a preference to individual underwriters; and that such preference would generally be given them on equal terms, by merchants who are not underwriters; but that those who underwrite themselves effect their policies at Lloyd's, in order that other policies may be offered them in return. The evidence before your Committee proves, that the two chartered companies generally charge a higher rate of premium than is paid at Lloyd's; that they will not admit the same clauses into their policies as are usual at Lloyd's; that they will not insure against capture and seizure in the ports of the enemy; that they frequently refuse what are called cross risks; that they will not write any ships of a description inferior to the first and second classes on Lloyd's books; and that with very few exceptions, they will not write more than from 12,000*l.* to 15,000*l.* on any one merchant ship. It does, however, appear, that they frequently take much larger sums on policies on ship or ships ; on risks to and from China' and the East Indies ; and on ships of war. The regulations under which they act, necessarily tend to contract their business within a narrow sphere, compared with the whole insurance business of the country ; but the effects of them are in some degree counterbalanced, by the confidence placed in their solidity, by their mode of payment when losses happen, and by their allowing greater advantages in the shape of discount, to those who transact business with them, than are allowed by individual underwriters. From these considerations many merchants who are not underwriters give them whatever sums they choose to take on all their risks; others resort to them when they have a larger sum to effect, than they can do with those underwriters to whom they are in the habit of shewing their policies;, and they also derive an accession of business, under the operation of their bye-laws, from the mercantile interest of some of their directors and proprietors. The opinion of the narrow scale on which they transact business appears to have become so prevalent, as to have reduced the number of applications made to them, and consequently, the amount of their business, below their own intentions or wishes; for their secretaries state that the companies are very much disposed to extend the scale of their insurances; and the practice so prevalent amongst merchants who are also underwriters, of interchanging their risks with each other for their reciprocal benefit, is assigned as a great cause of the limited proportion, which the business done by those companies bears to the whole insurance business of country. Still they are described by those who have considerable dealings with them as acting with great liberality ; as being advantageous and convenient to the

Left margin annotations:

Appendix,

Barr, Glennie.

Reed, Idle.

Glennie.

Reed, Throck-
morton, Hol-
land.

Holland,
Greathead.

Holland,
Greathead.

Glennie, Idle,
Rogers.

public; and as affording a useful competition with the
individual underwriters at Lloyd's.

The consideration of the means of effecting marine insurances at Lloyd's includes various points. The extent
to which insurances can be effected; the solidity of
the underwriters; the facility of recovering losses; and
the rate of premiums.

Some individuals have complained of the impossibility, and others of the difficulty of effecting insurances
on certain risks; but all the cases of the former class
have been satisfactorily explained; and it has been
proved that no such impossibility could exist amongst
persons of established solidity, and extensive connexions
at Lloyd's, unless in cases where the underwriters consider the premium offered inadequate to the risk: it has
been proved that 631,800*l.* was effected at Lloyd's, on
specie by the Diana frigate, from Vera Cruz; and that
some underwriters had no opportunity of writing a policy even of such magnitude. Attempts were made to
shew that during the autumnal months, particular
difficulty has been found in effecting insurances, owing
to the principal underwriters absenting themselves from
Lloyd's at that period; but it was proved that the leading underwriters when absent, left persons to write for
them; that some write at that season of the year in preference, conceiving that they are then writing to the most
advantage; and that the principal cause of the difficulty alledged, is the contest about the advance of premiums that constantly takes place on the approach of
winter. The evidence of the son of one of the masters at Lloyd's shews, that the number of subscribers to
that house, has increased since the year 1771, from 79

[margin notes:]
Rucker, Mol-
ling.

Simpson, Lond-
es, Barr, For-
syth, Russell,
Inglis, Glennie.

Angerstein,
Reed, Brown,
Halliday, Get-
ting, Mavor,
Nicholson,
Duraco.

Angerstein.

Rucker, Lind-
sey, Forsyth.

Angerstein,
Getting, Shed-
den.

Forsyth,
Mavor.

Angerstein,
Rogers.

Bennett.

to between 1400 and 1500 ; that near 500 underwriters take their seats there every day, and that many stand and write policies for want of greater accommodation. It also appears that many write at the Jamaica, the Jerusalem, and the Coal Exchange Coffee-houses ; as well as many others at their own counting-houses. A number of merchants and brokers, in the most extensive line of business, have declared that they were never unable to complete any insurances they received orders to effect ; and that they consider the present means of effecting marine insurances, as equal to every possible occasion that the increased commerce of the country can require.

The solidity of the underwriters at Lloyd's has been most unquestionably established. One merchant indeed stated, that he only consented to guarantee his underwriters, when required so to do by his correspondents, for fear of losing their business ; but could not state the profit and loss on his having so done. Another stated that he always refused to guarantee them, on account of the losses his house had formerly sustained by guaranteeing ; but he too, when called upon to produce a statement of those losses, declared that " he had never " looked into it." Statements of the proportion that the losses sustained by the insolvency of underwriters, bear to the amount of the property insured, were afterwards given in by various witnesses ; and shewed the following results :—On 8¼ millions, too trifling a sum to be worth making a charge of. On 8¼ millions, 1107*l.* 19*s.* 1*d.* subject to a further deduction by dividends not yet received. On between six and seven millions, 777 *l.* On five millions, 799 *l.* from which the dividends are to

(marginal notes): Angerstein. Angerstein, Reed, Brown, Warren, Idle, Rogers. Backer. Molling. Simpson. Angerstein. Reed. Halliday.

be deducted. One broker, who did not wish to state the precise amount of his returns, but declared that in the last year he had insured some millions, said that his merchants, during eleven years that he had been in business, had never lost 600*l.* by his underwriters. Another broker never had 300*l.* bad debts in the course of his business. Another on recovering 196,776*l.* had only a bad debt of 36*l.* 17*s.* 3*d.*; and another had recovered 200,000*l.* last January, without a bad debt of a single shilling. A witness who had carried on as extensive commission business as any house in London, declared that the bad debts he had made during twenty-eight years, were not worth mentioning; and that for the last few years he had made none; another, whose insurances exceed 800,000*l.* per annum, stated that his bad debts during twenty-four years, amounted to only 860*l.* Many who had not made any exact calculations represented their losses by insolvency as very trifling. It was proved too that in the course of the last war, the solidity of the underwriters was put to the test by various heavy losses; particularly the capture and condemnation of the Dutch ships, on the breaking out of hostilities between this country and Holland. The capture of the homeward-bound Mediterranean fleet, by the squadron under Admiral Richery. The condemnation of the American vessels by France and Spain, on the plea of their not being navigated with the papers required by treaty. The seizure of the British ships in the ports of Russia, by the late Emperor Paul; which were paid for by the underwriters in the first instance, though from one-half to two-thirds of the property was ultimately repaid them. Three different sweeps of the British vessels trading on the coast of Africa, were also made last war by French squadrons.

Getting.

Nicholson.

Shedden.
Rogers.

Meyer.

Idle.

Lyndsey, Barr, Lumley, Williams, Russell, Brown, Barnes

Angerstein.

Shedden.

Angerstein, Shedden.

Angerstein, Shedden

None of these events appear to have occasioned any failures worth noticing among the underwriters at Lloyd's.

Racker, Molling, Jones, Glennie.

Complaints were made by some witnesses of the difficulty of settling and recovering losses and averages at Lloyd's, which they said prevented houses abroad from sending orders for insurance to this country; and one

Racker.

merchant, a foreigner, established in business here within these five or six years, declared that the underwriters at Lloyd's were held in low estimation on the Continent. But other foreign merchants contradicted this assertion.

Grill.

A foreign Consul, who has been in business here more than 40 years, stated that he had never found the underwriters litigious, nor ever had occasion to bring an action against them; that his correspondents were perfectly satisfied with them; that he had never heard they were in low estimation on the Continent, but on the contrary, had no doubt in his mind that an English underwriter stands in very high estimation on the Continent, both in point of honour and character. Another merchant, who for 28

Meyer.

years past has carried on an extensive business in the commission line, chiefly to Germany and Holland, declared that all his insurances had been effected at Lloyd's; that he never found the underwriters litigious, but thought they had always settled their policies in a very honourable way, adding that his correspondents had always been satisfied, and that almost all his business was done for account of foreign houses. Many other witnesses

Angerstein, Reed, Shedden, Nicholson, Barnes, Warren.

gave testimony to the honour and liberality of the underwriters at Lloyd's, and enumerated various instances of their having settled claims to a very large amount for which they were not legally responsible; as well as of

their having dispensed with the production of those regular documents necessary to establish a loss, which in
the present state of Europe, the assured find it very difficult to obtain.

Several witnesses had transacted extensive business at
Lloyd's for many years without a single litigation ; and
stated that many law suits are occasioned by demands of
a fraudulent or suspicious nature ; by persons being employed to fill up policies, who have not sufficient skill
to define the risks with proper accuracy ; or are entered
into, in order to settle points of law, which can only be
set at rest by the decision of a court of judicature.   Particular instances of resistance to fair demands, on the
part of some individuals, may undoubtedly occur, but
the general conduct of the underwriters at Lloyd's in
this respect, does not appear to your Committee to furnish any ground of just censure.

It is almost unanimously admitted that the rate of premiums at which marine insurances are effected here, is
more moderate than in any other country.   One witness
indeed assigns the high premiums required here, as one
cause of the establishment of insurance companies in
America ; and states that cross risks or voyages from
America, to other parts of the world and back to America, have been effected there at two-thirds, and in some
instances at one-half of the premium paid in Great Britain ; but that risks to this country cannot be stated at
more than one-third less premium, and in many instances
nearly the same.   Another witness, who is lately returned
from a tour through the United States of America, where
he was sent with instructions to make particular en-

Marginal notes:

Getting.

Reed, Brown, Halliday, Getting, Grill, Shedden, Nicholson, Barnes, Meyer.

Angerstein, Throckmorton.

Angerstein, Getting, Barnes

Angerstein, Shedden.

Glennie.

Jones.

quiries respecting the marine insurance companies established there, states the rate of premium in America, to
Jones. be generally higher than in this country by one-third on
European and East India voyages; and only lower on
their coasting and West India voyages, which he says
are better known in America, as to the state of the
cruizers, and so on, than in this country. With this exception, (or rather contradiction between these two witnesses,) the position before laid down stands uncontra-
Simpson, dicted. The premiums charged by the companies in
Bridgman. the East Indies, are stated to be rather higher than here;
and no complaint appears to be made by the merchants
Rocker, Grill, on the Continent, as to the rate of premium charged by
Moyer. their London correspondents.

The premiums required by the underwriters at Lloyd's,
Angerstein, are generally lower than those required by the chartered
Reed, Shedden, companies; for as the business of the broker depends
Nicholson. upon his effecting the insurances of the merchant on the
Throckmorton most advantageous terms, he tries among the whole body
Nicholson. of underwriters to find those who will begin his policy
Angerstein, at the lowest premium, and the competition among so
Shedden, War- numerous a class of individuals, reduces premiums to the
ren. very lowest rate, at which they can be fairly afforded.
Nicholson. Indeed it is proved that many voyages are now actually
insured at, and some even under peace premiums.

Forsyth, Some of the underwriters are certainly persons of much
Angerstein, less property and respectability than others; but it ap-
Brown,
Getting. pears that when those of the former description accept a
Forsyth, Get- reduced premium, the most respectable underwriters are
ting, Shedden, frequently obliged to follow their example; so that it is
Warren. impossible to conceive any system better adapted to pro-

mote the general interests of commerce in this respect, than that on which underwriting is now carried on at Lloyd's.

At the commencement of the examinations taken by your Committee, they were led to imagine that a great increase in the number of foreign insurance companies on the Continent of Europe, as well as in the East and West Indies, and the United States of America, had taken place within these few years. The first witness Racker. called, stated, that there were from 30 to 35 companies at Hamburgh, the greatest part of which had been established since 1803; but admitted that the proportion of his correspondents who did their insurances abroad was very small, owing to many circumstances which compelled them to insure in this country. The second witness on the contrary declared, that the goods his house Molling. exported to the Continent, amounting to more than half a million per annum, were chiefly insured in Hamburgh, where the number of insurance companies had very much increased since he left that City; that losses were generally more easily settled there than here; and that he never heard any complaint of those companies; but he too concluded with saying, that scarcely any insurances were done at present on the Continent. On examining another witness it appeared, that although there had been Grill. more than 30 insurance offices at Hamburgh, six or eight years ago, there were now not more than five or six of them remaining; that some of them had closed their accounts because they found it not worth while to go on, and had paid in full; but that others, from heavy losses, had been obliged to declare their incapacity of paying in full, and had only paid from four to fifteen shillings in the pound.

Simpson,
Bridgman,
Lumley,
Russell.

With respect to the companies in the East Indies, there appear to have been seven at Calcutta, five at Madras, and one at Bombay, established mostly since the year 1797. Three of the Madras companies are stated

Bridgman.

to act no longer, from what cause is not mentioned ; but the credit of these companies in India does not appear to stand very high, as the agents for two of them in this City, have refused to pay losses for them, to so small an amount in one instance as 6,000*l.* because they had not funds in hand. Insurance companies were originally

Russell.

established in India, on account of the uncertainty of timely communication with Europe, and chiefly for the purpose of insuring what is called the country trade, or voyages from one port in the Indian seas to another,

Simpson.
Angerstein.

which it would not always be practicable to insure at all, unless they were insured on the spot. This trade alone is stated to be sufficient for the support of several

Bridgman.

insurance companies ; but the discontinuance of over-land dispatches, and regular packets from India to Great Britain, has thrown into their hands the insurance of a very great proportion of the consignments to Europe, which were formerly effected in Great Britain ; and

Simpson,
Bridgman,
Angerstein.

which can only be brought back into their old channel, by the re-establishment of the accustomed means of communication between the two countries.

The insurance companies in the West Indies are too trifling to deserve notice. The number of those in the

Jones.

United States of America, is stated to be about thirty, with capitals of from 44,500*l.* to 115,000*l.* Independent of the general causes which lead to the formation of such

Angerstein.

establishments in all commercial countries, such as the necessity of insuring short voyages on the spot, lest the issue of them should be known before the orders for in-

turance arrived, if sent to a distant country ; the diffi-   Glennie.
culty of effecting insurance in Great Britain, on vessels
not known and registered there except at an advance of
premium ; the desire of the merchants who are usually   Bridgman,
the proprietors of those companies, to retain the profits   Williams, Angerstein.
of their own insurances ; their wish to hold the policies   Molling,
which secure their property in their own hands ; and to   Angerstein. Williams,
transact their business themselves, rather than pay a com-   Angerstein.
mission for having it transacted by others ;—another
cause has powerfully contributed to their increase in
America, and that is the law which prohibits the British   Williams.
underwriter from paying in case of British capture.   A
great proportion of the export trade of America is carried on to the ports of the enemy ; and consists of articles either the produce and manufactures of the enemy,
or the produce of the enemies' colonies.   This circumstance renders her vessels liable to be brought in for adjudication by British cruizers, on suspicion of their cargoes being enemy's property ; and renders it inconsistent with the safety of the parties, to be insured in a
country where the law in such cases interposes an ef-   Angerstein.
fectual bar to the recovery of the loss.   It does not appear that any part of the marine insurances now effected
in America, is likely to be brought to Great Britain,   Williams.
either by the establishment of any new insurance companies, or by any other alterations in the present system   Angerstein.
of effecting marine insurances.   An alteration in the law
alluded to, is the only measure calculated to produce
such an effect.

It is not unconnected with this branch of the subject
before your Committee, to observe that the policy duty
for the year 1809, may be calculated to have been paid

Appendix,
No. 5. upon 175,598,000*l.*; as appears by the following statement, founded on the returns of that duty paid in London.

£311,787 Stamp-duty, at 5*s.* per
100*l.* covers property to amount
of - - - - - £124,714,800

£19,577 ditto, at 2*s.* 6*d.* ditto - 15,763,600

Policy duty paid in London on - £140,478,400
Scotland, Ireland, and the out-
ports, estimated at one-quarter
of London - - - - 35,119,600

£175,598,000

All estimates of British insurable property must be vague; the following, however, appears to be as fairly calculated as the nature of the case will admit.

Appendix,
No. 1. Imports, 1809, - - £30,406,860
Exports, ditto, - - 50,300,963
£80,707,823

Appendix,
No. 1. N. B. The above is exclusive of imports from the East Indies and China; but it is to be observed that the East India Company never insure either imports or exports.

Add difference between official and real value 30 per cent. agreeable to the evidence given by Mr. Irwin, Inspector-General of imports and ex-

ports, before the Lords' Secret Committee in 1797, " that taking all cir-
" cumstances with respect to the rates
" and values into consideration, he
" was of opinion that an advance of
· " near 30 per cent. might be added
" to the ancient estimates." - - - £ 24,212,346

Goods shipped coastwise,
   as per preceding statement of policy duty paid
   in London - - - - £ 15,763,600
Add one-quarter for Scot-
   land, Ireland, and out-
   ports, as per ditto - - 3,940,900
                               19,704,500

TONS.

Appendix,
No. 3.

Tonnage of British vessels
   entered outwards and inwards, 1809 - - - - 3,070,725
Deduct one-quarter for transports, colliers, coasters,
   &c. insured per annum,
   and for ships insured out
   and home on the same
   policy - - - - - 767,681

                 2,303,044 } 34,545,660
           at 15*l.* per ton }

Freight of 3,070,725 tons, at 5*l.* per
   ton - - - - - - - - - - - 15,353,625

                    £ 174,523,954

It must be presumed that many individuals remain

b

voluntarily uninsured, on a considerable proportion both of the ships, freights, and goods, in which they are interested, but to what amount it is impossible to ascertain; and on the other hand, that many of the foreign ships employed in the commerce of Great Britain, and their freights, are insured in this country; so that the one may probably serve as a set off against the other.

Appendix, No. 4.

Reed. Halliday.

The amount of the policy duty paid in former years, falls far short of that paid in 1809; but the cause of this deficiency is explained by the evidence given before your Committee, which states that the duty on policies was much evaded by the use of slips, till prosecutions were instituted by the Attorney-General in 1808, against several individuals for that practice. The fact therefore of less duty having been formerly paid, by no means proves that less insurance was effected.

Glennie, Idle, Rogers.

On referring to the Act of the 6th of George the First, your Committee find it provides, that if his Majesty, after the expiration of 31 years, shall judge the continuance of the two existing chartered companies hurtful or inconvenient, he may revoke them by his letters patent. Your Committee are no advocates for chartered companies possessing exclusive privileges, considering them as having a natural tendency to give monopolies to a few individuals, at the expence of the public at large. But the experience of near a century has shewn that the limited degree of mercantile interest possessed by these companies has counteracted the natural tendency of their institution, and the evidence given before your Committee, so far from proving that these corporations are hurtful or inconvenient, has on the contrary proved that they are convenient and advantageous to the pub-

Tie. Under these circumstances, the only ground on which your Committee could be induced to recommend to Parliament to abrogate their charters, would be a conviction, that by so doing, such ameliorations in the present system of effecting marine insurances might be made, as from a regard to the public good, ought to outweigh every consideration due to the interests of individuals.

Such ameliorations could only be produced in three ways: by adding to the number of the chartered marine insurance companies already established; by permitting the general establishment of joint stock companies for the same purpose; or by removing the present restrictions imposed by the Act of the 6th of George the First, against underwriting in firms or partnerships.

Very different opinions have been expressed by the witnesses examined before your Committee, as to the consequences of granting a charter of incorporation to the merchants and others whose petition is referred to their consideration,

It has been urged in favour of this establishment, that it would give additional facilities to our present means of effecting marine insurances, which it is contended are still wanting; that the confidence placed in its solidity, would bring more foreign insurances to this country; and that a new company would be obliged, by the increase of competition, to lower the premiums, and transact business on more liberal terms than the existing chartered companies. It has also been asserted, that a public board is less selfish, less acute in the pursuit of its own interest, and less careful of it, than an individual. The very great majority of the merchants of this metropolis

[marginal notes:] Rucker, Inglis, Gleanie.
Rucker, Mulling, Jones, Forsyth.
Rucker, Mulling, Jones, Gleanie.
Jones.
Forsyth.

Angerstein.

Inglis.

Forsyth.

Inglis.

who are subscribers to the intended new company, (which is represented as comprising nine-tenths of the commercial interest of the City of London, or so preponderating a proportion of it, that one witness declared he could not name half a dozen houses of note in this City who are not subscribers to it, without referring to some list of merchants,) has also been urged as a proof of the general persuasion entertained of its utility, by those who are most competent to form a correct judgment on the subject.

Angerstein, Reed, Mavor, Nicholson, Barnes, Rogers.

Angerstein, Reed, Brown, Halliday, Getting, Throckmorton, Mavor, Shedden, Nicholson, Barnes, Warren

Rogers.

Angerstein, Reed.

Brown, Nicholson.

Reed, Brown, Throckmorton, Mavor.

Nicholson.

Reed, Brown, Getting, Mavor Nicholson.

It has been contended on the contrary, that no new facilities for effecting marine insurances are wanting; and that if they were wanting, they would not be given by this new company, whose directors would avail themselves of the immense choice of business which the company would possess among its own members, to select the good risks, and reject the bad; that individual underwriters, deprived of a fair shew of good risks, would not find it worth their while to write the bad risks alone, and would be discouraged from continuing their present avocation; that then no means would remain of insuring the bad risks that had been rejected by the company, and thus the present facilities of effecting marine insurances, so far from being increased, would be diminished. That the incorporation of a company possessing so large a proportion of the commercial interests of this metropolis within its own members, would destroy the present system of competition, and establish in its stead a system of monopoly; and that when the individual underwriters were compelled to quit the field, the proprietors of this company might advance the rates of premiums as they pleased, and would enrich themselves at the expence of the public.

. It is denied that this new company would bring, any increase of foreign insurance, to Great Britain. It is contended in assertion, and proved by example, that though some persons may have engaged in this undertaking from a conviction of its utility, yet that the greater number have either not considered its consequences at all, or have been induced, by motives of interest, to join in a plan of which they disapprove. It is objected, too, that the directors of this company would have an undue controul over other mercantile houses, by the system on which they might think proper to regulate the credit given for premiums; that they might take unfair advantages of the opportunities they would have of becoming acquainted with the commercial operations of other merchants, by seeing their correspondence; and, in short, that this establishment would lay the foundation of a monopoly, not only of insurance business, but of commercial business in general.

Societies have lately been formed in this metropolis, by owners of transports and colliers, who insure each other's vessels. None but owners of good ships are admitted into these companies; the owners of bad ships being left, as one of the secretaries says, to insure them at Lloyd's, or where they please. It appears from his evidence, that by thus selecting the good ships only, and rejecting the bad, they had been able to insure each other at an expence of not more than 5*l*. 10*s*. per 100*l*. per annum; while the premium at Lloyd's on transports is 9*l*. and on colliers 18*l*. per annum. From this statement, some idea may be formed of the vast advantage of being able to choose the best description of ships; and some calculation may be made of the enormous profits that might be derived by this intended new marine insurance

Angerstein.
Reed.

Reed, Brown,
Throckmorton,
Mavor, Shedden, Nicholson,
Rogers.

Angerstein,
Reed.

Brown.

Reed,
Nicholson.

Cheap.

Wilson.

company, acting upon this system, and insuring property, as it is estimated they would do, to the amount of eighty millions per annum.

There appears to be a radical and irremediable vice, in the constitution of this new marine insurance company. The commerce of Great Britain is chiefly carried on, not for account of the merchants themselves, but for account of their correspondents abroad; who ship the produce either of the British colonies and dependencies, or of foreign countries, to be sold here on commission. Until the recent revolutions in Europe had thrown the trade of the Continent into new hands, as well as into new channels, the great bulk of the commerce of Great Britain was, and a great proportion of it still is, of this description. It is therefore the duty of the merchants to effect the insurances of their correspondents on the lowest terms possible; and this is likely to be best done through the medium of indifferent persons. The practice of a merchant being an underwriter, in the present open mart for marine insurance, can be attended with no disadvantage to the interest of his correspondents, because the rate of premium is regulated by the competition of the general underwriters at Lloyd's, which he has no power to controul: but if the merchants at large, by forming themselves into one or more companies or associations, were to take the insurance business into their own hands, and destroy individual underwriting, all competition would be at an end, and the rate of premiums be completely within their power. By forming such establishments, they would become at the same time agents and principals; they would have an interest directly opposite to that of the parties for whom they act; and the prayer of these petitioners is neither more nor less than this, that they may be permitted to do that by virtue of a new law, which the existing laws wisely prohibit and justly punish.

Whether the merchants form themselves into one large company, or many small ones, the effect of taking the business of the underwriters and insurance brokers into their own hands, will be the same, both as to depriving them of their present occupations and means of subsistence, and as to the general interests of commerce. The competition that at present exists, and keeps down the rate of premiums, though less narrowed than by the formation of one company, will still be greatly diminished. As men naturally associate most with those who follow the same pursuits as themselves, each of these associations would probably be composed chiefly of persons engaged in the same branches of commerce. If then any heavy calamity took place among the shipping engaged in any particular branches of commerce, the parties affected by this event, who would have to recover large sums as merchants, would themselves, as partners in these companies, be the parties on whom the losses would fall; and having few premiums derived from other branches of insurance business to set against the losses sustained in that particular branch, would be exposed to great risk of failure. Whereas the universality of the insurance business done at Lloyd's, and the limitations which the underwriters prescribe to themselves, as to the amount they insure on different descriptions of voyages, so divide the risks, that a calamity of this nature by no means affects them in the same degree. If such companies were permitted, it would be impossible to form any judgment of the prudence, or want of prudence, with which their business was conducted; an advantage which every

Reed, Halliday, Mavor, Shedden.

Angerstein.

Angerstein.

Lyndler, Angerstein, Reed.

Brown, Reed, Halliday, Shedden, Barnes.

broker has with every individual underwriter, in the present open manner of transacting business at Lloyd's ; and they might insure to an unwarrantable extent, out of all reasonable proportion to their capital, without the possibility of its being discovered.

Reed, Shedden.

A witness who acts as secretary to an insurance company, and whose attention of course has been much directed to this subject, says, that the country would be crowded with insurance companies in the first instance ; that with the superabundance of capital, and the disposition to speculation that prevails, fifty companies would be filled up in a short space of time ; and that the eagerness for business, particularly for speculative business, would in the first instance reduce the rate of premium very materially.   Your Committee think this disposition cannot be too strongly guarded against ; or that offices for marine insurances would start up in every street, as offices for lottery insurances once did, and would fail as often ; for they would probably adopt the same system as is now acted upon by the chartered companies, of allowing a large discount for prompt payment of premiums, and thus, instead of leaving their funds in the hands of the assured, as a security to them in case of loss, (the system of individual underwriters,) they would always have a large disposeable capital, ready to be invested in any objects of speculation.

Jones.

Mavor.

The effect of establishing insurance companies, as to the rate of premiums, may be correctly ascertained, by putting together the evidence of three witnesses respecting the companies in America ; and at the same time, the apparent contradiction in the statement of two of these witnesses, may be reconciled.   The first states these com-

Glennie.

panies to have been established in consequence of the high premiums charged in Great Britain; and that they made very handsome profits, by insuring on more reasonable terms. The second witness, recently returned from that country, says, that the premiums there, on the principal risks, are now one-third higher than here; and lays it down as a principle, that a public company is undoubtedly a dearer resort for insurances. The third witness proves that the merchants of New York, lately agreed at a public meeting, to encourage individual underwriting, in order to relieve themselves from the monopoly exercised by the companies. Thus it appears, that these companies began by writing on moderate terms; that by this means they beat the individual underwriters out of the field; and that then, they availed themselves of their monopoly, to raise the premiums higher than ever. · Jones. Bennett.

Another plan still remains to be considered, that of repealing the restrictions imposed by the 6th of George the First, against underwriting in firms or partnerships. It certainly is desirable that the best possible security should be given to the assured; it also appears reasonable to suppose, that the joint security of several persons, is better than that of a single individual; and some of the witnesses examined by your Committee, have expressed themselves to be of that opinion. To this, however, it has been answered, that theory and practice do not always accord; and it has been proved by those who have directed their observations to this point, that in cases of insolvency, where one of the partners of the house has been at the same time an underwriter, his separate estate has always paid a larger dividend than the joint estate of the partnership. This fact is not only proved, but satis- Glennie, Williams. Angerstein; Brown, Gietting Throckmorton, Shedden, Burnes.

c

factorily explained, in the following manner:—An underwriter is obliged to pay his losses within a month after they happen, but cannot begin to collect his premiums in less than a year. In the mean time, the payment of his losses brings him under considerable advances, which form a capital deposited for the security of those with whom he transacts business; and which it is absolutely out of his power to touch, or alienate. If he is under the necessity of stopping payment, it is generally found on winding up his affairs, that the premiums due to him form a fund sufficient, or nearly sufficient, to pay the losses on the risks outstanding, those on the risks run off to the period of his stopping payment having been previously paid as they became due. But if the underwriting account was rendered responsible for the commercial engagements of the house, by the whole being blended together, as would be the case if underwriting was carried on by partnerships, this advantage would be taken away, and the security of the assured be diminished, instead of being increased, by the change of system.

Your Committee are of opinion that this change has no more claim to favourable consideration in any other point of view; for it is open to many of the objections which have been urged against the other plans. It would tend to narrow competition, the extent of which depends upon the number of competitors. The objection of one partner, might defeat the disposition of another to settle a loss. The necessity of consulting an absent partner, might occasion great delay and inconvenience in effecting insurances. The assured would be obliged to outlaw an absent partner, before he could recover against the others; and this is a process so frequently resorted to by commercial houses, in order to gain time, that it is to be

---

Marginal notes:

Getting,
Throckmorton

Getting,
Throckmorton

Getting,
Throckmorton

Getting,
Throckmorton
Barnes.

Forsyth,
Glennie.

Reed,
Throckmorton
Rogers.

Aspenstein,
Barnes, Idle.

Brown,
Throckmorton
Barnes, Idle.

Barnes.

feared every litigious set of underwriters would take care, to have an absent partner, a subterfuge from which the assured is secured by the present system of underwriting by individuals only.

Brown, Barnes.

Your Committee having carefully considered the evidence before them, and compared it with the allegations in the petitions referred to their consideration, are of opinion, that although the trade and commerce of these kingdoms have so much increased since the year 1720, when the existing chartered companies were first established; and although those companies may not at present insure more than four parts in 100 of the ships, goods, and merchandize, insured in Great Britain, yet that the means of effecting marine insurance by individual underwriters, have kept ample pace with the increase of the trade and commerce of these kingdoms. They believe that no part of the insurance business now effected by the foreign insurance companies, would be brought to Great Britain by the establishment of more insurance companies here. They are persuaded that the present system of individual competition is best adapted to the interests of commerce, and to the genius of a free and enterprizing people. They find that this system was devised by the wisdom of our ancestors, at a period when the numerous failures of mercantile houses made it peculiarly necessary to secure the assured from the ruinous consequences of commercial speculation, which appear to be most effectually guarded against by the restrictions against underwriting in firms or partnerships; and that though they thought it expedient, in the then depressed state of credit, to accompany this measure with the incorporation of the two existing chartered companies, yet that in the very Act for their establishment, they declared their conviction of the pernicious tendency of joint stock companies and associations; in the most decided language) They are that under the present system, the commerce of these kingdoms has risen to its present height of unexampled prosperity ; and therefore they are not disposed to touch it with the rash hand of innovation, at the request of those who have an interest in the proposed change. They think this system is as free from defects, as any human institution can be expected to be found ; that the alterations proposed are likely to produce much greater evils than they are calculated to remove; and that parliamentary interference in matters of trade, ought never to be resorted to, but under circumstances of much more grave and urgent necessity, than have been made out in the present instance.

In confirmation of the foregoing statement, your Committee have annexed to their Report the Minutes of the Evidence taken before them ; together with the several accounts which they thought it necessary to call for, in order to elucidate the subjects referred to their consideration.

February, 1811.

CONSIDERATIONS

On the Dangers of altering the Marine Insurance Laws of Great Britain, in the manner proposed by a Bill, brought into Parliament for that purpose, and now depending in the House of Commons:

And, On the impolicy of granting, without the most accurate Legislative Enquiry, several Applications to Parliament for sanctioning certain self-erected Joint Stock Companies for Insurance of Lives, Insurance against Fire, and for the Purchase and Sale of Annuities.

PART I.

PRELIMINARY OBSERVATIONS

On the essential Distinctions between Fire and Life Insurance Companies, and Marine Insurance Companies.

MARINE Insurance being the mainspring of commerce, is now well understood to be, especially, so necessary to foreign trade, as to be justly considered its vital principle.

The nature and establishment of the laws which govern so important a concern, cannot then but be well worthy of the serious attention of every commercial state; and in England, where foreign trade is interwoven, in a manner, with her political greatness, these must be subjects of superlative importance.

They are now brought under the consideration of her legislature, *by a bold an Attempt at a Monopoly in favour of the petitioners for the establishment of a new Marine Insurance Company,* as ever distinguished the reign of monopolies, in earlier and less enlightened times.

Their petition, with one from the Globe Fire Insurance Company, for similar purposes, has been referred to a select Committee of the House of Commons, appointed to take the state of Marine Insurance into consideration; and their Report, accompanied by minutes of the evidence which they have collected, concludes with the following resolutions.

"RESOLVED, That it is the opinion of this Committee, that property requiring to be insured against sea and enemies risks, should have all the security that can be found for it, whether that security exists in chartered companies, or in other companies, or through individuals:

"RESOLVED, That it is the opinion of this Committee that the exclusive privilege for Marine Insurance of the two chartered companies should be repealed, saving their charters, and their powers and privileges, in all other respects, and that leave should be given to bring in a bill for this purpose:

"RESOLVED, That it is the opinion of this Committee, that, with respect to the two petitions which have been referred to them, it should be left to the discretion of the petitioners, to bring their respective cases under the consideration of the House, by bills for carrying into effect the prayer of their petitions, if they shall think proper so to do."

These resolutions leave nearly the whole subject to the

wisdom of the House. They encourage, rather than discourage, the object of the petitioners, since a decided opinion is given in the Report, in favour of *large Companies* for Marine Insurance, and no other objection is stated, even to their being invested with chartered rights, (which must always be, more or less, *exclusive* rights), than that no one Company should have any privileges or exemptions, from which any other company should be excluded.

Should the second resolution be adopted by the House, and passed unlimited and unrestrained into a law, it may be shewn, that the petitioners will attain the monopoly sought for, almost as effectually, as if it had been given to them with all the formality of the charter, with which they so boldly prayed to be invested.

The effect of the exclusive privilege of the two existing Chartered Companies, called the Royal Exchange and London Insurance Company, as it extends only to other *Companies*, has been to throw nearly the whole *legal* business of Marine Insurance into the hands of individuals; for what appears by the evidence taken by the Committee, to be insured by both these companies together, is in a general consideration unworthy of any notice.

Their charters, therefore, have produced effects diametrically opposite to the intentions of the legislature. They were *designed*, when granted, to give to the two companies a great monopoly, *but have, in effect, utterly destroyed the monopoly,* to which, as wil be shewn, that branch of trade is, in its own nature, but too much exposed; and have *thereby* mainly *promoted* its present flourishing condition.

How far the present Petitioners aimed at the erection of a new and more effectual monopoly, by the establishment of *their New Marine Insurance Company,* those who are acquainted with the motives and objects of the framers of the scheme, can have no hesitation in deciding.

They themselves have loudly proclaimed, *as is usual on such occasions,* that their views are directed only to the public good; but when the good of the commonwealth is to be advanced, only along with the private advantage of its promoters, there must always be room for much well grounded suspicion, whether the ostensible object be indeed the real object.

To the exclusive privileges demanded in their petition the New Marine Insurance Company have, *apparently,* abandoned their unjust pretensions. Maturer consideration has shewn them the inconsistency, and even the absurdity, of asking in one breath, exclusive privileges to be taken from two existing Companies, and in the next, to be conferred upon themselves. It has, however, not escaped their sagacity that if the second resolution of the Committee shall obtain the force of law, it will enable them, almost as effectually to accomplish their scheme, as if they had been formally erected into a chartered company for the purposes of it; not, indeed, by means of exclusive privileges, sanctioned by public law, but by a combination which would then no longer be unlawful.

This combination would enable them effectually to monopolize nearly the whole Marine Insurances of Great Britain, and consequently to destroy entirely the present system, together with all the individuals and their capital embarked in it.

These petitioners are now, therefore, straining every nerve without the doors of the House of Commons, to influence those within, to give the Resolution of the Committee that force; and the report of the Committee is certainly very favourable to their designs; but some observations may be made on it, which will materially alter the complexion it gives to the subject.

The general reasoning against monopolies is become trite, and is so well understood, that a word need not be wasted on the subject. It is a nicer and more undecided question, whether there may not be some branches of trade, which from their very nature require, that those who embark in them should be invested with extraordinary privileges. These are all, more or less, monopolies, because extraordinary privileges must always be, more or less, exclusive privileges. It is against the danger of their becoming entirely such, that the legislature has anxiously to guard in granting them.

Joint-stock companies, established by royal charter, or by act of Parliament, as described by Dr. Smith, seem to be the only proper institutions for conducting such branches of trade.

"To establish a joint stock company, however," says that learned author, "for any undertaking, merely because such a company might be capable of managing it successfully, or to exempt a particular set of dealers from some of the general laws which take place among all their neighbours, merely because they might be capable of thriving, if they had such an exemption, would certainly not be reasonable.* To render such an establishment perfectly reasonable, with the circumstance of being reducible to strict rule and method, two other circumstances ought to concur. First, it ought to appear with the clearest evidence, that the undertaking is of greater and of more general utility than the greater part of common trades; and *Secondly*, that it requires a greater capital than can easily be collected in a private copartnery. If a moderate capital were sufficient, the great utility of the undertaking would not be a sufficient reason for establishing a joint stock company; because, in this case, the demand for what it was to produce would readily and easily be supplied by private adventurers.

" The trade of insurance, (he continues) gives great security to the fortunes of private people, and by dividing among a great many that loss that would ruin an individual, makes it fall light and easy upon the whole society. In order to give this security, however, it is necessary that the insurers should have a very large capital. Before the establishment of the two joint stock Companies for Insurance, in London, a list, it is said, was laid before the Attorney-General, of one hundred and fifty private insurers who had failed in the course of a few years."

.. It has, however, been practically demonstrated, that in the trade of Marine Insurance, with the circumstance of being certainly of greater utility than perhaps any other trade, the other circumstance of requiring a larger capital than can easily be collected into a private copartnery, which the learned author says should appear with the *clearest evidence* to make the establishment of a joint stock company in any trade *reasonable*, does not concur. By the evidence taken by the Committee, it appears in the clearest manner, that the trade of Marine Insurance has been carried, with the commerce of the country, to the unparalleled extent it has now reached, not only without the aid of the capital of joint stock companies, but without even the *legal* aid of that of private copartneries. It may be safely averred too, that it is conducted at the lowest expence consistent with a reasonable profit for the labour and risk of those who are engaged in it, and with the maintenance of the capital set apart in the general distribution of stock, for the support of this branch of trade.

The new Marine Insurance Company may, at the same time boldly be challenged to produce to the Attorney-General, instead of a list of 150 names, any list of names, of private insurers, worthy of consideration who have failed within the last few years.

A little reflection will shew that, in times of war, and especially of the war which is now waged against commerce, the trade of Marine Insurance is not reducible to such a routine or uniformity of method, as Dr. Smith states to be the first and indispensable requisite to adapt any branch of trade even to the successful management of joint stock companies.

In times of such war, all the activity, the vigilance, and the sagacity of a great number of the most observing and inquiring *individuals*, all anxious for their several interests, have not been found more than are requisite for the successful management of that trade; the premiums whereof vary, not only with the sea-

sons, but with all the varying relations between Great Britain
and foreign powers, and between foreign powers with each other,
with the disposition and success of fleets and armies, and with
the greater or less protection afforded to commerce, they vary
also with the force, quality, and nation of the ship. An insurer
duly weighs all the shades of difference in the risk between a
ship built of English oak, or of American cedar or pine; between
a ship navigated by the hardy, bold, and skilful British seaman;
by the Portuguese or Italian; or by the feeble and helpless Las-
car. The Body of Insurers in London, accordingly, to obtain
such information as it is the interest of merchants to withhold
from them, have established a correspondence with all the
nations, and with almost every principal maritime place in the
world, which they daily expose to public view in rooms set
apart for that purpose, *at their own expence*. They maintain
an active correspondence with the Admiralty, both to receive
and to give information, when and where protection is
wanted for our own or for the trade of friendly powers, and
upon the general state of relations at sea. *They* have established, in all the principal sea-ports of the kingdom, Surveyors who examine into, and report, the age, the state, and the
condition of every ship at each time of entry or of departure.

Where such vigilance and such activity are necessary in any
business, it seems little capable of being reduced to a routine,
and accordingly *the existing Chartered Companies have, in a
manner, abandoned the pursuit of it*. Whether such vigilance
and activity could or would be equally exerted, by one, or by a
small number of joint stock companies; or whether, if equally exerted, their results might not, instead of being fairly
brought forward to the public view and used for public benefit,
be converted to the private advantage of such companies, may
easily be conjectured. The number of Insurers interested, who
contribute to this species of information, *alone* secures its publicity; but as almost every considerable merchant, in order to
obtain access to such a body of information, and to make
public such information, as it is for his interest to give, subscribes
to the establishment of the Insurers at Lloyd's, that publicity
is further insured even beyond the possibility of concealment.

Premiums of insurance, not only vary with all these, and
many other varying circumstances, they vary also with the
profit afforded by them *upon the whole* from year to year. If
the profits of insurers be insufficient to yield a reasonable recompence for their skill and labor, and to maintain the capital
set apart for that branch of trade in any particular year; or
should the business of two or three years together, as it sometimes happens, terminate in loss, premiums upon every description of risk rise, so as to afford them that reasonable and
necessary recompence.

Insurance, in general, as mentioned by Dr. Smith, naturally divides itself into two parts; Marine Insurance and Insurance of houses and of other fixed property from fire. There is another sort of insurance not mentioned by that learned author, the Insurance of Lives, and a trade akin to it, the Purchase and Sale of Annuities.

In the trade of Insurance of Houses from fire and these other last mentioned trades, (besides their having all the requisites which fit them for the successful management of joint stock companies, and which render the establishment of such companies, for the business of them, perfectly reasonable,) there is another important circumstance not noticed by the learned author, and that is, the length of their contracts, namely,' of the time necessary for the accomplishment of each single transaction. This circumstance operates in two ways:

First, by so delaying the issue, and consequently the ascertainment of the profit and loss of their undertakings, as altogether to unfit them for the enterprise of individuals, or common private copartneries, and accordingly none have embarked in them:

And, *Secondly,* by so prolonging the credit necessary to be given, as to preclude individuals, owing to the great uncertainty of the continuance of their security, from dealing with one another, or with common private copartneries, in those trades.

Well constituted joint stock Companies alone, therefore, whose security is unaffected by the uncertainty of the affairs of individuals, and whose permanence prevails against the certainty of their deaths, seem calculated to answer the purposes of those trades.

There are, however, two points of the greatest importance for the consideration of the legislature in establishing such companies,

First, That no one Company should be permitted to be so large as to prevent a sufficient number of them being appointed, so as to produce a competition among them, that should insure their accepting the lowest rate of profit consistent with a reasonable advantage on their respective capitals;

And *Secondly,* That their security and stability should be so ascertained, as to insure to the public the objects for which they may have been created.

The only proof perhaps of such security would be the deposit of their capital under legislative inspection.

With due encouragement every great town might, in process of time, have a joint stock company for itself and the surrounding villages and country, and for the insurance of lives and purchase and sale of annuities every considerable county.

The case is widely different with respect to Marine Insurances: though of vital importance to a country, where, as in England, foreign commerce has become necessary to her political existence,' the 'trade' in *them* must be confined to few principal maritime cities.' In York, Manchester, Birmingham, or Nottingham, a Marine Insurance probably never was effected. These, though some of the chief cities of the empire, furnishing an immense quantity of the most important exports, and working from the raw material, and otherwise consuming a no less important quantity of imports, are, by their situation in the interior of the country, precluded from dealing in Marine Insurances, which require to be conducted in sea-ports, where the earliest intelligence of nautical adventures naturally arrives.

Owners of ships, residing in sea-ports, prefer to insure on the scene of their business.

The maritime cities, which possess the advantages of situation and of access, naturally obtain a superiority in foreign trade.

London, above all,' from its peculiar advantages in these respects, but particularly from the operation of public commercial regulations and revenue laws, which draw to it *exclusively* the whole of the East India, and a great proportion of many other important branches of foreign trade, possesses such a pre-eminence over all the other maritime cities of Great Britain, that *her* market for Marine Insurance regulates that of the whole country. London, together with a very few other maritime cities, effects the whole of the Marine Insurances of the British Empire.

The impolicy of increasing this natural Monopoly by the erection of joint stock Companies in all, or any of these cities, but especially in London, whose market governs all the rest, must therefore be apparent. That London does govern all the market, and, in effect, herself alone enjoy a monopoly of Marine Insurance, is demonstrated by the Report of the Committee, which shews that nearly the whole duty on the policies of Marine Insurance, collected in Great Britain, is paid by London alone.[*]

In this situation of things, amid such facility and temptation, it is surprising that the merchants of London, who are well aware of the opportunity afforded them, have not made more frequent attempts to obtain charters from the legislature, for securing this natural monopoly to their own body.

---

[*] The exact proportion cannot be stated, as the distributors of stamps in the country, do not distinguish the amount of policy duty in their remittances. In 1809, £317,290 was collected at the office in Lombard Street, established for the convenience of Lloyd's Coffee House, and in all Great Britain, as far as the account can be made up, £348,592.

The charters of the Royal Exchange and London Assurance Companies, though they give them by law an exclusive privilege against other Companies for Marine Insurance, do not confer any such privilege for the insurance of lives or from fire, or for the purchase and sale of annuities.

The great utility of these trades, and the greater demand for them by an increasing population and commerce, than these two companies could supply, have therefore given rise to great number of associations larger than private copartneries; in London, especially, these have of late years wonderfully increased. But as they are almost universally without any legislative sanction, and, *therefore, without any legislative scrutiny,* they afford a very different security to the public, from what would be given by a number of well-regulated joint stock Companies, having that sanction, established throughout the country.

Such Associations, being subject to no legislative supervision, make rules and regulations for themselves, and having erected themselves into a Joint Stock Company, delude the public with splendid descriptions of their capital and of their security, though these are in fact, in most cases, of the most diminutive and slender description.

One thousand shares, for example, are arranged on a list of £1000 each, making an amount of one million; these are taken in greater or less numbers by, perhaps, five hundred persons, who set forth that they have established a Company for Insurance of lives, or against fire, or for the purchase and sale of annuities, with a capital of ONE MILLION. *This capital, however, is never set apart for the security of the public.*

Sometimes indeed, one per cent., scarcely ever more than ten per cent. is so set apart and invested in the funds, or in some public security for the payment of directors and clerks, and for the general purposes of the business. Taking five per cent. or one-twentieth part of each share, as the sum set apart, that rate, upon a million, would amount to £50,000. Each subscriber pays his five per cent. on his share or shares, and is *held liable,* for the remaining ninety-five per cent. or nineteen twentieths in case they may be wanted.

How much, or how little, such a Company differs from one with a capital of £30,000 must depend, not only upon the ability of each subscriber to pay the whole of his subscription, which may almost universally be questioned; but, also, upon the continuance of his ability to pay the remaining nineteen-twentieths, for which he is only *held liable:* and this ability the public have no means of ascertaining. It is sufficiently evident, however, that they remain in his possession, subject to all the fluctuations of circumstances and reverses of fortune,

2

to which mercantile men, who form the chief part of these associations, are liable; and when the whole property in such a
Company, has once changed hands, which, in the very nature of
things, must, in no very long period of time, be the case,
the original security is altogether lost.

The sum paid for the purchase of any of these shares will,
of course, be only the same as the deposit made by the original proprietor, and when a transfer of the whole stock has
taken place, there ceases to be the shadow of security that
the new proprietors possess one shilling beyond what they
have each paid for their shares.

*Finally, therefore, it appears that such an Association is changed
into a Company, whose boasted million has dwindled to one-tenth,
or one twentieth, or one-hundredth part of the sum.*

Thus, however magnificent these schemes may at first be
made to appear, it is quite plain they partake very much of
the nature of bubbles of a very empty kind. *And yet these
Associations now step boldly forward to the Legislature, and
demand to be recognised and sanctioned as public Bodies,
under the seemingly modest, but artful, request for leave to
sue and be sued in the name of their Secretary;* but, insecure
and unsatisfactory as they are, their first formation being generally supported by opulent and creditable merchants, whose honourable intentions may be unquestionable,
they have drawn to themselves a very considerable trade.
Even those who are aware of their insecurity, prefer the chance
of their honour and stability to being altogether without the
benefit of their trade.

How much more beneficial and solid would be joint stock
Companies, protected by the legislature, and having given
security by public deposit of their capital, is a subject well
worthy of the attention of that Legislature.

How magnificently soever the new proposed Marine Insurance Company have vaunted their boasted capital of FIVE
MILLIONS, every mercantile man in London knows it was
intended to be no other than just such a bubble as has been
described. If the Legislature had compelled them, had it
granted them a charter, to make a public deposit of their
capital, any one acquainted with the names which fill the
scheme lists of this proposed company, will smile when he
observes those which now grace these lists, and which such
an enactment would erase from their pages*.

* If the bill introduced by the framers of this project should pass into a
law, all these numerous other self-erected Joint Stock Companies will of
course be equally entitled to deal in Marine as in Fire Insurances, which is
probably the cause of their present anxiety to bring themselves into a state
which may enable them to offer some sort of practical liability to those who
may be pleased to deal with them in that trade.

PART II.

On the Impolicy of the Legislature's permitting self-erected Joint Stock Companies for the purposes of Marine Insurance.

THE TRADES of Insurance of lives, and against fire, and of the purchase and sale of annuities, have been enlarged upon as having a certain affinity to the trade of Marine Insurance.

It may now be shewn that the circumstance, not mentioned by Dr. Smith, namely, the time occupied in each separate transaction, which renders these trades *unfit for the enterprise of individuals or private copartneries*, is not of a length to have such disqualifying effects upon the trade of Marine Insurance.

The duration of the risk, or of each separate adventure of an insurer, and the length of time the assured incurs the hazard of his stability, are both shorter than in the greater part of ordinary trades.

The bodies of ships are seldom insured for time, during war; and when they are, the law, imposing the stamp duty on insurances, prohibits their being insured for longer than a year, to secure the renewal of that duty. In times of war, when premiums are high, the bodies of ships, or the freight money, are seldom insured for double voyages; that is, out and home. The assured must give, for a double voyage, a double premium, the whole of which would be lost to him should the ship perish, or be taken, on the outward voyage; he naturally, therefore, prefers to insure for a single voyage.

Goods, from their nature, can very seldom be insured but for a single voyage. The voyage to the Baltic, to the bottom of the Mediterranean, to the West Indies, to South and North America, to the Newfoundland Fishery, to Africa as far as the Cape of Good Hope, does not, out and home, on an average, exceed, at the longest, 6 or 8 months; and the termination of the outward voyage is generally heard of in little more than half that time. The voyage to ports in the Mediterranean nearer the Streights of Gibraltar, to France and Spain without them, to Portugal, to Holland, and to the Ports of the North Sea without the Baltic, does not exceed half the period of 6 or 8 months. It is on these voyages that almost the whole insurances of private merchants have to be made.

The longest voyages which are insured, are those to the East Indies and back; but, as the East India Company never insures, these bear but a small proportion to the whole insurances of the country.

The longest of these times does not exceed half the length of the credit the merchant receives from his clothier, his ironmonger, or any other of his tradesmen; as the credit he receives for the very merchandize insured.

Taking the average length of the voyages altogether, it does not exceed one third, or one fourth, of the usual length. of that credit. Practically, moreover, the merchant is often indebted to the underwriter, on which debt he has a lien for any loss; while the underwriter, though he does not receive his premiums sometimes for *years*, invariably pays his losses within *one month* after adjustment, in ready money, whereby his stability is almost daily put to a very strict test.

The duration of the risk, *on the things to be insured*, as it enables individuals to ascertain the issue of each transaction, in the trade of Marine Insurance sooner than in the greater number of ordinary trades, cannot then be a circumstance to render the establishment of a joint stock company in that trade *necessary;* and the length of the time, during which the merchant incurs the hazard of the stability of the underwriter, not exceeding on an average one-third or one-fourth of the usual length of mercantile credit, cannot be a circumstance to render the establishment of such a company *reasonable.*

The tradesman or manufacturer, besides, gives an absolute credit to the amount of the goods supplied to the merchant, while the merchant to the underwriter only gives credit for a *probable loss;* the chances against which must obviously be greatly in favour of the merchant; if the average of premiums be 5 per cent. it must be a hundred to five in his favour.

The credit for this *probable debt* must be very unreasonably objected to by the merchant, for 3, 6, or 8 months, who is himself taking an absolute credit for the very thing insured for 12 to 18 months; while at the same time he exacts from the underwriter payment of his losses at the end of one month after adjustment, and yet, if there be no loss seldom pays him the premium for 18 months, or even longer.

If there are then, sometimes, failures among underwriters,* as in other trades, no one will hesitate to conclude, when their mode of dealing is considered, that they must be much fewer and of less calamitous extent, than among merchants, who are not subjected to such tests, and who, by the longer credit they obtain from the tradesman and manufacturer, and even from the underwriter, are enabled to, and generally do, carry on their trade for a long period after they are absolutely ruined.

Those persons who devote their whole time and capital to underwriting are, besides, without the benefit of the statute of bankruptcy. The merchant has thus the advantage of holding liable the property an underwriter may, after having failed,

---

* By the failure of an individual underwriter, a few merchants MAY, now and then, lose £200, or £300. By the failure of a COMPANY, with whom they would be in the habit of insuring on one risk £10,000, or £20,000, an hundred merchants might be totally ruined, and involve the destruction of their industrious creditors.

acquire in all his future life. If underwriters are involved in bankruptcy, therefore, their bankruptcy must be the effect of dealings as *merchants*, and not as *underwriters*.

From this circumstance, no judgment can be formed of the comparative failures among merchants and underwriters ; but it is said, by persons conversant with the subject, and it partly appears by the evidence taken by the Committe, that, whenever an underwriter has been involved as a partner in the bankruptcy of a mercantile firm, his estate has always given a better dividend to his separate creditors, than any of the mercantile partners ; from which it may fairly be inferred, that the underwriting partner's transactions were not the occasion of their mercantile destruction.

To erect, in the trade of Marine Insurance, a joint stock company of merchants, who would so be exempted from the general laws which take place with respect to other insurers, would be more unjust than to erect a joint stock company in any of the branches of the trade of merchants ; because, insurers being already prevented from legally associating in private copartneries, and from the benefit of the statute of bankruptcy, are already thereby excluded from these important privileges of their neighbours.

If the duration of the risk, and consequent length of time the assured incurs the hazard of the stability of the assurer, afford no reasonable ground for establishing joint stock companies, in the trade of Marine Assurance, as little does the value of the things to be insured.

The value of ship, freight, and cargo of a West Indiaman, or vessel engaged in the South American trade, does not exceed from £20,000 to £60,000 ; these are of much greater value than ships engaged in the European or North American, or any other, except the East India trade; and (as the East India Company never insures) the ship, freight, and private trade of an East Indiaman, which are only to be insured, does not exceed the value of from £50,000 to £100,000. Let the largest of these sums be divided among only 500 underwriters, not half the number at Lloyd's (many underwriters insuring by procuration for two or three other persons), and it would not furnish a risk of £200 each on an average. Few judicious underwriters of the first rate, for practical prudential reasons, ever insure above £1000 on one vessel on the best risk, £1500, perhaps £2000, on an Indiaman; and on such a risk a small underwriter seldom exceeds £100, or £200, or £300, or £400, on an Indiaman:

The value of the things to be insured, therefore, is evidently quite suitable to the CAPITAL and power of the individual insurers, which the demand of the market of insurance has provided

If, indeed, there were practically much less facility, than there does exist, of insuring sums of £150,000 or £200,000, it might, in sound policy, be wiser to diminish that facility, than to increase it by the establishment of a joint stock company, supposing it would have that effect. Facility in insuring such vast sums on one ship, encourages the building and use of large vessels, which is politically unsafe; diminishes the number of seamen; incurs greater danger in the narrow seas around England; and occasions a heavier misfortune in case of loss. It is the opinion of many sensible persons, that it would be a wise law which prohibited the building of any merchant vessel above the size of 400 or 500 tons.

As the matter now stands, for £20,000 or £50,000, on a capital West India, or Brazil ship, sufficient insurers may be found in, perhaps, less than as many minutes. It may be remarked, that large sums are, or at least *ought*, only to be insured on fine ships; and on these, brokers will scarcely ever permit underwriters to insure any excessive sum, because they are anxious to divide such a risk among all their underwriters, to encourage them, and support their accounts against risks of a more indifferent nature.

If half the underwriters at Lloyd's, who, it must be remembered, are *necessarily* the Insurers of the whole country, be sufficient to insure at a risk of only £200 each, £100,000; nearly double the value of the richest merchant ships, except East India, that require to be insured, the security of that insurance is greatly enhanced by this circumstance: that though the law does, by the charters of the existing companies, prohibit private co-partneries in the trade of Marine Insurance; and therefore only a single name dares appear in the policy; yet (as that law never is, nor can be, enforced except in cases of bankruptcy,) that underwriters do unite in private copartneries and insure upon the capital of, and share the profit with, such co-partneries, is a fact so notorious, that to every merchant in London, the bare mention of it suffices for its proof. Two thirds, perhaps three fourths, of the underwriters at Lloyd's, insure upon the capital of some private copartnery.

Instead of the trade of Marine Insurance being supported then, as the Report of the Committee would make it appear by 1400 or 1500 individuals at Lloyd's, considering that some of them insure by procuration for two or three others, and those connected in private copartneries, it is in fact supported by, perhaps, four or five, or even ten times that number. These individuals form quite as respectable a body as the Exchange adjoining to them exhibits; and that they carry on their branch of trade, with all the economy consistent with its maintenance and security, is sufficiently demonstrated by the rate of the premium of Insurance, which, in the midst of the implacable war now waged against the commerce of the country, does not, IN ALL REGULAR AND ESTABLISHED TRADES, much exceed what it is in times of profound peace.

These observations may, perhaps, be thought *conclusive proofs of the insufficiency of the present system of Marine Insurance, and of the injustice and impolicy of erecting in that trade a Joint Stock Company;* for though (in the words of the learned author quoted by the Committee) it might be capable of thriving, yet to exempt one particular set of dealers from the general laws which take place with regard to their neighbours, merely because they would be capable of thriving, would certainly not be reasonable.

Should a large Marine Insurance Company be established, there can be little doubt that it would soon be divided into departments; there would be a magnificent building with halls and anti-rooms, with offices, for The Mediterranean, The West Indies, The Baltic trade, &c. In each of these might be seen *a little oligarchy of merchants,* engaged in every one of those different branches of trade, (since they would be the best judges of these several risks) for directors and managers. Is it not obvious how inconsistent all this would be with the enterprise of individuals? As, in insurance, all questions in explanation of the risk must be answered, if a merchant have a new scheme or adventure, he must declare it to this little oligarchy in his own branch of trade, who might obstruct his insurance, and hasten to the market of his enterprise and discovery before him.

This consideration would alone be an insuperable objection to a joint stock company of merchant insurers, were equal or even greater security and facility afforded by it.

London, as has been already shewn, enjoys a monopoly of the trade of Marine Insurance; and therefore to grant a charter of incorporation, to its merchants, through whose hands all orders for insurance must pass, would be infallibly to secure to them one of the most perfect monopolies that can easily be imagined. And as to the security which would be afforded by such a company, when contrasted with what is afforded under the present system, the superiority of the latter is apparent.

The capital of an Underwriter is of two sorts; his capital of money, or of property convertible into money, and his capital of premiums.

Although the Underwriter when he subscribes the policy, gives a receipt for the premium, the law so requiring, he does not, in point of fact, then receive that premium; he charges it in an account against the broker, and is, by usage, not entitled to demand any of the premiums he has insured for, till the end of the year. He is then only to receive the difference between the amount of them, and the losses, averages, and

returns he may have settled to the broker in the course of that
year. The broker gives a similar credit, to the merchant, for
whom he is responsible. These credits are, however, merely
nominal ; in point of fact, the Underwriter seldom or never
calls upon the broker, for reasons that will be explained
for a year and a half, often not for two years, which enables the broker to give a proportionable credit to the merchant.

If an underwriter meets with a loss, his account is balanced
with the broker upon the day the loss is publicly known at
Lloyd's, and he pays *in ready money, one mouth after adjustment*, whatever may be due for the loss. The solvency of an
underwriter is, therefore, put to the test upon every loss which
brings a balance against him ; this may happen to a principal
underwriter once in a week, and subjects him to sudden and
unexpected calls for money. His money-capital, therefore, he
invests in available securities, to be ready to meet such calls ;
his capital of premiums remains in the hands of the merchant,
and is drawn upon, through the broker, for the expences and
management of his business, the maintenance of his family, or
the increase of his money-capital, when his insurances are successful.

An estimate of the money-capital of the underwriters and
brokers (who must also be able to command capital) at Lloyd's
would be as difficult, uncertain, and probably as fallacious as an
estimate of the money-capital of the merchants on the Exchange
which it overlooks. Their capitals are, besides, a good deal
intermixed ; many of the merchants on the Exchange, however
illegal the practice may be, while they are negociating their
business in the square below, have a partner or agent assiduously engaged for them in the rooms of the insurers above.

To become at once an extensive Underwriter requires, as may
be seen from the manner the business is conducted, an extensive
capital. Underwriters and Insurance Brokers, like merchants
and other brokers are, however, as often persons, who from small
beginnings advance themselves, by the aid of industry and
frugality, those ancient handmaids of fortune, to wealth and
prosperity, as those who have commenced with great capitals;
but great fortunes among underwriters and brokers are less
frequently amassed, and are seldom so exaggerated as among
merchants ; a proof, that in their trades, the profit is not so
immoderate as in the trade of a merchant.

The capital of premiums may more easily be estimated. If
the number of underwriters be taken at 600, whose capital of
premiums is £30,000 each (sinking all the number above 600,
this will, by practical men, be known to be an under estimate) that will give a capital of 18 millions. Besides this capital

of premiums, there is to support it, the money-capital of all the underwriters, and to support the machinery of the business, the money-capital of all the brokers. Sinking the number of underwriters and brokers above 1000, it must be a calculation much below the truth, when the actual aid of private copartneries is considered, to take that capital at £6000 each, that will give a money capital of 6 millions. With respect to security then, how great must be the difference between the magnificent, but airy, 5 millions of the proposed New Marine Insurance Company and the real substantial capital of the Insurers of Lloyd's, who, be it always remembered, are, by the monopoly of London, the insurers of the empire, and almost of the world.

How much greater must be the difference between this real and substantial capital, the stock which is set apart in the general distribution of commercial stock for the maintenance of this branch of trade, and the 5 or 10 per cent. upon those airy 5 millions.

The more that the system of Marine Insurance of England is examined, it will afford to the patriot the greater satisfaction, and inspire the legislator with a salutary caution in giving sanction to new laws, whose enactment is urged by those who wished to overthrow this system for their private emolument.

If the merchants of London by the passing of the 2d Resolution of the Committee, unlimited and unrestrained, into a law, should be enabled to form themselves into a large joint stock association, such as has been described, they would soon monopolize the whole Marine Insurances of that city.

It is more than probable that they would then manage the business ill, and finally destroy it. Besides extinguishing from the state, two important classes of individuals, with the stock which it is their business to set apart, in the general distribution of commercial stock, for the maintenance of this, by far the most important of all trades, they would probably so lower the premiums as to destroy themselves.

If, after a few successful years, such an association should have so lowered the rate of premiums, as to afford only the interest of their capital (which in the New Marine Insurance scheme would have required no great amount) and the payment of their directors and clerks; and *then* such a calamity as the capture of a whole fleet, or the seizure of all the ships of one nation in the ports of another, *events which have happened*, a loss, perhaps, of three or four millions of money should be incurred, it is plain that that loss must be drawn from their *mercantile capital :* for the capital set apart for such an accident, which now remains practically in the hands of the merchants themselves, being extinguished and the occupa-

tion of the individuals, whose business it was to maintain it
gone, recourse can no more be had to its aid.

*What would be the difference of a Company with even 20. per
cent. upon 5 millions or 1 million of capital drawing upon THEIR
funds for the loss of a fleet of West Indiamen of only 200 sail, at
only £20,000 each, or 4 millions; and the Insurers of London
drawing that loss on 18 millions of capital in premiums, in the
hands of the merchants, and 6 millions of capital in money, in
their own hands, surely neither needs to be pointed out, nor to be
enlarged upon.*

The Committee in their Report, indeed, themselves say,
that if merchants were allowed to be their own insurers, the
premium would, probably, not *much* exceed the aggregate value of the losses on each class of risks. It does not exceed
that value at present, more than is barely sufficient to maintain the capital set apart for the trade, and to afford a reasonable profit to the individuals who wield it.

It remains for the merchants to shew the justice and policy of a law that would enable them to take that profit
from those individuals, with a view to keep it for themselves.

With respect to facility in effecting Marine Insurances,
in all probability it would be much lessened by such a company. There is no likelihood, that in three or four directors
would be found all the variety of opinion of risks, and competition for premiums, that is found among more than
a thousand contending insurers at Lloyd's. There is as
little probability that there would be equal facility of settlement of average or loss, where, perhaps, one mind is to judge
of the justice or reasonableness of the demand, as where many
are judges; or, if recourse to law be necessary, where the
wealth of a company, as where the purses of a few private
and divided* underwriters, are to be engaged in the contest,

* A remarkable instance has lately demonstrated the absence of that
monopoly which is alledged by the merchant promoters of the New
Marine Insurance Company, to be exercised by the insurers at Lloyd's. Several attempts (three at least) have been made by underwriters, who are
deeply engaged in late insurances to the Baltic Sea, which have terminated
in prodigious losses, to procure the establishment of a Committee, for the
investigation of such losses on their behalf; in other words, to oppose
more than the usual and natural difficulties to the recovery of these losses.
Yet though, perhaps, few things are more certain, than that a great many
of such losses are fraudulent, and though several of the most respectable
and leading underwriters were the promoters of the attempt, all their ef-
forts could not prevail over the natural indifference of so large and
promiscuous a body to bend it to their particular views, and the attempts
accordingly fell successively to the ground. It is due, however, to the good
sense and justice of many underwriters, also deeply interested in these Baltic
Insurances, to state, that they constantly and steadily refused to join in these
attempts, considering them as undue as unavailing.

C

from which much cost is inseparable. As to *usage*, that could only arise and prevail according to the pleasure of the company; it would, therefore, be always in their favour. ·

The effect of the existing law having, by the charters, prevented the merchants from securing the natural monopoly of London to their own body, and having thrown the business into the hands of individuals, has been then to give birth to two sets of labourers, besides the merchant, in the trade of Marine Insurance, Underwriters and Insurance Brokers. The merchant is obliged, for his own advantage, to furnish them with the profits of their trade, and thus to increase the industrious population, the commercial prosperity, and the wealth of the country.

It has been already often observed, that *London* enjoys an almost exclusive monopoly of the Marine Insurances of Great Britain, in other words, almost of the whole world. In this metropolis, therefore, these two classes of insurers have grown into consideration, and some of them into wealth and importance; who with their clerks, connections in partnership, and dependents, form a Commercial Body of a great many thousand individuals.

Her merchants, through whose hands all orders for insurances *must* pass, perceiving that, in order to carry on their trade, they must necessarily set apart in the general distribution of mercantile profit, which flows from the public, the fountain of all profit, first, *always* through the hands of the merchants, a portion for the maintenance of insurers; these merchants would be glad, (though they do not complain of the insufficiency of their present share in that general distribution), to increase it by appropriating to themselves the profit of insurers also. To be insurers, they have themselves individually neither spare capital, nor time, nor, under the existing laws, ability; but the monopoly enjoyed by the metropolis, having already brought the business of Marine Insurance into so narrow a compass, *her* merchants see that *it would be easy to secure the whole profits of that trade to themselves, if they could by address persuade the legislature to invest them, or to allow them to invest themselves with the exclusive privilege of dealing in it.*

The Legislature is too enlightened, not to know how prejudicial the success of such an attempt would be to the general interests of commerce, and consequently to our national prosperity; and could merchants see with the impartial eyes of statesmen, it would not be difficult for them to perceive, that its success would not be consistent even with their own interest.

Should such a Company, by the abrogation of the present law, become legal, there is no doubt it would be formed. It would

*be widely different in its effects from the joint stock companies
already described as existing for insurance of lives or against
fire.   These companies have no more employment than the public
may be induced to give them, from a confidence in their security
and honour, or than they can draw to themselves by the magnificent promise of their advertisements, the number of their hand-
bills, and the style of their placards ; but in respect to Marine
Insurance, as the members of a Joint Stock Company in that business would be the very persons, THE ONLY PERSONS who have
insurances to effect, and through whose hands all orders for insurance must pass, the case is widely different.*

Whatever may be the expediency of leaving all things relating to trade in their free and natural state, a point on
which all enlightened statesmen are agreed, there can be no
doubt that when, by the operation of laws and of commercial
regulations, trade has been diverted from its natural channels, and directed or accumulated by the force of those laws
and regulations, in any particular manner, or in any particular place, that other laws and other regulations must be
made, to counteract the evils which must inevitably follow the
first disturbance of that natural freedom.

The law of the charters of the two existing Companies,
though they themselves have sunk into utter insignificance,
has existed nearly an hundred years undisturbed; has produced, and is the corner stone of the present system of Marine Insurance, upon which a great fabric of commercial
laws and usages relating to that important branch of trade
has been raised ; and the passing of the law now under
the consideration of parliament, without limitation or restriction, must be at the risk of shaking that fabric to its very
foundation.

The framers of the law of these charters, indeed, did not
foresee its effects. Like the famous Act of Navigation, which,
though passed merely from a spirit of hostility to the Dutch,
has yet, in its effects, been one of the chief means of our
naval superiority, of our dominion over the seas, and of our
commercial prosperity : so these Charters, though intending
only to give a monopoly, have in effect prevented that monopoly of Marine Insurances, which natural circumstances,
heightened by commercial laws and regulations, would have
enabled the merchants of London to secure to themselves.

PART III.

REMARKS

On the Report of the Select Committee of the House of Commons on the subject of Marine Insurance.

The opposite reasoning of the following observations, from that of the Committee of the House of Commons, renders it unnecessary to follow their Report very closely.

The first division of it, " On the nature of the exclusive privilege conferred on the Royal Exchange, and London Assurance Companies, and the manner and extent of its exercise," may shortly be summed up in this.

That the Royal Exchange and London Assurance Companies have an exclusive privilege AGAINST OTHER COMPANIES *for Marine Insurance ; but having themselves sunk into utter insignificance in that branch of trade, the manner of their exercising it is unworthy of any notice :*

That their exclusive privilege, though of little value to themselves, has had a most important effect, in preventing the monopoly of Marine Insurance enjoyed by the city of London, from being converted by its merchants to their own purposes, at great hazard to themselves, and the risk of preventing the growth of that branch of trade :

That by that important and salutary effect, it has raised and fostered two classes of industrious and thriving individuals, who would otherwise never have existed in the commercial state, and an immense capital for the maintenance of this branch of trade, IT- SELF THE FOUNDATION OF FOREIGN TRADE, *which would otherwise never have been accumulated for its support, and been equally without existence in the commercial capital of the country :*

That they have, therefore, produced, though unforeseen by the legislature, those very effects, which its wisdom would have been exerted to produce by other apparently more direct, but perhaps less effectual, means.

The real motives which induced the Legislature to pass the law confirming these charters, no longer exist.

By the improvements of practice, merchants do not now pay insurers, " the consideration monies for insurances," until the risks are determined, and often have large securities consisting of such consideration monies in their hands, to indemnify them in case of the failure of underwriters.

" Failures" are now so rare, that no list of names can be produced of any that have happened of late years, worthy of consideration ; *and no instance can be produced of any merchant who has been " ruined or impoverished" by such failure of Insurers.*

The Committee, though they treat of the *nature and exer-*

cise, do not inquire into the *origin* of these charters, though they say, " the *intention* of the legislature in granting them has been defeated." The time of granting them was during the reign of the South Sea Bubble, when a sort of infatuation for schemes prevailed throughout England; and if it appear, as it does, on enquiry into the history of that bubble, that the grant of those charters was an attempt to cure the mania which then prevailed, as well with respect to insurance, as other schemes, it may, perhaps, however contrary to the opinion of the Committee, be safely asserted, that with the aid of other important laws since made, relative to the trade of insurance, the intentions of the legislature *have* been fulfilled.

Long subsequent to that time, wager policies were lawful, and so ill governed was the practice of insurers, that a broker would sometimes insure a ship without any order or interest, and when the merchant wanted a real insurance, would sell him the policy for a profit; but by the important act of 14 Geo. II. prohibiting and rendering void insurances where there is not a real interest; by the law prohibiting the insurance of enemies' property; and by the prevalence of a great body of commercial law, as applied to Marine Insurances, that business may now be truly said to be as respectably conducted as, perhaps, the nature of things will admit in any business, and that instances of frauds in Lloyd's Coffee House are full rarer, in proportion, than among merchants.

The calculation of the Committee of sums which *might* have been insured last year is very fanciful. No doubt these sums *might* have been insured, *had there been orders for so doing.*

As the calculation is quite an imaginary one, no time need be wasted on its consideration. If the Committee mean, that a proportion of *all but half* of the property requiring to be insured in the last year, went uninsured, the evidence proves directly the contrary; for all the insurances which were ordered were effected, excepting a stray order or two, unworthy of notice.

On the second division of the report, " The effect of the exclusive privilege upon Marine Insurance, and the state and means of effecting Marine Insurances in this country," much has been already said. The Committee observe, that Lloyd's Coffee house has a monopoly of the trade of insurance; but it has so no more than the Exchange has a monopoly of the trade of merchants.

London has the monopoly of Marine Insurances, and her Insurers must assemble some where. The only difference between *their* assembly, and that of the merchants, is, that as *their* business cannot be transacted in the open air, they are obliged to pay the " Gresham Committee," for the use of part of the same structure, which, by the munificence of its founder, the merchants frequent free of any expence; and that they do not admit within their walls any person without a certificate of character, a precaution which merchants cannot take with respect to their own body. Any respectable merchant, and all the partners of a firm, may be insurers, or may by one partner, or by a deputy, having a procuration, insure at Lloyd's, (which is as open to such as the Exchange,) as much as they please, or as much as their capital and connection can procure them.

They can only insure by deputy in a company. "The first merchants," says the Report, "do not and cannot attend Lloyd's Coffee House." If they cannot attend the Exchange of Insurance, which only a flight of steps separates from their own Exchange, it may be asked, how these "first merchants" can or will be able to attend a Company? Surely, it may be asked, where can its office be more commodically situated? Or how is it to diminish the MONOPOLY of Lloyd's, except by transferring it to itself?

Though individuals are prevented from *legally* associating in partnership in the trade of Marine Insurance, it has been observed, that they do in fact associate, and that, perhaps, the greater number of the insurers of London have partners, with whom they divide the risk and profit of the business. That circumstance, and the conveniences mentioned by the Committee, may be sufficient reasons for rendering legal a division of profits which does in point of fact take place. The effects of doing so, without limitation or restriction, need not be farther dwelt upon.

The circumstance of some Underwriters absenting themselves from their market during the autumn months, is dwelt on by the Committee as occasioning a necessity of giving an extravagant premium to those who remain. Not to dwell *here*, upon the improbability of men absenting themselves at a time when extravagant premiums, or in other words, *extravagant profits*, are to be had: or on the discolouration given by the Report to the length of these occasional absences; the fact is, that in the autumn months premiums begin to rise, till they double and treble, or increase yet more, from the change of the season. It may very safely be asserted, that if all the underwriters were brought back at that season, premiums would not be a shade lower. The principal underwriters too, generally leave a deputy to insure for them. The contest between merchants and insurers then runs high, but ends, almost uniformly, in favour of the merchant; for it is a common remark among underwriters, that the business of the autumn months is generally attended with loss. Insurances are then, as at other times, always to be done, an assertion completely confirmed by the evidence taken by the Committee.

The value of the things to be insured in these months, the

2

Committee may be thought, by practical men, to have over-rated. All ships sailing from the West Indies before the first of August, may be insured, without exception, to any amount a ship can carry, at a regular premium of 3 per cent. with convoy; from Jamaica 4 per cent. Ships that sail before the 1st of August are four-fifths of the trade. Any ship, to any amount she can carry, may be insured *out* to those colonies, at all seasons, for a regular premium of 3 per cent. with convoy. East India risks, in regular ships, do not vary at all. These instances may suffice to show the heightenings of the Report.

It is easy to prove, that in the last five months of the year 1809, the *whole business* of the country, as may be seen by the account of exports and imports, increased suddenly in a much greater proportion than was ever known. On the fairness of the Committee's having produced the accounts of a *single underwriter,* as a proof of their statement, and as a light to the House of Commons, it may be remarked, that there is no purpose which the particular accounts of some one underwriter might not be found to suit. The increase of the general trade of the country would be more than sufficient to account for the increase the account exhibited, which, like the accounts of all other underwriters, is governed by the judgment, or even by the caprice, of the individual.

As London enjoys the monopoly of the insurances of the kingdom, the laws which are wholesome for her, ought to govern the outports.

The Committee observe, that a Company consisting of the owners of eighty-three Transports, insured the sea risk for each other, and that their averages and *losses* came *last year* to one and one-quarter per cent. The Committee do not give an average of several years. It must be pretty plain, however, that if there were many averages, there could not be *one loss*, since one and one quarter per cent. on 83, would little more than pay for one loss. It seems not a little partial to state the charge for *one* year, and that too before the accounts were made or before the averages could be ascertained. *It may be asked too, what would be the consequence if these 83 transports,* THE PROPERTY OF SEVENTY OR EIGHTY INDIVIDUALS, *had been gathered together in one fleet and lost, other than the probable ruin of the whole of their owners? Or it may be asked where such a member of owners of transports can be collected, except in London!*

The same observation applies to the other society of eighty to eighty-four members, insuring 100 ships, which must also be a *London* society. The Committee state, that these persons insured each other, at *an expence* for last year of five and a half per cent. but the person who gives evidence, states, that the *losses* were not yet all ascertained; and it is very ambiguous from his evidence whether he does not mean that the *losses* alone came to five and a half per cent. Every person acquainted with the business of insurance knows, that averages are, upon the whole, full as heavy a charge as losses against insurers, if not heavier.

From the manner the evidence is stated by the person who furnishes the Committee with evidence of the existence of clubs in the country, it seems very uncertain whether these clubs be any thing more than *the Lloyds* of the place; for he says each member puts his name on the policy, and is liable for no more than the amount set against it.

These statements of the Committee are such leaps to conclusions, from such evidence, that it cannot but seem a little strange how they could have been made.

The third and last division of the Report, "Of the Importance of a better System to the Commerce and Revenue of the Empire, and to the Parties concerned," contains a still more extraordinary partiality of statement. Indeed, if the Report be meant to be a summary of the evidence and to guide the House of Commons, there is a downright suppression of a most material fact. In this division the Committee state the superiority, in their opinion, of *Companies* for Marine Insurance. They state there were 36 companies at Hambro', two at Stockholm, one at Gottenburgh, and five at Copenhagen, and enumerate a great many in America; but of the nature or success of these Companies there is no mention. The Consul of the Swedish nation, however, states in his evidence to the Committee, that there is but one company at Stockholm, whose business cannot be of great extent; and that of the 36 at Hambro', there are not above five or six remaining; *some have not found it worth while to go on, and others have failed and have paid from four to fifteen shillings in the pound.* Whatever may have been the cause of these failures, the suppression of the fact in the Report gives a very different feature to the case. To have inserted it would indeed have been *a most singular reason*, or *ground*, for the favour entertained towards *Companies* by the Committee.

The Report states, that "what gives the *best* insurance at the cheapest rate is the enabling merchants to insure one another." In which case, the *Assured* becomes the *Assurer*. It may however, by Parliament, be thought a wiser and better mode of insurance, to separate these two characters, which the monopoly of London already too much confounds, as much as the operation of laws can produce that effect; and to make insurance a division of labour, with a separate capital set apart by the labourers in it, for the maintenance of their branch of trade.

By that policy, existence must be given to a larger industrious population, and to a larger commercial capital, than would otherwise arise ; than if the merchants of London, enjoying the monopoly almost of the world, were to insure one another, and extinguish that division of labour, merely to engross profits of which their present share, already too much inclines to excess.

It has been the business of these pages to shew, that the law of the two existing charters, which is impotent as to the production of a monopoly to the persons who possess them, has corrected the monopoly, in this branch of trade, enjoyed by London, to the utmost ; namely, by prohibiting the association of the merchants who enjoy that monopoly, even to the number of two; and has produced that division of labour and that accumulation of capital, which, most probably, would otherwise never have been engaged in that branch of trade ; and that the enactment of the law recommended by the Committee, may pull down that system, and dry up a great fountain of our national wealth and prosperity.

If merchants were to insure one another, as their connections, acquaintances, and their mercantile knowledge too, are generally confined to their own branch of trade, they would, if permitted, naturally form companies in each branch. What would, it may be asked then, be the effect of a company of West India or Jamaica Merchants, insuring fleets of ships in *their own* trade, insuring *their own* goods and ships, (which very much resembles no insurance at all) if one of those fleets should be lost or taken? Instead of having, as now, recourse to insurers and the capital, which it is their business to set apart for the maintenance of their trade, and being fully indemnified for such a loss, *which has happened*, they would, in all probability, be utterly ruined, and involve a numerous body of industrious creditors in their general destruction.

With respect to the cheapness of Marine Insurances ; it is brought by the present system, with all its machinery, at least as far as respects the underwriter, to as great economy as perhaps it is capable of. It is an assertion that may easily be proved, that underwriters do not receive for gross profit, taking an average of successful and unsuccessful years, more than ten to fifteen shillings per cent. upon all the sums insured by them; or, in the language of the Committee, " the price paid for insurance does not exceed the aggregate value of all the losses and averages" *by more than ten to fifteen shillings per cent.* By that profit all the insurers, their clerks, and dependants, and the capital set apart for the maintenance of the trade, are to be supported. If the eighty-three transports, the sea risk of which cost 1¼ per cent. and the ninety coasters whose insurance cost, as far as the account could be made up, 5¼ per cent, and all the insurances of all the clubs in Great

D

Britain were to be thrown in, at the usual premiums, it would not alter this general rate of profit, one penny, perhaps not one farthing, in the hundred pounds.

A merchant, for handing an order for insurance to his broker, receives a *profit* of ten shillings in the £100; the broker, who merely sells the goods when arrived, receives always ten shillings, sometimes twenty shillings, in the £100, for selling them; and the merchant receives fifty shillings per cent. more for his management. If it be true then, that after all the perils of seas, fire, thieves, and the enemy, no more than ten to fifteen shillings per cent. remain to the underwriter for all his risk, capital, and anxiety; it is not very easy to suppose how his trade can be farther economised. It would not be difficult, however, to point out where, if greater economy in foreign trade is necessary, it might be more successfully practised.

The Committee state, as a proof of the difficulty in effecting Marine Insurance, that the *brokers* receive one fourth part of the total profits on *underwriting*. This is rather a confusion of terms; but the meaning of the Committee may be gathered more distinctly, when, as a proof of the want of economy in the present system, they state, that the *Brokerage* is *equal* to one fourth of the underwriter's profits. If the rate of these has been truly stated, at ten to fifteen shillings in the £100, one fourth of that rate may not be thought exorbitant for the brokers. But the Committee do not state, that the *profits of the broker* are equal to one fourth of the *profits of the underwriter*; though they seem rather to insinuate that meaning. Out of the *brokerage*, which, in the gross, may exceed one fourth of the profits of underwriting, the broker has to maintain his counting-house establishment, and to indemnify himself for the losses he sustains by the failure of merchants, and for the advances which he is obliged to make to them, which are both often very considerable.

Insurance brokers, different from all other brokers, must, by making themselves liable for the merchant, be *dealers in insurances;* their brokerage, therefore, which in the gross, may be, on an average, equal to eight or even ten shillings in the £100, can by no means be accounted as their profit, which is, in fact, greatly under that proportion. A broker who *sells* goods, receives sometimes twenty, never less than ten shillings in the £100, without any risk of the solvency of the merchant; but, whatever may be the rate of insurance-brokers' profits, it is a rate fixed by the merchants themselves, and settled in a manner, that gives colour to the *ingenious,* but not, on the part of the *mercantile* members of the Committee, *very ingenuous* statement of the Report.

2

It has been already shewn, that the merchant ought to be the paymaster of his agent the broker; but how that matter is really arranged, shall now be described.

When a merchant receives an order for insurance, he hands it over to his broker, and charges 10s. per cent. to his correspondent abroad, for " effecting" it. It is then agreed, between the merchant and broker, that whatever be the rate of premium, the latter shall have one shilling in the pound on that premium, for his skill and trouble, and for being answerable for the merchant; his brokerage thus increases with the risk of that responsibility.

In order to enable the merchant to retain the whole of these ten shillings per cent. for "effecting" an Insurance, (which is the proper fund from which the broker *ought* to be paid) it is agreed between the merchant and him, that the underwriter shall not be permitted to charge in his account against the broker, the whole premium inserted in the policy, but a sum less by one shilling in the pound. If the premium, for instance, be ten guineas, the under-writer charges the broker with ten pounds, but gives a receipt in the policy for ten guineas, which the broker charges in full to the merchant, and the merchant, increased by the ten shillings for " effecting," charges to *his foreign correspondent*, at whose expence the broker's commission is thus arranged.

When a broker pays an underwriter any balance that may be due to him, he deducts 12 per cent. from the amount. Underwriters, therefore, delay calling upon brokers till a great many risks are expired, scarcely ever sooner than for a year and a half, often for two years, in order to save that discount which they do not have to pay, should losses turn the balance in favour of the broker. The fear of the loss of this 12 per cent. on the balances, keeps them longer due to the underwriter, in the hands, apparently of the broker, but in fact, of the merchant.

It is evident, however, that in settling the premium *to be inserted in the policy*, the underwriter must, though nominally with respect to himself, raise it by the amount of these deductions to be made from it for the merchant and *his* broker. The Committee, in their Report, describe these as the fourth of the profits of *underwriting*; they are, however, mere contrivances of the merchant to conceal the real amount of *his own* profits; for to his foreign correspondent, or to any person unversed in the trade, it is thus made to appear that the underwriter receives the whole premium in the policy, and that the merchant receives no more than the 10 shillings per cent. for his own and his broker's trouble and reponsibility in " effecting" the insurance. To the Committee of the House of Commons it would seem to appear, that all this is a mere contrivance of the *underwriter and broker* against the *merchant*, whose charge of the ten shillings for " effecting" is not even mentioned in the report.

Though the profits of underwriters cannot, perhaps, be further economised, it does not seem so clear that those of the broker might not. It is a delicate matter for merchants, however to propose economy in that branch of the business, as it touches too closely upon their own profits; for it is a very common practice among merchants, who employ brokers, to receive sixpence out of the broker's shillings, and an equally common one to be their own brokers, by means of a clerk at Lloyd's, whereby the whole of these profits, however undue, are secured entirely to themselves,

When the great risk of insurance brokers, and the large advances they are sometimes obliged to make, are considered, they may not perhaps be overpaid. However that may be, there is something so unfair in the Report, in stating the manner in which the details of the business are arranged, as a conspiracy of the *Brokers* and *Underwriters* against the *innocent Merchant*, as causes of " diminution of his profits," or as " clogs upon his trade," that this explanation seems due to justice.

It may be thought therefore that the Monopoly, enjoyed by London, of the Marine Insurances of the country, notwithstanding the powerful law of the charters, *already* gives her merchants *too much power to secure to themselves undue profits in this branch of trade :* but how that evil would be *amended or removed* by their being allowed, *under the solemn sanction of the Parliament of the Kingdom to form themselves, for the express purposes of carrying it on, into large Associations,* cannot, it is conceived, be a matter of question to an unbiassed, serious, and disinterested inquirer into the grounds and the policy of this most important subject.

London, February 22, 1811.

THE END.

INDEX

Numbers in bold indicate the volume number

For Product Safety Concerns and Information please contact our EU
representative GPSR@taylorandfrancis.com
Taylor & Francis Verlag GmbH, Kaufingerstraße 24, 80331 München, Germany

www.ingramcontent.com/pod-product-compliance
Ingram Content Group UK Ltd.
Pitfield, Milton Keynes, MK11 3LW, UK
UKHW021116180425
457613UK00005B/110